CITY ON A HILL

CITY ON A HILL

A Portrait of
Shrewsbury School

David Gee

GREENBANK PRESS

Published by
Greenbank Press
Greenbank
East Horrington
Wells
Somerset BA5 3DR

First published August 2015

A CIP record for this book is available from the British Library

ISBN 978-0-9523699-8-1

Design & layout by Tom Sullivan, www.grand-design.eu
Printed by Hobbs The Printers Ltd, www.hobbs.uk.com

CONTENTS

To the colleagues and pupils
who were my fellow citizens
on the hill from 1958-2015

A city on a hill cannot be hid

St. Matthew 5.14b

It is neither ships nor walls
but men that make a city

*Nicias, Athenian general and
politician 470–413 BC*

FOREWORD

If allowed to offer Shrewsbury School from 1950-2015 as his specialist subject in each round of Mastermind, David Gee would win at a canter. Not only has he lived on the edge of his City on a Hill for most of the period covered by his book, but he has taught at 'The Schools' (as Shrewsbury School is known to Salopians) for fifty-four years. During that time he has been head of history and divinity, coached rowing and directed plays, been acting-Chaplain and the Housemaster of Severn Hill and, most importantly of all, master in charge of the Dayboys, who doubled in number during his tenure.

A formidable scholar himself, he has packed the book with information while insisting that it is a portrait of the school rather than a history. He does not sit in judgement on his contemporaries – although his description of the great eccentrics of the era is a delight – but gives an authoritative account of what Shrewsbury was like in the last half-century and how it is now. David Gee knows and loves the place and people. Portrait or History? *City on a Hill* is surely both.

The detailed picture of Shrewsbury will bring back memories for all who knew it in the second half of the twentieth century. However it has broader and more general interest. The great boarding schools have been hugely influential in our national life. For anyone interested in how they changed and developed in the twentieth century, City on a Hill provides the perfect case study, a close-up view of the dramatic winds of change that blew through the dusty cloisters of the 1950s and reinvigorated the system. It tells the story of how hierarchical closed institutions, with their own slang and arcane privileges, teaching the Classics much as they had done in 1850 and 1750, single-sex and keeping parents as far as possible at arms' length, became the co-educational, international schools of today with the breadth of study and the breathtaking array of sports, activities, clubs, charities, music, drama and expeditions described here in the final chapters. The history of the 'Public School Revolution', as David Gee calls it – breaking down barriers, expanding opportunities and combining traditional loyalties with a new spirit of individualism – is the background to this full-length and affectionate portrait of one of the great schools of England.

Eric Anderson
May 2015

PREFACE

The main focus of this book is on the developments which have taken place during the six decades between 1950 and 2010, but its scope is not strictly confined to that period. I have traced the antecedents of these developments when this seemed appropriate, and in particular I have provided an introductory chapter, containing a brief sketch of the first four hundred years of the School's history, attempting to identify the key elements of their legacy which have provided the basis, the context and a deeper understanding of what has followed. I have written rather more fully on the four decades (1908-1950) which constituted the immediate prelude to my chosen period. Basil Oldham and, more recently, Colin Leach have both written admirable and more detailed histories of those first four centuries as a whole. At the end of my period I have also recorded some of the more notable events and developments which have occurred, while this book has been in preparation, before Easter 2015.

These six recent decades exhibit a remarkable symmetry, for they cover the tenure of six headmasters, three of them, Jack Peterson, Donald Wright and Eric Anderson guiding the fortunes of the School in the first period of thirty years, and another three, Simon Langdale, Ted Maidment and Jeremy Goulding during the second.

My qualification for writing is simply that I have been a member of the Shrewsbury Common Room for all but the first eight of these years. There has been some danger that many details of this period could be lost: the School went through a period when the keeping of records became rather haphazard and inconsistent; inevitably the value of such records is greatly reduced by discontinuity or change of method; and the memory of current members of the staff and of those now associated with the School on a daily basis reaches back only to the beginning of the second half of my chosen period.

My principal objective has been to provide a record which is reasonably comprehensive in scope and as objective and accurate as possible. As the work has progressed I have become increasingly aware of the danger, on such a vast canvas, of omitting a name which deserves recognition, or an incident which requires a mention; I offer my apologies if such an inadvertent omission has occurred. I am acutely conscious that far more has been omitted than has been included. Although I have occasionally allowed myself some personal reminiscence, what follows is not intended to be an autobiography. Being a witness of many of the developments as they have occurred brings with it difficulties as well as advantages. Writing about recent events inevitably restricts perspective and requires particular circumspection and consideration. I have therefore aimed to follow the very proper convention, when dealing with persons who are still alive and with issues which are still relevant and sometimes controversial, of simply identifying the issues and presenting both sides of the case, without obtruding a strong personal opinion.

Another difficulty arises in preserving the distinction between a history and a memoir, particularly acute in a situation in which I have a personal memory of many of the circumstances and events which are recounted in this book. My overall intention has been, wherever possible, to maintain the degree of objectivity and balance characteristic of a history; but especially when dealing with personalities well known to me, it has seemed more appropriate to relax the literary and historical conventions a little and to allow the element of memoir to emerge. This will appear in the chapters dealing with the successive headmasters, and be rather more obvious in those dealing with the four Salopian 'characters'.

However, in surveying such a very substantial volume of material, an historian has to make a choice, which is in itself a form of bias, reflecting the writer's own knowledge and interests. Colin Leach remarks that there are four ways of telling the story of an academic institution, with the emphasis being placed variously on constitutional or on physical aspects of the school, on the men who shaped it, or on the alumni it produced. He quotes the Athenian general Nicias, who said that 'it is neither ships nor walls, but men that make a city'. I entirely agree with that assertion: accordingly I have adopted the third of these alternatives, and have chosen to focus on the visible, daily life of the School, on the personalities who have led and shaped it, and who have created, sustained and transmitted its distinctive ethos. I have not attempted a close examination of the voluminous hierarchy of minutes of govenors', housemasters' and head of faculties' meetings or of the documentation of financial problems and developments, which all require and deserve a separate history of their own. As my researches have continued I have found that my original intention of producing a conventional chronological account has given way to an examination of, and reflection on, what the School is like.

Future historians may, I think, identify a 'post-revolutionary period' in these sixty years, between the dismantling of the traditional hierarchical, cloistered, single-sex Public School at its beginning and the implementation of full co-education at its end. The first thirty of these years witnessed the characteristic strains and disturbances attendant upon 'The Public Schools' Revolution', but these had generally been absorbed and settled by 1980. They were followed by years of stability, success and steady expansion, in which, while there was greater attention to the interests and the welfare of the individual, together with a corresponding and very considerable expansion both of varied, extra-curricular activity, and of reciprocal links with the world beyond the School, the traditional ethos of the Public School and the strength of its community were preserved. One of my main purposes in writing has been to commemorate and celebrate that distinctive achievement.

By far my most important source has been the 140 issues of *The Salopian Newsletter*, more recently entitled *The Salopian*, which have covered the period between 1950 and the present day, which I edited between 1986 and 1999, and which altogether constitute the most consistent record of the activities of the School during those years. The articles which they contain are nearly contemporaneous with the activities which they describe and I have quoted from them freely. Basil Oldham's *History of Shrewsbury School* has provided reliable and magisterial information about historical antecedents, but his survey ceases at the Fourth Centenary of School in

1952. Colin Leach's *A School at Shrewsbury: the Four Foundations* provides an equally reliable and authoritative, and more attractively presented overview of the history of the School from its first foundation, and carries the story through to 1990, if understandably rather more sketchily after the resignation of Donald Wright in 1975. 'Jimmy' Street's *Changes and Chances*, Philip Cowburn's *A Salopian Anthology*, David Bevan's *Recollections,* Robin Case's admirable, imaginatively planned and beautifully illustrated 450th Anniversary booklet *Shrewsbury School 1552-2002* together with Michael Charlesworth's autobiography *Behind the Headlines* and his excellent booklet on the buildings of the Site all provide valuable additional insights and information. I am particularly indebted to Laurence Le Quesne, who has kindly allowed me to see his unpublished monographs on the Summer of 1959 and on *Donald Wright: The Age of Reform* which have been exceptionally illuminating, as have his contributions about Frank McEachran, the School Site and the Salopian Satirists, recorded in *The Salopian Newsletter* and elsewhere. On all of these he is the acknowledged authority.

I have arranged the material in this book in a series of sections, each dealing with a group of related topics. The section on the Historical Context contains a brief sketch of the history of the School before 1950, an account of the Public Schools' Revolution, another on the history and role of Day Boys, a survey of the development of the Site, a sequence of Salopian Celebrations, including anniversaries and Royal Visits, and a chapter entitled *View from the Pentagon*, which examines the contribution and the views of the six headmasters, only one of whom actually used that delightfully and deliberately misnamed hexagon as his study, but which came to symbolize the seat of headmagisterial authority. I have written an independent account of the headmasterships of Jack Peterson and Donald Wright and have interviewed the subsequent headmasters, asking them for their own perception of the main issues and developments of their periods in charge.

Then there is a section on Salopian institutions, including the Chapel, the Common Room, the New House and Basic Year.

The next section examines the *Genius Loci*. It contains a close examination of the Salopian ethos, a discussion of the characters and contributions of four colleagues who have embodied and shaped it during the last sixty years and the role which has been played in Salopian life by slang and satire.

This is followed by a section on the dramatic changes in the academic, administrative and social aspects of the School since 1950, the first two of which, taken together, have contributed significantly to the declining independence of the 'Independent School'.

The second part of the book deals with School Activities. Its purpose is to demonstrate the remarkable range, variety and standard of the achievement of members of the school, more impressive with each succeeding decade. The successive Newsletters present a horizontal view- a snapshot- at a given time; I have tried, where appropriate, to adopt a vertical perspective, to give an account of the development of these activities through the years, but in other ways I have relaxed some of the chronological constraints and although I have traced the antecedents of the five long-standing traditional sports, my principal objective has been to present a picture which is as recent and contemporary as possible, extending into the first half of 2015. Colleagues and pupils alike are understandably so immersed in their own activities, that they are often unaware of the wider picture. I hope that what is recorded here is as 'eye-opening' for readers as it has proved for me. It provides convincing support for the assertion that activities outside the classroom are often quite as important as those which occur within it in producing a well-educated and well-rounded individual: that this is one of the main attractions of the education offered in independent boarding schools; and that such schools are in the best position to provide it. In dealing with this material I have sought contributions from my colleagues most closely associated with the particular activity being discussed, who are, or were previously, in charge. In many cases I have interviewed my colleagues in person, in others they have contributed written notes which I have then edited and integrated with material supplied by others in order to produce a final draft. It has not proved feasible, without greatly extending the amount of time required for the preparation of this book, to contact everyone who might have something valuable to contribute about a particular topic, but I have tried to elicit a sufficiently wide range of assessments to provide a balanced appraisal of the material. I have acknowledged my debt to these contributors in a *Who's Who* section of the Appendix, which identifies them, together with other persons who are mentioned in the text. I offer my apologies to any colleagues whose opinion has not been solicited or whose contribution to any activity has not been adequately recognised.

The early chapters of this second part deal with Music, Drama, the Visual Arts and Craft, Design and Technology; the growing prominence and the excellent standards attained in all of them have done much to enhance the reputation of the School.

A discussion of other, primarily school-based activities follows. There is, of course, a section on sport; but since this now encompasses more than twenty different activities, I have decided to focus my attention principally upon the five 'traditional' and still most prominent sports, the Hunt, the Boat Club, Football, Cricket and Fives: and to limit any further comments on other sports to those, which on account of status, novelty or notable achievement require a specific mention. A Chapter on Outdoor Activities which, like so many other aspects of Salopian involvement, have expanded beyond recognition during these sixty years, concludes this section on the extra-curricular aspects of school life.

I have again applied the criteria of status, novelty or notable achievement in selecting items for particular comment in the ensuing chapter, which is entitled Societies, Conferences and Competitions.

Then the horizon steadily widens, to examine the proliferating and reciprocal links between the School and the wider world and to trace the civic, industrial and international areas in which these outward-looking initiatives have been developed, first with a chapter on the Civic Environment and another on the School's long-standing and evolving relationship with Shrewsbury House in Everton. The last chapter is concerned with Salopians in the Wider World.

The Appendix contains lists of the Headmasters and Housemasters, of the Chairmen of Governors, of Chaplains and Bursars, of Deputy Headmasters, of

Directors of Studies and Heads of Faculties, of the Missioners and Wardens of Shrewsbury House, of the Harvard Fellows, of Old Salopian members of the Common Room, of the Heads of School and of the Sidney Gold Medallists. The list headed *Who's Who* is primarily intended to identify individuals whose names occur in the text: the list entitled *Pillars of the Common Room* identifies colleagues who have served for ten years or more, together with those who have occupied prominent positions for a shorter period of time. It also includes the *Carmen*, the School Song, composed in Latin by Dr Alington, together with its English translation by Mark Mortimer.

Inevitably, in attempting to examine the component elements of a complex but integrated social organism, there is a risk of some overlap between the topics I have chosen. While attempting to minimise repetition I have preferred to give priority to the coherence and comprehensiveness of each chapter, indicating the location of related material in other chapters, where appropriate.

The methods I have adopted in compiling this record have been a mixture of private research on the one hand and interviews on the other. Sir Eric Anderson originally encouraged me to undertake the project and Colin Leach kindly discussed the venture with me. Several retired colleagues, including Alan Laurie and Robin Moulsdale, Michael Hart, Peter Hughes, David Main and Laurence Le Quesne helped me by contributing their memories and perceptions of the earlier years. Mike Morrogh and Robin Brooke-Smith facilitated access to the archive. Martin Knox made a helpful contribution to the section on the Support Staff. Peter Hughes, Richard Auger and Martin Cropper discussed academic developments with me: Mike Tonks steered me through the details of the Administrative Revolution: John Rolfe and his team in the Development Office provided me with information about the progress of fund-raising. Revd Gary Dobbie discussed the recent developments in Chapel. John Moore and I reviewed the very remarkable changes which have taken place in Music; I had similar consultations with Peter Fanning and Robin Case about Drama, with John Alford and Philip Woolley about the Visual Arts, and with Kevin Lloyd about Craft, Design and Technology.

In the field of sport, Paul Greetham discussed changes in organisation and policy with me; Willie Jones, Bob Parker, Peter Birch and Peter Middleton provided material about the Royal Shrewsbury School Hunt; Willie Jones' evocative verses eloquently convey the loyalty and nostalgia which the sport engenders in its participants. Nick Randall, who has compiled a most impressive archive of the history of RSSBC in the Club Room of the Boat Club and in the Sabrina Room of the Leander Club placed his vast knowledge at my disposal: it was reinforced by information from Roger Blomfield's *The History of Rowing at Shrewsbury* and by contributions from Simon Baxter, Philip Lapage, Steve Fox and Paul Manser. I was greatly helped by notes from or conversations with Robin Trimby, Mark Dickson, and Steve Biggins, for soccer, and *Shrewsbury School Soccer (1995)*, compiled by Mark Dickson, was an invaluable source. Mike Eagar, Martin Knox, Paul Nichols, Steve Holroyd, Andy Barnard and Paul Pridgeon contributed to the section on cricket and Seb Cooley and Andy Barnard to that on Fives. Mike Hughes (SH 1975-80) provided material both on cricket and fives. Mark Lascelles' contribution to the sections on all three sports, football, cricket and fives,was both extremely useful and a striking indication of his versatility on the sports field. Chris Etherington and Duncan Kirkby supplied me with material about Rugby football, Jim Sheppe talked to me about polo and Paul Kaye about mountain-biking. Nick David, as Director, was particularly generous with both time and information about the ever-expanding programme of outdoor activities.

In compiling the section on debating, I received valuable assistance from Richard Hudson, Laura Whittle and Dr Matthew Clark; on bee-keeping from Selby Martin and Andrew Allott; and on Astronomy from Steve Adams and Mark Elliot. Hugh Ramsbotham supplied me with an account of the origins of the Challenge of Management conferences, and Colm Kealy talked to me about their later development. Steve Adams (the Head of Science) and John Balcombe gave me a fascinating insight into the International Young Physicists Tournament, and I am grateful to Steve and other Heads of Faculty, Jerome Armstrong (Mathematics), Martin Kirk (Physics) Andrew Briggs (Chemistry) and Andrew Allott (Biology) for information about the School Olympiads in their respective subjects. Huw Peach gave me a splendid briefing on the Model United Nations and Charlie Oakley on the recent Salopian enthusiasm for Quizzes. Giles Bell provided a characteristically entertaining account of the adventures of the Social Services Group and of the Blue Chairs; and Lesley Drew introduced me to the imaginative enterprises of the Charities Committee. Dr John Godwin and Toby Percival unravelled the complexities I encountered in translating Latin Inscriptions. Adrian Struvé and Chris Conway were particularly helpful in contributing to the chapter on Shrewsbury House; and their assistance was reinforced by meetings with, and contributions from 'the Shewsy's' archive group and specifically from Revd Henry Corbett, John Hutchison and Henry Kennedy.

I have regretfully restricted the illustrations to the topics and activities discussed in the text: the range of the latter is so very extensive that it could scarcely be contained in one volume such as this. I record my gratitude to the many colleagues who supplied me with photographs of the school activities in which they are involved. I offer particular thanks to Annabel Warburg who helped me to search the Salopian Website Photographic Archive; and I owe a great debt of gratitude to Kate Bronner who contributed most of the photographs which illustrate the exteriors and interiors of the modern buildings. Particularly as regards the former aspect, the results testify that the sun shone brightly upon her enterprises and excursions.

I also express my grateful thanks to Chris Minns and Martin Knox for reading the whole text in draft and for their generous and painstaking participation in proof-reading - however the responsibility for any remaining inaccuracies or infelicities is mine - and to Richard Hudson for so kindly agreeing to publish the book and for his invaluable experience and consummate skills in doing so. Richard's own long association with the School, both as boy and master, and his participation in the wider activities of the Salopian Club, have enabled him to offer informed and positive criticism which has been equally invaluable and in which both Chris and Martin, with their long and reliable memories of the material, have shared.

From all this it will appear that this book is, to a considerable extent, a collaborative and community effort: and I think that it is both desirable and appropriate that it should be so. I do not claim it as a work of scholarship, but I hope that it will serve as a work of piety and pay appropriate tribute to my colleagues who have worked together to earn the accolade accorded to the School in the *Good Schools Guide* of 2003, 'A connoisseur's choice'. If the result also serves to fill a gap in the Salopian annals, to bring them up to date and to make a worthy contribution to them, I hope that it will thereby repay a small part of the debt which I owe to the Salopian community for the friendship, happiness and fulfilment which it has brought me over nearly sixty years.

CHAPTER ONE

HISTORY TO 1950

Shrewsbury School was founded, by Charter of King Edward VI, on 10th February 1552, at the petition of the local burgesses, to provide a Grammar School for local boys. It was one of many schools founded in the mid-sixteenth century which received endowments from recently dissolved religious institutions, in Shrewsbury's case, from the Colleges of St Mary and St Chad. The first decade of Shrewsbury's history is obscure, its first two headmasters shadowy figures, but the school was rescued from the possibility of early extinction by the appointment of Thomas Ashton in 1561, who may be regarded as its effective founding Headmaster.

Thomas Ashton (1561-1571) filled the school and established its national reputation. The enrolment of Philip Sidney, the son of the President of the Council of the Marches, in 1564, was a great *coup* for Ashton and, from the very first, boys from all over the country joined local boys as its pupils. By 1586 it was reputed to be 'the largest school in all England'. Ashton's own personal reputation as a producer of plays is known to have tempted Queen Elizabeth I to visit Shrewsbury, though regrettably she never completed the journey. Ashton managed to acquire extra endowments for the school and in his *Ordinances* (1578) laid down the principles for its government.

The two centuries which followed were marked by repeated disputes between the parties thereby involved in the running of the school. The Governing Body of St John's College Cambridge had the right to appoint the Headmaster, subject to certain restrictions, (many Headmasters, including Ashton himself, were Fellows of the College), but the Mayor and Bailiffs of Shrewsbury had the right to veto the choice. In the eighteenth century disputes became polarised and politicised between the Tory College and Headmaster on the one hand and the Whig Corporation on the other. The few really significant events which stand out in this period include the establishment of the School in the Old Schools building during Meighen's headmastership (1583-1635), the School's support of Charles I, during the Civil War, with a loan which has not been repaid, and the substitution of headmaster Chaloner by the nominee of the victorious Parliament. (Chaloner survived long enough to be restored, briefly, by Charles II.) Towards the end of the eighteenth century the School seemed to be in progressive and terminal decline. James Atcherley (Headmaster 1771-1798) was notoriously neglectful of his duties: the number of pupils had been reduced to less than a dozen, and a group of leading burgesses initiated a movement to reform the administration of the School by Act of Parliament.

The appointment of Samuel Butler (1798-1836) inaugurated more than a century of crucial importance for the school; he was the first of three great headmasters, whose combined tenure spanned 110 years. The Act of 1798 gave the Headmaster greater freedom of action and reduced the influence of the civic authorities. Butler quickly restored a proper academic curriculum with regular examinations; the numbers in the school rapidly and dramatically revived. Although Butler encountered a number of disciplinary problems, including a food riot and pupil disorders both in the town and beyond, the overall reputation of the school was retrieved and was recognized by the visit of the Duchess of Kent and her daughter, the future Queen Victoria, in 1832. Like Ashton before him, Butler recruited a pupil who was to earn international prominence and renown. Charles Darwin entered the school in 1818, though the strictly classical academic fare on offer was by no means to his taste. However, it is appropriate that the statues of two of the most famous Salopians, Sidney and Darwin, now stand at each end of 'Central', the School's principal avenue. Shrewsbury's reputation for excellence in the Classics had already begun to grow in Butler's time; and in 1831, Thomas Branckner, while still at school, won a University prize, the prestigious Ireland Scholarship.

Benjamin Hall Kennedy (1836-1866) came to be regarded as the greatest classical schoolmaster of the century, and his status and reputation proved crucial when the Clarendon Commission was set up in 1862 to identify and inspect the 'Public Schools'. Its task was distinguish and identify the schools which provided an élite and predominantly classical education to pupils who would be recruited from all over the country, who would normally proceed to Oxford and Cambridge and would subsequently play a prominent role in national life and imperial administration. The curriculum of these schools would differ from that of the many other schools whose principal objective was to provide a suitable education for the sons of the burgeoning middle classes, who would subsequently take the lead in a more restricted local and civic sphere. The status of Shrewsbury became a test case, well illustrated, in 1866, by an acerbic exchange of letters between the cricket captains of Westminster and Shrewsbury, the former denying and the latter vigorously asserting Shrewsbury's status as a Public School. This now famous verbal duel is recounted in its proper place in the chapter on cricket.

In the event, the Commission decided in Shrewsbury's favour. For the second time Shrewsbury could invoke an Act of Parliament, and in the 1868 Act the School was included with Eton, Winchester, Harrow, Rugby, Charterhouse and Westminster (and originally with two other London schools, St. Paul's and Merchant Taylors') as one of the great 'Public Schools'. Provision was also made in the Act for a new Governing Body, in which the membership would be broadened and the local representation diluted. By this time Kennedy had been succeeded by the third member of the great headmagisterial triumvirate, Henry Whitehead Moss (1866-1908). A Salopian himself, and only twenty-five at the time of his appointment, Moss was far-sighted enough to recognize that the School could never achieve the expansion he deemed necessary if it was still confined within the Old School Buildings in the centre of the town; and he was shrewd enough to ensure that a provision authorising him to move the School to a new location, within a radius of three miles of the centre of the town, was included in the Act.

It is easy to understand that the local authorities felt that they were progressively losing control of 'their' school. The proposals to move its location further reinforced this feeling. There was strong opposition by traditionalist Old Salopians in the town to the idea of any move at all. Each of a number of alternative sites attracted its advocates. Kingsland was by no means the most favoured. The final outcome was the result of a tortuous process in which determination, accident and compromise all played their part. Moss's determination was strengthened by the support of the new Governing Body; together they were firmly resolved that the School should be moved to Coton Hill. Accident played its part in the process when the news that Moss had administered eighty-eight strokes of the birch to a boy who came from a prominent family in the town resulted in questions being asked in parliament and in Moss being satirised in *Punch*. Feeling that their position had been weakened by the scandal, Moss and his governors were now willing to compromise, and the adoption of the Kingsland Site was the result of that compromise. The decision to move there was made by 1875 and the actual move took place in 1882. What is now the main school building had already occupied its position for well over a century and had had its own independent history, successively as Foundling Hospital, internment prison and workhouse. Now it housed what the townspeople had regarded as their local school; and as it loomed prominently over the town, they must have been painfully aware, in Colin Leach's vivid phrase, that it now represented 'a monument to the power of parliament'. It will already be clear that the sub-title of Leach's history of the school, *The Four Foundations*, was aptly chosen. After its creation in the reign of Edward VI, the School experienced three further leases of life, in its recreation by Ashton, its transformation by Butler and its transmigration under Moss. The recent introduction of co-education, certainly no less significant than these previous developments, may perhaps be seen as a fifth.

The development of the Kingsland Site, almost empty before 1882, is the subject of a subsequent chapter. When the long headmastership of Moss came to an end in 1908, the appointment of a young headmaster from Oxford, Cyril Alington, after a long, unbroken succession of Cambridge graduates, marked a definite change of tone. He appointed a remarkable group of enthusiastic and talented young men, whose social focus was located in the bachelor community of the New House. A reciprocal response to, and nurturing of each other's talents was combined with a willingness, unusual at that period, to devote their own private time to sharing their cultural interests with their pupils, outside the classroom and beyond the curriculum. The First World War claimed the lives of several of these idealistic young schoolmasters, but their legacy survived them and the spirit of the New House was to live on for another sixty years.

Prominent among them were Evelyn Southwell and Malcolm White, whose contribution and devotion to Shrewsbury and whose thinking, both at school and subsequently in the trenches on the Western Front, where both were killed in 1916, are vividly recorded in a memoir, *Two Men*, published three years later. When an initiative to reprint the book was made it 1954, it was claimed that 'what makes it a great book is that, reading it, there gradually shines forth a clear understanding of the special philosophy of the place, a philosophy which is passed from generation to generation in the School'. The distinguished historian H. A. L. Fisher once told a large audience in London that if they wanted to get an insight into a schoolmaster's philosophy of life, he would urge them to read *Two Men*.

There is a mass of evidence suggesting that there was indeed something distinctive and remarkable about the ethos of the School, and about the New House in particular, during the Alington years. R.A. Knox, who was briefly a member of that community, subsequently reflected,

Of the junior masters at Shrewsbury, I can honestly say that I never came in contact in all my life with a group of minds so original.

He wrote of the 'Golden Chains' which bound him to Shrewsbury and confessed that,

Shrewsbury had entered into me, I loved every stone of it: its ways, its atmosphere, its society, had come to be part of the machinery of my life.

But, of course, it was under the aegis of Alington himself that this atmosphere was created and nurtured. He recognized its distinctive quality, writing, in his foreword to *Two Men,*

The life of our Society from which they went was, for those few years, as nearly that of a happy family as any which the annals of schoolmastering can show.

And Alington made his own direct and specific contribution to it by his brilliant composition of the verses of the school song (the Carmen) and by delivering a series of inspirational sermons at Evensong, the so-called *Shrewsbury Fables*. The secret source of such an enabling atmosphere lay, as always, in the quality of personal relationships. Jack Peterson, who joined the school as a boy during Alington's headmastership, subsequently followed him, as an Assistant Master, to Eton, and finally returned in 1950 to be Headmaster of Shrewsbury himself, identified another source of this atmosphere. 'He always knew all about you, and he always cared.'

This atmosphere was easily detectable when I first joined the staff, and, soon afterwards, the community of the New House, in 1958, for Peterson was still Headmaster. Like Alington before him he had appointed a significant number of young men within a short space of time (including eight in one term) and like Alington, he too was willing to give his young colleagues their head and to support their initiatives.

The Salopian ethos which had been established during the headmastership of Alington, persisted during the reign of his successor, Canon Sawyer (1917-32), which was twice as long, and Philip Cowburn asserted that both Alington and Sawyer shared 'a quality of disinterested goodness.' Colin Leach concludes that Sawyer must have been 'a man whom it was impossible to dislike'. Sawyer was neither efficient nor businesslike (though the numbers in the school grew significantly during his tenure), and the stories about his forgetfulness are legion; but he was capable of inspiring great affection in both his colleagues and pupils. The account given, in a boy's letter home in 1929, of Sawyer's awkward and undignified, though public, descent in a fire-escape-harness from the fourth floor of School House, eloquently conveys the Headmaster's likeability: S.S. Sopwith's much-quoted application of a passage from Milton to describe the scene at a Masters' meeting convened by Sawyer and his senior master, Chance, equally indicates the Headmaster's lack of management skills:

> Chaos umpire sits,
> And by decision more embroils the fray,
> By which he reigns. Next him, high arbiter,
> Chance governs all.

When asked what he considered his greatest achievement at Shrewsbury to be, Alington liked to reply, 'Sending a crew to Henley' but it was under Sawyer that Shrewsbury first began to make its mark on the national rowing scene, recording several victories, which culminated in the crew's notable triumph of winning the prestigious Ladies Plate in 1932. To bestow the final accolade, the Prince of Wales visited the school in the same year, Sawyer's last as Headmaster. It is understandable that, looking back on the 1920s, a decade released from the tensions and tragedies of the First World War and not yet clouded by the threat of a Second, Salopians at school at that time should perceive it as a Golden Age.

Hardy (1932-44) was a Headmaster whose reputation has been enhanced by historical perspective. His obituarist, writing in the *Salopian Newsletter*, considered that 'he was the right man, in the right place at the right time'. It has been customary to emphasize the marked contrast between Sawyer and Hardy's styles of leadership. Indeed Philip Cowburn asserts that 'between their headmasterships lies the end of one era and the beginning of another'. But hindsight has produced a more nuanced and rounded picture. Hardy was austere on the public stage, a disciplinarian and an efficient administrator. Many of his pronouncements were peremptory. His displeasure when he discovered that the boys preferred watching films in the Alington Hall to taking the country walks on Sunday afternoons which he encouraged, was considerable: and the manner in which he expressed that displeasure was typical 'I frankly dislike these displays', he announced, 'and feel no disposition to sanction them in the future'. Many instances are, however, recorded of his kindness to individuals, and of his graciousness as host, in his new home in Kingsland House. He was also accustomed to invite colleagues to accompany him on his own Sunday afternoon walks, an invitation which, no doubt, proved an ordeal for some, but which provided a valuable opportunity for personal contact and exchange of views. Like Sawyer and indeed Alington before him, but for considerably longer, Hardy had to weather the initial unpopularity often encountered by new headmasters, but this situation was exacerbated by his insistence, in 1938, on compulsory P.T. for the whole school. Michael Charlesworth recounts that the boys set up an Action Committee to oppose the measure and that a manifesto denouncing it was published, but that swift concerted action by the praepostors nipped the protest in the bud. However, Hardy had much more serious problems, which it was imperative should be urgently addressed. The boarding fees had not been raised for over a decade and the school was running at a loss. Hardy's decision to curb the financial independence of the housemasters, many of whom were long-established in those positions, brought unpopularity in another, most influential quarter. To maintain the numbers in the school was a continuous and persistent struggle. Hardy's problems were compounded by the exigencies and deficiencies of war.

At one stage, in 1940, Hardy even had to confront the logistical nightmare of simultaneously providing accommodation, an academic curriculum and sports facilities for two schools on the same campus. Cheltenham College was temporarily 'billetted' at Shrewsbury, during the Michaelmas Term of 1939 and the Lent Term of 1940. The outcome was, in fact, remarkably harmonious and the situation produced some memorable highlights, notably when, on one day in November 1939, the Shrewsbury soccer XI beat Bradfield in the morning, and the Cheltenham Rugby XV beat Rugby in the afternoon, both matches being watched by the members of both schools. In the Lent Term both Salopians and Cheltonians took advantage of the exceptional weather conditions to enjoy ice-skating on the flooded Common and tobogganing down the School Bank.

Hardy also took three crucial initiatives in staffing: as the first lay Headmaster after a long, and almost unbroken succession of clerics, he appointed a School Chaplain; the financial situation demanded the recruitment of a full-time Bursar, and he also appointed a Director of Music. The origin of Music's ascent to its current very prominent position of universally acknowledged excellence can be traced back to this period. Hardy also separated the responsibilities of Headmaster and Housemaster of School House, soon transferring the latter to a colleague, Russell Hope Simpson, the length of whose tenure, first as House Tutor to Canon Sawyer and then as Housemaster in his own right remains unsurpassed, at twenty-four years. In view of the ever-increasing burden and complexity of Headmastership in the twentieth century, this delegation was a wise and inevitable step. When Hardy retired in 1944, both he and Shrewsbury had weathered the storm; soon even his strongest critics were willing to concede that he had been a great Headmaster.

At just under six years, Wolfenden's tenure of the Headmastership (1944-1950) was the shortest for more than two centuries. He came to Shrewsbury, while still under forty, after eleven years at Uppingham, already an experienced Headmaster, well-known for his interest and influence in educational matters far broader than the confines of those relating to any particular school. Frequent trips to London punctuated his headmastership, and it was said that one of his leaving presents from Uppingham had been a first-class season ticket for the new journey. Perhaps headmaster and school did not 'integrate' to the degree achieved by some of his predecessors, and this was recognized on both sides. Wolfenden disclosed in his autobiography that he considered that he had made very little impact on Shrewsbury where, in sharp contrast to Uppingham,

it seemed at first sight, the Headmaster was at best a constitutional monarch … while the actual running of the place was in the hands of a highly competent body of masters and boys.

However, this assessment does far less than justice to Wolfenden's achievement and the impact that he made. He was appointed headmaster at a time of great austerity, when there was a sharp rise in fees and a decline in numbers, but he handed over to his successor a school in which the entry lists were full. Like Hardy, he exerted strong and decisive leadership; he reformed an outdated curriculum; he forged closer ties with the town. He took the greatest care to keep - and to be seen to keep - in touch, by means of his regular Monday morning addresses to the school, his regular meetings with the praepostors and his equally regular tour of the sporting activities in the 'after twelve' period before lunch; and his great ability ensured that this appearance of having his finger on the pulse was also a powerful and positive reality. Perhaps the most significant element in Wolfenden's legacy lay in his appointments. He inherited a wartime staff in which many positions were temporary; subsequently he appointed seven new Housemasters and twenty new Assistant Masters – virtually half the staff- which ensured that his influence was to be felt for decades to come.

Peterson's appointment to Shrewsbury was greeted with widespread acclaim. It seemed to very many that the return of the most eminent Salopian of his age, a generation later, to preside over his school as it prepared to celebrate the Fourth Centenary of its foundation, could not be more appropriate. Jack Peterson's distinguished and versatile attainment, which is fully recorded in the chapter devoted to his headmastership, made him a fitting examplar both for the aspirations of Salopians in the future and an equally fitting reminder of the achievements of Philip Sidney's Renaissance school in the past. In the perspective of more recent history, it seemed that the 'Golden Age' of Alington and Sawyer would be restored.

This brief sketch of the first four centuries of the history of the School leads us to the period of sixty years on which the principal focus of this book is placed, enabling us to assess the legacy which forms the historical context for the developments which have occurred in these most recent decades.

In the sixteenth century the School received its royal foundation, an historic provision for Day Boys, and a close, if chequered relationship with the civic authorities, dating from the original constitution for the government of the School.

In the nineteenth century, arguably the most significant in the history of the School so far, Shrewsbury received a national reputation for academic excellence, specifically in the Classics, an acknowledged position as a leading Public School, and an incomparable campus, which was to provide the environment for further expansion.

In the early twentieth century the legacy was less tangible, but arguably no less significant, consisting in the emergence of a notably 'easy', positive and friendly relationship between the teaching staff and the boys, and in the pursuit of all-round achievement, already detectable in the school's earliest days, but revived and reformulated in the words of Alington's Carmen:

Arte, libro, remo, folle, gloriam petamus.

It is now time to examine the stewardship of that heritage during the last sixty years.

CHAPTER TWO

THE PUBLIC SCHOOL REVOLUTION

The changes which took place in Shrewsbury and similar schools in the third quarter of the twentieth century were generally so radical and far-reaching that they have commonly been described as 'The Public School Revolution'. If a boy at school in Shrewsbury in 1960 were to hold a conversation about school life with his Salopian grandfather, each would easily recognize exactly what the other was describing; if the same boy were to have a similar conversation with his Salopian son, such recognition would be established far less easily; in many respects it would seem to the fourth generation Salopian that his father was describing a foreign country.

This 'revolution' had three principal aspects: the breaking down of barriers; the expansion of opportunities; and greater recognition of the individual. It came to be accepted that every person, however junior, together with the school activity to which he chose to devote himself, was worthy of equal respect: and all these aspects of the revolution were closely connected, each promoting and reinforcing the others.

The term 'monastic isolation' is often used to describe life in the traditional public school. The adjective is appropriate enough, for they were predominantly single-sex institutions; like the monasteries they gave a high priority to religious observance and each day followed a disciplined and strictly observed pattern of activity prescribed on an hourly basis. The noun requires greater qualification: certainly there was isolation from the outside world; often the individual boy experienced painful psychological isolation, but paradoxically this internal isolation took place in an environment of a total lack of privacy.

One barrier which characterised the traditional public school was the fortress-like nature of the individual Houses and the baronial status of their Housemasters. Outside the classroom it was very unusual for boys in one house to visit, or even associate with, boys in another House. Encounters between members of different houses on the games field were nearly always competitive and adversarial, further reinforcing the separate identity of each House. At Shrewsbury in the 1950s assistant masters might enter the boys' boarding houses only by specific invitation and for specific purposes, perhaps for lunch or to take prayers in the evening. It was known for colleagues who were found, uninvited, in a House to be asked by the Housemaster to leave forthwith. The Housemaster was assisted by one other colleague, the House Tutor, whom he had personally invited to assist him. A generation previously it was not unknown for the House Tutor himself to be confined to the 'Private Side' during his tour of duty, to be called into action only when alerted to an emergency by the Head of House. Of course, the rigidity of this system was gradually being slackened even before the 'revolutionary' period and the isolation of the Houses was decisively ended by the inauguration of Central Feeding in 1969 and by the development of tutoring within the Houses, until finally virtually every member of the Common Room was assigned to a House, and the Housemaster presided over a team of half-a-dozen or more colleagues, who were positively encouraged to visit and participate in the activities of the House, whenever and to whatever extent they chose.

A second barrier existed between the boarders and the dayboys. A small minority in 1950, numbering fewer than sixty and at one point dropping to just over forty, dayboys had no house of their own. They occupied a hall in the Main School Building, now the staff Common Room, took lunch in the School Shop and usually went home soon after the conclusion of school periods and organised sport. They were regarded by the rest of the school as second-class citizens, an attitude clearly reflected in their being termed, in the school slang, 'skytes'. The allusion, of course, was classical, denoting Scythians or barbarians. The colleague assigned to supervise them was known, significantly, as The Master (rather than the Housemaster) of Day Boys. Their despised position, not surprisingly, stimulated an intense group loyalty among the Day Boys and a commensurate determination to achieve. Equally unsurprisingly, in the rapidly changing climate of the 1960s, this highly undesirable situation could not be, and was not, allowed to last. The routine of the school day was adjusted in order to abolish 'First Lesson' at 7.45 am, an institution which had proved so difficult for dayboys and their families. A deliberate policy to enhance the status of dayboys was adopted: a significant expansion of their numbers (which eventually trebled overall) was deemed to be essential for the future (and not least the financial future) of the School, and suitable accommodation was provided both for the boys and the member of staff who was now recognised to be their 'Housemaster'.

Parents were expected to confine their appearances on the Site to the beginning and end of terms and to Speech Day; the convention was that they should 'keep away' during term time. The consequence for the boy was long, unbroken separations from home, the prospect of which often made witnessing the emotional farewells, particularly between mothers and sons at the conclusion of the New Boys' tea-party, a truly distressing experience. Communication was by letter or by phone, the latter only if the boy was willing to wait his turn in a queue for the by-no-means sound-proofed house telephone booth. The increased willingness to welcome parents on a regular basis dates from the time of the so-called 'revolution'. The novelty of the idea was demonstrated by the uncertainty of the Headmaster in a Common Room meeting about how many parents to expect on one particular occasion and the ponderous answer of a colleague, "As a general rule, Headmaster, I think it would be wise to allow for two parents per boy!" Since then regular Parents Meetings for every year-group in the school, standing invitations to plays, concerts and matches, formal Exeats for the whole school at least three times a term with informal Exeats for family occasions in addition, together, latterly, with e-mails and the ubiquitous mobile phone have broken down any existing barrier between school and home. Of course, even in the traditional school, the Housemaster was *in loco parentis* but the demarcation between the boys' side of the House and the Private Side was clear and strictly observed: the Housemaster's study on the boys' side served as a kind of outpost in an alien environment. There, on the 'other' side, on a day-to-day basis, the monitors were in charge. But in the post-revolutionary era the Green Baize Door was flung wide open and the power of the monitors to compel obedience was broken; but by that time there is substantial evidence that many of them were more than willing to abdicate.

It was the rigid division between year-groups which constituted the most significant barrier which existed under the *Ancien Régime*. Entering the school was like experiencing a new birth and entering a new country. This impression was reinforced by the necessity to learn a new language. Progress in this new life was indeed acknowledged in common parlance. A Salopian became a 'one-year old, two-year old, three-year old, four-year old', and even – in the case of the Oxbridge Upper Sixth, 'five-year-old', at the successive stages through which the boy passed in the school. This new world was a hierarchical world of privileges and powers, populated by study monitors, bedroom monitors, house monitors, school monitors and, at the apex, the praepostors, each of these luminaries authorised to impose sanctions and enforce discipline in his own area of competence.

This hierarchy was suffused with the notion of privilege, and all these privileges were duly identified, formulated and recorded in a document known as 'The Pink Book': who might, or might not unbutton his jacket; who might carry an umbrella; who might take a companion for tea 'down town'; who might walk on this particular piece of grass; who might leap rather than walk sedately up a flight of stairs. And woe betide the delinquent who assumed a privilege which was not rightfully his; the least he could expect was the censorious and often repeated cry, 'It's not your privilege!'

Monitors were entitled to exact personal services from the most junior boys, the 'new scum', a practice known as 'douling', another classical allusion, from the Greek, 'doulos', a slave. The term survives in two of the oldest Houses, Rigg's and Churchill's, but it is now simply used as a term for the housekeeping tasks performed by junior boys. In bygone days the service could involve such chores as running errands, making toast, cleaning shoes and CCF kit and making beds for the monitors. The 'doul call' and the rather more polite, alternative cry 'one scum, please' were commonly heard in the Houses and obliged the particular category of juniors designated to run to answer it. But the best-known, most significant, and most contentious of these privileges was the licence given to the monitors to discipline members of their Houses by beating them. The practice varied a little from House to House. In the earliest years of our period the Head of House might have delivered a few strokes with a cane or a light mini-cricket bat, other monitors might apply a slipper to a pyjama-clad behind at bedtime. At the time of the revolution beating was spontaneously in decline, though the appointment of a group of progressive and enlightened housemasters at the beginning of the 1960s did much to accelerate that trend. The summons of a junior boy to the monitors' room, Headroom, a kind of schoolboy Olympus, might herald merely a friendly reception and a polite request to make toast, or result in punishment for some misdemeanour. Had a contemporary Third Former, (for the term New Boy is now considered to be degrading) been exposed to the rigours of such a system, he would not have been slow in invoking his human rights, his parents and the rigour of the law.

These monitors were, however, but minor gods. The prestige and the power of the praepostors was much greater. Their writ ran and their authority was acknowledged throughout the whole school. The Clarendon Commissioners in the 1860s had particularly noted and approved the responsible position of the praepostors at Shrewsbury, and the positive use which they made of their role as the representatives of the school to the Headmaster, and of the Headmaster to the school. The praepostors could apply the ultimate disciplinary sanction available to the boys: so-called 'postoring' involved the summoning of a miscreant who was considered to have committed a serious offence to the History Library, where he was confronted by the whole praepostorial body, each member of which gave him one stroke of the cane.

At the pinnacle of the hierarchy stood the Head of School, one of the privileges of whose exalted position was the right to request extra half-holidays for the school, not only from the headmaster, but from the visiting Judge of Assize. Originally this involved the exchange of written communications in Latin, which both the Judge and the Head of School were expected to be sufficiently competent to compose; latterly a master in the Classical Faculty might provide both letters! Most Heads of School were not only keenly aware of their eminent status, but also of the great responsibility which attached to it. A famous example of this sense of responsibility is recorded by Michael Charlesworth, in his biography of J.B. Oldham, where he quotes the reflections which a Head of School, newly appointed in the early nineteen-thirties, made in his diary as he contemplated his forthcoming year of office:

This is my domain for a year! For the last few weeks Solomon's prayer has been in my mind ... 'And now, behold, O Lord, I am but a child: I know not how to go out nor how to come in ; and how shall I rule over this people that thou hast given me? Therefore, give me wisdom, O Lord.

One of his successors, thirty years later, who had an equally strong and commendable sense of responsibility, was similarly conscious of his status. When confronted by a newly-appointed master, who having conscientiously learned the academic sanctions for late work, and who, quite innocently, and with constructive intent, suggested that he might be able to catch up by availing himself of the time available in Extra Lesson (detention), the Head of School exploded to an established member of the Common Room, "Good God, the young whipper-snapper! Does he know who I am?" It is impossible, for a variety of reasons, to imagine any recent Head of School echoing any such sentiments: another example of the revolution which has taken place.

A combination of significant factors led to the dismantling of this elaborate hierarchy. The challenging of authority in society at large could not fail to influence the thinking of the masters and the senior boys; and the influence of progressive housemasters, together with the flinging wide of the Green Baize Door dramatically changed the atmosphere within the Houses. At the same time the adherence to and interest in the system of hierarchy and privilege by the senior boys markedly slackened. Many were comparatively easily persuaded that the primary role of the monitor should be pastoral rather than disciplinary.

If the School was by no means completely isolated from social trends in wider society, the final barrier between the school and the wider world was still comparatively robust; it was buttressed by long, unbroken terms, frequent roll-calls and evening lock-ups, and by very restricted leave-out. The requirement for boys to wear school uniform in town immediately marked them out from their contemporaries in other local schools. This separation was reinforced by an extensive private language, the school slang; single-sex exclusivity was still demonstrated by the fact that female parts in school plays continued to be taken by junior boys. But as Laurence Le Quesne noted in an article in the *Salopian Newsletter* in 1963:

the insulation of the School is breaking down ... Shrewsbury no longer provides a completely satisfying self-contained world: people look through it and beyond it.

During the early sixties, boys from the School took part in a Social Services scheme in the town, girls were increasingly recruited for choirs and plays, house dances became routine, and long discussions took place in Housemasters' meeting about when and for how long girls should be admitted to the Site and to the boys' Houses on unofficial occasions. This access was, of course, not to be unrestricted and was to be carefully supervised. During the course of one of these discussions one Housemaster was heard to assert that "Girls are for Sunday afternoon"! By the end of the decade the opening of the Seventy Club for Sixth Formers, initially in 40 The Schools, but soon to be transferred to specially designed premises in Tudor Court, provided the official sanction and venue for the authorised entertainment of girl-friends.

The second aspect of the Public Schools Revolution was the expansion of opportunities. An examination of the School Fasti for any year in the 1950s will immediately reveal how limited these opportunities were. A comparison with the Fastis of the most recent decade illustrates the dramatic scale and scope of this expansion. In the academic sphere the Sixth Form curriculum was confined in a strait-jacket of Five 'Sides', Classics, Modern Languages, History, Mathematics and Science (with a General Side as a temporary expedient). Classics was still predominant, and although History challenged it numerically during the early 1960s, this was partly on account of the anomaly which compelled students of English to march under the historical banner. The curriculum of the Lower School was based on the Form Master system, in which a member of the Common Room taught his Form for a group of 'core' subjects, often some combination of Divinity, English, History and a foreign language. This arrangement inevitably came under sustained and eventually successful fire from those who considered teaching by specialists in each subject to be essential. In the event, the whole curriculum was radically re-modelled in the 1960s (although the Form Master element remained for many years), with the aim of providing free choice of a group of three subjects in the Sixth Form and setting by ability in a wide range of subjects in the Lower School.

These reforms were accompanied by the introduction of 'new' subjects, Economics, although only temporarily, being one of the first, and by the elevation of the status of others. Physical Education was accorded full academic status. Previously it had been supervised by retired senior NCOs; now the master-in-charge became a full member of the Common Room. This was not the first example of such belated recognition. Inconceivable as it may seem from today's standpoint, it was only a few years earlier that the names of masters who taught Music and Art, hitherto printed as an appendix to the Common Room list, had been fully integrated in it.

There was a similarly dramatic expansion in the field of sport. Again this had two aspects, the range of sports offered and the increase in the number of fixtures. The five traditional 'major' sports were the Hunt, the Boat Club, Football, Cricket and Fives. One early example of extension was greater provision for Rugby. Enthusiasm for other sports waxed and waned during subsequent decades, activity often depending on the proficiency and interest of a particular member of the Common Room, but the general trend was towards increase and variety. The total number of sporting activities now available to Salopians is nearer thirty than twenty. The concomitant proliferation of teams is equally significant, marking, as it does, a shift in focus from the exclusive training of a sporting élite to the provision of inter-school competition for the full range of ages and abilities. Before the 'revolution' the Fasti generally records matches for the 1st, 2nd and Under 16 teams. Now 3rd, 4th and 5th school teams commonly appear and 'A', 'B', 'C' and even 'D' teams have been constituted for the Under 16, 15 and 14 age-groups in the major sports. Other sports, too, now have a full range of inter-school matches. A girls' sporting programme, itself considerably expanded since its inauguration in 2008, has made a substantial further addition.

Expansion of opportunity on the sports field has been matched by the development of a wide range of other extra-curricular activities. These are fully considered in a separate section. However, mention should be made here of the prominence and phenomenal success, for nearly thirty years, of Basic Year, an outward-bound organisation inspired by the charismatic enthusiasm and idiosyncratic style of Michael Hall, under whom it virtually became a school within a school. The Rovers continued to flourish and the School began to participate in the Duke of Edinburgh's Award Scheme. There was also a marked revival of interest in debating and competitive public speaking.

By the end of the 1960s expertise in sport was no longer the principal qualification for prestige in the school, although such was the strength of Shrewsbury's classical tradition that scholarship had always carried its distinctive cachet. But now equal respect began to be accorded to achievement in a wider range of activity. School Firsts were no longer an exclusive accolade for sportsmen, the most versatile and distinguished of whom had formerly been entitled to have their names inscribed in the School Wall. Eventually a committee was constituted for the specific purpose of awarding School Firsts in recognition of commensurate achievement in music and drama and other cultural activities, for technical assistance in the theatre, for management of school teams, for other forms of service to the School as well as for social service in the wider community.

The third aspect of the Public Schools Revolution was a greater recognition of and provision for the individual. This was both the cause and consequence of the demolition of the hierarchy. It also reflected the changes which were occurring in the outside world in the sixties. One of its manifestations was the exercise of less compulsion. The obligatory, universal attendance in Chapel and the similarly universal and compulsory membership of the CCF had been the principal targets for complaint by the disaffected. Daily attendance at Chapel on weekdays had been the norm, apart from a secular Headmaster's assembly on Monday in the Alington Hall. At the beginning of our period there were two services on Sunday, at both of which attendance was compulsory. During the middle years of the sixties this requirement was gradually relaxed and finally the current arrangement of one compulsory service during the week, with another one on Sunday, was reached. Membership of the Combined Cadet Force had also been compulsory; indeed the military parade of the Shrewsbury School battalion was one of the principal features of the Speech Day weekend. Here, too, the element of compulsion was relaxed. At first, exemption was granted to a few senior boys who were permitted to substitute Social Services as an alternative; but gradually a range of non-military Outward Bound activities virtually replaced the former system, leaving participation in the Corps as the voluntary choice of a minority. Another significant reduction in compulsion was the removal of the obligation for the whole school to attend certain specified school matches.

The increasing use of first names, rather than surnames, both between boys and also when masters were speaking to pupils was another indication of the recognition of the individual, as was the discarding of masters' gowns for everyday teaching and the removal of the dais upon which they had been accustomed to sit. There has also been a gradual, progressive and moderate relaxation of the strict regulations concerning school dress, allowing some expression of individual style and taste, and boys were allowed to wear casual clothes rather than school uniform when visiting the town.

One further important aspect of the recognition of the individual resulted from the demolition of the hierarchy. When the senior boys were no longer required, or disposed, to be the primary agents of discipline, and appropriate space became available in Houses after the inauguration of Central Feeding, it was possible to focus on their individual interests, too, by the provision of private study facilities in bedsits. This further reduced both the opportunity and their inclination to supervise their juniors.

A number of specific features of the revolution at Shrewsbury should be noted. The changes here occurred rather late, but with dramatic speed, so that quite quickly Shrewsbury, which seemed to some to have been falling behind, appeared to have taken the lead. That this was so was largely due to two factors. The first was that, in the fifties, Shrewsbury was experiencing a 'neo-Alingtonian age', reinforced not only by the success of Paul Dehn's remarkable *Masque*, which celebrated traditional Salopian values, but even more so by the after-glow of the Queen's visit in 1952 to celebrate the Fourth Centenary of the foundation of the School, which many saw as an endorsement of the *status quo*. The second was the dynamism and vision of Donald Wright, who succeeded Jack Peterson in 1963. It is too easy, but somewhat misleading, to over-emphasize the contrast between the two regimes. Historians tend to divide their seamless and intractable subject into 'periods', which are, of course, essentially artificial; but the seeds of significant change can often be discerned in the period prior to that which is generally held to be characterised by it. This is certainly the case in the instance of the hand-over between Jack Peterson and Donald Wright; but this mildly revisionist assertion in no way detracts from Wright's impressive and crucial achievement. Another factor is that such disenchantment as there was among the boys had been fairly successfully contained and managed. The Art School, in particular, provided an invaluable refuge for senior boys who felt alienated by and from the traditional system. In a wider perspective there was a certain geographical isolation which insulated Shrewsbury from the earlier impact and pace of change experienced in metropolitan areas. Two Salopian masters who in 1968 attended an early showing in London of the iconic film *If*, which satirised the traditional public school, laughed loudly as they recognized humorous and familiar characters and features; but they noticed that the rest of the audience was sometimes silent: to them, it appeared, the plot was too fantastic, or too outrageous, to be funny. It seemed to be an entirely different world. But by then Shrewsbury, too, was in the throes of rapid and dramatic change.

CHAPTER THREE

DAY BOYS

'Dayboys' is used in this chapter to indicate a group of boys and 'Day Boys' to refer to their House, the institution.

Dayboys have always played a significant part in the history of the School. Indeed Edward VI's charter was granted at the petition of the local burgesses to provide a free education in grammar for the sons of local citizens. But from its earliest years the School acquired a national reputation and boarders joined from all over the country, lodging with the Headmaster and his assistants or with other citizens in the town. Oldham states that there is no known evidence as to *when* the masters' boarding houses were first established, though it is recorded that between 1754 and 1770, when Newling was Headmaster, he had more than sixty boarders in his House. Butler had overall control of three groups of boarders and Kennedy had two – Senior Hall (Doctor's) and Junior Hall (Gee's). The Second Master had a House, presided over, in the final years of the Old School, by Revd G.T. Hall, which was eventually established on Kingsland as Rigg's Hall. At the same time Revd C.J.S. Churchill and T.A. Bentley also accommodated a few boys in their houses in the town, but it was not until the school moved to Kingsland in 1882 that boarding houses as we would now recognize them came into existence.

Historically, the relations between the boarders and the dayboys have not been easy. Parity of esteem and a desirable degree of integration have only been fully developed and established during the last forty years. Oldham notes that 'to some degree a barrier had always existed between [the dayboys] and the boarders'. He attributes this partly to a misconception of the original intention of the foundation and partly to chronic tensions between the School and the municipal authorities. Dr Kennedy was aware of this barrier and regretted it, but considered it inevitable. He attributed it not to any difference in social status, but rather to the fact that the experience of boarding inevitably made for greater social cohesion. The dayboys, he thought, were 'lacking in sociality'. This was not the only manifestation of the perceived barrier. Many of the dayboys were placed in the 'non-collegiate class' in which the element of classical studies was much reduced. They played their games on a different field from other members of the school and even had their own separate 'pack' in the Hunt. Thus the barrier operated both inside and outside the classroom.

When the Public School Commissioners visited in the 1860s, they recommended that the dayboys should be regarded as being at all times 'under discipline' and that they should be required to wear their 'mortar boards' in the town, in order to place them on equal terms with the boarders. But the later recommendations of the Commissioners reinforced rather than weakened the barrier. Although the removal of the burgesses' privileges, in the ensuing Public Schools Act, including that of claiming a free education for their sons, was intended to promote equality, it understandably increased local resentment, and the migration of the school from its premises in the centre of the town to the newly acquired Site in Kingsland greatly exacerbated that resentment. It is in the years immediately following these developments that the barrier between boarders and dayboys was at its strongest and most obvious. The epithet by which the boarders were accustomed to refer to dayboys – 'skytes' (Scythians and, hence, barbarians) - was an eloquent expression of the view they held of them.

Oldham asserts that 'A.H.Gilkes was the first to set himself definitely to bring together the two sections of the School'. Gilkes (1873-85) was an Olympian among the assistant masters of the time, commanding great respect and exerting influence in proportion. But the process he initiated proved to be difficult and lengthy. It was marked by the appointment in 1904 of a master to exercise general supervision of the dayboys and the change of nomenclature, which occurred much later, from 'the Master of the Dayboys' to 'the *Housemaster* of the Dayboys', was a further very significant step. The achievement of a dayboy, H.C. Owen, in becoming Head of School in 1934 also reflected an improvement in the position of Day Boys. But in the first half of the twentieth century the dayboys still occupied an inferior position, both in terms of status and of numbers; and their own awareness of this situation engendered among them not only a powerful *esprit de corps* but an equally powerful incentive to achieve.

These aspirations were carefully nurtured by a series of housemasters who devoted themselves to the task of obtaining parity of esteem for the dayboys. In 1949 Stacy Colman took over a House which was small in number but which already possessed a strong community spirit. He was struck by the absence of the rivalry and clannishness which might have been expected among the products of different local preparatory schools. It was a good move to appoint an eminent scholar to preside over a community of boys whose background, as sons of mainly professional families, enabled them then, as it always has since, to make an important contribution to the academic standards and achievements of the School. A fine musical tradition was established, and it was at this stage that the sons of Masters began to play a prominent and distinguished role in the fortunes of the House.

Under Basil Saint (1961-66) the scholarly tradition and the feeling of strong community were reinforced and four developments were to provide important growing points for the future. Parents began to appear more regularly at social functions previously restricted to members of the House; a formal luncheon was provided for dayboys in the School Shop; the first House Dance was another foray into the social possibilities of a House rooted in the local community; and the new Headmaster, Donald Wright, signalled his full support and encouragement for Day Boys as a vital element of the School.

Arnold Ellis (1966-71) was able fully and most imaginatively to exploit the possibilities which this favourable climate and the work of his predecessors had created. He was greatly assisted by the lively presence of his wife, Margaret, and by the motherly concern which she showed in the welfare of the boys. An important feature of Arnold's housemastership was the regular Parents Meetings, an initiative which was further developed by his successor. The strengthening of the links between the House and the local community from which it was drawn constituted Day Boys' unique contribution and was a source of strength to the school as a whole. The numbers in the House began to rise sharply, a feature which was partly responsible for the marked predominance of the House in sport. A House photograph towards the end of Arnold Ellis' reign is graced by twenty-six sporting trophies, and his parting gift to his successor, in his last week as Housemaster in 1971, was victory in all three soccer competitions – First House, Second House and Under 16 House.

The particularly distinguished, but still primarily athletic record of a group of dayboys between 1969 and 1973 did much to enhance the reputation of the House, and soon this achievement was diversified. In the two years between 1974 and 1976 dayboys won nine places at Oxbridge, three of them being awards. Two winners of the Sidney Gold Medal between 1971 and 1976 were former members of the House, and between 1972 and 1982 there were three dayboy Heads of School. Meanwhile Day Boys was developing, and managed for several years to maintain, an unchallenged pre-eminence in instrumental music.

A number of important financial and administrative developments greatly facilitated the cumulative achievement of these housemasters and their pupils. The Governing Body had determined on a policy of expansion and this in turn required an increase in pupil numbers. A rise in the number of Dayboys would produce an equally significant increase in income without the degree of capital expenditure required to accommodate a commensurate expansion in boarder numbers. In 1967 'First Lesson', a single period which had traditionally occurred, before breakfast, at 7.45 am, was abolished. Thereafter the first teaching period was to occur (after Chapel) at 9.15 a.m., an arrangement which obviously made dayboys' attendance at the School much easier. These developments were quickly followed by the inauguration of Kingsland Hall in 1969. This enabled dayboys to take lunch in their own area of the Hall, like the members of every other House. It also made it convenient for them to remain for tea after afternoon lessons in the winter and sport in the summer; and this in turn facilitated their attendance at society meetings in the evening and encouraged the habit of completing their *Top Schools* (homework or 'prep') at school.

Powerful external factors, both social and political, were also at work. The influx of professional families into the town (and, in particular, the major expansion of Shrewsbury as a medical centre) provided a supply of strong applicants for places in Day Boys – and Eric Anderson further enhanced the quality of the entrants by offering competitive places in addition to those allocated on the basis of priority of application and qualification in the Common Entrance examination. At the same time intense and prominent political debate about the future of Public Schools suggested that the position of those schools would be most secure which could demonstrate a close association with and service to their local communities.

David Gee (1972-83) inherited a house of 83 boys. The number of dayboys, 42 in 1961, had almost doubled in the course of a decade. By 1972 Day Boys, as a single unit, was becoming rather too preponderant in the School. His instructions were to cut the size of the House down to what was considered to be the optimum level - that of the average boarding house plus five. During the first four years of his tenure, he did just this. But the arrival of Eric Anderson in 1975 heralded a reversal of policy. Anderson considered that historical tradition, the ever increasing demand for places in Day Boys from the rapidly growing professional element in the town, the academic reinforcement which a strong Day Boys' House could provide, the advantages which would accrue to the school from a firm rooting in the local community at a time of political uncertainty and the clear social and educational advantages of strengthening such links, were cogent factors which recommended a doubling rather than a reduction in the size of the House. Accordingly, between 1975 and 1983 Day Boys' numbers grew again from less than 70 to 123. Members of the House were required to complete their Top Schools in the House first on two, then on three, and finally on four days a week. The policy was, as far as practicable, to integrate dayboys fully into the life of the school, so that, in effect, they became 'boarders who happened to sleep at home'. It was considered that this was the most effective way in which to achieve parity of status and esteem with the boarders and also to allow dayboys to profit as far as possible from the communal and social advantages of boarding school life. Such a policy required full co-operation from parents who were made fully aware, at the time of their registration, of the inconvenience to family life which would, on occasions, inevitably ensue.

The very rapid increase in numbers during these eight years caused considerable problems in the provision of study accommodation. The two large studies adjacent to Day Boys' Hall in the Main School Building soon proved totally inadequate, and the strategy of taking over more and more classrooms on the ground floor, thereby reducing the number of rooms available for teaching, was a hand-to-mouth expedient which was clearly both undesirable and unsustainable. Eventually a Day Boy annexe was established in the Poplars at the junction of Ashton and Butler Road, raising its own problems of the supervision of this remote outpost. The solution adopted was to move the whole house to the Old Sanatorium building on Port Hill Road, which had been adapted to provide all the facilities of a boarding House, other than bedrooms. Now dayboys had their own studies, changing rooms and common rooms, with space for further expansion, within a well-defined territorial base they could call their own. The migration, 'the Great Trek', occurred on the wintry morning of Friday 16th February 1979. The dayboys simply picked up their belongings and carried them across the Site to their new home. It was well over thirty years since a House had changed location in this way. Their Housemaster moved to occupy accommodation immediately adjacent to the new house which was officially opened, very appropriately, by the Mayor, Councillor George Marston, who had himself been a dayboy and who was the father of two dayboy sons. The members of the House promptly took advantage of their new location beside the Athletics track to win the Athletics Cup in Lent Term 1979. The last time Day Boys had done this was in 1893.

This migration was a crucially important milestone in the development of Day Boys. They now had their own House and their own resident Housemaster. Establishment in their own House seemed to enhance both their status and their achievement. But if the problem of accommodation had been solved, the administrative problems caused by their growing numbers remained. School House provided the obvious model, with its internal division at that time, for purposes of competition, into Doctor's and Headroom. Whereas the boarding houses on the Upper Common had taken the names of their Housemasters, those on what had come to be called the Lower Common, Ridgemount and Severn Hill, were topographical. Accordingly it was decided that the two sub-divisions of Day Boys should be called Port Hill and Radbrook. Assistant Housemasters were appointed to supervise each half, and when the numbers of dayboys in the Lower School became sufficient, junior teams were also fielded for each. Dayboys of earlier generations, still resident in the town, were insistent that the purple colours under which they had served, when a despised minority, should be retained; so it was agreed that Radbrook should inherit the existing colours of purple and white, and Port Hill should wear purple and black, the idea being to indicate both unity and difference. After a few years, however, experience having shown that the latter colours were difficult to distinguish on the field, Port Hill adopted completely different colours of red and orange, then to little protest from the town. A more important question was whether the two rapidly growing sub-divisions of Day Boys should remain as one House, when they had developed to full size, or whether two separate Houses should be established. The latter alternative was adopted. As it happened this last development coincided with the retirement of their Housemaster, and in January 1984 the two new houses of Port Hill and Radbrook were established, Port Hill in the part of the building nearer to Severn Hill and the town, with their respective Housemasters resident in the private houses immediately adjacent on each side. Subsequently separate Assembly Halls and additional study accommodation for the two houses were built between the main building and the Athletics track. The thirtieth anniversary of the separation of the Houses was marked by a dinner in Kingsland Hall on 3rd October 2014.

Unsurprisingly, many of these developments had been controversial. Full integration required full commitment and the question of how far it was reasonable to take this commitment naturally arose. One major issue was whether dayboys should be required to attend Chapel on Sundays, and if so, whether this should be every Sunday, on prescribed and limited occasions, or not at all. The requirement that dayboys should, as a rule, complete their Top Schools at school, had also been contested and subsequently relaxed. The extent to which the school rules imposed upon the boarders should be extended to dayboys was another recurrent issue, not least in so far as the rules on driving cars were concerned. The obligation to wear school uniform in town had occasionally led to circumstances in which dayboys, cycling home in the evening, had been attacked, or at least menaced, by groups of local boys from other schools. This problem was reduced when, in the 1980s, neither dayboys nor boarders were any longer required to wear school uniform in town. When Day Boys moved from the Main School Building to its new premises on Port Hill Road, it was feared that this relocation on the periphery of the Site might tend to marginalize dayboys' contribution and reduce their influence in the school – a concern which has proved entirely ungrounded. When two separate Day Boy houses were established in 1984, it had been argued both that it was more appropriate for the town house to be administered under the authority of one housemaster, in order to ensure consistency of policy and to avoid comparisons being made and preferences expressed between two institutions whose conduct would inevitably be closely monitored by local parents. It was also argued that from a purely social point of view a constituency drawn from one local municipal community would be more appropriately reflected in one school community rather than two. Subsequently, however, this latter point has been addressed by the formation of a vigorous Day Boys'

Parents Association and by regular social events in which both Houses participate. More recently the respective merits of an arrangement by which Day Boys have two Houses of their own and the alternative arrangement in which they would be distributed between the existing boarding houses have been discussed, the debate stimulated by the fact that in the three recently established girls' houses the latter alternative, dictated by the inevitably small current number of daygirls, has been adopted.

Whatever its own internal standards of excellence, a good school must accept the obligation of setting these standards to work in the wider community, and indeed aim to set a higher standard than that accepted in society as a whole. Dayboys, occupying a middle position between the more protected conditions of a boarding school and the less protected conditions of society at large, have historically acted as front line troops in that educational process. Conversely they have helped to mitigate and reduce any tendency towards an 'ivory tower' mentality in the school as a whole. However the significance of this mediating role has been significantly reduced during the last forty years by the more general breaking down of the monastic isolation of the traditional boarding school and by the reciprocal and ever-increasing practice of placing the facilities of the school at the disposal of a wide range of local teams and interest groups.

If the collective role of Day Boys in this respect has become less significant, the distinctive educational challenge presented to the individual dayboy in a boarding school remains unchanged. Writing in 1976, their Housemaster asserted that their position provided them both with the opportunity to derive the maximum benefit from life at a boarding school and also with an insidious temptation to waste it. The dayboy stands to gain a great deal if he commits himself fully to life in a boarding school, in terms of the benefits from its strong communal life, its freedom from external distractions, and its generous provision of extra-curricular facilities. These, taken together, provide a totality, richness, and variety of experience not generally available in a Day School. But to take full advantage of these assets requires both considerable self-discipline and sound judgement to be exercised at a comparatively young age. It is easy enough to spend the time available for sport and cultural activities at school completing Top Schools and then to pass the evenings in front of the television at home. It is not always easy to find a balanced response to the different claims of parental authority on the one hand and the school authorities on the other, particularly if their priorities conflict. Nor is it easy to deal with the tensions caused by restrictions imposed by the school, when a dayboy witnesses every day the greater freedom enjoyed by his neighbours and contemporaries at home. In all these respects potential difficulty and positive opportunity are finely balanced. But it is arguable that overall it is within a judicious and disciplined dayboy's capacity to enjoy the best of both worlds.

During the first decade after the inauguration of Port Hill and Radbrook the total numbers in the two Houses together stabilized in the range of the hundred and twenties but during the 1990s reached peaks exceeding 140 on three occasions: 148 in 1997, 143 in 1998, and 145 in 1999, before dropping back, in the first decade of the present century, to the former average around 125. The catchment area from which the boys were drawn extended ever more widely into the countryside, with some boys commuting from as far afield as Much Wenlock, Wellington, Welshpool and Wolverhampton. Writing in 1994, to mark the tenth anniversary of the two Houses, one of their Housemasters commented that each House now had 'its own particular feel and characteristics and certainly a very strong loyalty' and that 'the premier fixture in any season is the local derby which is contested as vigorously as any major inter-school event'. He also records with satisfaction that,

the current status of Port Hill and Radbrook was well expressed by a new third former who, on being asked if he was in Day Boys replied, in a rather puzzled way, "No, sir, I'm in Radbrook."

Colin Leach, commenting at a comparatively early stage in what must be surely be the most significant period in the development of Day Boys in the recent history of the School, makes the interesting observation that,

it is not too much to describe this welcome and important trend as being, in a sense, a return to the Schools' origins.

CHAPTER FOUR

THE SCHOOL SITE

The school campus, or 'The Site' as it has always been known, is one of Shrewsbury's greatest assets, and the arrangement of its buildings around a vast carpet of greensward helps to inculcate and reinforce a sense of identity and community. Neville Cardus described the scene which lay before him as 'the most beautiful playing fields in the world' and Laurence Le Quesne, in a fine article in the *Salopian Newsletter* identified space and surprise as the two key elements in its magical impact.

But in 1882 the twenty-seven acres purchased from the Council were common land, neither mown nor levelled. A great task lay ahead before they could be used for sport. The account which follows traces the development, both in acreage and construction, which has occurred during the last hundred and thirty years. The purchase of The Beck in 1890, the Craig and Chance fields in 1891 and of the Withers Field beyond in 1912 produced an area similar to that with which we are now familiar, extending the School Site beyond the present location of Oldham's towards Port Hill Road, and eventually quadrupling the acreage owned and occupied by the School. So far as construction is concerned, there is much evidence at Shrewsbury to support another of Laurence Le Quesne's interesting assertions that "it's one of the many curiosities of the English Public School system that most of its buildings are hideous, but most of its landscapes are beautiful."

The development of the Site may be examined in a series of distinct phases: the establishment of the original nucleus of buildings; the provision of a number of boarding houses to the south, along Ashton Road; and a similar and mainly subsequent construction westward along the northern perimeter, in an area now called The Moser Precinct. Then, after a further period of thirty years in which there was little building, each of five headmasters made a significant contribution to the rationalisation, expansion and enhancement of the already-established pattern. The current extent of the Site is 110 acres, roughly the same size as Vatican City, so the School can claim to be 'a city on a hill' indeed!

The original nucleus of the School lay in the immediate proximity of 'Central', the avenue leading towards what is now known as the Main School Building. This had been built in 1758 as a Foundling Hospital; subsequently, during the War of American Independence, it had served for the internment of Dutch prisoners of war; finally, in the nineteenth century it had become the local workhouse, 'a house for the correction of the idle poor'. The earlier associations of the building were considered unfortunate and they provided an argument for those who opposed the move of the School to Kingsland: but these objections were overcome and in 1882 the building was thoroughly renovated and adapted to provide classroom accommodation for the School.

School House was built by the Governors, a few yards to the east, to house the Headmaster and his boarders. Rigg's and Churchill's were constructed, by their first Housemasters, at the far end of 'Central', on land leased to them by the Governing Body. Most of the Houses built around the Top Common were given their Housemaster's names, for example, Churchill's Hall: but since Rigg's Housemaster in 1882 was himself called Hall, the House was given the name of a predecessor who had presided over one of the boarding houses in the Old Schools. Chapel, immediately to the west of the Main School Building, was under construction but not yet completed in 1882. Uncovered Fives courts, a photographic dark room, a carpentry shop and the school shop all belong to this very early period on Kingsland. A boat house had been erected in 1881.

The next stage in the development of the School took place along Ashton Road, very soon after the original occupation of the Site. Moser's was built in 1884, and in the same year Chance's House was established at 13 Kennedy Road. It has traditionally been known, as befitted a Classical School, as 40 The Schools, because it was built *forte*, by Chance! When Chance retired as Housemaster in 1925 the boys were moved to Severn Hill (this early antecedent explains Severn Hill's precedence in the order of Houses in the Brown (now Blue) Book. (A description of Brown Book will be found in the chapter on Administrative Changes.) In 1889 the two existing private Houses at No. 6 The Schools were adapted to become a boarding house, with F.E. Bennett as Housemaster, but the House came to be identified by the name of one of his successors, W.H. Moore. Boys from this House, too, were finally transferred to Severn Hill, and Severn Hill teams were being encouraged by cries of 'Moore's!' well into the 1970s. Arguably, the House currently known as Severn Hill was established and acquired its present identity in 1943, when boys from both Moore's and Chances were united there under J.H. Tombling. In 1900 Ingram's was built by Revd F. Sergeant, but came to be called by the name of its second Housemaster, F.M. Ingram.

Further developments in this area included the construction of the Alington Hall in 1909 and the building of the New House in 1911 to accommodate bachelor masters, adapted in 1978 to become a Sanatorium. A War Memorial, with a statue of Sir Philip Sidney, and the Moss Gates were both erected in 1923. Thereafter there was no other significant building in this part of the Site until the construction of the Gymnasium in 1938, converted into the Ashton Theatre in 1984.

Another line of development took place, west of the original buildings, in the Moser Precinct. In 1882 the baths were installed and in 1904 the (Old) Darwin Building (now the Art School) was built to house the Sciences. An Armoury followed in 1909. Although always intended to be a temporary edifice, it was only finally demolished in 1965, to make way for the Lyle Building. Oldham's was built in 1911, and funded by a loan of £17,749 16s and 7d from Lloyd's Bank to its eponymous Housemaster; and in 1916 the Moser Building was completed, its foundation stone having been laid in 1914 (by an early example of remote control) by King George V, from his carriage in the centre of the town. In 1938 the opening of the New Darwin Building, now the Biology building, completed that phase of building in the precinct. Meanwhile, still further to the west, first Ridgemount (1921) was purchased and then Severn Hill (1925) was re-purchased from private owners.

One initiative, though it occurred just off the Site, was to have considerable significance for the School and for the development of the RSSH in particular. Building along the by-pass road beyond Kingsland House threatened very soon to close the School's direct access to the countryside, a route which, as we have noted, the Headmaster, Hardy, very much wanted to keep open. In 1934 a field, identified as No 24, came up for sale on the other side of the road. Encouraged by Hardy, the governors made a cautious offer for the field; but during the Easter holiday another potential buyer put in a strong challenge and the opportunity for purchasing it seemed about to be lost. Hardy, who, making an analogy with a contemporary burning political issue, called the field the School's 'Danzig Corridor' to the open country, acted decisively on his own initiative. Enlisting the help of a number of Housemasters, Mitford, Whitfield, Tombling, Street and Hope-Simpson, together with the Bursar, Tippetts, he bought the field for £1,000, each of his associates contributing £100 or more. Field No. 24 thereafter became known as 'the Housemasters' Field'. The field was only conveyed to the Governing Body in 1945, when its original purchasers were reimbursed. Further projected building developments, beyond the field, placed the Governors under great pressure to sell it, and they eventually did so in 1979 for £50,000, having secured legal guarantees that the area would remain as a green space and a right of way in perpetuity.

Between 1938 and 1966 there was no major building project on the Top Common, but in the first half of the 1950s the Withers Field was levelled so that the surface came up to that of Chances. The result was one great playing field, stretching from the Miniature Range to the gardens of the houses on Port Hill. The long-desired running track was completed in 1956 and a year later the Stott Pavilion was constructed beside it. Provision was also made, in the Home Farm area in the 1960s, for Design and Technology and for a CCF office, the Craft Centre itself being completed in 1969. Meanwhile, the visit of Her Majesty the Queen in 1952 had been marked by the creation of the Queen's Terrace, to the north of the main school building, at the top of the School Bank.

The two main directions of building development having been established in the first fifty years of the School's relocation on Kingsland, first to the south and then to the west, there was a thirty-year pause before a third major phase of development began, also lasting about fifty years. These additions, enhancements and adaptations were not focused on specific areas, but tended to 'fill in' the existing pattern, always with the aim of building on the periphery of the Site, in order to preserve the central space. These developments are now most clearly considered, in the order in which they occurred, under five headmasters in turn.

During the Headmastership of Donald Wright (1963-75) there were three building developments of great importance. The Lyle Building was completed in the Moser Precinct in 1966, to house the then fashionable academic grouping of The Social Sciences (History and Geography). On the ground floor the classrooms were separated by screens, rather than solid walls, to permit the equally fashionable practice of 'team-teaching'. Kingsland Hall, to accommodate Central Feeding, was so cleverly sited, alongside Kingsland House, an eighteenth-century building, that it was scarcely visible from the upper, and merely a discreet presence on the lower areas of the School Site. The Science Building, built in 1974 to house Physics and Chemistry, was located immediately in front of Oldham's on the edge of the Upper Common. Also worthy of mention was the inauguration of a Sixth Form Club, located initially in No 40 the Schools, but subsequently moved to Little Tudor, which was extended to provide a club room with upstairs bedsits for senior students, with a warden occupying the original house, the whole complex being renamed Tudor Court.

Under Eric Anderson (1975-1980) the main theme was a carefully considered rationalisation of the use of existing buildings to provide greater efficiency. The first example of this was the abandonment of a plan to divide the School House building, physically, into two independent Houses, a scheme which was becoming as unworkable as it was expensive. In 1976 the Old Darwin Building became an Art School; and in 1979 Day Boys moved from their accommodation in the ground floor of the Main School Building, as described in the previous chapter. Meanwhile The New House, in Ashton Road, became the new Sanatorium. As the result of a generous donation by Mr T. Semaan, Squash Courts were also built and inaugurated in 1979.

During Simon Langdale's Headmastership (1981-88) the existing gymnasium was adapted to become the Ashton Theatre in 1984, a new sports hall having been erected nearby in 1983; and in the far south-west corner of the Lower Common a new boarding house, The Grove, was constructed, opening in 1988.

Under Ted Maidment (1998-2001), the Craig Building, for Information Technology, was constructed in 1996, and all-weather sports pitches, inaugurated in May 1998, between the Stott Pavilion and the Day Boys' Houses, replaced the Athletics Track. The Darwin Statute was erected outside the Main School Building in 2000, and a new Music School, the Maidment Building, was completed in 2001 in the south-west corner of the Top Common, on the rising ground above Kingsland House. It was a fitting memorial to the Headmaster's enthusiastic interest in and support of music, and, as had also happened in Sawyer's last year, the final accolade was conferred by a visit from the Prince of Wales in 2001 to inaugurate the building.

Major developments during the Headmastership of Jeremy Goulding (2001-2010) included the provision of the Neville Cardus Cricket Centre in 2006 on the ground between Ridgemount and Severn Hill and the construction of the Gemini Swimming Pool, as an extension of the Sports Hall and its adjacent changing rooms, in Summer 2007. This, in turn, allowed the conversion of the Old Baths into a Sixth Form Common Room, called *Quod*, in the Moser Precinct. A new boarding house adjacent to the Grove had originally been intended for occupation by boys, but when the decision was taken to admit girls to the Sixth Form, it was first used to provide temporary accommodation for the members of Severn Hill and Ridgemount, while their own houses were being thoroughly refurbished, and then adapted for the use of the first Sixth Form girls, who occupied it in 2008, when it was named Mary Sidney Hall.

Subsequently a second house for girls, Emma Darwin Hall, absorbed and made imaginative use of the whole Tudor Court complex. It was planned during Jeremy Goulding's Headmastership but was completed and inaugurated during that of his successor Mark Turner in 2011. The later decision to move to full co-education from September 2014, and the consequent further shift in the balance of numbers in the school from boys to girls, required the provision of a third house and it was announced that the membership of the Grove would be gradually reduced, to be converted for use by girls from September 2014. In March 2015 a further announcement was made that Moser's, too, would be converted from a boys' to a girls' house. The most recent and ambitious building project, the construction of a 19-classroom teaching block at the top of the rising ground between Ridgemount and Oldham's, is currently in progress and is due to be completed in the summer of 2015. The architect is Adrian Hoare OS (S 1976-1980).

One change to the external appearance of the Lower Common occurred when the Chance Pavilion was burned down (through suspected arson) in August 2005. As Will Hughes, then Director of Sport, noted, this misfortune ironically led to a little more playing space and good practice areas for football and rugby. However, the loss of the pavilion was keenly felt, not least because it had provided a suitable memorial to Arthur Chance (Master 1880-1925) who had led the initiative to turn the common land of Kingsland into suitable playing fields for the School. The new pavilion, a neighbour to the Stott pavilion at the north end of Chance's field, was built with the generous help of David Chance (O 1970-75) who had a family link to the original Chance family.

While these more obvious and visible changes have been taking place, there has been a continuous improvement of the living conditions in the individual boarding houses, starting with the provision of bedsit accommodation, made possible, after the inauguration of Central Feeding in 1969, by the adaptation of areas previously occupied by domestic staff. Many houses have built small extensions and linking corridors between different wings of their buildings. In some cases, most recently in Ridgemount and Severn Hill, as noted above, there has been such a thorough internal reconstruction and refurbishment that a temporary vacation of the premises was required, followed by a virtual re-opening of the House.

CHAPTER FIVE

SALOPIAN CELEBRATIONS

Returning, in 1982, from the festivities which marked the centenary of the School's move to Kingsland, Roger Dixey (JHT (S) 1935-40) wrote, "If there is one thing among many others that Shrewsbury School can do really well, it is to organize a celebration." During the last sixty years there have been frequent grounds for celebration, falling into two principal categories: those which mark the anniversaries in the history of the School itself or of its famous members; and, as befits a royal foundation, visits by or contacts with the Royal family. In some instances, of course, the two observances have coincided.

During the last sixty years there have been four occasions on which there have been Royal visitors to the School: and the previous four hundred years record only three. On 31st October 1832 the Duchess of Kent, accompanied by her daughter Princess (the future Queen) Victoria visited the School, still located in the Old Buildings. Oldham relates that the Duchess and the Princess were received under the archway by Dr Butler and his wife, to the accompaniment of the ringing of the bells of St Mary's and the firing of gun salutes from the river, and then escorted to Top Schools, where they were welcomed in an address (in English rather than the customary Latin) by the Head Boy; that the flowers ordered for presentation to the royal guests arrived too late; that Dr Butler used pre-arranged signals with his mortar board to moderate the cheering; and that the visitors took luncheon in the Headmaster's House.

Twenty years later, in 1852, on an occasion which ranks as a contact rather than a visit, Dr Kennedy, learning that the royal train was to pass through Shrewsbury, waited on the platform to pay his respects to Queen Victoria and the ten-year-old Prince of Wales. He presented a suitable educational tome, an elaborately bound copy of Radclyffe's *Memorials of Shrewsbury School*, to the future King Edward VII; and when it was thoughtfully returned to the school by Queen Mary, in 1946, as a memento of that earlier royal visit, it was remarked that it was in absolutely pristine condition! Delighted by the graciousness of his reception by the royal pair, Kennedy decreed an extra holiday for the whole school.

Princess Louise, Duchess of Argyll, the fourth daughter and sixth child of Queen Victoria and Prince Albert, was the first member of the Royal family to visit the School in its new location on Kingsland, when on 19th January 1898 she arrived for morning coffee; but the main object of her visit to Shrewsbury was to open the new High School.

Another royal contact occurred in 1914, when King George V laid the foundation stone of the Moser Building, by means of an electric current, transmitted from the Market Square when his carriage paused for the purpose.

The plaque set into the wall of the Moser Building records the circumstances:

> HIS EGO FUNDAMEN DOMIBUS, QUAS, ADVENA, CERNIS
> TESTIFICOR REGIS ME POSITUM ESSE MANU;
> NEC TAMEN IPSE ADERAT; VIS EMINUS IGNEA TACTU
> EMICAT, IN IUSSUM SUBSIDEOQUE LOCUM
> A.D. V NON. IUL. ANNO SCHOLAE CONDITAE CCCLXIII

> I, the foundation of these buildings which you observe, stranger,
> Bear witness that I was laid by the hand of a King,
> Not that he was present in person, however,
> A fiery energy (electrical current) sprang out
> And by his touch and assistance
> Laid me in the designated place.
> On the fifth day before the Nones of July
> In the 363rd year from the founding of the School

The date in the Latin inscription appears to refer to the year of the completion of the Moser Building (1916), although the King's visit occurred two years earlier.

Robin Case recounts the story that, as he presented a model of the proposed building to the King, Basil Oldham was tempted to change the course of the cable to his own adjacent greenhouse, so that he could claim to have the only greenhouse whose foundation had been laid by a king!

In Canon Sawyer's last year as Headmaster, 1932, the Prince of Wales visited the School to mark the Golden Jubilee of the move to Kingsland. A service was held in St Mary's, after which the Prince lunched with the Mayor and other notables at the Castle. Subsequently he was received at the School with an address by the Head of School (this time in Latin, but with an English translation provided for the Prince). He inspected a Guard of Honour, commanded by Major J.M. West, laid the foundation stone of the school wall, distributed prizes in the Alington Hall, and departed by means of the river ferry, another guard of honour being provided by six school eights lining the ferry rope.

The fourth centenary of the School was celebrated, in June 1952, by a series of events spanning the greater part of a week. On Tuesday 17th June the Combined Cadet Force was inspected by the Colonel of the Shropshire Light Infantry, Major-General J.M.L. Grover, CB, MC. On Wednesday 18th the first performance of Paul Dehn's Masque *Call-Over* took place. On Thursday the School assembled at the top of Pride Hill to witness the presentation of the High Cross to the town, which was inscribed as follows:

Municipio dilecto regia schola Salopiensis, sede non fide mutata

If the following loose translation is accepted, 'To our esteemed town from Royal Shrewsbury School, changed in its location, but not in its allegiance', the inscription makes a veiled, but reconciliatory reference to the fierce dispute surrounding the move to Kingsland seventy years previously. That evening a dinner was held for the civic and county authorities and for members of the school Common Room in the Alington Hall.

A reader of the Masque *Call-Over* to-day may well find it rather dated; but it was an eloquent and deeply moving portrayal of the ethos which pervaded the School at the time. Writing at the time of its production, S.S. Sopwith, Housemaster of Oldham's (1932 - 1947), claimed that 'it embodied the ideals, however trivial and however high, of a public school.' The play starts with Edward VI, the founder, calling the roll of the Salopians who are to appear; and in the scene which follows, John Smith, a new boy, apprehensive at the prospect of all the challenges which are to confront him, overwhelmed by the overbearing encouragement of the leading participants, and intimidated by a group of matrons who 'love to see little boys ill' is guided by Sir Philip Sidney, who has replaced King Edward on his plinth, to join in all the various activities of the school, athletic and academic. The first part of the production concludes with advice which still has strong relevance to the contemporary Salopian faced with an ever-widening range of opportunities:

> So in harmony we sing:
> Try your hand at everything.
> Spend the first odd year or two
> At finding out what you can do.
> Then whatever you are best at
> You can safely spend the rest at.

The second part of the Masque opens with a meditation on the theme of Time. John fears that he will be unable to find the time to take part in all the enterprises to which he has agreed; but Sir Philip counters:

> it is more than probable
> That Time, before you have been here very long,
> Will find you.

After meeting Philomathes, a lover of learning, and Polymathes, the educated man, representing respectively the Salopian as he arrives and as he leaves, and who differ, it seems, only in the way in which they hold their hats, John asks to meet real Salopians. These are represented first by Judge Jeffreys and Charles Darwin, and subsequently, in Part Three by Andrew Irvine, who died on Everest in 1924 and by a fighter pilot, whose name is Legion. They represent those who have displayed the courage that is needed to make a sacrificial response to the challenges they faced. The word 'need' reminds John of the equally sacrificial gesture of the dying Sir Philip Sidney on the battlefield of Zutphen and of his words to a common soldier, also mortally wounded, when he ordered that a cup of water which had been brought for him, should be given to the soldier instead: 'Thy need is greater than mine'. These examples provide John with the courage to face his own challenges and at his first Call-Over he confidently answers his name.

The Masque was produced by Arnold Hagger and the music was composed by John Stainer.

On Friday, June 20th the Fourth Centenary celebrations continued, following the precedent of the Prince of Wales' visit twenty years previously, with a Service of Thanksgiving in St Mary's, at which four bishops were present, the sermon being preached by the Rt Revd Tom Longworth, Bishop of Hereford, an Old Salopian and former Moserite. On the following day, Saturday, the focus of the celebrations moved back to the Site. There was a Call-Over, a Chapel service, a demonstration of massed PT and a cricket match against the Saracens. A buffet luncheon was provided in marquees on Central, Lord Tedder gave an address from a dais in front of the School Building, and the Headmaster gave a Garden Party. Old Salopians were subsequently invited to supper in their respective Houses, and the evening was concluded by a firework display on the Common. On the Sunday morning two services of Matins were provided in order to accommodate as many visitors as possible; but Evensong, at which Dr Alington, who had been invited back for the occasion, preached one of his Shrewsbury Fables, was restricted to members of the School.

By far the most significant of royal visits was that by her Majesty the Queen and the Duke of Edinburgh on 24th October 1952, forming the second part of the Fourth Centenary celebrations. Her Majesty had particularly asked to see a normal school day. There was considerable amusement in the Common Room at the lengthy, elaborate and meticulous arrangements which were set in hand to make it so. An eye-witness of the occasion records how the royal visitors were received in a respectful and impressive silence as they were accompanied by the Headmaster down Central to the dais which had once more been erected in front of the Main School Building. As her uncle had done before her, the Queen inspected a Guard of Honour, on this occasion commanded by Major M.G. Powell. After the Governors and the Officers of the Old Salopian Club had been presented to her Majesty in School House, the royal visitors witnessed a display of massed PT, visited Oldham's, watched fives and football matches (one of the players scoring a well-timed goal), and watched the Hunt set off on a run which would subsequently be named 'The Queen's'. They visited the carpenter's shop and a number of the support staff were presented; they viewed exhibitions of science, art and photography, and then moved to the library, where Basil Oldham was presented and Her Majesty accepted a superbly produced copy of *Shrewsbury School Library Bindings*. (It is related that only on the previous day, when the volume had been laid on a table in the Common Room for colleagues to inspect, many of them having already done so with nothing but admiring comment, one master, sharper-eyed than all the others, noticed that the first 'r' was missing from the word 'Shrewsbury', embossed in gold on the front cover, leading to an extremely rapid and equally miraculous rectification.) The Duke of Edinburgh received a presentation copy of Paul Dehn's Masque. The members of the Common Room were then presented to the royal couple at a sherry party.

David Bevan records the frenzied activities behind the scenes in his *Recollections*:

The boys, wearing their blue suits, formed a double line on Central to greet HM. Very shortly afterwards they all had to take part in a massed PT display. They were therefore instructed to wear their PT kit, instead of underclothes, beneath their blue suits. Their gym shoes had been left in form rooms, allotted by houses, in the School Building...The Queen was escorted to the School House and during this brief pause in the proceedings, the boys dashed into the School Building, changed into PT kit and were on parade again, in ranks and sized. This was the last Shrewsbury PT display.

Lunch was taken in School House, where Her Majesty sat between the Head of School and the Senior Praepostor. She then proceeded to the terrace behind the School Building, overlooking the town, to find the whole School massed on the bank below. The inauguration of the Queen's Terrace is recorded on a plaque on the wall, inscribed thus:

HANC GESTATIONEM ANNO SCHOLAE FUNDATAE
QUADRINGENTESIMO EXSTRUCTAM
PRIMA INGRESSA EST
ELIZABETHA II REGINA
A. D. KAL. NOV. MCMLII

UNDE TRAHAM MOLES RUDIS, ADVENA, QUAERIS.
DISCE OLIM DOMINAE ME TETIGISSE PEDES.
TUM VERA INCESSU PATUIT REGINA. QUIS UMQUAM
CONTEMNET TITULOS ABSTULERITVE MEOS?

This terrace, constructed
On the four hundredth anniversary
Of the foundation of the School,
Was first entered by Queen Elizabeth II
On 24th October, 1952.

You ask, stranger, how I, crude structure,
Derive my name.
Know that once the feet of my Lady touched me
By her gait she then revealed herself to be a true Queen.
Who ever shall despise or remove my claim?

Jimmy Street, Second Master at the time, records that when Her Majesty asked for an English version, Stacy Colman composed an Elizabeth Quatrain and sent it to the Palace in a private letter, which he subsequently obtained the Queen's permission to reproduce:

MEERE EARTH, I TAKE MY TITLE FROM A QUEENE
SITHENCE MY SOVRAN LADYES FOOTE AND I
MET, AND HER GRACE MAJESTICALL WAS SEENE.
WHO DARES DISDAIN OR GIVE MY CLAIME THE LYE?

The inscription reveals interesting parallels with that on the Moser Building recording the initiative of the Queen's grandfather.

Our witness tells us that Her Majesty was rather overwhelmed by the enthusiasm of her reception, all the more tumultuous when it was announced that she had requested three days extra holiday. There was a short service in Chapel, after which the Duke commented on the fine quality of the vigorous singing, and then the royal visitors, leaving from School

House, retraced their steps up Central to their waiting car, this time to the accompaniment of prolonged and vigorous cheering. Their last glimpse of the school included an incident with a typically Salopian flavour: two boys attempted to 'thumb a lift' at the Moss Gates! The School basked in the after-glow of the Queen's visit for the rest of the decade; it seemed to endorse the restoration of the Alingtonian tradition which was perceived by many to have taken place.

Our next royal visitor was Queen Elizabeth, the Queen Mother, who, during the course of a series of engagements in the Shrewsbury area, came to the School on 5th November 1969 to take luncheon in Kingsland Hall, which had been officially opened by Lord Bridgeman a month previously on 4th October. The *Salopian Newsletter* reported that she was accompanied by the Lord Lieutenant, the Mayor and Mayoress and the High Sheriff, all accommodated at an extended High Table. Boys, as was the normal practice, served at the table, but no doubt for this particular table they had been selected with more than usual care (the publisher of the present volume was one of them!). Afterwards Her Majesty had coffee with the Praepostors in the Moser Building and managed to meet a much greater number of people than had been planned during the course of a couple of hours on the Site. David Bevan was presented to the Queen and found himself tongue-tied. He recalls:

'How long have you been at Shrewsbury?' she asked. There ensued an abashed silence on my part. 'Come on, Mr Bevan', she said, 'You can tell me.'

The centenary of the School's arrival on Kingsland was celebrated in 1982. The centrepiece was a *son et lumière* pageant, entitled *Move Over Mr Moss*. Performed with the School Building as a backdrop, it recorded scenes from the School's history in the intervening years. The setting was Tom Wheare's idea; the script was by Michael Charlesworth and the director was Robin Case. With over sixty actors and many technical problems to be overcome, the challenge was a daunting one, involving, as it did, a dramatic reconstruction of the Great Fire of 1905, and all the additional hazards of an open-air production. Scenes presented included Alington's appointment of Cardus, Sawyer's forgetfulness, the celebrations in 1932 after the victory in the Ladies' Plate, the persecution of the Kingsland Bridge toll-keeper, Mr Dunn, by members of the School (in Chapel the boys were accustomed to modify the words of the General Confession to 'We have done unto Dunn the things we ought not to have done'), Hardy's efficiency, Peterson, the archetypal Salopian, Wright's dynamism and Anderson's enlightened and constructive consolidation.

Eric Dehn, writing in the *Salopian Newsletter*, records:

The finale showed the modern world of sailing and judo, squash and tennis, archery and artistry, fencing and bee-keeping, climbers descending the sheer face of the school buildings, wielders of guitars, wooers of girls... There were somersaulting, vaulting, hitting, kicking, catching every shape of ball, pursuing activities as multifarious on the ground as there were suddenly thereafter multi-coloured fireworks in the sky.

Predictably, rain fell during the first performance, but entirely failed to dampen the enthusiasm of the audience. Dehn concluded his review with this final reflection:

We used to live rather segregated lives, belonging to our own House, walking and talking only with our contemporaries ...[here] we were privileged to feel together a joint pride in a Salopian past and faith in a Salopian future.

A fine photographic exhibition, entitled *The Kingsland Years*, was mounted by Michael Charlesworth. The school orchestra gave a concert in Chapel. All the members of the winning 1960 Henley crew, with their coach, Peter Gladstone, appeared on the river. All the surviving headmasters and their ladies, the Wolfendens, the Wrights and the Andersons, were present at the occasion. 550 guests attended a Dinner Dance in Kingsland Hall. At morning chapel on Sunday, the lessons were read by Lord Wolfenden and Donald Wright; and Michael Charlesworth gave the sermon. On September 18th, as another facet of the celebrations, the School entertained the town of Shrewsbury. Local dignitaries were invited to a festive lunch in Kingsland Hall, and in the afternoon the School was 'open for anyone who cared to come and look around'. About 500 people came.

Princess Margaret followed her sister and her mother to the School on 13th May 1984. The main purpose of her visit to Shrewsbury had been to open the County Library in the Old School Building; but she followed the Queen Mother's precedent by lunching at a Head Table in Kingsland Hall with local dignitaries and school praepostors. The royal toasts were proposed - and drunk in cider. Her Royal Highness subsequently visited the Ashton Theatre (which had recently been opened) and the Art School.

The celebrations for the Millennium had a strongly academic character and a distinctively Darwinian emphasis. The members of the Common Room considered educational aims for the twenty-first century at a conference chaired by Nicholas Barber (OS SH 1954 - 1958), addressed by a galaxy of eminent guests and covering a comprehensive range of academic, social and technological issues. The Sixth Form was convened to consider the prospects of the future in a Darwinian context and *The Wildlife of a Gentle Man* was performed in the Ashton Theatre. On the last day of the Michaelmas Term 1999 a celebration lunch took place in Kingsland Hall. The Headmaster presented a Millennium Tie to every current member of the School. The customary Carol Services were replaced by a Millennium Assembly in the Alington Hall, its content a mixture of the sacred and the secular. A Millennium Ball was held, also in the Alington Hall, on 8th July 2000: and on September 9th, continuing the Darwinian theme, the whole school assembled on Central to witness the unveiling of the Darwin statue by Sir David Attenborough. The statue is the much admired work of the sculptress Jemma Pearson. It depicts Darwin as a young man standing on the Galapagos islands, with a marine iguana, unique to those islands, together with other fauna, at his feet. The plinth was designed by John Pringle (Ch 1964-69) whose work was to feature even more prominently in the subsequent Salopian celebration recorded in the next paragraph. In his speech on this occasion Sir David suggested that,

surely no school in this country, or indeed in Europe, or even – I would suggest – in the world, has had a more distinguished or influential pupil.

To conclude the Darwinian theme, Charles Darwin himself appeared in Chapel during the weekday services of February 2009, reincarnated in the person of Mr Robin Case, to deliver a biographical reminiscence to mark the 150th anniversary of the publication of *On the Origin of Species by Means of Natural Selection*. Robin's impersonation was so convincing that a fourth former approached one of the masters after the service to enquire, "Sir, was that really Charles Darwin?"

Our most recent Royal visit occurred when The Prince of Wales visited the School in the afternoon of 21st February 2001 to perform the official opening of the new Music School, the Maidment Building. The Queen's visit had concluded the 400th anniversary celebrations and the Editor of the *Salopian Newsletter* noted that in reality the Prince's visit inaugurated the 450th year of the School's history, which had actually begun eleven days previous to his visit, on February 10th. Entering the school grounds through the Moss Gates, the Prince paused to admire the new Darwin statue, before being driven to the Science Buildings, where the Chairman of the Governors, the Headmaster and the Mayor were presented. Accompanied by the Head of School, his Deputy and the School Captain of Music, the Prince then walked down the paths leading to Kingsland House and up again to the Music School, which were lined by boys, staff and parents, pausing to chat briefly with as many groups as he could. The Bursar, the Second Master, the Housemaster of Oldham's Col. Nick Jenkins, (who had been one of the Prince's contemporaries at Trinity College, Cambridge), and the Director of Music, John Moore, were then presented. As Prince Charles entered the Music School, the Brass Ensemble played a fanfare composed by a pupil, Anthony Wiles. After the architect, John Pringle, and the principal contractor, John Kirkland, had been presented, His Royal Highness toured the practice rooms, where various ensembles were practising. He then entered the main auditorium to hear a performance of the first movement of Haydn's Cello Concerto by Andrew Hughes (an appropriate choice, as the Prince plays the cello). Having unveiled a plaque and declared the building open, Prince Charles then left to complete his other engagements in the area, to the sound of a second fanfare, this time composed by another pupil, Jamie Walton.

The most recent celebration of a school anniversary took place in 2002 to mark the 450th anniversary of the foundation of the School. In February, the members of the Common Room were entertained to dinner by the Governing Body. On March 10th (a month later than the actual date of the signing of the Charter) a service of Thanksgiving was held in St Chad's Church, at which the Charter was laid, for rededication, on the altar. The social celebrations opened with a luncheon at the Worcestershire Cricket Ground and were followed by an Anniversary Ball on July 6th and by a dinner, attended by 180 Salopians, at Haberdashers' Hall in London, at which Michael Palin was the principal speaker. On October 5th there was a Chapel service at Shrewsbury, after which five Headmasters, Donald Wright, Eric Anderson, Simon Langdale, Ted Maidment and Jeremy Goulding assembled for an historic photograph in the Masters' Garden. After a celebration lunch in Kingsland Hall, the school football XIs played the Old Salopians, marking the beginning of the celebrations of the Old Salopian Football Club's centenary, and the new rowing tank was opened. The School Play, *Tumbling Tom Ashton*, directed by Robin Case, was presented in the Ashton Theatre.

CHAPTER SIX

A VIEW FROM THE PENTAGON

Shrewsbury has been exceptionally fortunate in experiencing a succession of headmasters who, for more than two centuries, have bequeathed an unbroken record of effective and dedicated service in promoting the welfare of the School and in enhancing its reputation. The quality and the length of the contribution of the 'Great Triumvirate' of Butler, Kennedy and Moss (1798-1908),which spanned the whole of the nineteenth century, is widely considered to be unequalled among schools such as ours. In the following centuries the tenure of the headmasters has been shorter; there were ten headmasters between 1908 and 2010, four before 1950 and six after; but each of them left a positive legacy, responding appropriately to the rapidly changing social, educational and political circumstances in which the School was placed. They have successfully weathered the remorseless pressures of government intervention, ever more burdensome administrative and legal requirements, invasive assessment procedures, financial stringency and media intrusion. They have also had to manage a revolution in communications and increasingly aggressive 'parent power' in an age of consumerism and direct personal accountability.

Alington, Sawyer, Hardy and Wolfenden presided over the fortunes of the School in the earlier part of the twentieth century; Jack Peterson, Donald Wright, and Eric Anderson's headmasterships covered the next thirty years, and Simon Langdale, Ted Maidment and Jeremy Goulding's headmasterships covered the last thirty. It is with the tenure of the last six that this book is primarily concerned.

Jack Peterson died in 1978 and Donald Wright in 2012. I have accordingly written my own account of their headmasterships, though in the latter case Laurence Le Quesne's magisterial analysis of 'The Years of Reform', an unpublished monograph which he has kindly allowed me to read, will surely be regarded as the definitive account, and I gratefully acknowledge my debt to him. I have considered it much more appropriate and much less presumptuous to invite the remaining headmasters to speak for themselves. They have all been kind enough to allow me to interview them; I have made a draft based upon our conversations in each case, which I have returned to them for amendment and approval. The views attributed to each headmaster are, therefore, authentic; but I have, of course, included assessments, appreciations and examples based upon my own experience and upon the experience and tributes of other colleagues, which the modesty of each of our subjects in turn would not have allowed him to introduce or to endorse.

John Magnus Peterson: Headmaster 1950-1963

Jack Peterson's appointment as Headmaster in 1950 was greeted with widespread acclaim. To many, his status as an Old Salopian and his distinguished record, both as a schoolboy and at the university, made him an ideal candidate. It seemed to them that it could not be more appropriate that the most eminent Salopian of his age should return, a generation later, to preside over his school as it prepared to celebrate its Fourth Centenary. Born in 1902, Jack had entered the School in 1915, spending the earlier part of his schooldays under Alington, the rest under Sawyer. He was Head of School for two years, a member of the first XI for both football and cricket, and also of the fives IV, in the last of these teams for four of his years at school. Having won a scholarship to Oriel, he emerged from Oxford with a double first in Classics, blues for Fives and Football and with the captaincy of the University XI to his credit. Subsequently he was appointed by Alington to the staff at Eton, where he served as a highly successful Assistant Master and a much-loved Housemaster. Alington also officiated at his marriage. Jack Peterson's versatile attainment made him a fitting exemplar both for the aspirations of Salopians in the future and an equally fitting reminder of the achievements of Philip Sidney's Renaissance School in the past. In his obituary tribute to Peterson in the *Salopian Newsletter*, an Old Salopian recollected that when he entered the School as a new boy he already knew that his headmaster was 'the living legend of a scholar-athlete'.

Eton's farewell to Jack Peterson, recorded in the *Eton Chronicle* at the time, provides very touching testimony to the impact he had made there, the affection in which he was held and the deep regret at his departure.

> At Shrewsbury your boyhood days
> *Non sine gloria* were spent
> (Your modesty would look askance
> At a straightforward compliment)
> A Shropshire Lad, as one might say,
> In training for this greater day.
> Scholar and athlete, you must go
> Where duty summons you, to rule
> (All Eton wishes you good luck)
> Over a royal, ancient School,
> An O.S., who deserves to be,
> And is, by courtesy, O.E.
>
> You leave the Thames, (no longer "sweete")
> To dwell by fair Sabrina's streams,
> But we may confidently hope
> That you'll remember in your dreams
> School Yard, the Field, the Chapel bell,
> The Fives Courts, where none played so well.
> Eton has been in Shrewsbury's debt

Since, three and thirty years ago,
She "borrowed" from her C.A.A*
And, therefore, as a *quid pro quo*
But with sad hearts, we now send back
Her son - affectionately, Jack.

(The Revd Cyril Argentine Alington moved to Eton as Headmaster, having been Shrewsbury's Headmaster between 1908 and 1916.)

Jack Peterson was admired – even loved – at both the schools in which he spent his professional life. In his memorial tribute to Peterson, Michael Hoban, his colleague at Shrewsbury and thereafter Headmaster successively of St Edmund's School Canterbury, of Bradfield and of Harrow, remarked that he had found Jack's goodness 'daunting' (the quality of 'shared goodness' was a characteristic to which the *Times* obituary also referred, significantly, and was an echo of the similar quality which contemporaries recognized both in Alington and Sawyer). Hoban admired Jack's compassion and his understanding of colleagues and boys. 'One learnt from him about God. It was not that he ever pushed God at you, he just showed you a lot about him'. Hoban considered him

the straightest man I ever knew ... deviousness was entirely foreign to him. He was the 'genius loci' of an intimate community ... a man whom one would be ashamed to let down.

But Peterson was also an intensely private man, and very shy. He came to Shrewsbury as a widower; the loss of his deeply-loved wife intensified both his shyness and his loneliness, and except to the senior boys whose responsibilities necessarily brought them into regular contact with him, to many of the Salopians of the time he seemed a dignified, but remote figure. He did not stand on that dignity: it was the natural consequence of his achievement and his character. He wore these achievements with great modesty and humility; and he had no ambition to make his mark upon the wider educational stage.

To his junior colleagues he was both kind and encouraging. He startled more than one of them (myself included) by the advice which he offered at their first meeting, "Never become a headmaster". Though not himself by disposition an innovator, he was willing to give them free rein, and would willingly entertain and support the ideas and contributions they offered. Many of them (again including myself) can cite instances of personal kindness which revealed how closely he followed individual fortunes and empathised with individual feelings. And how he could laugh! I can remember him, as my neighbour among the basses in the Concert Choir, dissolving into helpless mirth at my strained and distinctly unmusical attempt to reach the high notes in *Belshazzar's Feast*.

I vividly remember one particular occasion upon which I was the recipient of Jack's characteristic kindness. It was the custom, in the 1950s, for one or two coachloads of boys to travel to Henley to support the crew. Shortly before my arrival on the staff the practice had been suspended, owing to misbehaviour on the coaches in the previous year. But after a year's suspension it was resumed, and a notice was posted on the Common Room board inviting masters who were willing to accompany the coaches to inscribe their initials.

Having never previously been to Henley, I saw this as a marvellous opportunity to get there and I duly signed up. My older colleagues were wiser than me; and when, after a day or two, mine were still the only initials upon the notice, Russell Hope Simpson, the Senior Master, intervened, very reasonably urging upon the Headmaster how unwise it would be to allow an inexperienced junior colleague like me to take sole charge of the venture. My name was taken off the list; well-established colleagues stepped into the breach, and I was very disappointed. That year the 1st VIII was victorious at Henley. On Friday afternoon, when the crew had reached the Final (the Regatta ended on Saturday in those days), the Headmaster came out of his School House study as I was going into Third Lesson and called me over. At first hearing, his question was rather perplexing, indeed dangerous:

"Are you averse to playing truant?"
Somewhat nervously, I replied, "Why do you ask?"
"Well", said Jack, "it looks as if the crew are going to win this year, and I shall have to go to Henley again to-morrow. Would you like to come with me?"

And so I did. He cooked breakfast for me in Kingsland House, drove me to Henley (in his Alvis) and took me, on the launch, along the course behind the victorious Salopian crew.

'Marketing' was unknown, at least in the context of Independent Boarding Schools, in those days. The number of applications for entry to the School during Jack Peterson's time far exceeded the number of places available. An Old Salopian, looking back on his time at the school during Peterson's headmastership, asserts that

The spirit and achievements of the School during his reign – and especially the spirit – do not suffer by comparison with what went before and came after; and the choice of staff being by far the most important single function of the headmaster, the list of Jack Peterson's staff speaks volumes.

Even Peterson's sternest critics endorsed this opinion. Three of the eight colleagues who joined the staff in the Michaelmas Term of 1958 together contributed over a hundred years of service to the School.

The visit of Her Majesty the Queen, to mark the Fourth Centenary of the School in 1952, seemed to confirm the feeling, certainly shared by many of the staff, that all was very well; that this was a successful, happy and caring community, with every prospect of remaining so. But towards the end of the decade there were increasing signs of unrest, particularly among the senior members of the staff. In the nature of the case, it was they who were most affected in what they perceived as the Headmaster's indecisiveness and weak administration. To address this situation, the Housemasters obtained Peterson's permission to hold meetings in his absence in order to submit firm proposals for his approval. There was criticism of the Headmaster's patience with and tolerance of a particularly wayward colleague, and some feeling that discipline in the School was beginning to slacken. More generally there was the perception that Shrewsbury was standing still, while other comparable schools were moving forward. Certainly none of these criticisms was intended to impugn the headmaster's universally admired personal qualities.

It was a disciplinary matter, trivial in itself, which brought these matters to a head in the summer of 1959. Some boys broke out of their house during the night, with great labour removed all the chairs from the school building, and arranged them on the Common to spell out 'Tiffin', the name of a school whose crew had unexpectedly defeated our own 1st VIII (the latter, in the perpetrators' view, being much too loudly vaunted and overprivileged), at Henley Regatta the day before. The culprits failed to own up when called upon to do so – in fact their identities were not generally known for over thirty years. It is arguable that Peterson mishandled the affair; certainly some Housemasters and others found the sanctions he imposed on the school and the extra responsibilities involved in implementing them extremely tedious - the last straw at the end of a long summer term. An informal meeting of some of them, with other senior members of the staff, decided to apprise the Chairman of the Governors of their views; he in turn invited the Headmaster (who was a personal friend of his) to 'consider his position'. Subsequently a full meeting of the Governing Body supported the Headmaster and invited him to extend his tenure in office. Many other members of the Common Room resented an initiative taken, without their knowledge, by some of their colleagues, claiming that it did not represent the feeling of the teaching staff as a whole. While acknowledging that the initiative had been motivated by the genuine intention of promoting 'the good of the School', they felt that the Headmaster had been shabbily and unjustly treated and that he deserved greater loyalty. The issue remained divisive for many years.

There would be wide agreement with Michael Charlesworth's judgment that Peterson's reign as Headmaster witnessed the 'apotheosis of the Public School'. However, to say that Shrewsbury at the time was unresponsive to the changes which were occurring in other schools and in wider society would be a misleading conclusion: and the contrast between the traditional stability which characterised the greater part of Peterson's tenure and the dynamic movement which marked the first years of his successor is often too starkly drawn. Peterson's last years at Shrewsbury saw the leasing of Talargerwyn, the first Parents' meeting, a School Dance (at the announcement of which it was reported in the national press that 'five hundred boys cheered') and the institution of the first Exeat. It was a period which was able to contain, if not to welcome, the journalistic initiatives of the future editors of *Private Eye*. Inevitably the events of 1959 had resulted in a shaking up of the 'Old Guard' and perhaps, most significant of all, it was Jack Peterson who, in a flurry of new housemagisterial appointments, selected among them three men, Alan Laurie, Robin Moulsdale and Michael Hart, who were to be the principal agents of the crucial changes which took place in the mid-1960s, and who were already setting their powerful influence to work before Peterson himself retired.

It is true, however, that Jack was uncomfortable and disorientated in the changing atmosphere of the 'Swinging Sixties', remarking that 'I don't really understand these boys' and expressing hearty dislike of the emerging phenomenon of 'The Angry Young Man'. His address to parents on his final Speech Day in 1963 contains his appraisal of the true nature and aims of education, and they may very appropriately stand as his own epitaph:

Ultimately it is not a question of what a man says, nor indeed of what he does, it is a question of what he is.

Arthur Robert Donald Wright : Headmaster 1963-1975

Donald Wright's portrait in the Alington Hall is particularly successful in revealing the character of the man, depicting the thinker's brow, the kind eyes, the firm mouth and chin. Colleagues who worked with Donald have often remarked upon the contrast between the upper and the lower part of the face, conveying two aspects of personality which cannot always be made to work effectively together but which in Donald's case were successfully integrated and harnessed: the idealism suggested by the eyes and brow and the determination evident in the mouth and chin. Alone among his fellow headmasters portrayed in the hall, Donald is not wearing academic dress: an appropriate departure, for in many other ways, in both provenance and style, Donald did not conform to the traditional mould of Salopian headmasters. He had been educated at Bryanston, a school as liberal as Shrewsbury was then conservative. There he had been much influenced by his own headmaster, Thorold Coade. The reader of Coade's collected papers *The Burning Bow* can learn much about the context of Donald's thinking. Unlike most of his twentieth century predecessors, Donald had not served his apprenticeship as headmaster in another school: he came to Shrewsbury straight from his housemastership at Marlborough; and he was the first headmaster of Shrewsbury not to be a classicist.

His arrival in 1963 inaugurated a period of marked change both in the style and pace of headmagisterial activity. Colin Leach writes that Donald was

a man whose instinct was to turn everything upside down, rattle it and see whether it could be made to work better ... he gained with a few the reputation of acting first and asking afterwards ...(but) *he saw what had to be done, found the means – human and financial – and did it.*

Everyone at the time noted the symbolic contrast between the means by which Donald and his predecessor chose to travel across the Site from their residence in Kingsland House to School House, in which the Headmaster's study was still located, Jack upon an ancient bicycle, Donald by fast car along a newly tarmaced road (which inevitably became known in Salopian circles as the M1); Donald certainly conveyed the impression that there was an urgent job to be done and that he intended to waste no time in doing it!

Donald's first impression of the School was of an unduly conservative, narrow and introverted institution. His aims were to broaden the curriculum, to expand extra-curricular opportunities, to discard antiquated customs within the School out of tune with the spirit of contemporary society and to break down the barriers between the School and the outside world.

This humane and liberal programme would imply extensive building, in turn requiring a thorough overhaul of the financial management of the School. Another unusual feature of Donald's headmastership was that he was able to combine an impulsive nature with a willingness to find and consult experts (another pair of characteristics which cannot always be made to work together, but which did in Donald's case). He took expert advice in all three of these crucial aspects of his activity, educational, architectural and financial, and he welcomed new ideas. The consequence was that his own initial ideas were often shaped, modified and sometimes diverted from the course originally intended, but their general direction (in both senses of the word) remained his.

New subjects were introduced into the curriculum, together with greater flexibility of choice between them. Much more substantial provision was made for Science, and a more generous allocation in the timetable was given to non-specialist subjects and private reading: so-called 'minority time' was to account for one-third of the whole.

Donald was particularly concerned to encourage wider reading; and it was no accident that his wife Helen, in addition to her responsibilities as a hostess and the mother of their five children, should initiate the tradition that the Headmaster's wife should preside in the School Bookshop. Laurence Le Quesne, who has written the authoritative account of Donald's headmastership in his monograph *The Age of Reform*, shows how his remodelling of the Moser Buildings, in which the library was situated, epitomises the whole character of Donald's activities:

The old Shrewsbury insulated itself as far as possible from the world outside: the way in which the Moser Building turned its back on the magnificent view was entirely typical of this. ARDW wanted to make Shrewsbury face outward to the world, which was exactly what was achieved.

The three major building projects in Donald's time were the Lyle Building (1966) to accommodate the 'Humanities' in a subject centre which originally featured moveable partitions between the classrooms in order to facilitate the 'team teaching' which was very much in vogue at the time; Kingsland Hall (1969) for central feeding, which had a crucial impact upon the social life of the School; and the new Science Building (1974) which remedied a long-standing deficiency both in classroom accommodation and in laboratory facilities in a vital component of the School's educational programme. The provision of the Craft Centre (1969) testified to Donald's wish to widen that programme. The building of Tudor Court (1972) demonstrated his awareness of the need to provide better social facilities for the Sixth Form, just as the remodelling of the Moser Library was intended to facilitate the widening of their intellectual horizons. Major improvements in the classroom accommodation in the School buildings were set in hand. An extension to the Chapel completed the list of new building in Donald's time; the conversion of the Darwin Building into an Art School was planned during his headmastership, but finished only in 1976, after he had left Shrewsbury. An extensive interior reorganisation of School House was designed to enable the division of the house into two independent communities under the same roof. But the plan was soon seen to be impracticable and was aborted by his successor. Donald's building programme alone would qualify him as one of the most influential headmasters of the century ... *Si monumentum requiris...* but that was only a part of his impact.

He was never afraid of new ideas; Laurence Le Quesne again remarks on his 'taste for intellectual and spiritual adventure' and it was in Chapel that this characteristic was most regularly seen, in his invitation to a whole series of challenging speakers, both clerical and lay, to address the assembled school. It was, after all, the age of Bishop John Robinson's *Honest to God*, of Tillich and Wren Lewis; and perhaps the most dramatic example of Donald's determination that Salopians' experience of religious practice should transcend what they saw and heard in the confines of their Victorian Chapel was his decision, implemented near the beginning of his headmastership, that the whole school should be conveyed, in a procession of Longmynd coaches, to attend the principal Sunday morning Eucharist in the newly consecrated Coventry Cathedral. The logistics of this major excursion had been carefully, though, as it turned out, not quite flawlessly worked out. A reconnaissance had identified a suitable 'comfort stop' at Sutton Coldfield, where adequate facilities were sited in a capacious lay-by. Accordingly the long procession of coaches turned into the lay-by, only for the discovery to be made that the facilities were closed on Sundays. There was no alternative but to 'set on towards Coventry'!

The first half of Donald's headmastership was the time in which the antiquated customs of the School were discarded. The boys' hierarchy was dismantled, the chores required of junior boys were now to be for the benefit of the community as a whole and personal 'douling' (or fagging) officially came to an end. Corporal punishment of boys by boys ceased. The elaborate system of privileges, carefully recorded in a document known as 'Pink Book', was discarded. These developments have been fully recounted in the Chapter on 'The Public School Revolution'. All this was not exclusively Donald's work; some of it had already been initiated by colleagues and by the boys themselves before his arrival; but Donald welcomed and encouraged it. His direct influence is more obviously to be seen in the end of compulsory membership of the CCF and in the reduction of the number of obligatory attendances in Chapel each week. The greater element of informality which characterised his reign was also to be seen in the ending of the requirement for masters to wear gowns for teaching, in the removal of the teaching dais from classrooms and in the changes in the seating arrangements within the rooms, where circles or 'open squares' of desks, with the teacher seated in the midst of his pupils, round the square or circle, became as common, at least in the Sixth Form, as the traditional format of the single individual facing serried ranks of pupils.

He had a major impact upon the composition of the Common Room. Michael Charlesworth records that by 1975 Donald 'had made seventy appointments to the teaching staff and had selected all the housemasters except one'. He also recruited as new members of the Common Room graduates from universities other than Oxford and Cambridge, and others who had had experience in other professions than the specifically academic.

He was keen to break down barriers between the School and the 'outside world'. He encouraged exchanges both of masters and of boys with other schools, both in the local maintained schools and in the independent sector. One exchange, between a group of Sixth Form students from Shrewsbury and a corresponding group from Manchester Grammar School, which took place early in Donald's headmastership, proved particularly stimulating and valuable. Michael Charlesworth again notes that Donald's vigorous support of a bursaries scheme was intended to widen the social group from which Salopians were drawn. Donald encouraged colleagues to take a period of sabbatical leave, whenever that was a viable option; he particularly made a habit of suggesting a sabbatical to a colleague if he intended soon to appoint him to a housemastership. He strongly advocated the importance of the Day Boy element in the School and promoted a significant increase in their numbers. He took a keen interest and made a decisive intervention in the development of Shrewsbury House in Everton. His own vigorous participation in the affairs of the Headmasters' Conference, culminating in his appointment as Chairman in 1970, brought him such prominence in educational circles that Shrewsbury was often referred to as 'Wright's School', its reputation providing a parallel with that of Kennedy's Shrewsbury at the end of his tenure as Headmaster, exactly 100 years previously. The editor of the *Salopian Newsletter*, writing shortly after Donald left Shrewsbury in 1975, comments that

in this forum (the HMC) *as in so many others, he has been Shrewsbury's best known ambassador, travelling untiringly, present at conferences, meetings, committees and dinners all over the country: it could be plausibly argued that no headmaster of Shrewsbury has ever been so well-known as he has.*

Donald's personal dynamism was the engine which drove all this immensely varied and comprehensive activity, but this engine was fuelled by financial expertise. He was acutely aware of financial issues and exigencies (the inauguration of the Friends of Shrewsbury dates from his time) but he was equally aware, in this area above all others, of his need for expert advice. If he, as the driver, occupied the most conspicuous role, the contribution of the two 'technicians' he found to assist him was absolutely crucial and entirely indispensable. Micky Jones as Bursar and Pat Young as financial controller, set the course and provided the means for the programme of reform and expansion upon which Shrewsbury embarked and which has been continued ever since. They are the three architects of the modern Shrewsbury.

All the colleagues who served with Donald and all the recent historians of the School are unanimous in their assessment of the vital role which Donald played in guiding Shrewsbury through the turbulent sixties and seventies and reshaping it from the traditional public school which he found, to become the exemplar of what Laurence Le Quesne has called 'the New Model Public School' which he bequeathed to his successor,

[transforming] Shrewsbury from a conservative and old-fashioned school running gently downhill to a school with a reputation as one of the most liberal and adventurous public schools in the country. He did it with a vigour and conviction that at the time took Shrewsbury to the head of the convoy ... He was a good and generous man ... who changed Shrewsbury more than any other headmaster of the twentieth century ... and changed it very much for the better.

Colin Leach writes of

twelve wholly remarkable years ... when the arts, drama, music were encouraged to flourish, when the green baize door mentality was successfully challenged in a way that allowed dialogue and friendship to flourish in the vertical as well as the horizontal plane.

The editor of the *Salopian Newsletter* suggests that

The period 1963-75 may, in perspective, be compared to the period of Alington's headmastership from 1908-1916 — a period of remarkable expansion; a period marked by the broad vision of what a school should be in the contemporary world; and a period of strong and positive leadership from the top ... that Shrewsbury came through this time as a happy and constructive community, is a great tribute to the leadership ... in all the teasing problems of organisation, curricular reform and administration, he has never lost sight of the fact that education is about people.

While agreeing wholeheartedly with all these judgments, I would offer one other, final reflection. There is always a subtle balance to be kept in any school between the interests of the individual and of the community. Donald Wright shifted the focus of the School markedly onto the interests of the individual boy, onto his unique identity, his choices, his problems and his potential, establishing another new balance between the community and its component members. This 'new deal' has been maintained, developed and carefully guarded ever since. For that, too, Shrewsbury owes him another debt of profound gratitude.

William Eric Kinloch Anderson: Headmaster 1975-80

When Eric Anderson became Headmaster in 1975 at the age of 39, he had already been Headmaster of Abingdon School, an English master at Gordonstoun (where the Prince of Wales had starred in his school plays) and a housemaster at Fettes, where his pupils included a future editor of the *Financial Times* and a future Prime Minister. He had not thought of moving from Abingdon until Walter Hamilton, Master of Magdalene College, Cambridge, and Shrewsbury's Chairman of Governors at the time, cornered him at the Headmasters' Conference and, peering at him lugubriously over his spectacles, said, "Young man, I think you ought to be the next Headmaster of Shrewsbury."

Poppy and he (they were very much a husband and wife team) were not at first inclined to apply, but when they eventually paid an incognito visit to the Site, their resolve to stay where they were was shaken by what they saw. The natural and friendly manner in which boys and masters greeted each other on the Drum (the space in front of the Main School Building) was impressive, and everything suggested a community at ease with itself.

The next five years strongly reinforced those first impressions. Indeed Eric said much later that of all the schools he worked in he would most have enjoyed being an assistant master at Shrewsbury. It was a Common Room of individuals, many of them highly able, all of them dedicated to the job, a few of them eccentric in ways that great schoolmasters can be. On the surface nothing was taken too seriously; but beneath the humour and fun there was serious intent. And no school, he thought, had a better team of Housemasters than Shrewsbury in the seventies.

At the beginning the Andersons had the uneasy feeling, however, that their liking for the Common Room was not reciprocated. Shrewsbury seemed wary of the Headmaster and happy to see him tucked away for the evening in the secluded house down Canonbury, outside the school grounds, to which Donald Wright had moved a year or two before. The final straw was to hear from an applicant parent that he had decided on another school because at Shrewsbury neither of the two boys showing him round had known where the Headmaster lived. That was not how the Andersons wanted it to be. They loved School life and they intended to be part of it. So, almost immediately, they persuaded the Governors to sell 9 Canonbury and to buy 17 Ashton Road, much nearer the heart of the School and right opposite Ingram's. Mike Eagar, the Housemaster, was aghast: "Good Lord, the head man is going to see what time my boys put their lights out." He did, and most of them were not put out early – but he never commented on that to the Housemaster.

Shrewsbury's response to the winds of educational change blowing through the public schools in the last twenty years had been belated, but when it finally began it had been both rapid and radical. The dramatic changes which then occurred had stemmed and diverted the main current of unrest, but a nucleus of disaffected Sixth-Formers remained to whom the apparent prospect of firm government offered by the new Headmaster was unwelcome. Speech Day that June (1976) saw windows all over the Site decorated with swastikas. For the Headmaster there were three consolations: the symbols were in foam rather than paint; they turned out to be the work of a single dissident boy; and the Chairman of Governors was highly delighted: "It shows you are tightening things up a bit, just as we hoped."

There was a problem too with a small group of masters. Rather late in the day the sixties' philosophies of the encounter group, of flower power and the ashram had reached Shropshire. "Why do you insist that we must do?" said one master to the Headmaster. "Is it not enough for us to be?" In Anderson's view that was not enough. Such ideas threatened the traditional educational values for which the School ought to stand.

The problem needing quick solution, though, was School House. Complicated difficulties had arisen from the attempt to divide it into two Houses, Doctor's and Headroom, each with its own Housemaster. The original plan, to divide the House vertically into two separate independent Houses, would have worked, but foundered on grounds of cost at a time of high inflation. The decision had then been taken to divide the House horizontally, with Doctor's on one floor, Headroom on another and most of the public spaces available to boys from both Houses.

This cheaper plan had led to difficulties of accommodation and administration, and the prolonged renovations were not complete at the start of the school year. It had not even been possible for both Housemasters to assume their responsibilities at the same time. They were both excellent men, but they did not see eye to eye. One was at the liberal end of the spectrum and the other a middle-of-the-road traditionalist. It was easy to see that boys sharing the same common room were not going to think it fair that disciplinary action should be different for boys involved in the same incident, and in a School where House loyalty is intense, sharing facilities between two Houses is at the best of times unlikely to be harmonious.

The way out of this muddle, Anderson decided, was to revert to a single, albeit over-large, School House, with one overall Housemaster and an Assistant. No-one among the possible candidates in the Common Room was prepared to take on what seemed an impossible challenge. So the unthinkable happened, and a Housemaster was appointed from outside. Tom Wheare, who came from teaching at Eton and went on to be Headmaster of Bryanston, by dint of being everywhere and sleeping very little, with the vigorous assistance of Richard Field, put things right within two years.

The previous decade had transformed the School's facilities and earned Anderson's predecessor the title of "Wright the Builder". It was obvious to the new Headmaster that his task was by comparison unglamorous. After a decade of extensive and successful building, his priority was simply to make the best use of the School's facilities, new and old. In an article in the *Salopian Newsletter* he described this process as "All Change".

The biggest change was the relocation of Day Boys. This rapidly expanding House, which Eric was keen to encourage to grow further, had progressively crowded into most of the ground floor accommodation in the Main School Building, thereby steadily reducing the number of rooms available for teaching. By contrast, the Sanatorium, at the Severn Hill end of the site, was capacious and grossly under-used. To move Dayboys into the old sanatorium made obvious sense, especially when it was realized that the New House, formerly the residence of bachelor masters, could be adapted to provide more than adequate medical facilities. There was room in Kingsland House for displaced bachelors to move into individual flats, above the Masters' dining room, drawing room and bar which were already established there.

Underway when Anderson arrived was the refurbishment of the Old Darwin Buildings, made redundant by the move of Chemistry into the New Science Building the year before. With the aid of a brass band and a funny speech by Willie Rushton, this was reopened as the Art School. The school's first computer appeared in the room adjacent to the Swimming Pool. It was second-hand and massive, a gift from the directors of Smith's Crisps. For a year or two, as the Headmaster pointed out at Speech Day, it remained prudent to take its results with a pinch of salt! The transformation of the old gymnasium into the Ashton Theatre was planned and Jon Barnsley appointed as architect, but this project was completed after Anderson had left; so only the Squash Courts, the gift of the Semaan family, stand as a bricks-and-mortar monument to his years as Headmaster.

In fact, his priorities lay elsewhere. Donald Wright had advised the Governors that, in appointing his successor, they should look for a man who was well qualified to promote the academic standards of the School, and Eric quickly realised the wisdom of that advice. There were some very able boys at Shrewsbury, but not enough of them. The majority seemed to lack the urgency and academic 'edge' which are required to produce and maintain the highest standards. He once said that the Shrewsbury Masters were abler than the boys – whereas in the best schools the boys can more than give their teachers a run for their money.

So he devoted a lot of time to meeting personally for half-an-hour the parents of every potential applicant. He started a cricket festival which brought boys and parents from four eminent prep schools to Shrewsbury. He persuaded the Governors to introduce Sixth Form scholarships with the aim of attracting able boys from the Welsh hinterland – although that scheme took some time to bear fruit. The expansion of Day Boys was also a part of the drive to raise academic standards.

By 1975 the number of Day Boys had grown significantly,so that it had become by far the biggest House. The options were either to reduce those numbers to a point which would produce fair inter-house competition, or to increase the numbers to the point where Day Boys could divide into two Houses for competitive purposes. Anderson opted decisively for the latter. There were historical, political, social and economic reasons for this decision, which are fully discussed in the chapter on Day Boys; but the most relevant factor in the present context is that there was also an excellent academic reason. Shrewsbury had become an increasingly important professional, specifically legal and medical, centre; there was keen competition among these professional families for places at the School, and their sons were likely to make a very significant and positive contribution in the academic sphere, which indeed they proceeded to do.

The comparatively remote location of Shrewsbury, far from the nucleus of its most formidable competitors in the south, caused a degree of complacency, induced, he thought, by an ignorance of standards rising elsewhere. So he encouraged invitations to mainstream speakers, ranging from former Prime Ministers Wilson and Heath, to academics like David Butler the psephologist, A.L. Rowse and Walter Marshall the director of Harwell. Less mainstream but at least as diverting were James Irwin the astronaut and an Oxford lexicographer who was a many-times winner of the *Times* crossword competition.

Eager to keep Shrewsbury in the eye of those with able sons to educate, Anderson himself was a regular visitor to prep schools and did a lot of after-dinner speaking to groups as diverse as the Wrekin Burns Society and the Master Cutler's Feast in Sheffield. After a speech to a huge annual gathering of the combined Rotary Societies of the area, his host thanked him warmly as he sat down:

That was wonderful. Thank you very much. You were far funnier than last year's speaker, Jimmy Tarbuck - and we had to pay him.

Eric was a schoolmaster at heart. He valued scholarship - he had produced the Oxford University Press edition of Sir Walter Scott's *Journal* - but he genuinely loved the wider aspects of School life. In an age becoming increasingly obsessed with educational targets, he was sometimes quoted approvingly for saying, "The best things in education cannot be measured." Boys and masters were left in no doubt of his enthusiasm, and his wife's, for everything that was going on in the School.

Rowing had been in the doldrums. But with Nick Bevan as coach of the VIII Shrewsbury again became a force to be reckoned with on the river. Anderson still remembers as a great moment the victory at National Schools when the Headmaster of Rugby, father of stroke John Woodhouse, cycled maniacally down the towpath shouting himself hoarse for Shrewsbury. The Andersons had become keen on rowing at Abingdon and loved the sport. Nor did it escape the Headmaster's notice that a school's performance on the river becomes a vital element in its reputation. Alone among school sports, rowing puts a school into the top league, up against the finest national (and at Henley, international) opposition in the full glare of critical evaluation and publicity.

He also welcomed the School's increasingly ambitious involvement in drama, though he recognised that full development would depend on a properly designed, dedicated theatre space. That project was under consideration, with Jon Barnsley appointed as architect, during his headmastership, but was completed only in 1984 after his departure. Both Andersons were theatre-goers, particularly to Stratford, where Poppy later became a Governor of the Royal Shakespeare Company. But Eric also liked the way drama nurtured self-confidence, stimulated team spirit and taught the invaluable lesson that hard work is required and that no great achievement comes without effort. Anderson regretted that he failed to stimulate musical activity in the same way. Music had to wait for the 'eighties for proper momentum to be gained and the 'nineties for distinction to be achieved.

The Salopians of his day, according to Anderson, were straightforward and genuine, good to talk to and easy to get on with. They met adults easily, were sociable by inclination and had a distinctively Salopian sense of humour. He has happy memories of their companionship on the Sponsored Walk and of the competition, initiated and judged by Poppy, for the largest blister of the day. Poppy and he were surprised, but also touched, when on their very first Sunday at the Schools, a boy turned up on their doorstep and offered to show them the way to the Chapel. They treasured a letter from one of the many new boys they had to tea. It read: "Thank you very much for inviting me to tea. I had enormously underestimated how much I would enjoy the occasion". The hospitality to boys, masters and visitors offered in the Headmaster's house was unceasing. Michael Charlesworth records that in their first year they had 282 guests to dinner. All new boys came to tea in their first term. Eric and Poppy Anderson did their utmost to ensure that Shrewsbury was a happy ship.

Poppy was even more vital in this respect than Eric, but theirs was a team effort. As a member of the staff in the school bookshop Poppy took full advantage of the opportunity to chat easily with the boys. She started teaching Scottish Country Dancing on Saturday evenings and filled the Alington Hall with a huge congregation of boys, which included, she suspected, most of those whom their Housemasters were keen to see well occupied outside the House on a Saturday evening. Eric refused to become office-bound and combined walking their sheepdog, Dusty, round the Site with watching afternoon games. Both of them went on Basic Year exercises. Everyone recognised that that they had their fingers on the pulse of the community. Its harmonious operation was further enhanced when they were followed from Abingdon by Ron Harrison, a superb Bursar, outstandingly competent and versatile, universally liked and respected, a man with whom the Headmaster enjoyed one of the best working relationships of his life.

There were two initiatives, during Eric's headmastership, which explored an international dimension. The Shah of Iran, as part of the modernisation of his country, favoured a plan to set up boarding schools on Western lines at which Persian boys could be well educated without going abroad. With Sir Eric Drake, the former head of BP and then a Shrewsbury governor, advising them to go but to be careful what they signed up to, the Headmaster and a group of colleagues spent a week in Iran and produced a blueprint for the first of the new schools. The British Council, through whom it was to be submitted, thought the plan excellent but delayed passing it on, "as there is a spot of religious trouble at the moment." That quickly escalated into the arrival of the Ayatollah Khomeini and the Shah's fall from power. So Shrewsbury on the Caspian remains unbuilt.

A more fruitful scheme was the institution of the Harvard Fellowship. As a result of the Headmaster's friendship with Peter Gomes, the Plummer Professor of Christian Morals at Harvard and Preacher to the University, it was arranged that a young Harvard graduate would be selected annually to spend a year as a member of the Shrewsbury Common Room. Since 1978 the succession of these graduates, unbroken apart from one year of visa difficulty in 2012, has furnished Shrewsbury with an invaluable resource of talent and whole-hearted participation, a window on a wider world and more recently, advice on preparing for entry to American universities.

It had quickly become apparent that the Headmaster of Shrewsbury was the master of his brief; and this widely-accepted opinion had not escaped the notice of the Provost and Fellows of Eton. One of them, Walter Hamilton, was also, embarrassingly, Chairman of Governors at Shrewsbury. When the headmastership of Eton fell vacant in 1980, Anderson was invited to apply. He did not seek the post and hesitated about letting his name go forward, acutely conscious of the brevity of his five-year tenure at Shrewsbury. However governors and colleagues alike conceded that he was eminently well qualified to take on this greater challenge. Michael Charlesworth even visited a local betting-shop to place a £10 stake on his appointment. Nevertheless the departure of Eric and Poppy was witnessed by the Salopian community with the greatest regret. The high esteem in which they were held was matched by the deep affection which they had developed for the School, for Old Salopians, for Shrewsbury and for Shropshire. This affection, tinged with nostalgia, is eloquently conveyed in the Headmaster's words at his final Speech Day, which I have quoted in the chapter on the Salopian ethos; and the visible demonstration of it was their purchase of the old primary school in Bedstone in South Shropshire in which to spend their holidays. Eric Anderson followed Cyril Alington to Eton, Jack Peterson returned from Eton to Shrewsbury; and in this most recent exchange Eton was, once more, greatly in Shrewsbury's debt.

Simon John Bartholomew Langdale: Headmaster 1981-1988

Simon Langdale's arrival at the School in January 1981, as a Cambridge graduate, signalled the second break in the succession of seven Oxford-educated headmasters which has dominated the last century – a break which was prolonged by the appointment of Ted Maidment, another Cambridge graduate, to succeed him in 1988. Simon's first impression of Shrewsbury was of a school which was independent in every sense of the word, doing very well in its firmly-established way; and he shared his predecessor's view that it could really get along equally well without a Headmaster, an impression which was corroborated by the fact that there had been three *interregna* during the course of the previous decade. He concluded that in this going concern no sharp change of direction was necessary: all that would be required was the occasional touch on the tiller.

His first task was to get to know a huge constituency of colleagues and boys, of governors, parents and preparatory school headmasters, in an area which was virtually unknown to him (he had only visited the school once before) and far distant from the schools of his own earlier experience. He had been a boy at Tonbridge, an Assistant Master and Housemaster at Radley and most recently, for seven years, a most successful Headmaster at Eastbourne College. A senior colleague observed to him, perhaps somewhat ambiguously, that, in contrast to this earlier experience, "Salopians are thickest in Cheshire". Plans had already been made at Eastbourne for Simon and Diana Langdale's three children to be educated in the South and consequently Diana had to fulfil an exacting dual role both in sustaining regular contact with their children and supporting their activities, and in playing a lively and varied part as hostess, as the *doyenne* of the school bookshop and the Chapel flowers team, and in attending the myriad social occasions which required her presence as the Headmaster's wife; all this she did with indefatigable cheerfulness.

Simon quickly recognised that the ablest Salopians were brilliantly taught, but that the School also needed to pay particular attention to the needs of the less able boys. He was conscious, too, of the need to maintain a judicious balance in the Common Room between the specialists, entirely and properly absorbed in their chosen spheres of activity on the one hand, and the all-rounders who played an equally valuable part in sustaining the life of a boarding school, both outside as well as inside the classroom, on the other. More broadly, a significant number of external academic changes took place in the 1980s to which the School needed to respond. The acme and hallmark of academic achievement for Salopians had previously been the winning of an Entrance Award at an Oxford or Cambridge college. This aspiration, which had permeated all academic activity at Shrewsbury, was weakened first by the discontinuation, in 1984, of the 'Seventh Term' Upper Sixth in which to prepare for the Scholarship Examinations, and subsequently by the phasing out of Oxbridge Entrance Awards and Examinations during the course of the next decade. Meanwhile the National Curriculum had been formulated and its consequences for Independent Schools had to be carefully evaluated. Preparations were in hand for the full implementation of a new 16+ examination, the GCSE, which was to be inaugurated in 1988. These were the problems which Simon and his Director of Studies, Lyndon Duffield, had to face. It seemed that the rock-like stability of the long-established system of O levels, firmly based upon a secure foundation of factual knowledge, was being replaced by shifting sands in which, in many subjects, the subjective opinion of the candidates would play a greater part. There was a suspicion, too, that passing the new examinations would generally be easier. Simon was concerned that the academic diet should be suitable, challenging and rewarding for Salopians of all levels of ability.

He also noticed, on his arrival, that the accommodation in the boarding houses was unduly cramped, and he considered that a new boarding house would be needed in order to reduce the numbers in each established House. The planning and the construction of the new House proceeded and was completed during Simon's headmastership, but 'The Grove' was finally inaugurated, in the south-western corner of the Site, in the first week of Ted Maidment's tenure, in 1988.

A rather less ambitious, but very much needed initiative was completed more quickly, when an imaginative reconstruction of the existing gymnasium transformed it into a 250-seat theatre. Simon had been very well aware that the lack of such a theatre constituted a serious deficiency in the School's facilities, and he gave enthusiastic support to the project, fully realizing the many educational advantages of drama as a team enterprise, in nurturing the self-confidence of those who participated, and in strengthening the communities of those involved in the activity. The new theatre, appropriately named the Ashton Theatre after Thomas Ashton, the sixteenth-century Headmaster who was the effective founder of the School, was officially opened, equally appropriately, by Robert Hardy, the distinguished actor and son of a previous, much more recent Headmaster, Henry Harrison Hardy (1932-44). A new Sports Hall had previously been constructed, immediately adjacent to its predecessor. Much more capacious, it has been able to cater for the ever-expanding variety of Salopian sports; it has also proved altogether indispensable, in an age of ever-proliferating examinations, as an examination hall, though its precise and very prominent location and architectural impact on the Site have not escaped criticism.

These structural developments required careful resourcing and management and the financial resources required were bolstered by an Appeal, launched to mark the Centenary of the School's migration to Kingsland in 1882, bequeathed to Simon by his predecessor, and managed with characteristic devotion and self-effacement by Adrian Struvé. The supervision of these projects naturally fell to the Bursars, and Simon was exceptionally fortunate in being able to rely on the expertise of two outstanding Bursars, Ron Harrison, whom Simon remembered as possessing the unusual characteristic in a Bursar of being 'prone to think of things that people would like and then suggesting them' and Derek Crompton, who was not only extremely competent, but also an excellent manager of his staff, regularly to be seen around the Site, keeping a close and encouraging eye on what was going on.

Apart from the Appeal, another crucial factor in the financial stability of the School was the steady flow of Fees in Advance; these, in turn, depended on the number of parents accepting Guaranteed Places for their sons. Simon remembers that although the number of entries to the School remained healthy, it was always difficult to find the last 10% of entrants. He recognised that in the question of recruitment to the School, the relationships with Preparatory School headmasters were of paramount importance; he took immense care to cultivate these positive relationships and learned to rely upon their judgment. On grounds much wider than the purely financial, he was very much in favour of accepting boys who, although they might struggle to meet the required overall pass mark in Common Entrance, nevertheless had good references from their headmasters as being likely to persevere successfully, contribute positively both inside and outside the classroom and maintain a good standard of behaviour. Simon derived much pleasure from seeing this confidence repeatedly vindicated.

The further development of Day Boys was an important feature of the School during Simon's time at Shrewsbury. Their presence was, of course, based upon long historic tradition, but it also seemed natural to the Headmaster who, in his own schooldays, had been familiar with a similar mixture of dayboys and boarders. This arrangement produced obvious financial and academic advantages, but Simon's clearest impression of Day Boys during his headmastership was of the extent of their pre-eminence in music.

Simon attached particular importance to the role of Chapel, believing that its status, and the quality of the observances which take place in it, reveal a great deal about the nature of a school. Whatever an individual's private beliefs might be, he considered that the existence of a School Chapel was a sign that the things of the spirit truly matter, that a prescribed time in which to ponder them is a vital part of education and that attendance at Chapel was an obligation which the staff as well as the boys should be encouraged to accept.

Simon remembers Salopians as providing congenial company, particularly in small groups; he found them independent-minded, frank and straightforward in conversation. He noticed that a boy at Shrewsbury was allowed to pursue his own interests, though he suspected that laggards were not always kept up to the mark; and he considered that in larger groups standards of behaviour could occasionally require monitoring. He improved the standards of courtesy in the School – not least by his own example; and he expected both colleagues and pupils to observe such standards. He noticed the fierce competitiveness of Salopians on the games field, and followed the example both of Alington and of Peterson by his own vigorous participation in the Fives Court. On two occasions he sustained minor injuries there, necessitating brief reliance, on the first occasion, on crutches, and on the second occasion on a golf buggy. The boys regretted the disappearance of the latter, which followed upon his recovery, for while he was using it they were confident that they knew exactly where he was. He attracted the rueful admiration of his colleagues by his prowess on the croquet lawn. He also turned out for Staff golf and football teams, in the latter instance as goalkeeper; but his performance in goal did not always escape the critical strictures of the professional pundits on the touchline!

His colleagues particularly remember the punctiliousness with which he recorded his appreciation of their individual contributions, on significant occasions, by sending them a personal hand-written note of thanks. Another characteristic was his gentle humour. On one occasion he and I were teaching in adjacent classrooms, for he took care, when his other commitments allowed, to maintain his own, albeit restricted, teaching timetable. Our classes were separated then only by the far from sound-proof partitions which had originally been installed in the Lyle Building. As we emerged simultaneously at the end of the lesson, he said to me, 'Doctor, I'm afraid that there was one point that you were making that we didn't quite manage to get down'. His talent for defusing confrontation and controversy was illustrated on another occasion when I approached him on some, no doubt, entirely insignificant matter, now long-forgotten, which had aroused my fierce indignation, when he responded with the memorable but emollient injunction, 'Pursue it, David; pursue it!'

One of Simon's most marked characteristics was his concern for individuals. He numbers among his happiest memories of Shrewsbury the experience of seeing boys who were grappling with difficulties gradually overcoming them by dint of their own persistence, sustained by encouragement from others. He was also extremely appreciative of the contribution of his Housemasters, fully supportive of them, remembering, from his own experience, the pressures as well as the rewards of the position, and recognising their vital influence in nurturing and maintaining the pastoral quality of the School. Simon Funnell, who served in two schools with Simon Langdale as his headmaster, and subsequently became a headmaster himself, records that, 'he was firm and fair in a job in which it is extremely difficult to be either for very long'. It was a judgment, widely endorsed by Salopian colleagues, which Funnell was uniquely well qualified to make.

It was this concern for individuals which proved to be a crucial factor in determining the course of Simon Langdale's own future career. In his search for funds to allow a very promising boy to remain at the School, Simon was able to solicit and engage the support of the Rank Foundation, and in doing so was greatly impressed and attracted by its work in finding and funding a secure future for young people who otherwise appeared to have no such prospect. Just as he was beginning to think that it was an appropriate time, both for him and for the School, to consider a move, he was invited to accept the directorship of the Rank Foundation which he had so much admired.

Funnell's further judgment that Simon and Diana Langdale were the kindest of people would find similar wholehearted endorsement in the experience of those who came to know them during their time at Shrewsbury. He is also right in observing that while serving as headmaster, Simon never lost the instincts and the awareness of a schoolmaster and a housemaster. Far more important than 'the safe pair of hands' which it is universally agreed Simon brought to the Salopian tiller, was the civilised atmosphere of courtesy and concern for others which he so diligently nurtured, of which he was the exemplar, and which is his enduring legacy.

Francis Edward Maidment: Headmaster 1988-2001

Ted Maidment's thirteen-year tenure as Headmaster was the longest since the resignation of Jack Peterson in 1963, and during the quarter of a century which had elapsed between them heavy external pressures had developed which Ted's predecessors had not had to face. Ted was given no specific brief by the Governors and they had identified no specific problem which needed urgently to be addressed. He shared the impression of his two immediate predecessors that Shrewsbury was very much a going concern. Ted's previous experience as a housemaster at Lancing and as headmaster at Ellesmere had reinforced his awareness that a school must always be understood and developed in its historical, social and geographical context. At Ellesmere he had seen the need for radical measures and had taken them. He had little previous acquaintance with Shrewsbury itself (although he came with the advantage of established links with local preparatory school headmasters), but quickly came to the conclusion that no such radical measures were needed here. The internal structure, organisation and composition of the school were essentially sound.

His approach to his new school was pragmatic, but he perceived that academic standards would need to be kept sharp, that Shrewsbury would have to fight hard both to preserve its status as a national school and also that it would need to compete vigorously to attract its full share of the dwindling number of Preparatory School boarders who still provided the overwhelming majority of entrants to the School. He also realized the importance of maintaining and cultivating good relationships with the press.

He believed that it was both possible and desirable that Shrewsbury should preserve its status as a leading national boarding school for boys only. He considered that its considerable geographical distance from its major competitors, many of them in the South, could be turned to advantage; and that there were excellent potential recruiting grounds in the North, the North East and in Scotland. He felt that he could focus on this aspect of policy, since there were no significant internal problems in the School to distract him; and he judged it vital that the School should be perceived by others as a vibrant institution, well able to compete in any aspect and at any level, but as one which also enjoyed the advantages of its geographical location, well removed from the problems and temptations of the metropolitan areas.

Ted was prepared to take risks in order to implement this policy and to maintain Shrewsbury's prominent position, and his instincts were often fully vindicated. The most notable of these risks was his invitation to OFSTED to use Shrewsbury School for its first full inspection of a major independent boys' school. The procedure was elaborate, the necessary administrative preparation was monumental; and the report, for good or ill, would be widely noted and discussed in the national press. The result was outstandingly successful, and Ted acknowledged that this success was due, in no small measure, to the meticulous and indefatigable contribution of his Director of Studies, Richard Auger.

A new approach to fund-raising for the School was also pioneered during Ted's headmastership. In the *Salopian Newsletter* of May 1991 he had written,

In the past, the School has tended to focus on particular requirements by means of appeals. In our view the time has come for a broader and more continuous approach.

'The Friends of Shrewsbury' had been inaugurated in 1965. In November 1991 the name of this fund-raising institution was changed to 'The Shrewsbury School Foundation', in order to reflect this change of approach. Chaired by Ronny Utiger and directed by Ian Edwards, whose innovative skills were of crucial importance, the Foundation established a new pattern of fund-raising which has been very widely followed by similar schools. Membership and contributions were no longer to be devoted to one specific project, but rather to provide on-going and flexible support for a whole 'menu' of objectives.

A third initiative which very much intrigued the educational press was Ted's decision to prolong the summer term, at a time when elsewhere it was being progressively curtailed, in order to provide a period of teaching freed from the restraints of examination syllabuses, to allow constructive preparation for the academic year ahead, and to restore some of the summer term's desirable and traditional extra-curricular activities after the constraints imposed by the national examination timetable had been concluded. Although this experiment was not widely copied by other schools, it too attracted considerable notice and was much discussed.

Ted was concerned that Shrewsbury should extend its range of contacts with Prep Schools, not least in the South. Prep School teams came from far and wide to take part in the competitions organised by Mark Dickson, the master-in-charge of football: and, like so many before them, the competitors and their parents were captivated by the beauty of the Site and impressed by the warmth of the welcome which they had received.

Richard Field was appointed School Registrar in 1998, the first occupant of the post, but during the greater part of his headmastership, Maidment was happy to see his housemasters compete to persuade visiting parents to register their sons for their own House. The interview with the Headmaster, the gracious initial reception by his secretary and the social ease and straightforwardness of the boys who showed them round the School all contributed to the frequency with which parents chose Shrewsbury for their sons.

The results achieved by this combined and concerted effort speak for themselves. Ted had inherited a school of 664 boys; he bequeathed one of 697, and during his headmastership there were several terms in which the number of pupils passed the 700 mark. This was largely due to his strong and confident leadership; and long-serving colleagues could not fail to notice a parallel in the way in which Ted Maidment's name was instantly coupled with that of the School in the 1990s, as Donald Wright's had been in the 1960s. Other schools wanted to know what Shrewsbury was doing. The aspiration defined in the School's Carmen was being vigorously pursued: *ut per ultimos Britannos nomen celebretur.*

Ted is quick to acknowledge that this achievement depended crucially upon the quality and reliability of the key members of the Common Room. He was very well supported by a succession of his Second Masters, whose role is always crucial in preserving the ethos, strength and integrity of the community. He had a huge regard for his Bursar, Derek Crompton, both for his financial acumen and for his excellent supervision and management of his staff. He had a strong team of housemasters, and his own housemagisterial appointments, some of them surprising and unexpected, were generally acknowledged to have been fully vindicated. His successive housekeepers, Mrs Ann Gray and Mrs Mags Jones, also provided him with the supportive domestic environment needed by a bachelor headmaster. Without the confidence engendered in all these areas by support within the School, the external initiatives we have been considering could scarcely have been attempted.

All the headmasters with whom we are concerned were well aware of the importance of Chapel. Ted was no exception, and like Simon Langdale before him, he strongly impressed the obligation of attendance at services upon the members of the Common Room. He was very well supported, too, by his successive chaplains, David Allcock and Gavin Williams, of whom the latter served in Chapel for the greater part of Ted's headmastership. Ted particularly appreciated Gavin's ability to present the Christian message clearly and attractively in terms which seemed relevant, cogent and contemporary to a teenage audience. He believed that the historical, doctrinal and scriptural context of Christian teaching still had its own intrinsic value, at a time when the increasing tendency was to place the greatest emphasis upon its ethical aspect. Ted's revival of the custom of the School's annual service in St Mary's was another example of his contextual awareness.

The buildings and the other additions and alterations to the Site which form part of Ted's legacy include the IT building, opened in 1996, and the provision of the all-weather surface opposite Ridgemount, although the latter, while providing very welcome facilities, involved the loss of the athletics track. The erection of a fine statue of Charles Darwin, at the north end of Central, outside the Main School Building, corresponding to (but not directly facing) that of Philip Sidney at the south end, was another reminder of the historical context of the School. However, the most significant physical and structural reminder of Ted's headmastership is the new Music School, appropriately named the Maidment Building, which was opened by HRH the Prince of Wales, in 2001. It constitutes a permanent reminder of Ted's wholehearted support for and commitment to the musical life of the School. Himself a former Choral Scholar of Jesus College, Cambridge, Ted performed as a soloist in the School and elsewhere and his appointment of John Moore as Director of Music inaugurated a period in which Salopian music has acquired a national reputation.

The pressure of government intervention, of legal requirements and external assessments was beginning to play a significant role during the 1990s, but the full force of the veritable deluge of administrative procedures and of the extensive proliferation of external examinations was not to be felt until the next decade. As we have seen, Ted met the challenge of OFSTED head-on and appreciated the value of the Children Act in providing an appropriate safety net for the care of children away from home, although it had not been primarily designed for application in fee-paying boarding schools. He recognised that League Tables needed to be taken on board, even though they could not adequately reflect the full picture of academic achievement in the particular circumstances of each individual school. He felt that Shrewsbury compared well with its competitors, and particularly so in the Oxbridge entrance results, which indicated that during these years there had been a substantial number of Salopian candidates of high quality.

All six headmasters were concerned that members of the Salopian community should be aware of and attentive to the respect which should be accorded to each other as individuals. Ted expected that they should acknowledge each other appropriately as they moved about the Site. He did not quite manage to make good his claim that he would learn all 664 names of the boys and identify their owners during his first term in the school, but it was a valiant aspiration and a significant indication of his policy. No-one could fail to be aware of Ted's presence in the School, and, like Donald Wright before him, he wanted the School to buzz, to be alive. To this end he took several initiatives, ranging from the institution of a Scholars' Dinner to a series of measures to promote European awareness, including the appointment of a member of staff for that purpose, and the introduction of a series of European Conferences in which each House represented the interests of a different European country. Although this particular format has subsequently lapsed, the idea has been most successfully developed and extended by the School's Model United Nations team. The introduction of an Indian Scholarship for boys from the sub-continent was another outward-looking initiative. On a more trivial level, the presentation of a Millennium Tie to all members of the School at the turn of the century, and an attempt to establish a World Record by persuading the staff and boys alike to join in holding the lead, a hundred yards long, on which the Headmaster was taking his dog, Louis, for a walk, was another example of Ted's attempt to reinforce the sense of community. The 'free-style' format of the 2001 school photograph, in which the teaching staff, the support staff and the pupils were all gathered informally, in a crowd, on the grass in front of the Pentagon, was a further example of Maidment's awareness of and emphasis upon community values.

Ted was extremely shrewd and he kept his finger firmly on the pulse of that community. He took care to keep himself well-informed of opinions and developments all over the Site, and even in the far-flung domain of Severn Hill, as I discovered on a number of occasions, when I was the Housemaster. Once, when a parent, concerned about the increasingly cramped conditions in the House, generously offered the services of his in-house architect, to draw up plans to provide extra accommodation to improve the situation, he and I agreed that this should be presented to the Headmaster as being entirely his own independent initiative. He accordingly did so. As they subsequently pored over the plans together in the Pentagon, Ted observed drily to our would-be benefactor, 'I don't suppose the Doctor is entirely innocent!' Ted also, not infrequently, showed himself to be very capable of springing a dramatic surprise. My own appointment to Severn Hill, as a Housemaster who had already retired after the stipulated period of twelve years in another house, was just one example. Originally intended as a stop-gap position for one term, my tenure proved to be remarkably elastic. At a stage when Ted and I had agreed on two years, some parents came to see the House, after their interview with the Headmaster, and naturally asked me how long I would be staying.

'Two years, I think', I replied.
'Oh!', they said. 'The Headmaster told us just now that it would be three!'

In the event, it proved to be seven.

Ted remembers Salopians as being very much at ease in social situations, frank and straightforward in conversation, and he considers that, once again, context has played a significant part in shaping these Salopian characteristics. The School attracts a wide social mix of pupils; its immediate environment is an urban one which enables its pupils to keep well in touch with the wider world, but this in turn is set in a neighbouring rural environment which provides Salopians with an experience during their years at school differing markedly both from that of boarders marooned deep in the countryside and also from that of their contemporaries at Independent Schools in metropolitan areas. Maidment believed that Salopians, therefore, are able to compete successfully in this metropolitan world, when they encounter it, as they often do; but they are in it, not of it; they are 'plunderers' rather than residents born and bred.

Ted has two outstanding memories of his time at Shrewsbury. One is of the laughter in the Common Room and particularly of the festive sense of togetherness upon the triumphant conclusion of the inaugural OFSTED inspection; the other is of an occasion, entirely different in mood and circumstance, but in which that same sense of togetherness and mutual support was equally displayed, after the tragic death of one of the boys. Ted declared in a Headmaster's Assembly that he had never felt more proud of the School than he did then. What he did not say, and perhaps did not realise, was that the quality of the response and the strength of the community spirit displayed on both these occasions was a real, but unspoken tribute to him also.

Jeremy Wynne Ruthven Goulding: Headmaster 2001-2010

When Jeremy Goulding became Headmaster of Shrewsbury in 2001 he had already been Headmaster of two other schools, Prior Park College, Bath, and Haberdashers' Aske's School in North London. He was one of two among the six headmasters with whom we are concerned who had had significant previous experience of Shrewsbury. Jack Peterson had been a boy at the school; Jeremy Goulding had been a member of the Common Room for eleven years, as an Assistant Master, and successively as Head of the Religious Studies Faculty and Housemaster of Oldham's.

The news of his appointment was widely welcomed by those who had already served with him as a colleague and knew him to be a man of high principle, affable, considerate and approachable, with a deep devotion to and great affection for the School. Jeremy himself initially had some apprehension about returning to Shrewsbury, and to many former friends in the Common Room, as Headmaster; but this was quickly dispelled by the warmth with which he was received, and he experienced absolutely no difficulty with colleagues previously his seniors, who were generous and warm-hearted in their welcome.

In some respects his previous association with the School made his task considerably easier: he had already assimilated its ethos and traditions and he knew his way around the Site. His experience as a housemaster had provided him with an invaluable insight into the day-to-day working of the School. He was returning to a place which he loved and in which he had spent golden years of his earlier life. However, although he well understood that the Headmaster's position and perspective would inevitably be different from that of an assistant master, it took him time to acclimatise to the new role and relationship, albeit in familiar surroundings. Shrewsbury differed from the two schools in which he had previously been headmaster in that it was both a single-sex school for boys and predominantly a boarding school; he knew – and relished the prospect - that his position would require total immersion in the affairs of the School, seven days a week.

He discovered that in some ways Shrewsbury had not changed at all during his twelve-year absence. The Site had its own powerful personality; and the ethos which permeated it was equally powerful and immediately recognisable. In other ways, however, there had been fundamental changes which had made a considerable impact on the life of the School. It is not overstating the case to say that an electronic revolution had taken place during those years, and this had far-reaching implications for the functioning of the community. The whole method of communication had changed radically; additions to the Headmaster's correspondence seemed to arrive almost continuously, making it ever more difficult for him to escape from his office. The Headmaster countered this by making a deliberate effort to be seen about the Site and was well-known for the diligence with which he put in an appearance whenever possible at every conceivable Salopian occasion. He felt that the immediacy of e-mail and mobile phone contact wrought subtle changes not only in methods of communication, but also in the way the School functioned, sometimes making a more significant difference than might have been imagined. Just two examples made the point. First, instant phone communication from boys to their parents (and, importantly, vice versa) meant that boys new to Shrewsbury no longer had a period in which they could immerse themselves wholly and independently in the School's boarding environment. This could make the process of settling in and acclimatising far more difficult than it needed to be. Second, it became natural, because so instant and convenient, for colleagues with matters of mutual concern, or differences of view, to resort to the use of e-mail to express their opinions, sometimes to groups of fellow members of staff at the same time, rather than to seek each other out for personal, individual conversation. Such messaging could be useful and constructive; on other occasions, however much unintended, it could be the reverse.

Jeremy believed that his personal relationships with the members of the staff were of vital importance. He made a deliberate point of looking out for colleagues to whom he was aware that he had not spoken for a while. He considered that with mutual respect and trust even the trickiest issues could be negotiated and he learned by experience that he could indeed trust members of the Common Room to share such issues and respect the confidences involved. Pupils and colleagues towards whom he had to act in a disciplinary capacity were gratefully aware that this was always done in a manner which indicated his concern for them as individuals.

Hospitality was frequently offered by Jeremy and Isobel at the Headmaster's house, and guests were not infrequently greeted by the Headmaster emerging from the kitchen wearing a cook's apron and brandishing a cooking implement. Sunday evening discussion groups on ethical and philosophical matters were regularly held there for any who wished to attend and the Headmaster tried hard to maintain a regular, if strictly limited teaching schedule in the junior forms. A fine cellist, he was sometimes to be seen taking his place in the cello section of the school orchestra and was very occasionally coaxed into participating in chamber music recitals.

All this clearly represented a deliberate attempt to play a full part in the daily life of the School and in this Jeremy's wife Isobel made her own invaluable contribution, not merely as a hostess, but in further substantial involvement as a teacher of both Classics and Religious Studies and as a House tutor. Her daily presence in the Common Room enabled her to maintain relationships with her colleagues as easy and friendly as those which she had established with her pupils in the classroom and the House. At the farewell gathering of the Common Room at which leaving members traditionally make short speeches, Isobel relished the opportunity finally to be able to speak in her own right. This was an appropriate recognition of her conspicuous success in fulfilling the dual role of her own individual contribution and the supportive role of the headmaster's wife. Senior colleagues could not fail to be reminded of the similar success of an earlier 'team effort' launched from the Headmaster's house at the time when Jeremy and Isobel were first appointed to the School. Richard Hudson, in a valedictory article in *The Salopian*, comments that Isobel

combined a warm and outgoing personality with a natural discretion, qualities which fitted her ideally for the role of headmaster's wife ... without a shred of ego, willing to roll up her sleeves and get on with whatever job needed to be done

and he quotes the tribute of one of her recent pupils that Isobel was *'one of the nicest people on the planet'*, sentiments which so very many members of the Salopian community, colleagues and pupils alike, would wholeheartedly endorse.

It was the saddest of ironies that a headmaster who was so well-known for his willingness to consult and so obviously considerate of the feelings of others, should have found himself the target of the sharp criticisms arising from the most significant and far-reaching development during his headmastership – the admission of girls to the Sixth Form in the School.

Unsurprisingly, the proposal to develop a co-educational Sixth Form was, at the time, highly controversial. My intention in what follows is to explain the controversy, as I have understood it, as clearly and accurately as I can, for the sake of a fair and balanced historical record. That an initiative of such significance would be highly controversial was inevitable: it is no light matter to make such a breach in four and a half centuries of established and respected tradition.

Two separate issues emerged, though the focus shifted in time from the first to the second. The first was the nature of the decision itself and the second was the manner of its implementation.

The introduction of girls to the School had been an idea often raised during general speculation about its future, but although there was a clearly observable trend to adopt this measure in many similar schools, it was not part of any specific agenda when Jeremy Goulding was appointed. However, there was increasing concern over the steadily declining number of boy boarders in preparatory schools. For many years they had provided the overwhelmingly predominant source of recruitment to the School. Extensive and detailed research by the Headmaster and his colleagues convinced him that this was a problem that needed urgently to be addressed, for the sake of the future health of the School. He recommended the admission of girls, to the Sixth Form only, to the governors, as a long-term solution, rather than as a temporary expedient.

Other options had been carefully considered and had been presented to the governors by the Headmaster in a briefing paper. These alternatives included the admission of boys to the School at the age of eleven or the implementation of full co-education from the start, at the age of thirteen, across the whole age-range of the school. A more radical option would be to reverse the policy of growth which the school had adopted for a generation and to embark upon a deliberate reduction in its numbers. Some governors, however, hoped that the problem might prove temporary, that any shortfall might be assimilated and overcome, and that vigorous marketing of the School might make it possible to maintain the *status quo* in all its essentials.

At the full Governing Body meeting at which the Headmaster's recommendation to admit girls into the Sixth Form was discussed, a large majority of Governors spoke in favour. It was stressed that such a proposal, far from simply being an expedient to forestall a potential deficiency in numbers, would bring great enrichment, in social and cultural terms, and some Governors considered in academic terms also. The Headmaster felt that the proposal not only allowed greater flexibility in recruitment (the established procedure for the admission of boys would be unaffected and their intake would not be curtailed at any level), but also that the whole character of the School in the years before the Sixth Form could be maintained unaltered. Given that the Headmaster's recommendation to admit girls into the Sixth Form was endorsed by a large majority of Governors, it was decided that the recommendation should be approved and implemented without further ado.

Some Governors, however, believed that although a recommendation had been submitted, it ought to be subject to further deliberation; they considered that there should be further and more extensive discussion within the Governing Body. On hearing that a decision had been made, they took the view that a delay should take place between the formulation of the decision and its implementation, in order to gauge, guide and moderate the reaction. Three resignations followed upon these differences in perception and another upon the grounds of conflict of interest.

Thus, it was the swiftness of the decision which became the other focus of controversy. Even though it had been foreseen that the announcement of such an historic change would excite criticism from some quarters, a near-unanimous decision at the crucial meeting indicated that the case had been conclusively made and that a decision in favour of the option to take girls, into the Sixth Form only, had become inevitable. That being so, it was considered that it would be best to make a public announcement immediately, to avoid speculation and inaccurate leaks of information, and that it would be imperative enthusiastically to promote the vision of the cultural enrichment of the Sixth Form which the prospect seemed to offer. Some Governors, very widely experienced in the worlds of business and finance, including the Chairman, Sir David Lees, reinforced the judgment that it was important that implementation should follow as soon as possible, doubt and irresolution being notoriously damaging to the stability and future prospects of any corporate activity.

It is undeniable that the suddenness of the announcement did cause considerable problems. One unfortunate consequence was the difficulty experienced by some Housemasters in explaining the decision to parents, especially to those who had entered their sons for the School on the basis of a different prospectus. The situation in which the Registrar found himself was particularly regrettable. He had been devotedly and most successfully advocating Shrewsbury's status as the leading boarding school for boys within a wide geographical area; and he felt very strongly that the abrupt change of policy had placed him in an impossible position. In the wider Salopian community only a minority expressed strong criticism; but understandably this was at its most vocal and extreme among those Old Salopians who had been loyal to the School and most devoted to its long-established traditions, many of whom felt that an opportunity should have been provided for the opinion of that wider community to be expressed, before the decision was made.

Deeply held and strongly articulated though the criticism was, the Governors and the Headmaster perceived and understood that this was not the view of the majority. The advocates of the measure considered that it was courageous, of fundamental value and vital for the continued prosperity of the School. Perspectives and assessments change even during the short span of a decade as governors, staff and pupils come and go. Some of the earlier critics now acknowledge that the measure has been vindicated by very considerable success, while others continue to regret it deeply. The whole context of the discussion has also been changed by the recent decision to proceed to full co-education. Whatever their individual opinions may be, few would deny, as I suggested when I introduced the topic, that this was one of the most momentous decisions in the history of the School. In the narrower environment of the Site itself, it was a tribute to the personal relationships established by the Headmaster that although the decision was, no doubt, seen to be equally controversial when communicated to the Common Room, any dissent felt there was muted and it was generally received in a co-operative spirit, indeed, in many quarters it was greeted with warm enthusiasm.

The 'Great Matter' has, of course, tended to overshadow the Headmaster's other objectives and initiatives. Well aware, as he always was, of the need to keep the School full, he also recognised that it was not rigorously selective in academic terms and that there was an advantage in maintaining the diversity of the population and in exercising some flexibility in the admission of boys with good personal references who seemed likely to make a positive and talented contribution to the Salopian community (albeit not primarily as academics) and to derive full benefit from it. At the same time he considered that it was vitally important to maintain the academic 'edge', and to take particular care to attract and nurture the 'high-flyers'. Accordingly he strove to maintain and support a talented staff in order to achieve these high standards not only in academic, but also in a wide range of extra-curricular activities. A judicious balance such as this was difficult to maintain, but he felt – and the record shows – that Shrewsbury was successful in attaining both of these objectives (not least, for example, on the academic side, in the record of Oxbridge successes), and he found it unhelpful that the rigid categories of the League Tables failed effectively to record and reflect this diversity of achievement.

A major effort was made to improve and expand the facilities of the School. A new boarding house, originally intended for occupation by boys, was adapted to provide accommodation for the first Sixth Form girls, and a second boarding house for girls was planned and under construction. An extensive programme of refurbishment of existing boarding houses was completed, an initiative which, by means of a generous benefaction by the Worth family was extended to the fives courts. The Neville Cardus Cricket Centre and a new swimming pool were major additions to the amenities of the Site: the provision of these facilities was made possible by the exceptional generosity of Alan Palgrave Brown. The building which formerly housed the swimming bath was adapted to become a Sixth Form Common Room, which was called 'Quod'.

Far beyond the confines of the Site, the setting up of Shrewsbury International School in Bangkok has proved to be an outstanding success, enabling both Shrewsbury Schools to enjoy a rich partnership, manifested in educational and cultural collaboration. Jeremy Goulding and the then Chairman of the Governors, Sir David Harrison, together with fellow Governor Andrew Hillman, were heavily involved in the initial negotiations and in the early development of the International School, necessitating frequent trips out to Bangkok.

But in the final analysis it is the people, not the systems or the buildings, which create the character of the school. Jeremy remembers Salopians as being attentive to convention but not constrained by it, characterised by much sensitivity and generosity of spirit, with a distinctive sense of humour, always revealing a brightness of wit which is colourful, lively, creative and which, although indefinable, is instantly recognisable. He remembers Shrewsbury as a place where individuals and personalities mattered and where its pupils were encouraged to find their own temperament and character. Visiting parents repeatedly reported that they recognised and admired these qualities and influences in the boys and girls who showed them round.

He derived satisfaction from seeing the first girls complete their Sixth Form education at Shrewsbury and appreciated the generosity which the members of the Common Room had shown in receiving them; satisfaction, too, from the mix and range of achievement in the School, with an academic 'top end' which could more than match its major national competitors. Applications to the Sixth Form by both girls and boys continued to be very strong and the all-round performance of the first members of the co-educational Sixth Form seemed to vindicate and exemplify the aspiration of social and cultural enrichment which had always been one of the Headmaster's principal objectives.

Always keen to stress that the achievements of the School were the result of the collaborative effort of his colleagues and their pupils, his happiest memories included the celebration of a varied range of outstanding Salopian achievements, in music, drama and sport, all of which received national recognition, and among which the triumph of the Football 1st XI (against Repton) in the Boodles ISFA Cup requires particular mention. But to a former oarsman, the moment when he sprinted through the Stewards' Enclosure at Henley, throwing headmagisterial dignity to the winds, to discover that the Shrewsbury VIII had won the Princess Elizabeth Cup by a hair's breadth ,provided an indelible and treasured memory of their outstanding achievement, which encapsulated for him all that he valued about the spirit of Shrewsbury and Salopians.

There was a marked resemblance in style between Cyril Alington, Jack Peterson and Jeremy Goulding, which almost constitutes a tradition. Peter Fanning noticed it when observing Jeremy in Chapel:

catch him at rest in the Chapel, illuminated by one of the Chaplain's spotlights, and the beatific profile put one in mind of no-one so much as the late Cyril Alington ... ascetic, intellectual, almost metaphysical – pondering a world removed from timetables and tolling bells and Top Schools

It was a resemblance which extended to Jeremy's preaching in Chapel, as will be seen in the appropriate chapter. Peter also highlights the punctiliousness with which the Headmaster discharged all his manifold duties; and Goulding also trusted others to do their job. Peter observes that '(this) sense of being empowered, to get on and do the job themselves was the hallmark of Jeremy's time in the experience of many staff' (that too was a characteristic of the Alington and Peterson years). Peter also considers that 'the Full Monty' of success which the School recorded during his headmastership 'did not occur by chance. For apart from his excellent appointments, it was Jeremy's style that helped to furnish it all'. Peter quotes the words of one notable Old Salopian that Jeremy's years at Shrewsbury should be remembered not simply as 'Goulding Years' but 'Golden Years'. That is an opinion with which many of Jeremy's colleagues would wholeheartedly agree.

His self-deprecating humour is one of the qualities for which both his staff and his pupils will remember Jeremy Goulding. A typical example of this occurred on the occasion on which, after an unusually long absence necessitated by a visit to Shrewsbury International School in Bangkok, he returned to the Common Room for the regular Monday morning meeting and, for a formal apology for his absence, substituted the following words: "Good morning, ladies and gentlemen. My name is Jeremy Goulding; and I'm the Headmaster." His final appearance before the School in the Alington Hall contained a similar example of his engaging style. Standing there, in his academic gown, he was astonished when two senior members of the School appeared on the stage and presented him with an oar, engraved on the blade, in the approved manner, but with a record of his time at Shrewsbury substituted for the names of the crew. Nonplussed at first, he finally slung the oar over his shoulder, and walked off the stage to thunderous applause.

Michael Lindsay Charlesworth

One other man presided over the fortunes of the School during the sixty years with which we are concerned. Michael Charlesworth was Acting Headmaster on three occasions, in the Summer Term of 1972, during Donald Wright's sabbatical; in the Summer Term of 1975, after Donald's resignation and before the arrival of Eric Anderson; and again in the Michaelmas Term of 1980, after Eric's departure for Eton and before the arrival of Simon Langdale in January 1981. Michael records in his autobiography *Behind the Headlines* that when the Governing Body were looking for a successor to Donald Wright, the Chairman asked him whether he would like his name to be considered, but that he replied 'in the negative'.

Michael experienced and contributed to nearly every aspect of Salopian life. A boy in Oldham's between 1932 and 1937, he went on to Magdalen College, Oxford to read history and subsequently served in the war, before returning to Shrewsbury as an Assistant Master in 1947. He was Housemaster of School House between 1955 and 1961, and after a period of absence abroad, during which he was Headmaster of Lawrence College, Pakistan, he again returned to Shrewsbury in 1967. He was subsequently appointed Second Master, a position he retained until his retirement from the staff in 1981. In this third Salopian incarnation he played an astonishing variety of roles, not only as Acting Headmaster, but successively as temporary Housemaster, in turn, of Rigg's, Moser's and Churchill's, Acting Bursar, an efficient and well-liked form master, a fund-raiser and Editor of the *Salopian Newsletter*. In retirement he made a major contribution to Salopian literature, producing a biography of Basil Oldham, *Heads and Tales* (an account of Shrewsbury in the twenties and thirties), a booklet about the School's buildings, monuments and other landmarks, a history of the chapel, two war books, *Marching as to War* and *Two of the Few*, and most importantly his own autobiography *Behind the Headlines*. All these, like the present volume, were published by Richard Hudson under his Greenbank Press imprint. Michael was an athlete, actor, playwright, impresario and producer of plays, with an encyclopaedic knowledge of Salopian lore and an unmatched range of Salopian friendships and contacts. He served as President of the Old Salopian Club and he was regarded by many as 'Mr Shrewsbury', the embodiment and the guardian of Salopian values and traditions. One of the headmasters with whom Michael worked considered him to be 'the best all-round schoolmaster I have ever met'. He was for many years a governor of Moreton Hall, where one of the boarding houses bears his name.

The three terms in which he served as Acting Headmaster had their own distinctive character. The position of headmasters of Independent Schools combines power and isolation. The power arises from the very considerable patronage a headmaster has at his command, the promotion which he can confer and the influence which he exerts upon the careers of his assistant masters; the isolation derives partly from that power, but also from the necessity of avoiding any suspicion of favouritism. Headmasters are of course required to make decisions and to formulate policy. As all headmasters know, each decision and initiative can offend as many colleagues as it pleases. As Acting Headmaster, Michael Charlesworth was released from all these restraints. Patronage, promotion and policy could, in most cases, very properly be deferred until the following term. Isolation was both unattainable and unnecessary. And there could be no question of autocratic rule: an Acting Headmaster is truly *primus inter pares*, whose principal responsibility is to keep the ship of state on an even keel. Both Eric Anderson and Simon Langdale have recorded their impression that Shrewsbury could get on very well without a headmaster. In the long term, that is of course an entirely impracticable prospect, but that they formed that impression was in itself a tribute to Michael, and it was reinforced by the experience of those colleagues who served with him.

CHAPTER SEVEN

CHAPEL

Shrewsbury is a religious, as well as a royal foundation; and compulsory corporate religious observance has been a central feature of the School's life throughout its history. However, it was scarcely to be expected that the School would be unaffected by the progressive secularisation and decline in church-going in society at large. Two other factors, within the School itself, have necessitated change: there has been a considerable increase in the number of pupils who have been brought up in cultural traditions other than the Christian, or with no religious faith at all; and with the marked increase in numbers in the school, Chapel can no longer accommodate the whole school together. The capacity of the fixed seats in the nave and the gallery is 520 and the pupil roll is currently over 760.

The consequence of all this has been twofold. The number of occasions on which a Salopian is obliged to attend Chapel has been reduced: and there has been a shift in emphasis in the nature of the observances which take place there. This is reflected in the change from doctrinal instruction and scriptural exegesis to wider aesthetic, intellectual and moral contemplation of the eternal values of Beauty, Truth and Goodness, and to more frequent lay participation in the services, by both staff and pupils. They have, in turn, contributed their own experience and perceptions of how they have found meaning and value in their own lives. Essentially the focus of the study and practice of religion has moved from the narrowly confessional sense to the wider philosophical and literal sense of the word, 'what binds things together'. In tune with this development, the current chaplain, the Revd Gary Dobbie, wrote, upon his appointment in 2003,

I believe that the chapel should be a place of ideas and should keep open a spiritual understanding of life, in a way which is challenging and creative. I very much want the boys to be involved in what happens.

He has consistently pursued this objective. In the foreword to the booklet of Chapel services which was produced in August 2008, Gary wrote,

I seek to convey a spiritual understanding of life, that there is a bigger perspective, another league table of value, in the light of which all our doings will be seen in their true perspective: that human beings are more than just material entities – that we have a spiritual nature and a spiritual destiny … Chapel challenges us to live for the big idea, to find a beautiful idea on which to base our lives. And yes, it celebrates the unique contribution of Jesus Christ to the search for value and self-fulfilment.

In considering the history and development of Chapel during the last sixty years, it seems appropriate first of all to consider the people involved, the chaplains, assistant clergy, the choir and other lay participants; next to examine the relaxation of compulsory attendance and the changes which have been made in the pattern of services; and finally to trace developments in the structure, interior arrangement and decoration of the building.

Shrewsbury has had ten chaplains since the post was instituted in 1933, after the appointment of a lay headmaster. Previously nearly all Salopian headmasters had themselves been in Orders, and their own regular appearances in the pulpit had provided them with the opportunity to exert a powerful influence upon the moral tone and standards of the School. Among them, in comparatively recent times, Cyril Alington was outstanding. In his Shrewsbury Fables, a series of sermons preached at evensong and presented as recollections of dreams, he found a captivating means of presenting profound moral teaching set within a specifically Salopian context and environment.

The tenure of each of the first three chaplains, the Revd A.L.E. Hoskyns-Abrahall (1933-36), the Revd Prebendary E. Moore Darling (1936-37) and the Revd H. Beevor (1937-41) was comparatively brief, but that of the Revd Guy Furnivall (1941-66) lasted for a quarter of a century, and these were to prove to be the last years in which the traditional features of the public school chapel, compulsory daily attendance (twice on Sundays), twice weekly voluntary communion services, together with systematic scriptural exegesis and doctrinal instruction were to be seen in full operation. This teaching was reinforced by the regular appearance, as visiting preachers, of a whole succession of senior clergy, including many bishops and archdeacons.

Stability, then, was the keynote while Guy Furnivall was chaplain. The whole school could still be accommodated in chapel. Congregational singing, nurtured by the weekly Friday practices, was particularly strong, and it received favourable comment from the Duke of Edinburgh on the occasion of the royal visit in 1952. Guy was remembered for his sincerity, simplicity and humility; and for his total lack of egoism. A Salopian who was himself later to be ordained recorded the powerful impact which the sight of Guy saying his prayers in chapel had had upon him. Guy himself was encouraged by the comment of a visiting Lutheran pastor that the chapel had seemed to him to be a 'holy and humble place'. The impact of this traditional Christian worship and teaching was further strengthened by the tradition of thrice-weekly addresses by members of the Common Room in Lent, and by the production of a Passion Play every five years. Shrewsbury was a quite strongly religious community at the time; and it was significant that the number of ordinations among Old Salopians was sufficient to warrant a separate section in the Salopian Newsletter in which to record them.

Alistair Conn (1966-1973) became Chaplain at a time when Donald Wright's 'wind of change' was sweeping powerfully across the Salopian scene. Donald had previously demonstrated his strong support of corporate worship by transporting the whole school to a service in Coventry Cathedral on one occasion. Now he similarly signalled the importance he attributed to the Chaplain's position by requiring the whole school to witness the full ceremony of Alistair's induction and institution by the Bishop. This was a period of vigorous discussion about the role of Chapel and about the compulsion and frequency of attendance. There was much pressure to reduce the element of compulsion: and on one occasion the whole Housemagisterial body adjourned to Lake Vyrnwy Hotel to discuss the issues at length. Michael Charlesworth writes that Donald was *a very fully committed Christian, determined that the presentation of the Christian religion should continue, but prepared to rethink Chapel services and their content, without in any way abandoning the central doctrines. Chapel was launched into an experimental phase, sometimes involving boys in the conduct of services. Departing from the run-of-the mill missionary/general/ bishop as preachers, he brought some outstanding and challenging men to the pulpit.*

A moderate degree of relaxation was conceded, a reasonable compromise being reached between compulsory and voluntary services. The recently authorised provisional liturgies were used, and perhaps most important of all, informal communion services in Houses were introduced.

Paul Lucas (1973-78) remembers that he inherited a 'mixed grill' of different kinds of services during the week and that this prompted him to develop 'themes', such as 'the Maze', 'Hands', or 'Fire' in a series of addresses during the course of a particular term. In Chapel itself, he recognized the fragility of the compromise which had been reached between traditionalist and progressive views. It was a time when the failure of a visiting preacher to find the right pitch to create a resonance in his audience might be signalled by a concerted creaking of the benches. Paul commented,

It takes a very special blend of acting flair with sincerity, of passion with intellectual rigour, to get past the defences of a parade of Salopians

but he valued and continued the regular provision of House Communions, which,

in the candlelit halls of the boarding houses in the quiet of the evening, remain in my mind as the best bits of the Christian life of the School.

David Allcock (1978-1993) was Chaplain for fifteen years. If Guy Furnivall's tenure represented the last period of traditional Public School worship, David's tenure saw the consolidation and widespread acceptance of the contemporary format. David was a perfectionist, and an inspirational preacher who applied the skills acquired in his earlier career as a textile designer to the pattern of corporate worship. These skills were seen at their finest on the great occasions which he planned to mark the Salopian calendar – Harvest Festival, Remembrance Sunday, the Carol Services and the Leavers' Service. David's ability to place his teaching in a Salopian setting was reminiscent of Alington, and few who heard his deeply moving sermon at one Leavers' service, when he referred to the Leavers as his 'Salopian Swallows', will forget it. David's ability to capture a mood amounted to genius. His sensitivity to that mood and the importance he attached to it are recorded in his own words:

Shrewsbury is a strange animal. One of the most important skills which a chaplain has to cultivate is the sense of just where it is at any moment in is growth. A marvellous animal – at times cantering along magnificently, it can suddenly snort and rear if the great beast is being badly served or ill directed.

David's patience, sensitivity and imagination ensured that these were calmer days in Chapel. But on two matters he was adamant: he was strongly against any attempt to make Sunday worship voluntary; and he was convinced that the visible support of the staff at Chapel services was an essential prerequisite for any secure growth in spirituality in the school.

Tom Mendel's tenure as Chaplain (1993-1995) lasted less than two years, and turned out to be an experimental interlude between his previous and later experiences as a chaplain of the Anglican Church in Europe; but during his time at Shrewsbury he invested the services with dignity and colour, always stimulating and occasionally mystifying his congregation with his subtly constructed sermons.

Gavin Williams (1995-2002) had joined the staff as Assistant Chaplain in 1992 and succeeded Tom Mendel as Chaplain three years later. Gavin was another inspirational preacher, who earned the respect of his congregation by his sincere and challenging sermons, spiced with wit and humour. His message, while always relevant to the contemporary situation and well attuned to his audience, was always firmly based on biblical teaching and Christian moral principle. He presided over a period of calm and stability in chapel, reminiscent, in some ways, both in style and atmosphere, of Guy Furnivall's day, but fully cognisant of, and responsive to, the intellectual and social changes which had taken place during the intervening generation.

There was an interregnum, during the Michaelmas Term of 2002, between Gavin Williams' departure in July and the arrival of Gary Dobbie in January 2003, in which David Gee, as a Lay Reader, was Acting Chaplain. The observance, in Chapel, of the 450th anniversary of the foundation of the school, took place during that term. Otherwise, quite properly, no attempt was made to modify the established style and pattern of the services. The obvious major problem, with a layman in charge, was how to maintain the tradition of Sunday communions, to which David attributed great importance. This was effected partly by visits from local clergy to perform the consecration, and partly by implementing the Bishop's permission for David to administer the bread and wine in chapel, after they had been consecrated earlier that morning at a service in St Chad's.

In the ten years since his appointment in 2003, Gary Dobbie has fulfilled many of the objectives he then identified. He has harnessed a wide range of aesthetic media to expand the resources and environment of School worship; and he has presided over a greater degree of participation both by staff and pupils. Readings of poetry and individual musical performances have become regular features of the main services on Sundays, many of which have been adapted to include some special feature such as acts of commemoration of the School's founders and benefactors, of former members of the staff and school, or the dedication of new works of art. Special service booklets have been produced to mark these significant occasions and a wide range of commissions has brought painting, ceramics and sculpture to the chapel. The overall result has been a transformation of its interior appearance fully described at the end of this chapter.

The ten chaplains have usually had the assistance of other ordained members of the Common Room, and a particular tribute must be recorded here to Michael Tupper's long and faithful service. Mention must also be made of the distinctive exuberance of Hugh Brooke, and of the individual contributions, in turn, of Paul Lloyd, Tom Williams, Ian

Browne, Neil Britton, David Hart and David Stanton.

The tradition of inviting eminent ecclesiastics, headmasters and chaplains of other schools, to preach in chapel, always interspersed, of course, with contributions from ordained members of the Common Room, was consistently maintained until the mid-1960s. The name of the preacher for each Sunday was printed in the Fasti for the forthcoming term, the entry sometimes establishing a bleak contrast with the paucity of other non-ecclesiastical fixtures in the week.

The later 1960s witnessed a series of less orthodox, but always challenging, series of addresses from visiting preachers, both clerical and lay. In the restless 1970s the hazards of installing a visitor in the pulpit who might fail accurately to gauge the receptivity of his congregation led to fewer invitations and greater reliance upon the 'home team', except on well-defined special occasions. These included the annual visits of the School to St Mary's, the ancient location of school worship, but now a 'redundant' church, devoid of pews. Since the move to Kingsland and the establishment of the Chapel there, the School's visits to St Mary's had been intermittent. During Jack Peterson's headmastership, in November 1951, the practice of an annual School evensong at St Mary's had been restored, after an interval of nineteen years, but was subsequently allowed to lapse. In 1990 the tradition of an annual visit was revived, but for a service of Mattins, rather than Evensong. This now raises considerable logistic problems, for all the seating has to be brought from school, but it has provided a rare opportunity for the whole school to worship together and has also revived the tradition of inviting a distinguished visiting preacher, notable among whom, in recent years, have been the Dean of St Paul's and the Cardinal Emeritus of Westminster. That Cardinal Cormac Murphy O'Connor was able and willing to celebrate Mass in the School Chapel before preaching to the school in St Mary's on 13th September 2009, not only indicates the degree to which inter-denominational barriers have been dismantled, but must surely mark an historic moment not only in the annals of the School Chapel but in the much longer tradition of Salopian religious observance.

Music, of course, has always played a central role in Salopian worship. It was given a great and vigorous boost by J.B. Johnson, Director of Music between 1933 and 1950, who took particular care fully to involve the congregation. The institution of a weekly Congregational Practice on Fridays provided an invaluable opportunity to extend the repertoire of hymns, to teach the boys a congregational part in the Canticles and to enliven the singing of the psalms by imaginative and idiosyncratic rendering of certain verses: *hail -stones and coals of fire* and *Who is the King of Glory?* immediately come to mind. This tradition was maintained by Johnson's two successors, John Stainer and Stan Lester, who continued to take immediate charge of Chapel music themselves. In 1962 it was recorded that there were four *Te Deums*, two *Benedicites*, one *Benedictus* and two Evening Services in the repertoire for the Congregation.

In the late 1970s, however, Chapel music began to develop as a semi-independent activity, marked by the appointment of a member of staff whose principal function was, specifically, to train the Chapel Choir. A deliberate campaign to attract leading choristers from cathedrals to move on to Shrewsbury was initiated. The Chapel Choir began to make regular reciprocal visits to sing evensong in local cathedrals. These initiatives have been continued by Denny Lyster, Richard Dacey, Chris Argent, Simon Dearsley, Kathryn

Burningham and Alex Mason until the present day. The reputation of the choir has been particularly enhanced by its performance at the Carol Services, which have attracted an increasing number of visitors. Two Carol Services (rather than one) were deemed to be necessary as early as 1968; and subsequently provision has been made for three. The appointment of Alex Mason, with his previous experience as Organist and Master of the Choristers at St David's Cathedral, together with the stronger and more mature contribution the girls bring to the soprano and contralto parts in Choral Singing, has enabled the Chapel Choir, now numbering sixty, to reach a higher standard and offer a wider repertoire than ever before. The persistent and increasingly difficult problem of finding sufficient unbroken voices had previously been eased only by recruiting boys from Kingsland Grange Preparatory School. The admission of girls to the School, first to the Sixth Form and in 2014 also at the age of thirteen, finally solved it. According to Basil Oldham, the first School choir was formed in 1864, before the move to Kingsland. A hundred and fifty years later, its present successor is in fine fettle!

Another example of lay participation in worship is the much more prominent role of staff and pupils. Members of the Common Room frequently give the address at weekday chapel services; it has become customary, during the last twenty years, for a member of staff who is also leaving to speak at the Leavers' Service in the summer and together these 'Leavers Sermons' have provided a treasury of wise and memorable reflection; and in the summer term it has now become customary for Upper Sixth Formers, about to leave the School, to reflect, in weekday chapel services, on their experience of life and on Salopian life in particular.

The debate about compulsory attendance at Chapel was at its fiercest in the late 1960s and early 1970s. The result was that the tradition of 'obligation' (to use a more emollient word) has been maintained in principle, but significantly relaxed in practice. Opponents of obligatory attendance argue that it is out of tune with contemporary society, that adolescents are entitled to choose for themselves, that Christianity is only one of many frameworks of religious belief and that there is a risk either of indoctrination on the one hand or lifelong alienation on the other. Proponents of obligation argue that attendance at Chapel is only one of many aspects of compulsion (attendance at lessons is, of course, another) which are necessary to provide a full and effective education; that every community requires a location in which it can assemble to formulate and examine its values; that the moral teaching and aesthetic experience which are inseparable from Chapel worship have an instrinic educational value to which every adolescent ought to be exposed; and that, though attendance may be compulsory, everyone present is free to evaluate the experience for himself. Much of the 'steam' has been taken out of the controversy by the steady reduction of the occasions on which attendance in Chapel is obligatory. In 1958 the School assembled in Chapel at 9.30 a.m. (after First Lesson and breakfast) on four weekday mornings – Tuesday, Wednesday, Thursday and Saturday. There was a Congregational Practice, also in Chapel, on Friday and an Alington Hall assembly on Monday. Now the general requirement is to attend one service on a weekday and one on Sunday, together with an occasional Monday School Assembly.

Closely connected with the question of compulsion is the pattern and the provision of the services. In practice, the change in the character, scope and frequency of the services has done much to quieten the debate over compulsion. On Sundays, before 1965, an early voluntary communion was followed by Mattins and Evensong, both the latter compulsory in theory. As early as the late 1950s some of the evensongs had been made voluntary. By the 1960s, nearly all of them were. The experimental character of the decade between 1965 and 1975 was reflected in repeated changes in the pattern of the services. Sometimes only the Sunday morning service was compulsory, at other times only Evensong was. As the numbers in the School grew, separate services for senior and junior boys were introduced. The compulsory morning service alternated between Mattins and a School Communion. At one stage those who did not wish to communicate were allowed to leave at a certain point in the service, an expedient which was quickly discarded.

Between 1978 and 1981 the current pattern and provision of services was gradually formulated and stabilised. By 1978 there were three choices on Sundays – a said communion at 8.30 am, and on alternate Sundays Mattins at 10.15 am and Communion at 6.45 pm or Communion at 10.15 am and Evensong at 8.45 pm. A further reorganisation in 1981 retained the early morning said Communion, at 8.15 am, with either Sung Eucharist or Mattins at 9.40 am. Thereafter, there has been a School service either in the morning or in the evening, but not both; and if the morning service was Mattins, a shortened, voluntary service of Communion would generally follow. During the eighties and nineties, Compline, in the late evening, became another alternative, sometimes being used to accommodate those for whom it had been impossible, as a result of the growing numbers in the School, to find room in Chapel for services earlier in the day. Currently there is usually only one service in Chapel on Sundays.

The occasions on which the school is in session on Sundays have been reduced by the institution of Exeats of one week in the Lent and Summer Terms and of two weeks in the Michaelmas Term, all including a Sunday both at the beginning and the end. This 'loses' three Sundays in the latter and two Sundays in each of the former terms. 'Coach Weekends', usually occurring twice a term, further reduce the number of Sunday services in Chapel. School Communions take the place of Mattins on two or three occasions each term.

Some general observations may be made about these changes. Since 1978 the weight of preaching and expounding the scriptures has been moved to the weekday services, which normally consist of an address, a prayer and a hymn. Different sections of the School attend one of these services on Wednesday, Thursday or Friday. The addresses are given by lay members of the staff as well as by the Chaplain. The discontinuation of a Congregational Practice means that congregational participation is less significant than it used to be (one notable, splendid and comparatively recent exception is the singing of the *Libera Me* from Fauré's *Requiem* in the Remembrance Service); and psalms have almost entirely disappeared from the Salopian liturgy. 'Relevance' has become an increasingly important criterion in the services, with its attendant danger of lapsing into triviality and banality; and perhaps something has been lost in terms of the subliminal and numinous impact of the traditional service. But there is a much wider acceptance of Chapel's legitimate place in Salopian life than was the case forty years ago. Writing in the *Salopian Newsletter* in 1991 I noted that the Salopian congregation is *receptive and indeed appreciative when the fare is good, but proves a stern critic when what is offered seems inadequate, patronising or irrelevant*

and that is still the case today.

As the School has continued to expand, so that neither the Chapel nor the Alington Hall can accommodate the whole pupil population, Kingsland Hall is the only building in which the whole School community can be assembled, and the need for a suitable space in which the values of the School can be expressed and communicated to everyone regularly and simultaneously in a comfortable environment seems ever more urgent.

During the course of the last sixty years there has been a series of significant changes in the interior arrangement of the Chapel, but only comparatively minor changes have been made to the structure itself. When the organ was refurbished in 1962, the opportunity to provide a musicians' gallery was seized: a location which has sometimes been used to very good effect by brass groups and notably by trumpeters on 'state occasions'. During a week in the Easter holidays in 1965, employing skills honed in earlier and similar enterprises in support of the School Mission in Liverpool, a group of fifty masters and boys completed the major operation of painting the walls of the nave white and the roof of the chancel sky blue, producing a much brighter and lighter effect. In 1967, profiting from a generous donation in memory of Sir Humphrey Haslam, the north transept was extended and redesigned and a new vestry built. But although the desirability of a more ambitious extension to enable the Chapel to accommodate a significantly larger school was never far from the minds of a succession of headmasters and chaplains, this has not yet occurred.

However, there has been a series of significant changes in the interior of Chapel. During the 'experimental' period of the late sixties and early seventies, the Victorian reredos at the east end was covered by a curtain, in front of which a large wooden cross was suspended. The old choir stalls disappeared and a moveable altar was installed in the sanctuary. At the end of the decade, however, these changes were partly reversed. The curtain and the cross were removed, the reredos was once more exposed to view and the new choir stalls were transferred from the chancel to replace the six front pews on either side of the nave. During the last ten years a still more radical rearrangement has taken place. The Choir has been moved to the extreme eastern end of the building beneath the reredos, and new choir stalls have been provided by a bequest of Christopher Argent, a former Organist and Choirmaster. They are illuminated by lanterns in the style of an Oxbridge college, installed across the width, rather than the length of the assigned area, the effect being not only to accommodate a much larger choir but also to place it facing the congregation.

This latest change, if perhaps the most obvious, was only one of the many which have transformed the interior of Chapel within the last ten years. In the re-painting, much use has been made of Pugin red, juxtaposed with blue, with the intention of creating a numinous atmosphere and producing a sense of mystery. The angels on the Chapel ceiling, previously scarcely visible, have been repainted in muted tones and are now sensitively lit; stars have been painted on the chancel roof. A series of seventeen ceramics, on porcelain plaques, have been contributed by Victoria Dark and fixed to the wooden panels which line the north wall of the nave. Victoria also designed the white ceramic bowl, on its plinth, which serves as the new font, and which stands in the Ante-chapel.

At the east end of the Chapel, the six niches which stand on either side of the reredos have been filled by frescoes of St Francis of Assisi, St Cecilia, St Winifred, St Chad, St Nicholas and St John, painted by Aidan Hart. His triptych of the Transfiguration, the Resurrection and the Ascension stands beneath the East Window, and a re-lighting programme has been completed to show off these works of art to their best effect. A further work of Aidan Hart, an icon of the Annunciation, has been placed in the Ante-chapel. An icon of St John the Forerunner was presented by the father of Artem Bocharov (SH 2001 - 2006) in thanks for his son's recovery from leukaemia, and is placed next to the font.

A sculpture of Lazarus by Max Baccanello (OS) (Rt 2001-2006) stands at the east end of the south side of the nave, at the entrance to the south transept, flanked, on the other side of the nave, by a fifteenth-century image of the Madonna and Child. This has been in the School's possession for more than a century. Having been displayed in a Florentine palazzo for four hundred years, it was brought to Chapel and dedicated by Dr Alington in 1909. Max Baccanello has also contributed the image of the Bound Lamb in the Ante-Chapel. One of the most recent developments in Chapel was the design and installation of contemporary windows by Steven Robinson in the north transept in 2013.

The Shrewsbury School embroiderers have also made a substantial contribution in Chapel, having produced an altar-rail kneeler, kneelers for the occasional wedding, with cushions for the seats of the Bishop, the Headmaster, the Chaplain and the Assistant Chaplain, with kneelers to go with them. The embroiderers have also made altar frontals, a hanging at the rear of Chapel and the Pulpit Fall. Jane Dillon produced a set of altar cloths in memory of Sebastian Hudson (M 1996-2000). She also contributed fifty pew runs in memory of Charlie Kershaw (S 1998-2003) and a final set of four runners has been provided for the crossing. And finally, after many years' sojourn in St Mary's, the Headmaster's and Chaplain's stalls were returned in December 2014 and restored to their traditional place in Chapel.

Jeremy Goulding observes that a distinctly Alingtonian quality seems consistently to have been preserved in the contributions delivered from the Chapel pulpit; its essential character is that the message – the good news – is expressed, not in abstruse doctrinal terms, but in a recognisable and meaningful Salopian context. In the first of the following two passages, each of them part of an address delivered to Salopian leavers and their parents, the preacher compares leaving school to preparing a ship for a voyage, and refers directly to Alington's fables:

These recent years -five years for most of you – have been spent stocking, rigging and provisioning the ship and learning the art of seamanship: and now is the time to set sail. And what is the cargo with which your ship is stocked? Much of it consists in what you have done, what you have gained and what you have learned: but much the most valuable part, for you as well as others, consists in what you have given. Dr Alington made the point in two of his most famous sermons, no doubt delivered from this very spot. In the first, he tells of the coinage which is issued to the boys for their journey money, in copper for what they have done for themselves, in silver for what they have done for others, in gold for what they have done for God. In the second, he dreams of a fire in Chapel, blazing there in the sanctuary, in which a Salopian, due to leave school, throws all the symbols of his achievement, books, prizes, ties, scarves, oars and bats, hurling them into the blaze, only to see the flames leap ever higher, till finally, when he has nothing else to give, he jumps in himself … and finds that, far from being consumed by the fire, he is refined and transfigured by it. It is an appropriate image for a school like ours: for, at its very best, it is the intensity of the community life which produces such strength and which nurtures such refinement. And one of the most valuable lessons which this city set on a hill affords, is that it is what we have given that we have truly gained.

And the second address strikes an Alingtonian note exactly:

Late of a dark, silent evening, as the moon breaks through the clouds and lets its pale light through the limes on Central – limes whose branches have sheltered so many Salopians in their day – stop and sit for a time with your back to one of the trunks, look up and listen very carefully. For if you listen very carefully indeed, you will begin to catch an unmistakeable exchange between those two sculpted figures, from one end of Central to the other.

It happens more frequently than you might guess, heralded in the night stillness by the faintest, whispered, creaking of the one, adjusting, just a fraction, his noble Elizabethan, armoured stance to ease the unremitting pressure of statuesque stillness – particularly with that Zutphen shot-injured thigh: and the other, taking a touch of tension out of his energetic, stretching stride, which can be so very tiring, even for a youthful Galapagos explorer.

During the day they see it all and hear it all; they see and hear quite a lot in the evenings too, more than you might imagine.

The preacher goes on to describe the scene by day, and continues

By evening, gatherings and concert-goers, pizza cars and hungry, chattering purchasers; assignations and secret conversations; some late at night; some even later at night – all witnessed, knowingly yet unknown from just above.

And then there is that time, on a chill November Sunday, when they all come from morning chapel and gather, quiet, attentive, praying, as far too many names are read and Salopian thoughts are stirred, and footfalls echo in private memories, too private for words.

The preacher next describes the scene from the Darwin statue, in its turn, and then asks:

And the exchange between those two along Central? About how fashions come and go, and life seems ever busier; and how the deeply important things, like kindness and thoughtfulness and virtue, don't change, mustn't change; and how it was when they first came to Shrewsbury.

Opportunity, they talk of opportunity; how seizing the good moment is still all-important, and life-changing and deeply Salopian, and leads to discovery, sometimes beyond one's wildest expectation.

Time present and time past
Are both present in time future

It is one of the functions of addresses in Chapel to convey an ethical message and to express it in terms which are familiar and meaningful to the specific audience; and if, indeed, there is a distinctive Salopian ethos, although immensely difficult to capture in prose, I suspect that its themes can be distinguished in the poetic, dream-like quality of the two passages quoted above.

CHAPTER EIGHT

THE COMMON ROOM

The location of the Common Room has changed twice during the last sixty years, in order to accommodate the steady growth in numbers of the academic staff. It has occupied rooms both on the right and the left of the principal entrance to the Main School Building and also on the first floor; nowadays even the much greater space afforded by Old Day Boys Hall becomes remarkably crowded during morning break.

Statistics relating to the membership of the Common Room can be misleading, since it is composed both of full-time and part-time staff. The number of the latter group has varied widely, sometimes exceeding more than a dozen and, just occasionally during the last sixty years, Brown Book has not always made a clear distinction between the two components. Consequently the most reliable and significant criterion on which to base any measurement of the growth of staff numbers has to be based largely on the full-time members of the staff. There were 41 full-time members of the academic staff in Michaelmas Term 1950 ;in the Michaelmas Term of 2013 there were 103; in the Michaelmas Term of 2014 the total number of members of the Common Room had risen to 123. An appraisal of the figures at regular intervals shows a steady growth overall of seven or eight additions to the staff in each decade, but with twice that rate of increase in two five-year periods, first between 1970 and 1975 and then between 2000 and 2005. The overall totals at ten-year intervals, are as follows: MT 1950: 41; MT 1960: 49; MT 1970: 55; MT 1980: 69; MT 1990: 75; MT 2000: 82; MT 2010: 96 and MT 2014: 123, recording a rise of nearly 30% over the last four years.

These figures naturally raise the further question of how the staff/pupil ratio has changed during the last sixty years. A juxtaposition of the average number of the staff in the previous decade, with the number of pupils in the School at the end of that decade, shows a gradual increase in the staff/pupil ratio, as follows. Numbers of pupils to each full-time member of staff in 1960 were 10.9; in 1970: 10; in 1980: 9.3; in 1990: 8.9; in 2000: 8.5; in 2010: 7.3 and in 2014 5.4.

The academic background of the staff has also become considerably more varied. Teachers of art, music and physical education have always had their own separate professional qualifications, but so far as teachers of the 'core' academic subjects are concerned, the monopoly of Oxford and Cambridge degrees remained virtually unbroken until the middle of the 1960s, with many recruits to the staff before that time having been Scholars or Exhibitioners of their Oxbridge colleges. Within the next ten years new members were drawn from the universities of the northern cities, from King's College and Imperial College London, from St Andrews and from Queen's University, Belfast, until by 1975 graduates from fifteen different institutions, other than Oxford and Cambridge, had joined the Common Room. One notable feature of the 1970s was the recruitment of staff who had already had experience of other professions, for example in business and the diplomatic service. Both these tendencies have developed further in the last forty years, the appointment of a number of former army officers during the last three decades being a notable feature. In the Blue Book of 2014 over fifty different higher education institutions are represented and the record shows that only 23 teachers, less than a quarter of the total, were educated at Oxford or Cambridge, but it also shows that exactly the same number, 23, had taken a higher degree, whereas a doctorate was virtually unknown among members of the Common Room in the first two decades of our period and formal teaching qualifications were also very rare.

Until 1978 the full-time members of the Common Room were all male. This monopoly was first broken by Lucy Tanner, who was appointed for two years and stayed for three. In the 1980s a number of women were appointed to the part-time staff, some of them destined to serve for the long term. But the 1990s is the decade in which a nucleus of female staff consisting of Mylène Sourbès, Caroline Pringle, Dympna Nightingale, Sara Hankin, Liz Caney, Jay Upton and Hilary Laver was fully established in the Common Room. This contingent tended to number six or seven at any one time; but a steady increase has been apparent during the last decade. In 2012-13 female staff accounted for just under 20% of the total full-time complement. In order to cater for the introduction of full co-education in September 2014, however, most of those appointed to the staff during the last twelve months have been women. In the Michaelmas Term 2014, 78 members of the 123 members of the Common Room were men, and 45 were women, bringing the percentage of female members of the staff up to 35%. However, in a longer perspective, it should be noted that the part-time staff is and has always been predominantly female in composition.

Another significant feature of the composition of the Common Room has been the employment, on a temporary and generally on an annual basis, of teaching staff from overseas. Here the pioneers were the Harvard Fellows who, having first been established in 1978, have continued, with one year's interruption, until the present day. They were followed by European Fellows and, more recently, the contribution of the latter has been replaced by colleagues with more specific roles, the Eastern European, Bordeaux and Hispanic (Rosario) Fellows. This diversity has greatly enriched the teaching staff. For the two decades following 1990 a youthful element was introduced into the Common Room each year by a succession of 'gap-year' students - 'The Gappers'. These young men were usually from Australia, New Zealand or South Africa. They were good sportsmen, duly recommended by their schools, who had decided to spend a year in the United Kingdom, developing their coaching skills in their chosen sports and giving general assistance to members of the teaching staff. Their number varied between two and five each year. In the last few years they have been replaced by young sports graduates from our own universities on temporary appointment.

In the Common Room as a whole and in the longer term, changes in the academic structure of the School have led to consequential changes in the criteria for appointment. In the 1950s a significant proportion of the staff was employed as Lower School Form Masters and would generally have been expected to teach English, History, Divinity and a foreign language to their forms. In the last thirty years the search has been for specialists, selected for their ability to teach a specific subject or a closely related combination of subjects, such as two foreign languages or the physical sciences. This shift in emphasis, together with the establishment of specialist teaching areas, often at a considerable distance from the Main School Building, as in the Lyle Building, the Science Building and the Kennedy Building,

Aerial view of the site.

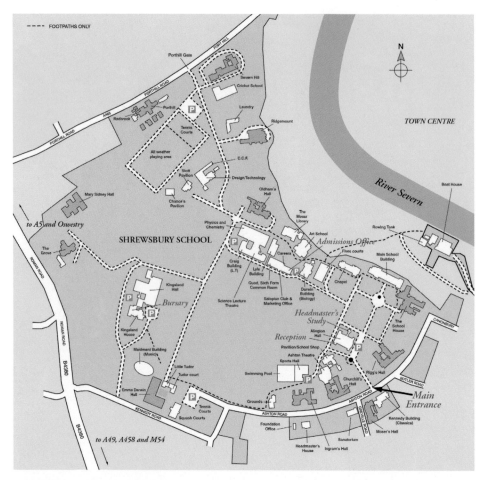

Plan of the Shrewsbury School site.

Speech Day

The most famous of Willie Rushton's (Ch 1950–1956) cartoons of the School, richly justifying the assessment of his contemporaries that 'he had highly developed antennae for the absurdity of the human scene'.

The statues above represent Philomathes (left) a lover of learning and Polymathes (right) the educated man. The photographs below are of James Plaut (S 2010–2015) as a Third Form entrant to the School in 2010 (left) and as Head of School (right) in 2015.

SHREWSBURY SCHOOL

FASTI FOR SUMMER TERM, 1955

Apr.	Tues.	26	Term begins.
	Wed.	27	
	Thurs.	28	
	Fri.	29	8.30 p.m. Da Vinci Society. Talk by L. C. Lloyd :
	Sat.	30	" Shropshire Buildings "
May	Sun.	1	*S. Philip and S. James. Easter III.*

Preacher : Rev. F. T. Horan, Vicar of Huddersfield (Matins).

Mon.	2	
Tues.	3	
Wed.	4	
Thurs.	5	
Fri.	6	
Sat.	7	1st XI *v.* Market Drayton (away).
		2nd XI *v.* Market Drayton.

Sun.	8	*Easter IV.*
		Preacher : Rev. C. G. Furnivall (Matins).
Mon.	9	Examination for Bright History Prize.
Tues.	10	
Wed.	11	2nd XI *v.* Mr. M. L. Charlesworth's XI.
Thurs.	12	
Fri.	13	
Sat.	14	1st XI *v.* Shrewsbury Town (away).
		2nd XI *v.* Shrewsbury Town.
		Rover Camp.
		7.45 p.m. Forum Society : M. L. Charlesworth, Esq.

Sun.	15	*Easter V.*
		Choral Communion.
		Preacher : Rev. M. H. Tupper (Evensong).
Mon.	16	Junior Challenge Oars begin.
		Visit of P.S.A.B. Representative.
Tues.	17	
Wed.	18	1st XI *v.* Shropshire Gentlemen.
		2nd XI *v.* Ellesmere College.
Thurs.	19	*Ascension Day.*
		7.45 a.m. Holy Communion.
		9.20 a.m. Chapel.
		Whole Holiday.
Fri.	20	
Sat.	21	1st XI *v.* O.C.S. Eaton Hall.
		2nd XI *v.* King's School, Worcester (away).
		Kingsland Ramblers *v.* Shrewsbury Accountants.
		8 p.m. Debating Society.

Sun.	22	*Sunday after Ascension.*
		Preacher : The Ven. E. Treacy, M.B.E., Archdeacon of Halifax (Evensong).
Mon.	23	
Tues.	24	Scholarship Examination begins.
		Field Day.
Wed.	25	Scholarship Examination.
		'A' XI *v.* King Edward's School, Birmingham.

64

Fastis for the Summer Term of 2015

WEEK B

Sunday 3rd May

All Day	5th Sunday of Easter
All Day	RSSBC: Wallingford Regatta, Dorney Lake (1st VIII, 1st 4X, J16A, J15A)
10:30 am	Cricket: HMC T20 Round 1 (Shrewsbury School, Oswestry School, Ellesmere College & Queen Mary's Grammar School, Walsall)

Monday 4th May

9:00 pm	Extended Coach Weekend ends

Tuesday 5th May

All Day	13+ Scholarship Entrance Examinations begin (end Thursday 7th May)
All Day	Spanish: AS and A2 Orals (end Thursday 7th May)
7:00 pm	Careers: Fourth Form Event: "Careers in Business": Kate Daubney
	(Science Lecture Theatre)

Wednesday 6th May

All Day	Athletics: English Schools Athletics Association Track and Field Cup, County Round, Oakengates (Third and Fourth Form)
9:00 am	Physics: PHA3X (AS Physics EMPA Practical Exam) (Gym)
2:00 pm	Rounders: 1st IX v Old Swinford Hospital School
2:00 pm	Cricket: 1st XI v Denstone College
2:00 pm	Cricket: 2nd XI v Wrekin College 1st XI
2:00 pm	Cricket: U16A XI v Wrekin College 2nd XI (depart Alington Hall 1.10pm)
2:15 pm	Tennis: Boys: 1st VIII v Ellesmere
2:15 pm	Tennis: Girls: 1st XI v Ellesmere College (depart Kingsland Hall 1.30pm)
4:00 pm	Swimming v Lucton School (Depart Kingsland Hall 3pm)
4:20 pm	Cricket: U15A & U14A XIs v Wrekin College Twenty20 (depart Alington Hall 3.15pm)

Thursday 7th May

1:30 pm	Cricket: U15A & U14A XIs v Cheshire U15s & U14s
2:00 pm	Athletics: Achilles Relays, Iffley Road, Oxford (depart Kingsland Hall 10.30am)
2:30 pm	Tennis: Boys: 1st, 2nd VI, U15AB VIII v Repton School
8:45 pm	Christian Forum: "Fear is not an option": Mr Mike Keep (Quod)

Friday 8th May

9:00 am	Physics: PHA6X (A2 Physics EMPA Practical Exam)
4:00 pm	Girls Cricket: U14A XI v Packwood Haugh Prep School (Gym)
4:15 pm	Cricket: U14B, U14C & U14D XIs v Packwood Haugh Prep School (depart Alington Hall 3.50pm)
7:15 pm	House Quiz Finals (Ashton Theatre)

Saturday 9th May

All Day	Open Day for prospective Third Form entrants
All Day	RSSBC: Shrewsbury Regatta (All Crews)
10:00 am	Athletics: Shropshire Schools Track & Field Championships, Oakengates (depart Kingsland Hall 8.30am)
11:30 am	Cricket: 1st XI v Repton School (depart Alington Hall 8.30am)
2:00 pm	Cricket: 2nd, 3rd, U15A, U15B & U14C XIs v Repton School
2:00 pm	Cricket: U16A, U14A & U14B XIs v Repton School Twenty20 (depart Alington Hall 11.30am)
2:00 pm	Cricket: U15 Girls XI v Malvern College
2:00 pm	Girls Cricket: U15A XI v Malvern College
2:00 pm	Tennis: Boys: 1st, 2nd & 3rd VI v Warwick School (depart Alington Hall 12.20pm)
2:30 pm	Tennis: Boys: U15AB & U14AB VIII v Warwick School
6:00 pm	Duke of Edinburgh Award: Group A Bronze Practice Expedition Weekend (return 6.00pm Sunday 10th May)

Notes:

16

Sixty years on. A comparison of the School Fastis for 1955 and 2015. The 1955 Fasti covers one month: the 2015 Fasti cover one week!

Headmasters

JM Peterson (OS) 1950–1963
Portrait by Edward Halliday

ARD Wright 1963–1975
Portrait by R. Tollast

WEK Anderson 1975–1980
Portrait by David Poole

SJB Langdale 1981–1988
Portrait by Peter Edwards

FE Maidment 1988–2001
Portrait by Alastair Adams

JWR Goulding 2001–2010
Portrait by Nick Bashall

JM Peterson 21st June 1952

*(Left to right) JWR Goulding, FE Maidment, ARD Wright, WEK Anderson,
SJB Langdale in the Masters' Garden, 5th October 2002.*

Four Salopian characters

Hugh Brooke
(Master 1933-1969)

Frank McEachran
(Master 1935-1960) who taught part-
time in his retirement until 1975

Mark Mortimer
(Master 1958-1994)

Michael Hall
(Master 1967-1995 and 1996-1997)
who also continued to teach part-time in
his retirement

Four Salopian`Senators

Russell Hope Simpson
(Master 1924–1965)
Housemaster of School House. Senior Master

David Bevan
(Master 1929–1969). Housemaster of
Ridgemount. Second Master

Michael Charlesworth. OS
(Master 1947–1961 and 1966–1981).
Housemaster of School House. Second Master

Richard Raven. OS
(Master 1960–1993). Housemaster of
Severn Hill. Second Master

*Wing–Commander
Ron Harrison,
Bursar 1976–1986*

*Gerry Sturges,
School Boatman
1954–1988*

*Ken Spiby,
Head Groundsman
1957–1994*

*Mike Stone,
Catering Manager
1969–2002*

A discussion group at Shrewsbury House in Everton ('The Shewsy'), with members of the School on a Sixth Form Social Studies Course taking part.

Members of the School assist the Headmaster (Ted Maidment) in taking his dog, Louis, for a walk.

The Day Boy Houses in 2015 comprising the Old Sanatorium building in the background, with Assembly Halls for Radbrook (left) and Port Hill (right), each with the Housemaster's house alongside. Since this picture was taken the athletics track has been replaced by an all-weather pitch and by a tennis court.

Led by their Housemaster, the Dayboys pick up their belongings and walk to their new accommodation. February 16th 1979.

Summer Term 1968

Back row (left to right): M.A.Mackinnon, M.A.Eagar, M.M.Jones (Bursar), S.D.Baxter, A.McHaffie, A.J.Bowen, R.J.Jones, J.R.Drummond, D.C.Christie, F.M.Hall, M.R.Rutland, R.P.Murray, B.Storey

Third row: M.W.Cross, Revd A.A.Conn, A.C.Grant, S.Lester, M.Mortimer, R.W.Trimby, R.N.E.Raven, A.G. Phillips, G.E.L.Spragg, B.R.Coulson, J.J.Crowhurst, G.Garrett, R.Kelsey, B.C.Pitt, J.B.Lawson

Second row: W.J.A.Mann, A.W.Fowler, Revd M.H.Tupper, L.R.Edbrooke, A.W.Laurie, A.C.Struvé, A.R.B.Moulsdale, F.L.Duffield, P.Gladstone, D.M.Main, A.D.Ellis, D.E.P.Hughes, R.M.Blomfield, D.H.Gee, J.H.Alford

Front row: A.L.Binney, M.L.Charlesworth, R.M.Connell, J.H.Woodroffe, M.G.Powell, D.J.V.Bevan, A.R.D.Wright (Headmaster), A.J.Hagger, W.E.Matthews, A.E.Broadbent, D.E.Brown, F.R.Ewing, H.L.B.Saint, F.McEachran.

Summer Term 1993

Back row (left to right): D.B.Nightingale, J.H.Upton, S.L.Saxton, J.M.Irwin, Revd G.J.Williams, R.N.R.Jenkins, B.W.Hewitt, A.P.Pridgeon, H.R.W.Peach, M.J.Lascelles, A.J.Allott, J.S.Taylor, M.W.R.Worster, Z.T.Kovacs, M.E.M.Caney

Fourth row: M.A.Schützer-Weissmann, A.S.McK.Went, T.Kidson, M.H.Hansen, M.S.V.Partridge, C.M.Pringle, G.StJ.F.Bell, D.W.N.Aston, M.J.Barratt, M.M.Morrogh, J.F.Moore, J.R.Burke, S.M.Holroyd, M.S.Sourbes, P.R.Scales

Third row: R.J.Kendall, J.Balcombe, J.M.Gladwin, W.G.Harvey, R.H.Dacey, P.N.Woolley, R.Brooke-Smith, J.Godwin, J.M.Williams, P.H.Lapage, D.R.Field, P.A.Fanning, P.D.Morris, D.Kirkby, D.Nickolaus, C.J.Minns

Second row: R.E.W.B.Field, P.T.Holgate, R.Parker, H.M.Ramsbotham, R.E.D.Case, I.J.Walton, S.W.Martin, A.W.Hayes, P.F.Cann, M.D.Dickson, S.B.Roberts, C.W.Conway, G.C.Woods, Revd D.Allcock, J.H.Furniss, R.G.Roscoe

Front row: M.W.Knox, C.J.Etherington, J.R.Drummond, J.B.Lawson, M.Mortimer, R.Auger, D.J.Crompton (Bursar), F.E.Maidment (Headmaster), S.S.Caney, D.H.Gee, R.N.E.Raven, S.D.Baxter, F.M.Hall, M.E.Ling, I.H.W.Lacey.

The Salopian Community 2001

Royal visits

Her Majesty, accompanied by the Headmaster, Jack Peterson, inaugurates The Queen's Terrace, October 24th 1952.

Her Majesty and HRH The Duke of Edinburgh take their leave.

The Headmaster, Donald Wright, presents David Bevan (Second Master) and the Hon. Mrs Bevan and M.M. Jones (OS), the Bursar, and his wife Mrs. Alison Jones, to her Majesty Queen Elizabeth The Queen Mother, November 5th 1969.

The Headmaster, Simon Langdale in conversation with HRH Princess Margaret with two of the Praepostors, Rodney Spiby (DB and Port Hill) (centre) and Rupert Harvey (S) completing the group, May 13th 1984.

The Prince of Wales addresses the audience with members of the School orchestra in the background and the headmaster in the foreground (left) after inaugurating the new Music School, February 21st 2001.

Traditional Buildings: Boy's Houses

Churchill's Hall 1882

Oldham's Hall 1911

Modern Buildings: Girl's Houses

Mary Sidney Hall 2007

Emma Darwin Hall 2011

Converted House

The Grove 1988. The Grove was a boys' house from 1988 to 2014 and was then converted into a girls' house.

The new Academic Building: Hodgson Hall

An impression of the new Academic Building, named Hodgson Hall after its principal benefactor. The scaffolding round the actual building has just been removed and it is due to be opened officially on October 3rd 2015.

The Statues

Sir Philip Sidney

The statues of two of the most famous Salopians, erected at each end of 'Central'. Sir Philip Sidney (1554–1586) was a member of the School from 1564 to 1568. Charles Darwin (1809–1882) was a member of the School from 1818 to 1825.

Charles Darwin

The exterior. Chapel was completed in stages during the the 1880s.

The interior. which has been redecorated and transformed during the last decade.

Traditional Interiors

The History Sixth being taught by Laurence Le Quesne.

A study

House lunch

Changing

Before lights out

Modern Interiors
The Girls' Houses

A lounge in Mary Sidney Hall.

A double bed-sit in Emma Darwin Hall.

The Hall in Emma Darwin Hall.

Modern Interiors
The Boys' Houses

The Television Room in Ridgemeount.

A double bed–sit in Severn Hill.

The Irvine Room in Severn Hill. A.C. ('Sandy') Irvine was in Baker's and Moore's (1916-1921) whose boys were subsequently transferred to form Severn Hill. Irvine died on Everest in 1924 and his ice-axe, discovered on the mountain in 1933, is preserved in the room named after him and can be seen in the photograph, displayed in its case on the wall (left).

The Moser Library.

The Art School.

The Design Centre.

Music

The Maidment Building.

The Chapel Choir on their visit to sing Evensong in St George's Chapel, Windsor. (The Director of Chapel Music and Assistant Director of Music, Alex Mason, is on the front row extreme left).

John Moore, who has recently celebrated 25 years as Director of Music.

Robert Collins (S 2006–2011) as soloist in the Joseph Horowitz Oboe Concerto with John Moore and the School Orchestra in Birmingham Town Hall, February 2011.

has inevitably reduced the social cohesion of the Common Room.

Fifty years ago there was a strong sense of seniority and hierarchy and, as a result, much greater formality in the Common Room. The use of surnames, rather than Christian names, was still commonplace, at least between senior and junior members. It was not unknown for a senior colleague to report one of his juniors to the Headmaster for some administrative deficiency, or even to reprove him for being inappropriately dressed and instruct him to go home and change. It is very difficult to imagine either of these circumstances occurring nowadays. Gowns were worn both for teaching and for Common Room meetings. If, at morning break, one had urgent business with a colleague who was already engaged in conversation, one could ensure that he could not get away, without interrupting his current conversation, by tying the sleeve of one's own gown to his. Common Room meetings were extremely formal. A colleague with less than two years' standing would have been ill-advised to make an unsolicited contribution. In the middle of the Common Room stood a solid table with eight places. The Headmaster sat at the head of the table; the other places were occupied, by convention, only by very senior members of the staff, nearly always senior Housemasters or others of equal and acknowledged *gravitas*. The remaining members of the Common Room sat on chairs which lined the walls, the whole arrangement producing a kind of concentric effect, with authority located at the centre. When a vacancy occurred at the central table, whether or not one was qualified to fill the vacancy was a matter which had to be gauged very carefully. This convention was finally breached by Mark Mortimer, who, (although qualified by seniority, would certainly never have claimed any qualification in terms of *gravitas,)* suddenly took it upon himself to sit opposite the headmaster, in a prominent position from which he was well able to demonstrate his amusement at the absurdities which often characterised such meetings.

Another example of the operation of a strict hierarchy was the convention governing the occupation of seats in Chapel. The stalls at the west end of Chapel, both downstairs and in the gallery, were strictly reserved for the exclusive use of members of the Common Room. There was a further restriction. The stalls downstairs were similarly reserved for senior members only. There came a time then, when the decisive question was whether one could properly move downstairs; the usual solution was for the Chaplain or the Senior Master to take one aside and suggest that such a move might be appropriate.

Relationships in the Common Room during our period were generally very harmonious, as the Bloxham Report, thoroughly examined in the chapter on Ethics, had testified; it recorded that there were no obvious cliques and no intolerant and diehard reactionaries. Social, as distinct from professional, relationships between colleagues were facilitated and enhanced by means of termly Guest Nights, regular Dining-In Nights and the opportunity for weekly encounters at the *Little Brown Jug,* which was an informal gathering for drinks, once a week, usually at the end of a full school day. Its location varied, but originally it took place in the rooms of a master willing to act as host. After the refurbishment of Kingsland House in 1969, the tradition was continued in the masters' bar provided there. More generally, necessary communications between masters were made directly, whenever possible by personal encounter, without intermediaries, or else by word of mouth on the telephone. To all outward appearances the Common Room was a placid environment even if, swan-like, colleagues were paddling furiously beneath the surface or, like stage-managers, were rushing about frantically behind the scenes.

It was only when half-term reports were placed upon the Common Room table that frustrations tended to emerge. In the first half of our period an A4 envelope was provided for each form or set, containing each individual boy's report, arranged in alphabetical order. The brief reports had to be hand written. Colleagues sat round the table, repeatedly asking questions such as 'Where's VB?' or 'Have you finished with the Third Form?' or expressing irritation if the previous plunderer of the envelope, having selected the reports of the boys he happened to teach, had failed to replace the contents in alphabetical order. The trick was to find a time – very late evening or very early morning were favoured - when attendance would be likely to be sparse, only to find that an inconvenient number of colleagues had had the same idea. As deadlines for completion approached, the room became crowded, frustrations increased and mistakes were made. Obviously, with a number of contributors to each report, mistakes could not easily be rectified. Crossings-out were not uncommon, followed by brief written apologies along the lines of 'Sorry, wrong report' (inserted in brackets). Fortunately half-term reports did not routinely have to be sent home.

End-of-term reports, which consisted of separate sheets for each set and subject, were eventually collated by the boy's tutor or housemaster, arranged in a logical sequence and linked by a treasury tag in a folder. Housemasters of the 1970s may remember a prolonged and futile discussion (sadly typical of end-of-term meetings) when the alternative uses of the treasury tag were doggedly advocated by those who thought that the treasury tag should be threaded through the reports and the front cover only, those who insisted that it should be threaded through the reports and the back cover only, those who thought that it should be threaded only through the subject reports and neither cover, and those who maintained that it should be threaded through the reports and both covers. I believe that I manifested considerable impatience on that occasion; and at length the Headmaster brought the exchanges between the exhausted combatants to a halt, with the strangely prescient words, 'I shudder to think what David Gee will write in his memoirs!' These end-of-term reports could be typed or hand written, according to the individual master's preference, and dealt with at home; but even in these circumstances problems could arise. On one famous occasion, a member of staff spilled a glass of wine over the edge of a large pile of reports. Unwilling to undertake the chore of doing them all again, he adopted the slightly less drastic, but also scarcely less time-consuming expedient of carefully cutting the edges off the stained reports sheets, only to evoke the curious enquiry of the boys' parents at the Parents' Meeting which followed, 'Why are Mr X's reports smaller than everyone else's?' The present system of submitting reports electronically has its own particular problems, but at least the tensions inevitable when a number of colleagues were competing to record their remarks on the same sheet of paper have been avoided.

Apart from the difference of opinion over the treatment of the Headmaster in 1959, which went through its most important stage during the holidays, there was only one other brief interlude, in the period with which we are concerned, when the characteristic equilibrium of the Common Room was disturbed. This was over the institution known as The Trimmers. The Trimmers was a private dining society, whose existence was supposed to be secret, founded to honour the Salopian who arguably exercised the greatest political influence ever wielded by one of its former members in the entire history of the School.

This was George Savile, Marquess of Halifax, who presided over the House of Lords during the interregnum between the departure of James II and the succession of William III in 1688/9. He was credited with exercising the crucial influence in ensuring that the political revolution which then took place, 'The Glorious Revolution', deserved its name by being bloodless. Halifax was a political moderate who aimed to trim the sails of the ship of state during his time at the helm, in order to restrain the excesses of the Whigs on the one hand and the Tories on the other. He set out his policies and principles in his political testament entitled *The Character of a Trimmer.*

The object of the members of the society which took his name was less elevated but entirely understandable, namely to alleviate the burdens of schoolmastering and to vary its routine by indulging in the pleasures of fine wining and dining in congenial company. The best description of the organisation, procedures and activities of the Club is given by Jimmy Street in his book of autobiographical memoirs *Changes and Chances.* There was a President, whose principal functions were to invite guests and propose toasts, a Treasurer and a Cellarer (as one would expect), a Manciple who kept detailed records of each occasion and recorded those who had attended, and a Librarian, who took charge of the two substantial volumes of *The Character of a Trimmer,* with uncut pages, which had been presented to the Club. The sartorial emblem of the club was a black tie with owls (symbolic both of wisdom and of nocturnal activity) embroidered in silver thread on the bow. The only initiation rite required of those newly elected was to cut some of the pages and to be ready to answer questions about their content, in the extremely unlikely event of being called upon to do so.

Perhaps it was not entirely surprising that in the more 'open' society and rapidly changing world of the seventies, such an institution should attract criticism from some quarters. The membership of the Common Room was much smaller in those days, and some of its members felt (rightly or wrongly) that it was inappropriate that an exclusive Club of this nature, which contained a significant and influential proportion of the masters, should exist. There was a suspicion that election to the Club implied some kind of official approval and perhaps even an indication of future promotion, and that it was, in effect, a kind of shadow 'Establishment'. The Club members, on the other hand, would strongly deny any such intention or significance and maintain that the sole and perfectly legitimate purpose of the Club was civilised dining. However it was an obvious target for the characteristic Salopian brand of satire. Summonses to the Trimmers' meetings (couched in archaic language) and inadvertently left beside the duplicator, were intercepted, printed and circulated; their menus were lampooned (*'ye stuffed owles with all ye trimmings'* appeared as one of the dishes on a spoof menu); the locations at which their dinners were held were discovered and the proceedings interrupted by telephone messages. It is well known that closed societies – and particularly closed academic societies – are susceptible to such violent, if essentially trivial storms in a pedagogical teacup, but this was particularly unedifying, and particularly remarkable, too, in that it was so very untypical of Shrewsbury; an exception which proved what was otherwise an admirably inclusive and harmonious rule. Jimmy Street had himself described the Trimmers and its proceedings as 'rather childish'. The same view may reasonably be taken of the response which it provoked. The Headmaster stepped in to reduce the temperature, and the Trimmers lapsed into obscurity.

There has been a very considerable change in the status of Housemasters, too.

When the School first moved to Kingsland in 1882, Housemasters generally built their own houses, having leased the land from the Governing Body. That was still the case thirty years later when, in the classic instance, Basil Oldham borrowed £17,749 from the bank, incurring that personal debt in order to fund the construction of his House. Until Hardy's time as Headmaster, Housemasters were still entirely responsible for all the routine financial arrangements in their Houses. They recruited their own pupils, collected the fees from parents, employed domestic staff and provided the catering, the result being that they ran their houses either at a personal profit or a personal loss. The establishment of Central Feeding in 1969 was a further infringement of the totality of their control. The intimacy and exclusiveness of breakfast, lunch and supper under one roof had been important factors in maintaining a family atmosphere in a community of which the Housemaster was the head. At about the same time the established tradition of allowing only one other member of staff, a single House Tutor, in effect the deputy Housemaster, to come and go in the House as he pleased, without specific invitation, was replaced by an arrangement in which all members of the teaching staff were assigned to a House. This meant that five, six or even more colleagues became part of the establishment of each House. While providing considerable benefits in terms of pastoral care and oversight, this inevitably dimmed the spotlight which until then had been sharply focused on the Housemaster. (The tradition of using the Housemaster's name or initials to identify Houses, their members and their teams had persisted until times in living memory.) During the last two or three decades, the recruitment of boys (and most recently girls) to the Houses has been increasingly subjected to centralised supervision and allocation, the process marked first by the appointment of an official Registrar and subsequently by the development and expansion of his or her office.

In his Report to Parents on Speech Day in 1992 Ted Maidment provided an evocative insight into the role of the Housemaster, which in spite of the changes I have listed, still pertains today:

Housemastering. There is no job like it. It is the worst and the best of all schoolmastering jobs. The restlessness of it, the minute-by-minute knock on the door, the 24-hour a day responsibility. Awesome. The conviction that this door, however tempting it may be, can never be closed. But it is also the best of jobs. Deep and lasting friendships which headmasters by the very nature and distance of their tasks can never achieve. The chemistry of the situation has a permanent effect. People remember their housemasters and what they said: the tolerance, co-operation and discipline learned, the standards achieved, the quality of the communal life in a house, leave a permanent impression.

Giles Bell, who served a fourteen-year term in School House, quotes one of his predecessors as remarking that 'working in a school like this and not being a Housemaster is like going out for a meal and missing the main course'. That was a view which, for most of the period with which this book is concerned, would have found widespread acceptance, but would, I think, be rather less generally adopted today.

Throughout the twentieth century the Housemasters' Meeting had been – and was acknowledged to be – the principal source of authority and executive action in the School. The gradual construction and development of a Senior Management – recently renamed Senior Leadership – Team, during the last twenty years, again resulted in a perceptible diminution of the Housemasters' status. These were all internal changes; but an equally significant development was the more frequent use of e-mail. The accepted traditional view had been that the Housemaster really was *in loco parentis* during term-time. Parental interventions were unusual and unwelcome, parental visits to sons already in the School were rare. Now such visits are frequent and positively encouraged; and the institution of Exeats three times a term (the half-term Exeat being over a week long in the Lent and Summer Terms and over two weeks in the Michaelmas Term), together with the universal availability of mobile phones, ensure that close contact is maintained with home in most cases. Similarly, e-mail and text messaging have made parental interventions with the Housemaster commonplace. No one can doubt that parents have every right to take a close interest in the education of their children; and there are many reasons why parental involvement is to be warmly welcomed. One inevitable effect, however, when Housemasters may have to deal with as many as a hundred e-mails a day, is that their autonomy is further and significantly weakened. Since 2008 the problems and pressures experienced by Housemasters have been shared by Housemistresses, of whom there are now three. One notable feature in the role of Housemasters is that Sara Hankin has the distinction, so far unique, of having served as Housemaster (she insisted on the title) of a boys' House, Port Hill (2002 - 2007), and subsequently of a girls' House, Mary Sidney Hall (2008-2012).

In spite of the many significant changes which have taken place in the Common Room during these last sixty years, in its numbers, its composition and in the distribution of authority within it, the dedication of its members and their openness to their pupils remain as strong as I have ever known it. It is they who inherit, maintain and transmit the character and the tone of the School.

CHAPTER NINE

THE NEW HOUSE

The New House provided a notable example of the prevailing ethos at Shrewsbury during its final years as a traditional public school. For sixty-five years, between 1913 and 1978, it housed a community of five bachelor masters, each of whom occupied his own set of rooms - a sitting room and a bedroom - but who a shared a common dining room and a common bathroom. The whole situation produced, in effect, a continuation of the style of life which its members had experienced at school and at university. The common bathroom produced an incongruous collection of memories. There were two baths, which had been named 'Quanta' and 'Qualia' by Southwell. One was, by common consent, reserved in the morning for the Senior Member's cold bath, an ordeal which followed a prolonged period of filling it, while he shaved. When the moment for his immersion came, his junior colleagues, alarmed by the frantic gasping which always ensued, were in constant dread that the experience might prove fatal for him. The other bath was not infrequently occupied by his photographic prints, for he was an enthusiastic and accomplished photographer.

The inhabitants were looked after by a series of housekeepers, Mrs Butler Lloyd, Mrs Billany, Mrs Morgan and Mrs Butter, who in the earlier days supervised their own team of housemaids; but latterly the cleaning of the house was conducted under the overall supervision of the Domestic Bursar. Similarly, the finances of the House were originally entirely independent of the School, but these, too, were eventually taken over by the Bursar's office. A further development was the decision, taken in 1957, to allow a group of non-resident masters to join the residents for meals, doubling the numbers and providing further stimulation for what was characteristically witty and stimulating conversation round the dining table. The two groups were, thereafter, usually described as the 'inmates' and the 'outmates'. Earlier, David Brown's room in the New House had also provided the venue for meetings of 'The Little Brown Jug', described in the previous chapter.

Most of the members of the New House were young men, but a succession of older colleagues provided an element of stability and a brake, discreetly exercised, if only by their mere presence, on the wilder examples of their juniors' exuberance. K.B. Banks (1921-36), J.R. Hope Simpson (1948-65) and A.W. Fowler (1961-78) all lived in the New House for fifteen years or more; V.K. Chew (1946-57) and P. Gladstone (1952-65) for more than ten; and a dozen others for at least seven. During the two World Wars, sojourns in the New House were, in the nature of the situation, much briefer; and after the introduction of Central Feeding in Kingsland Hall, with the consequent withdrawal of dining facilities from the New House, the character of the establishment was drastically altered. This led, again, to a whole series of briefer tenures, until, in 1978, the building was finally converted for use as a Sanatorium. But in its heyday, for the shorter period of just over fifty years, the New House was a key location for those who wished to keep a finger on the pulse of Salopian affairs.

The community displayed a consistent character throughout its existence. Stacy Colman remembered it as *a place of hospitality, disputation, song and friendship, [which] produced an exhilarating mixture of energy and informality … it was open, accessible and unpretending.*

David Bevan recorded

a tradition of wit and a light-hearted but total dedication to the job … we were not serious, but we were not frivolous; cheerfulness abounded with industry.

and David Main endorsed the impression given by his seniors:

No-one was allowed to take himself too seriously … life was lived to the full, both enjoyably and conscientiously.

These characteristics had, of course, been infused into the New House by its very first inhabitants and notably by 'The Two Men', Evelyn Southwell and Malcolm White, who came to Shrewsbury together in 1910, entered the New House together in 1913, left the staff together in 1915 to serve in the War, and were killed, within days of each other, in 1916. Their respective contributions to Salopian life were as considerable as they were inseparable. They were commonly referred to as 'The Men' and they habitually referred to each other as 'man': 'Man, that's good' was an everyday observation. They had many common interests. Both were expert oarsmen: Southwell had taken the first Salopian crew to Henley in 1912; White was a versatile all-round sportsman. Both were keenly interested in music: White was an accomplished violinist, Southwell played the piano. In the classroom, Southwell's ability to communicate his love of literature, and particularly of poetry, enabled him to achieve the notable feat of encouraging his Fifth Form pupils each to contribute to an anthology of poems they had written, which was subsequently published. He was an inspirational, rather than a systematic teacher, switching from Greek, to Latin or French (for which he had a passion), as the spirit moved him. White

had that perfect control of boys which enabled him to bring the atmosphere of a Christmas party into the form: he would teach sitting among the boys or standing on the window-sill and swinging from a cord.

It was well said that no-one who had been taught by either Southwell or White would ever forget the experience: their spontaneity, openness and hospitality won them their pupils' admiration and devotion.

W.F. Starkie, a Moserite between 1909 and 1912, who was one of their pupils when they first arrived at Shrewsbury, pays the following tribute to them in his book *Scholars and Gypsies*, which clearly conveys the lasting impact they made.

It was the partnership at Shrewsbury of those two men, picked representatives of the two great universities, that produced the deep spiritual change in all of us who had the privilege of consorting with them, and this came about mainly through the music of Bach. Every Sunday evening we devoted to playing the concertos and sonatas for two violins, and the works of Vivaldi and Purcell.

We gave our performances in White's or Southwell's rooms before a select and appreciative audience of masters and boys. And when I look back at my years of adolescence at Shrewsbury I find that my friendship and close association with these two men meant more to me than anything else in the world.

Their own devotion to Shrewsbury is eloquently revealed in their subsequent letters from the Western Front; and three extracts from White's letters are quoted below. The idealism and nostalgia which they exhibit do not resonate easily in our more cynical age, but they still have a great power to move the reader and provide an outstanding example of the intense devotion which the School still seems able to inspire:

I always think (and sometimes say) that there has never been anything quite like the life which our common household has lived at Shrewsbury these five years, with its intimacies, enthusiasms and mutual appreciations

Do you think that we all continue to have our part in the place after death, even when not remembered? I am very jealous of mine …I cling to the idea of becoming, after death, more completely a part of Shrewsbury than when I was an unworthy, active member of the community; not by what I've done there, but by how much I have loved it.

and most poignantly, in a letter written four days before he was killed:

Oh Man, I can't write now. I am too like a coach before Bumping Races or Challenge Oars. So, Man, good luck. Our New House and Shrewsbury are immortal, which is a great comfort.

This wholehearted commitment to the School which was displayed by so many members of the New House was often veiled under a cover of high spirits and light-hearted ebullience; and this, too, was a characteristic which spanned all the years of its existence. Annually, on 5th November, White let off fireworks in the garden, dressed in a scholastic gown and a broad-brimmed felt hat. David Bevan remembered an incident, when a thunderstorm threatened while he and his colleagues, in full ceremonial dress, were waiting to go on parade, when Stacy Colman and George Simmons

drew their swords and rushed into the garden where they enacted the confrontation, on Mount Carmel, of Elijah the Tishbite with the priests of Baal.

On another occasion a resident appeared downstairs dressed only in a fez and figleaf.
    While Hardy was Headmaster a competition called the 'Suckers' League' was initiated. The winner was the member who submitted the most obsequious remark with which he was prepared to approach him. On one occasion the winning entry was

Headmaster, I have completed my corrections. I wonder whether it would be in order for me to take my Mother to a performance of The Messiah?

The Headmaster, Hardy, was noted for the inimitable style of his administrative notices. His regular 'Beginning of Term' notice was a fine example and contained the prescription: 'Chapel seating is to be detailed by Masters through previously circulated lists'. This sentence was 'sung antiphonally by certain junior masters to the chant of Psalm 51 at uproarious gatherings in the New House'.

A later generation maintained the spirit of the House in different, but equally flamboyant ways. In the 1960s it was still the customary practice that Housemasters were selected from members of the staff in order of their seniority in the Brown Book. In 1961 Easter was spent at School. In a sudden and uncharacteristic display of decisiveness just before the end of term, Jack Peterson announced the appointment of five Housemasters during the course of one Common Room meeting on Maunday Thursday, apparently ignoring the greater seniority of two members of the New House, who duly considered themselves 'passed over'. The 'Passover Party' which resulted that Easter weekend was among the most memorable in its history. More generally, the New House was renowned for its generous hospitality. Its annual summer garden party, at which its members collectively reciprocated the hospitality they had received during the year, had earned wide renown; invitations to it were greatly prized and eagerly accepted. The garden, which had been devotedly and expertly cultivated by the Senior Member, was at its magnificent best. It was customary to serve an alcoholic fruit punch. On the appointed day the windows of Churchill's and Moser's were lined with boys eagerly anticipating a sight of the resulting casualties. On one occasion the results were so dramatic that the New House inmate who had prepared the punch was banned by the Headmaster from ever doing so again. On other occasions, however, arrangements were less than meticulous. A colleague who had been invited to dine in the New House found, on his arrival, that none of his hosts was present. He waited during the stipulated pre-prandial period, until the housekeeper brought in the supper and placed it on the hot-plate. After waiting a little longer, he sat down to the meal, in solitary state, and finished it. Since no one else had appeared even then, he sat down, wrote a thank-you note, placed it in an envelope, propped it up on the sideboard – and departed.

Daily conversation around the table was, as David Main remembered, punctuated by the recitation of *Spells* by Frank McEachran, the lamentations of the Senior Member about the inadequacy of the Fourth Form's Latin construe, and heated discussions about the relative speed and prospects of crews on the river. Another diversion was a competition among the junior members to be the first to manoeuvre Russell Hope Simpson, who, (in common with other more recent staff members of a certain age,) was prone to the repetition of certain favourite anecdotes, to utter his iconic phrase 'the whole school gasped', the invariable conclusion of his description of the occasion when a visiting adjudicator of the House Music Competition made an incredible and totally unjustifiable decision. An alternative version of this procedure was to lead the venerable Basil Oldham, who was an occasional visitor, to pronounce the word '*incunabula*',which he was renowned for being able to utter as one syllable.

The table itself served other purposes. David Main remembers that 'many a pocket-hatched duckling cheeped and stretched its wings (and did other things) on the dining room table'. David Gee, flushed by his crew's first victory under his aegis as a novice rowing coach, unwisely placed the trophy, an enormous silver object, topped by a silver Neptune, complete with trident, upon the table before breakfast, only to be ordered, gruffly and peremptorily by the Senior Member, to whom coaching triumphs were a matter of routine, to 'Take that thing off!'

But ducklings were not the only examples of Peter Gladstone's introduction of fauna into the New House. His dog Moses, and later Néné, his Irish 'boghound', together with a badger and a vixen all joined the menagerie in the New House Ark, to receive Peter's enthusiastic, if not invariably successful training. Bronco, the badger, was the most famous of these other residents. Peter persuaded Bronco to accept a collar and lead, and visitors to the upstairs sitting-rooms might be startled by a snuffling sound and the sight of a pile of cushions being propelled, without any apparent agent, along the upstairs corridor, only to discover that Bronco, concealed behind them, was collecting them to construct a den. His colleagues wagered that Peter could not spend a whole night with Moses, the badger and the vixen all at large in his bedroom. He persevered valiantly, but lost the bet. In the early hours of the morning, he crept quietly downstairs and locked them in the cellar.

By the time that Peter Gladstone and David Main left the house to take up their housemasterships in 1965, the 'glory days' of the New House were coming to an end; but in the nineteen-seventies Michael Ling and Richard Higson manfully maintained its remarkable and distinctive reputation for a combination of meticulous scholarship, unremitting industry and quirky ebullience. But its days were numbered …

CHAPTER TEN

BASIC YEAR

Basic Year was one of the most characteristic, and certainly one of the most prominent features of Salopian life during the last quarter of the twentieth century. This was due, above all, to the enthusiasm, charisma and meticulous devotion of Michael Hall. He took full advantage of the very favourable and temporary circumstances of the time. It was a period when the dangers of hill-walking had come to be properly appreciated, but before the full imposition of inhibiting Health and Safety regulations; and when the sanctity of the time allotted to extra-curricular activities on Thursday afternoons was still jealously preserved. The competition from other activities at that time was not as strong as it was later to become. External examinations had not yet imposed their straitjacket on teachers and pupils alike; and the former had not yet been fully subjected to the full weight of contemporary bureaucratic obligations. All these conditions enabled Basic Year to flourish.

In the mid 1960s National Service had been abolished and the justification for compulsory military training in schools like Shrewsbury was far less obvious. Also, abolition of the obligatory requirement both for attendance at Chapel and membership of the CCF were the two prime targets both for educational reformers and for restless schoolboys. Donald Wright set up a committee, consisting of Arnold Ellis (then the Officer Commanding the CCF), Alan Laurie and Peter Hughes to consider the situation. The outcome was that membership of the CCF became voluntary and part of a new structure of extra-curricular activities for each level of the school. 'Basic Year' was the name assigned to the programme of camping and hill-walking devised for second-year members of the School, the Fourth Formers. These radical changes made Shrewsbury a pioneer among similar schools. There was an element of irony in the fact that participation in the Basic Year was to be just as rigidly compulsory as participation in the CCF had been. Michael demonstrated a ferocious obstinacy which allowed no-one to evade its demands and requirements, coupled with a concern for those in genuine difficulty, claiming that the fact that no Fourth Former could escape produced a valuable *camaraderie*, a sense of togetherness, that 'we're all in this together'.

Michael Hall was greatly influenced by his very considerable experience in Scouting: indeed, for several years he was the District Commissioner for Shropshire. He was adamant, too, that all military features should be removed from the new scheme. There was to be no drill, no parades, no uniforms, no Officers or NCOs. This determination presented serious problems, for the CCF had been greatly assisted by funding and facilities provided by the Army. These remained essential if a full and challenging programme for Basic Year was to be maintained. Fortunately it proved possible to persuade the Army that it was both legitimate and worthwhile to support the activities of Basic Year, while close and harmonious co-operation between the leaders of Basic Year and the Officers both of the reduced CCF and of the local Army authorities provided a sound foundation upon which Basic Year could develop.

Michael Hall participated in Basic Year for a total of twenty-six years, and he was

Master-in-Charge for the last twenty of these, between 1973 and 1993. For the first six Michael Cross led the organisation. These were experimental years and much of the later success of Basic Year is owed to Michael Cross' leadership at this time. In his Memoirs, *Around the World in Forty Years*, Michael Hall devotes six chapters to Basic Year and distinguishes five consecutive periods in the development of the organisation: The Early Days 1967-73; First Years in Charge 1973-79; The Rise of the Instructor 1979-85; The Golden Years; 1985-1990; The Later Years; 1990-93. A further chapter is devoted to an Overview.

His philosophy was that our contemporaries are much too cosseted by the comforts of 'civilisation'; and that to place adolescent boys in unfamiliar situations in which they have to face up to the vagaries of nature, to be confronted with challenges which might be unwelcome, to have to recognise and appreciate risks and to make a careful assessment of them, together constituted an invaluable element in an all-round education. He considered that such experiences not only developed self-reliance and self-awareness but also required concern and responsibility for others in the pursuit of shared goals within the framework of a team.

At the heart of Michael's thinking was the balance and tension between the educational value of calculated risk and the requirement for every reasonable safety measure to be taken. His first priority, on taking charge, was to find means to finance the provision of proper equipment, boots, tents and cooking utensils. There were regular inspections to ensure that the kit was adequate and in good order. He insisted that a meticulous reconnaissance was carried out before every exercise, that everyone taking part was fully briefed and that all groups should stick together, under all circumstances: 'a split group is a dead group'. He demanded rigorous checking and roll-calls of names at the end of every exercise and at every possible stage during its course, asserting that to fail to notice an absentee was nothing short of criminal. Emergency telephone numbers were always provided. Reviewing his period in charge, Michael wrote,

We have had some accidents (very few serious ones) and have to balance these against the real value of the challenge we have given to thousands of boys. My touchstone has always been that if I had to stand on oath in a coroner's court, could I justify my actions and decisions? If there is any doubt, then the opposite decision must be taken.

The range of activities available in Basic Year gradually expanded. Camping and hill-walking were central; and the skills which were required were developed by pioneering, building with ropes and spars, and instruction in the erection of tents. Cycling exercises had to be abandoned as road traffic became more dangerous. An assault course was constructed near the river. 'Circuses' were installed in which boys moved from one physical challenge to another on the basis of strict timing. There was training with map and compass, culminating in an orienteering exercise on Cannock Chase. Instruction was given in First Aid. There was bridge-building and rafting; and later canoeing and climbing activities were added. There were night exercises; and field days were spent on exercises in the Berwyns in the Michaelmas Term, in Radnor Forest in the Lent, and at Talargerwyn in the Summer Term. There were weekend camps in preparation for the annual summer camp, held initially at

Cwrt-y-Gollen, but subsequently at Cantref, near Crickhowell, which had been specified as an integral part of the Basic Year programme from the very beginning. Michael fully endorsed the assertion that 'if you have camped with somebody, you know him for life' and he believed that camping taught participants to work as a team and to help one another in the good times and the bad.

Basic Year was organised with supreme efficiency. In its heyday Michael managed to attract a substantial number of fully committed colleagues to assist him. All their names are carefully recorded in his memoirs, and he is generous in his tributes to them. Among the most prominent and long-serving were Selby Martin, Barry Storey, Alan Hayes, Richard Field, Peter Cann, John Furniss, Richard Auger, Gilbert Roscoe, Gawen Harvey and Mark Twells. Many of these, at various times, took charge of a patrol. Before 1974 there were four patrols; thereafter there were six. Four groups of boys, with five or six boys in each group, made up the patrol. The groups were formed strictly on an alphabetical basis: it was held that it was good for boys to learn to cooperate with companions whom they would not necessarily have chosen. At summer camp, however, the groups were constituted, so far as possible, on a House basis, and there was keen competition for the inter-house Camp Cup, awarded at the end of the year.

Instructors, drawn from the Fifth, Lower Sixth and Upper Sixth Forms, played an increasingly important part in the scheme as the years went by. Their role was to accompany, supervise and assess their groups, rather than to lead them, but they were on hand to intervene in case of emergency. The more senior the instructor, the greater the responsibility; but every instructor was made aware of the crucial importance of accurately recording the composition of every group as it passed his check point on a particular exercise. The instructors too were trained and consulted by their seniors and by the masters in charge of patrols. Great importance was attached to the selection of the Deputy Head of Basic Year, chosen from the Lower Sixth Instructors after extensive consultation, for invariably he became the head of the whole organisation. Michael took great pride in asserting that the boy who held this appointment had greater responsibility than any other among his contemporaries; and that the Upper Sixth boy in overall charge had responsibility equal to that of the Heads of Houses and the Head of School; indeed, in several instances, he *was* the Head of School. He would, of course, have completed the Basic Year programme himself, as a Fourth Former, and then have had two years' further experience as an instructor upon which to draw.

Michael believed that rewards were a more effective incentive that sanctions. Among his idiosyncracies was a firm belief in the powerful incentive of chocolate (a predilection for swimming in ice-cold lakes was another – he claimed that over 2,000 Salopians had swum in Llyn Cau) and the distribution of chocolate played a prominent part in Basic Year. One of his colleagues discovered 'Freddo Bars', customarily wrapped in paper printed with excruciating jokes. This could scarcely have been more fortunate or appropriate, for 'Fred' was an abbreviation of Michael's first name, and also his nickname. Freddo Bars played such an important role, that when domestic supplies ran out, they were ordered from Australia! But there were also Shop Teas to be awarded, rising in a hierarchy of desirability, from Special Purple Shop Teas, to Super Gold Shop Teas, and Atatürk and Double Atatürk Shop Teas. (Atatürk was Michael Hall's cat – for most people this will be a necessary explanation;

one of my most amusing memories of editing the *Salopian Newsletter* was the occasion when, very mysteriously, in proof, the phrase, 'Atatürk is Michael Hall's cat' appeared at the bottom of every page!) But sanctions were applied when necessary, ranging from the most trivial, folding maps, straightening tent pegs, cleaning mess tins and mending survival bags, to Extra Field Days and the dreaded sentence to clean latrines.

Basic Year also developed its own private language, of which the names of the chocolate prizes and the shop teas formed part; to these were added such phrases as 'wet and weedy', 'hurry up chop chop', 'bright-eyed and bushy-tailed', 'festering in bed', 'tired but happy'. Returning from an exercise soaked to the skin, boys were reminded that 'the rain is all in your imagination' and were, rather inappropriately admonished, 'Don't be wet, don't be weedy, don't be spare: make the most of Basic Yare'. And an incantation, amounting almost to a motto, was developed:

> Basic Year is fun, fun, fun
> Lots of rain and not much sun
> Summer Camp is best of all
> It's organised by Michael Hall

It is easy to see that Basic Year, in its numbers, with its distinctive ethos and with the devoted allegiance which it had inspired in many of those who participated in it, had, in its 'golden years', virtually become a school within a school, and it is equally obvious that it would find it difficult to survive, without serious modification, with the onset, subsequent proliferation and increasing rigour of Health and Safety legislation. Indeed, Michael began to experience difficulties while he was still in charge. It became more difficult to recruit committed staff to the scheme, as the bureaucratic and administrative pressures on his colleagues continued to grow. The introduction of an Adventuring scheme for Fifth Formers, admirable in itself, broke the continuity of training for Basic Year instructors; the 'sacrosanct' status of Thursday afternoon for activities such as Basic Year was increasingly infringed, while an ever-increasing variety of other activities competed to make use of the allotted time. Commitment to other desirable activities, such as music and drama, increased the overall pressure on the boys, which was further increased by the exacting and ever-expanding demands of the examination system. Finally, the Welsh farmers, over whose land many of the Basic Year activities had taken place, were under pressure themselves, and they became increasingly fractious and uncooperative.

Mark Twells took over from Michael Hall in 1993 and experienced a stressful five years as the shadow of 'Health and Safety' loomed ever larger. There was immense pressure to remove every element of risk from such activities. The paper-work required in compulsory 'risk assessments' proliferated. Qualifications were required for masters conducting hill-walking expeditions and very few members of the staff had even the most basic certificates, but gradually Basic Year was brought into step with the 'guidelines for mountaineering activities' required by the British Mountaineering Council.

Inevitably, Basic Year had its critics, as well as its enthusiasts, and it did not escape the lightly satirical pen of Mark Mortimer:

Each year I get camp service in,
        some twenty hours, not longer,
the bulk of it spent drinking gin
        in potions ever stronger,

while through an alcoholic haze
        I view the troops, and wonder
how *they* endure for six whole days
        the regimen they're under:

the food (designed to keep you slim),
        the ceaseless exhortation
to join the early-morning swim,
        the Lats (or constipation?),

the crowding, three in every tent,
        those laden treks they go on,
the giddy heights up which they're sent,
        the Freddo jokes … and so on.

The answer is, they've got no choice:
        we'd bear it, if we had to.
(It's fortunate that we're not boys,
        or else we might be made to!)

But what about the others there
        who supervise the training?
Each one of them's a volunteer:
        that surely needs explaining.

You'd think that nobody would go
        if able to avoid it:
but those Instructors look as though
        they really quite enjoyed it.

It's strange how easily we'll bear
        what ought to cause revulsion,
provided it's our own idea:
        what irks us is compulsion.

That's why, when all is said and done,
        while those who help afflict him
find Basic Year's a lot of fun,
        it isn't for the victim.

Mark's argument, though valid and characteristically humorous must be set against the substantial collection of tributes paid to Basic Year. While many of these, no doubt, were by volunteers, others were by converts. One of the boys wrote, appreciatively, to Michael that '(Basic Year) gave me the opportunity to prove that I could be trusted'; and one of Michael's colleagues reported that

For myself, Basic Year has provided a breadth of experience far greater than any other activity in the School. It is this diversity of experience which makes Basic Year so important a part in the life of the School and has enriched my life and no doubt that of many others.

Even those whom Mark would identify as 'victims' commonly regale each other, with masochistic relish, with tales of the vicissitudes they experienced during Basic Year. Over 3,000 boys took part in the organisation. It was unique to Shrewsbury School and gave a huge amount of self-confidence to generations of Salopians. Michael himself should have the last word:

We gave Fourth Formers memories …the majority felt that they had coped with the elements, their companions and, most important of all, with themselves: and we gave senior boys real responsibility and the experience of true leadership.

CHAPTER ELEVEN

ETHOS, IDENTITY AND COMMUNITY

Every school has its own ethos, the product of its history, of its members and their relationships, of its environment and its purpose. In some schools the ethos is paid little attention, in others it is a subject of analysis and a source of pride. Shrewsbury, I think, falls into the latter category, and the aim of this chapter is to consider what can be discovered about the ethos of independent boarding schools in general, and of Shrewsbury in particular. The philosophical distinction between body and spirit provides a clue to what is meant by an ethos. The 'body' of the school is composed of its day-to-day structures and routines, all of which are – and need to be - susceptible to change. But its spirit animates, informs and survives them all. The older the institution, the stronger its ethos is likely to be. A visit to an ancient cathedral produces a numinous effect because it awakens an awareness that in that very place countless generations of people have assembled with the common purpose of worship, which makes it holy. There one is surrounded by an unseen 'cloud of witnesses' each of whom has played his part in that common purpose. The same is true of a school. If any reminder is needed of that, one has only to sit quietly in the School Chapel and reflect that the number of those who gave their lives in only the first of the great wars which scarred the last century would fill every single place. Evelyn Southwell wrote from the trenches of the First World War that,

the younger of us would be wondering how the school would carry on, when this and that place was empty – having not learnt from experience that a school is the only immortal thing on earth and the only thing about which certain platitudes are true.

For a further reminder, it would simply be necessary to leave the Chapel, to take a few steps and look down at the river flowing beneath our hill, always moving yet always the same, constituting another image of the immortality of a school. My contention then, is that Shrewsbury has a powerful ethos, that it is susceptible to analysis, and that is eminently worth preserving.

The interrelation between an established ethos and the people who inherit, mould and transmit it has long been a subject of great fascination to me; and the topic is crucial if a proper understanding of the last sixty years is to be achieved. Mark Turner, the present Headmaster, describes the various attempts which have been made to identify the component parts of the ethos as 'a geographical concept (in Shrewsbury's case derived from a beautiful Site), as an historical concept, as a subtle blend of innovation and tradition, and as the combined product of outstanding personalities'. When, upon his arrival, he commissioned a survey of attitudes towards, and evaluation of the School, one of his questions invited comments on what should and what should not be changed. He reported that 'the answer that came back most strongly was that the Shrewsbury spirit, or *genius loci*, should be protected at all costs.'

Change, however, is a sign and indeed a condition of life, and all great institutions, religious, political or educational, must change or die. In effecting such change judiciously and successfully the crucial prerequisites are the achievement of a balance between change and stability, together with an understanding of and sensitivity towards the nature of the institution in which the change is to take place. David Allcock's observation on the vital role of sensitivity, which I have quoted in the chapter on Chapel, comes to mind in this respect. Two previous historians of the School and one Headmaster have commented on this subtle but vital balance; and it is interesting that they were all closely associated with Oldham's Hall, (one as a pupil, and two as its Housemaster), often perceived to be the most traditional of Shrewsbury's Houses. Basil Oldham, Colin Leach and Jeremy Goulding constitute our first group of witnesses. Basil Oldham writes:

Respect for tradition and custom gives a sense of historic continuity and so provides a stable element in school, as it does in national life ... it is only the unthinking who condemn as meaningless an adherence to that which has been inherited from the past ...

It is indeed as true of institutions as it is of individuals, that when they lose their historical awareness, their corporate or personal memories, they risk losing their identity, but Oldham also warns that

customs, of course, must develop and circumstances change (and) tradition must be broken if it comes to stand in the way of progress.

Jeremy Goulding, in an address in Chapel in 2010, during his last term as Headmaster, announced:

My theme is remembering. It is about treasuring and respecting the important things of the past, in order to step forward with confidence into the future

and there is a distinctly Alingtonian touch in a later passage:

Come into this building in your own time, when no-one else is here – no-one else as far as you may judge. I'll warn you, the benches are always gently on the move, believe me, they are, you will hear them ... whether there seems to be a draught by way of cause, or no perceptible cause at all. It is as if there is a sort of flexibility in this building, which moves and bends a mite with the grain of so much noble, ancient oak. And such flexibility seems to me to be rather nicely Salopian.

The penultimate sentence seems to illustrate the point exactly.

It is a commonplace that even during the course of one school career, Salopians (like all schoolboys) have tended to look back on the School as it was when they arrived as 'the good old days' and regret the changes which have subsequently taken place. Colin Leach, too, vividly expresses the tension which tends to exist between nostalgia and realism. When reviewing his own schooldays in the 1940s, he comments, 'However bitter on occasion the vintage, perhaps we had the last of the wine', but in his history of the School he concludes,

The school of Charles Darwin, if any school in the land, should know that one survives by evolution...... Pride in a noble tradition is justifiable; attempting to preserve a tradition artificially would not be.

Lord Wolfenden, when Headmaster, referred to this tension when he commented that Old Salopians manage to hold in conjunction two contradictory views, that the School was the same as it had always been and that since they left it had gone to the dogs!

What are the conditions which shape and inform the ethos of an Independent Boarding School? I shall examine three. Freedom is, perhaps, the most important. Community life, the shared experience and enterprise it involves and the mutual care and tolerance it requires, is another. The third is the range of opportunity which, together with aspiration for excellence in each aspect of endeavour and the concentration of the environment, produces an intensity requiring self-discipline and effective allocation of time, if it is to be used to advantage.

Walter James, the eminent educationalist, in a magnificent address to The Friends of Shrewsbury in the late 1960s, soon after the formation of that organisation, offered the finest evaluation of Independent Boarding Education I have encountered. Freedom was the keynote:

... to feel that one has a part in a school which is free, which is an enterprise created naturally out of a wealth of free, human choices, and is at the same time excellent, outstanding, yet humble in the wisdom of an ancient faith, can be no small satisfaction ... It makes a strong appeal to a certain kind of men, maybe limited in number, but men of quality, men ready to say this place is worth a life. It is a great school only because it attracts such men.

This freedom is also an essential component of good teaching, which is the informed communication of an academic enthusiasm. Freedom, enthusiasm – and sometimes a hint of eccentricity – go together; it is no accident that the four Salopian characters I have chosen to commemorate in another chapter were all great teachers, very different in style, but free to indulge their own idiosyncracies and thereby to make an indelible impression upon their pupils, and in many cases to motivate and even inspire them. This awareness of freedom, of enablement, produces a sense of devotion and dedication to the task which makes teaching a vocation. And, quite apart from this atmosphere of freedom within the school, James observes that,

The school is buoyed up by favouring choices: the parents choose a particular school, usually after long consideration of the matter, in an extremely competitive and expensive market.

So far as the second aspect, the community life, is concerned, James asserts that it is

the great gift that the public schools have given to English education ... [the school] teaches as much through its community life as it does in the classroom. The English excel in schools, in colleges, in regiments, in clubs. They have a genius for brotherhood. Unity of purpose and companionship are the essential characteristics of a public school ... Community and brotherhood grow most easily and naturally in an independent community [for] there is no confusion of loyalties. Everyone's responsibility is personal, understandable and complete ... we have to remember that there are in the whole modern world only a few schools as good and as embracing in its concern for the boys as this one. This school and its fellows are a rare and very English creation – perhaps one of the best things the English have done – something certainly to defend and cherish.

Shared experience is a vital component in building a sense of community; and it operates in two quite distinct but connected ways, in the shared experience with the historical past and the shared experience with present contemporaries, both teachers and pupils. A judicious balance is also required in weighing individual against community interests. Alington told a story which indicates that where mutual respect exists, the relationship between master and pupil is able to transcend the disciplinary encounters which are a necessary feature of school life, and which can often lead to a lifelong friendship. He had invited a boy to breakfast one morning, had discovered in mid-morning that the boy had been guilty of a misdemeanour and had beaten him, and had still honoured an arrangement to play fives with him before lunch. I was reminded of that story, during a conversation, only a few months ago, with an Old Salopian, whose Housemaster I had been, when we were reminiscing about instances of the 'cops and robbers' aspects of School life. 'Of course', he said, 'it was all a Machiavellian conspiracy'. He meant that confrontations about minor breaches of discipline, far from leading to mutual antipathy, turn out, in retrospect, to have been a form of bonding, part of the shared experience.

Of the range of opportunity, Richard Hudson, the current editor of *The Salopian*, observed, in 2011, that

Part of the modern genius (loci) must stem from the blurring of traditional cultural boundaries between sport, academia, music and the arts ... which activities should take priority over which is a matter of constant debate, even contention. But it is from just such tensions that the vitality of the school flows.

And Walter James, again, surveying the range of these activities, encompassing academic scholarship, sport, music and drama, commented that,

As we think of all these things, we find them merging, becoming just parts of the life of the school as a whole. It is not religion only, nor scholarship, or any of the other factors only, it is the joining together of all of them in a common life.

Members of staff I have interviewed have emphasised, time after time, that the qualities which distinguish the recipient of an independent boarding school education are those which are acquired outside the classroom: self-reliance, responsibility, skills needed to live happily in a close community, the ability to cope with the intensity of varied activity, and learning to work together in extra-curricular enterprises, cultural, sporting and adventurous.

Vinoj Srinivasan, an Indian student at Shrewsbury in 2007, was one of the top five entrants in the Hobson's/Metropolis Boarder of the Year Award. In response to the question 'In what respects has your UK education prepared you to take a positive role in the wider world when you leave school?' he made the following observations:

The chief thing I have learnt from life at a boarding school is to say, 'yes'! I have really enjoyed being part of so many activities at Shrewsbury that I would not have experienced without deciding to try them. I believe this positive attitude has been enhanced by my experience as a boarder ... Boarding school has prepared me to face challenges head-on rather than try and avoid them ... I firmly believe that the boarding environment has helped me to appreciate the needs of others. You have to be considerate when you are in close proximity to 79 other boarders ... People say that boarding schools are not the real world, but that depends on the outlook of the people around you. If the people around you are outward looking, then the world will come to you ... Boarding has taught me that you can never stand still ... You are never alone as a boarder and that gives you a strength that perhaps otherwise you might not know you had!

It is time now to turn to the specifically Salopian ethos and to introduce another group of witnesses to make their individual appraisals. They are arranged in three categories, those imbued with the ethos, those informed about the ethos, and those merely acquainted with the ethos, casual visitors who caught an inkling of it.

Philip Cowburn asserted that affection for one's school was one of the characteristic features which emerged in Public Schools in the late nineteenth and early twentieth centuries; and both staff and pupils in the twentieth century have been conspicuous in expressing their love for Shrewsbury not least in the phrases which are used (and sometimes borrowed) to apply to it: a 'land of lost content', 'blue remembered hills', 'pastures green and fields of gold'. Of course, the 'golden chains' which Ronald Knox felt bound him to Shrewsbury, were not composed of landscape alone, but of friendship also. He records that

Shrewsbury had entered into me: I loved every stone of it; its ways, its atmosphere, its society had come to be part of the machinery of my life.

It is easy to discount the warmth of such expressions as being characteristic of a particularly sentimental age, but they were to be echoed, more than sixty years later, by observers from a different generation, who were able to make a more objective assessment, as we shall see.

In 1964 there was an enterprising and illuminating exchange of Sixth Formers between Shrewsbury and Manchester Grammar School, who, on returning to their respective schools, recorded their impressions. One of the Mancunians, while arguing, naturally enough, that the great disadvantage of Salopians was that they were cut off from everyday reality, divorced in their formative years from 'normal life', also commented:

At Shrewsbury, I got the feeling that the sense of partnership (between staff and boys) really meant something, has a positive and tangible expression. Of course, I don't just mean academic partnership, which every good school has: I mean social, twenty-four-hour-a-day co-operation ... the mutual attitudes of boys and staff are shatteringly different when the same people raise you as teach you ... Salopians always know that without good staff relations their whole educational system would collapse.

Sir Eric Anderson spent only five years of his distinguished career at Shrewsbury, but he was in an admirable position to combine knowledge and objectivity together with the wide perspective of a headmaster, when he appraised the Salopian ethos. Speaking on Speech Day 1980, he remarked

The atmosphere of a School … is all-important, but maddeningly not really within his [the Headmaster's] control … I love the atmosphere of Shrewsbury – the faintly concealed enthusiasms, the friendliness of boys and masters, the devastating individual and corporate sense of humour.

Having then spoken warmly of the friendship he had found here, he added

[Poppy and I] shall miss … the Site: white figures on green fields, the smell of grass and mud and wet leather in the dying minutes of house matches; the bell ringing for evening school in winter and the cosy glow of classroom lights shining out into misty air; the stupendous chestnut on the school bank, aflame with white candles; the splash of oars and the creak of sliding seats; the breath-taking beauty of the bend of the river from the school bank at all seasons and the startling townscape on the other side where

High the vanes of Shrewsbury gleam,
Islanded in Severn stream

And he went on to express the fear that his experience might prove to be the same as that of Dr Alington, who wrote:

I do not think I ever expected to be quite as happy at Eton as I had been at Shrewsbury, and to be honest, I do not think I ever was.

Anderson himself records that it was his very first impression of the easy and positive relationships between the staff and the boys which he found attractive about Shrewsbury. More generally, even casual visitors seem to have formed the same impression:

Anyone coming here from outside could not fail to remark, gratefully, on the general amenableness of the boys in the School

Walter James declared, when he visited the school forty years ago,

I remember chiefly an outgoing friendliness, an easiness and kindness unspoilt by what used in those days to be called 'side'.

And after Sir Richard Southern, a distinguished historian and President of St John's College Oxford, had visited the School as Guest Speaker on Speech Day, 1975, he sent the following letter to the Acting Headmaster, Michael Charlesworth:

The impression which the school made on me on that lovely day has left a memory which I

shall always cherish – it was like a scene from an ideal world. I expect it is not always like that, but to be capable of being so is an achievement of high quality.

When a group of Salopian Housemasters returned from a visit to competitor schools in the South in 2011, one of them recorded:

We returned with a renewed sense that there is something very special about the Shrewsbury atmosphere.

It is striking how often it is an autumnal scene which stimulates the most powerful feelings of nostalgia; the fallen leaves on Central and the poppies lying on the grass after the Remembrance Service in November; and one powerful image which recurs in my own mind is of mud-plastered boys kicking a seemingly endless series of penalties into goalmouths increasingly obscured in the encroaching dusk in December, to determine the final outcome of House matches, as the moon rises slowly over the river.

The supreme example of this Salopian nostalgia is expressed in Ronald Knox's poem, published in *The Salopian*, in memory of Evelyn Southwell. Although a tribute to an individual at a specific time, it is powerfully evocative of our location and of an ethos transcending the particular circumstances in which it was written:

> Players before an empty house
> October's pageants go,
> That now no plaudits can arouse
> From you, who loved them so
>
> By you unheeded, as of old
> The tyrant autumn breeze
> Will strew our pavements with the gold
> It plunders from the trees:
>
> Unmarked by you the swallows' flights,
> Cloud-shapes, and chimney-tunes,
> And friendly blaze of schoolroom lights
> On mist-wreathed afternoons.
>
> There is no light on hill or plain,
> No sigh of wind or wood,
> But seems as if it watched in vain
> To hear your 'Man, that's good!'
>
> But where on some unchartered shore
> Fearlessly you look down,
> A nearer pilgrim than before
> To that Eternal Town.

How you must cry aloud, in praise!
God send one echo through,
To cheer the dull and dusty days
That sunder us from you.

These impressions span a period of sixty years, and in the century which has elapsed since the first of them was recorded, there does indeed seem to have been a remarkably strong feeling of community and common purpose in the Common Room and an unusually easy and positive relationship between the masters and the boys.

Alington perceived and recorded an exceptional cohesion and dedication among his younger colleagues. Writing about Evelyn Southwell and Malcolm White in the foreword to the memoir *Two Men*, he observed

There is one thing I know they would wish me to say, and that is that the life of our Society from which they went was for those few years as nearly that of a happy family as any which the whole annals of schoolmastering can show.

It is widely held that the young schoolmasters in the New House at that time, by nurturing and encouraging cultural and intellectual interests beyond the confines of the academic curriculum, established that distinctive family feeling.

Canon Sawyer, Alington's successor, was 'a man whom it was impossible to dislike', and his biographer, Rupert Martin, commented on:

His own extraordinary knowledge of, and sympathy with the individual boy ... he aimed at knowing each boy as a separate human being, and since it was natural for him to look for the best in everyone, he rarely failed to find and develop it.

In the eighteen years after the resignation of Sawyer in 1932, Hardy and Wolfenden faced immense problems arising from the prospect, duration and aftermath of war. It took some time for the very considerable achievement of each of them to be recognised, and the criticisms of established members of the Common Room, not least of the perceived neglect of the Alingtonian tradition, was often unjust. But with the appointment of Jack Peterson as Headmaster in 1950, regarded by many as the embodiment of the Salopian ideal, it was widely felt that the tradition had been restored.

The focus once more was on concern with the individual and good personal relationships. Though Peterson's shyness and modesty made him seem a remote figure to many of the boys, and his indecisiveness, together with his perceived administrative deficiencies, understandably frustrated his senior colleagues, there was universal admiration and affection for his character and principles. Particularly through his kindness to and encouragement of his junior colleagues, his example permeated and informed the whole community. His remarks to parents at Speech Day, during his last term as Headmaster, reveal the man:

Virtue is not something that can be taught or learnt in the classroom: it must be acquired slowly and often painfully ... And of course, an example must be set, too. This is the frightening thing about schoolmastering: the young cannot all see their way through a quadratic equation or a Latin Unseen, but they can all see through a sham. Ultimately, it is not a question of what a man says, nor indeed of what he does, it is a question of what he is. This, surely, and nothing less than this, is the aim of education in the true sense. This preoccupation with the individual boy and the good life is what makes schoolmastering exacting always, frustrating frequently and occasionally, very occasionally, infinitely rewarding.

On being invited to take over a boarding house in 1960, the housemaster-elect asked Jack Peterson, who himself had been an outstandingly successful and much-loved housemaster at Eton, "What does a housemaster do?", to which Peterson's reply was both extremely simple and extraordinarily challenging: "Love every boy in the house and make sure that each one knows it."

Donald Wright unconsciously echoed Peterson, when asked by one of the Bloxham researchers what he considered to be his greatest problem as Headmaster. After a long pause, he replied, "The sheer impossibility of loving everybody." Donald was absolutely explicit on the question of the relationships between masters and boys:

I am convinced that there is nowadays only one authority whereby a boarding community of boys can retain stability and develop purpose, and that is the respect which boys have from knowing that there are men about them who really care and who enter into discussion with them: thereby comes an understood and appreciated atmosphere which makes it unreal for boys to identify masters only with authority.

Ten years later, at the end of the 1970s, Michael Charlesworth considered that the School appeared to have settled down after the comparative 'turbulence' of the previous decade, and asserted that

The key was the network of personal relationships, which criss-crossed the body politic, both through the formal tutoring system and in so many other ways, based on shared interest and activities.

The Bloxham inquiry, set up in 1967, was specifically concerned with that precise area of values and relationships which is the subject of our present discussion. It is time to examine to what extent its findings, published in 1973, are consonant with and reinforce the picture so far presented. An important part of the data was gathered from questionnaires completed anonymously by Sixth Formers. These were taken to thirty-nine different schools during the course of 1971. The researchers reported that the Shrewsbury questionnaires had been more carefully and fully completed, and with greater engagement with the issues, than at many other comparable schools.

In the written report, the participating schools were given pseudonyms; the pseudonym allotted to Shrewsbury was Hartfield. The overall conclusion was that Hartfield appeared, by a very significant margin, to be the most contented of all the schools visited. In general terms, this was attributed to a judiciously liberal and generally consistent tenor of school policy across the many facets of school life. The report summarised this in the educational jargon which was fashionable at the time. It asserted that the School

Had steadily and consistently moved from positional to personal control in relationships, from rigid to fluid control of boundaries and from extrinsic to intrinsic modes of motivation.

To express this in more direct and accessible language: teachers now exercised control by force of character and the respect they earned rather than by prescriptive sanctions; boundaries in rules and status both internal, within the school itself, and external between the school and the wider world, had become more flexible (the researchers considered that Hartfield was much more aware of, and open to, the wider world than many comparable schools, and a significant element in the Common Room had already had experience in other professions); and that more choice and less compulsion were exercised in an expanding range of activities, allowing masters and boys freely to share a common interest.

The Bloxham report placed great emphasis on the quality of relationships among the staff and the frequent hospitality they offered each other; it also stressed the importance of the staff discussion group – the Friday Club. It observed that the quality of the relationship between the Headmaster and the members of the Common Room was mirrored in that between the staff and the boys, and vice versa. The Second Master told the researchers,

We stand or fall entirely here by the network of personal relationships we establish throughout the school. We can keep everything going … if the boys feel there is always someone they can talk to.

The report concluded that

There is something about Hartfield – the way it does things, its 'structure', its 'culture', which both releases the best qualities in its masters and also permits those qualities to be seen by the boys

It was perceived that there was less social distance between the masters and the boys than at similar schools. Both the high level of the masters' academic qualifications and of the sporting prowess of the staff (Hartfield had more than its fair share of Firsts and Blues) enabled them to be seen as 'competence models' by their pupils. Here again the power of example was at work. This high degree of competence, trustworthiness, openness in expressing their opinions, approachability, willingness to listen to their pupils and to help with their problems were the qualities which boys most greatly appreciated in their teachers.

The report further concluded that Salopian relationships both within the Common Room and between the teaching staff and the boys were the most constructive which had been encountered in its whole field of research and, of course, that finding reinforced the very characteristics which Salopians themselves had claimed to identify. The great attention which has been taken subsequently to preserve and enhance pastoral care, not least in the universal application of the system of personal tutors, has ensured that the quality of relationships which the Bloxham researchers observed has been fully maintained. It will be apparent from all this that there is indeed a strong and distinctive Salopian ethos.

However this situation has encountered a series of challenges, particularly during the course of the last couple of decades. Some of these challenges are inevitable and unavoidable, many are the result of government intervention or market forces; others, once perceived, can be mitigated.

The first of these challenges is the stark reality that the traditional sources from which members of the School have been drawn are drying up. The constituency of parents who are both financially able and by inclination disposed to support a child at Shrewsbury for five years is rapidly dwindling. The tendency to select a school to which the parents have easy access grows stronger; and Shrewsbury is not well placed, geographically, to recruit from the most affluent areas. The competition from similar schools grows ever fiercer; the preparatory schools which for many years prepared and delivered a suitable and reliable supply of thirteen-year-old entrants are experiencing competitive pressures as never before. The logical consequence of all this, accepted by many, but not all, as the only solution, is that the exclusive reception of boys only, and only at thirteen, and only British boys, had to be broken. Of course, there were many powerful educational arguments for doing so, but the fundamental rock-solid fact remained. No entrants, no school: no school, no ethos.

Next, there is a group of factors which presents both welcome opportunities on the one hand, and challenges to the School's identity and ethos on the other. The growth in size, eminently desirable in that it makes possible the provision of state-of-the art facilities, which are essential in a period of intense competition, inevitably presents a threat to the cohesion of the community, particularly when there is no longer any building in which the whole community can conveniently gather. The immense value of such provision was very clearly demonstrated in very the successful expedient of erecting a huge marquee in which the headmaster, governors, teachers, parents and pupils, could all be accommodated on the three most recent Speech Days in 2013, 2014 and 2015.

The increasing cultural diversity, represented by the current members of the School, provides exciting opportunities for enrichment both of academic and social education. In today's 'global village' the modern Salopian is indeed unquestionably enriched by contact with contemporaries from different cultures and ethnicities. However, this inevitably reduces the possibility of producing an ethos firmly based, as previously, on the common background and experience of the entrants. Many new members of the School nowadays have not been accustomed to pursuing their academic studies in the context of participation in the wide range of sporting and other extra-curricular opportunities which have been a traditional feature of English preparatory and secondary boarding schools.

The greatly increased participation of parents, both by regular visits, by easy communication by mobile phone with their children and by frequent e-mails to the staff, is greatly to be welcomed in that, at its best, it harnesses the interest and co-operation of those who are the natural and principal agents of the education of their sons and daughters in the widest sense of the word. There are, and always have been, difficulties when the values, standards and practices of home life differ markedly from those which the School tries to uphold. More than one Headmaster has emphasized (and has been teased by his colleagues for repeatedly doing so) how crucial it is that the 'triangle' of communication, consistency and co-operation in the school-parent-child relationships should not be broken. However, the contrast between the situation in the 'traditional' and in the 'contemporary' public school in this respect is stark. The responsibility of the teaching staff for their pupils in the 'classical' age of the public school was almost total. There was minimal parental participation – indeed it was sometimes positively discouraged – and the trust reposed in the school, its mores, curriculum and procedures was also total. There was greater freedom for the school to act and to teach and greater insulation from less desirable trends and influences in wider society. The school and its staff really were *in loco parentis*. They were in a much stronger position to set and maintain a standard.

The overall shortening of the length of sojourn at the school, both by pupils and by members of the common room, is a still clearer threat to the maintenance and transmission of an ethos. The admission of both boys and girls at Sixth Form level means that there is a sizeable minority in the school who only experience what it is to be a Salopian for rather less than two years, although the intention, once the first mixed cohort reaches the Sixth Form in 2017, is to reduce the number of Sixth Form entrants accordingly. The members of the Common Room remain immensely loyal and the attraction of prolonged service at Shrewsbury remains strong; but, consonant with the spirit of the age, the proportion of those who view their stay at the school rather as constituting a valuable step in their personal career, than as a long-term commitment, is steadily growing. A careful balance between the long-term and the short-term members of the Common Room is essential, or as a senior and greatly respected member of the Common Room expressed it when he left the staff in 2013, a balance between the 'standing' and the 'rolling' stones, if Shrewsbury's human architecture and the ethos which pervades the building is to be preserved. All these last three tendencies tend to reduce the strength of the community and to impinge upon the preservation of the ethos.

Government intervention is also a serious threat to the strength of the community. The deluge of educational directives, required assessments, and health and safety regulations saps the energies of members of the Common Room and diverts their attention from their primary responsibility, which is to deliver a first-class education; and by far the greatest and ever-increasing expansion of staff at the school has been in the administrative sector. Rigid specialisation and equally rigid prescribed syllabuses and assessments add to the load. The result is that the members of the Common Room can scarcely find the time to raise their heads from the mountains of paper which confront them, to seize the opportunity to escape from the administrative tread-mill, and to harness the energy and inclination to socialise with and entertain their colleagues. Their attention is diverted increasingly from people to paper.

Ted Maidment addressed the situation in his Speech Day Report of 2000.

There are dangers. Too many hurdles, too many points of assessment could smother genuine academic qualities, qualities such as interest, imagination, a real commitment to ideas. Will there be time for excellence? … Ultimately, the success of a school is not to do with statistics, league tables, analyses, charts, vectors. It is not to be found on paper, documented in black and white. It is to do with the feel, the ethos of the place and particularly it is to do with the pupils, the boys.

In the fifteen years since he expressed that warning these pressures have become still greater and the questions which he raises more urgent. Will there indeed be time for excellence? Will there be time for the nurturing of the community? The Salopian community was a prominent theme of Ted Maidment's final Report to Parents in May 2001. He referred to the School Photograph which had recently been taken, which in the words of the Editor of the *Salopian Newsletter* depicted 'a community of boys, academic and support staff living on a glorious site with common purpose'. Ted commented

> *The whole point about Shrewsbury is that* everyone *plays a crucial part in the success of the place ... 'Our' school photograph included all boys, all the staff and absolutely everyone who works here, standing informally on Central and in no particular order. It speaks volumes about Shrewsbury. Our way , not my way ...*

This brings us back to the original question of how to combine stability and change in order to produce an effective and harmonious process of evolution. Many of the major factors involved are no longer within our control; we have to work within the restrictions set by legislation and the pressures of marketing, but I believe that there are feasible responses to the challenges I have outlined which are able to mitigate their deleterious effects. It is not a change of direction, but a change of emphasis which needs to be considered. The most important agents in such an endeavour are the members of the Common Room.

Most crucial of all these responses would be an emphasis on the importance of personal encounters and an effort to substitute these for electronic communications wherever possible. Time needs to be found for regular social opportunities for the staff to meet. Termly guest nights, regular 'dining-in' nights, the convention that one evening a week, after school, would be designated as a time when staff members could meet their colleagues socially in the bar all made a significant contribution to the cohesion of the community.

A second important response would be a clear statement of the School's values. The *Blue Book* outlines a code of conduct. Both to reinforce this and to place it in context, consideration might be given to a formulation of the values which form the basis of such a code, to be presented to members of the School regularly on suitable occasions in Chapel and in assemblies. If the presentation of ethical teaching in the terms of Christian scripture and doctrine which had such a profound effect in the era of great preaching is no longer thought to be appropriate for an international audience drawn from several religious traditions, an equally powerful means of presenting a set of values is desirable, perhaps in the form of an examination of the School's mysterious motto. One everyday application of such a formulation might be specific attention to the maintenance of good and considerate manners and another to the promotion of equally specific forms of service to others in the wider community. Such an emphasis would be of particular importance at a time when it is sometimes alleged that the Independent Boarding Schools have lost their moral compass, that the confidence they instil and the competition they encourage are applied primarily to ruthless self-advancement.

A third response might be to ensure that all the members of the community are thoroughly familiar with their Salopian heritage. The School has a long and distinguished history which marks it out from the great majority of co-educational secondary schools. In the last 150 years, as I have tried to indicate earlier in this chapter and in the historical section of this book, it has been numbered among the great schools of England – and by extension, if the widely acknowledged estimate of the excellence of English education is held to be justified, of the great schools of the world. It is up to our present generation to emulate and perpetuate this reputation.

Lastly, it should be recognised that the transmission of this heritage is primarily the responsibility of the members of the Common Room. Much of their time is spent in complying with administrative procedures. If some of it could be devoted to a consideration of purposes instead, that might well work to the general advantage. Here, again, our predecessors have something to teach us. The 'Friday Club', the discussion club which, famously, never had any minutes, and never met on Fridays, might be due for resurrection. It produced some challenging ideas and provided a compass to check our progress.

So what, then, are the components of the Salopian ethos? Its foundation is the easy relationship between the staff and the pupils, which, it may justifiably be claimed, really is distinctive. They genuinely seem to enjoy each others' company; there is mutual respect, but it is informal, tinged with humour and reinforced by the satisfaction which all derive from shared endeavour, academic, cultural or athletic. There is a curriculum which caters for pupils of every kind and level of ability, in which it is possible for everyone to find an activity which brings enjoyment and fulfilment. The School offers superb pastoral care. The result, as one master remarked to me the other day is that 'it is difficult to find an unhappy Salopian'. The staff are exceptionally committed to their vocation. The pupils are amenable and realistic. Overall they may lack something of the polish and the drive of their metropolitan contemporaries, but they are natural and genuine, not least because they realise that they are cared for at Shrewsbury as individuals. And the setting for all this is a Site which in its beauty and in its construction seems ideally suited to house a contented community.

And what are the characteristics of Polymathes, the Salopian who has been moulded by this ethos, upon the completion of his education at school ? Sir Eric Anderson observed that 'Salopians have always had the reputation of being agreeable people'. What is it that makes them so? Straightforward, independent-minded, possessed of a quirky sense of humour, with a friendliness and social ease which makes them welcome in every company – these are qualities, frequently identified by observers, which occur repeatedly in this book. And is there such a thing as an Ideal Salopian? Probably not. *Quot homines, tot sententiae.* But here is the view of a recent, particularly thoughtful Polymathes, who makes an impassioned plea for tolerance and deplores the occasions on which it is absent.

Being an individual is key … someone who can look at authority and decide for himself when it has gone too far and whose opinions don't need to be swayed by the majority; someone who doesn't frown upon other people who aren't like himself; someone willing to break the often mundane routine to do something different, but who doesn't allow hedonism or boredom to get the better of him.

It is such openness, responsiveness and sensitivity both to ideas and to people, lightened by an engaging sense of humour, which make Salopians such excellent companions, make them so willing to foregather in later years and which pay such an admirable tribute to the School which nurtured them.

CHAPTER TWELVE

FOUR SALOPIAN CHARACTERS

It has commonly been held that University Common Rooms and famous Public Schools have traditionally provided a safe haven for eccentrics; indeed it has been asserted that its ability to accommodate its fair share of such colleagues is one mark of a great public school. Equally current is the idea that eccentricity in these institutions, and perhaps less obviously in society as a whole, is on the decline. Eccentricity flourishes where there is tolerance, security and freedom; and there is certainly a case for concluding that regulation, inspection, the requirement to attain prescribed standards and the imposition of rigid syllabuses stifle inspiration, reward conformity and consequently discourage eccentricity in independent schools.

During the last sixty years, four colleagues emerge clearly as the leading Salopian eccentrics, Hugh Brooke and Frank McEachran, Mark Mortimer and Michael Hall. As indicated in the foreword, I have thought it appropriate in this section, as personal memories come to the fore, to relax the degree of formality required in a history, and I propose to refer to Brooke and McEachran as *Brookie* and *Kek* and to Mortimer and Hall by their given names, Mark and Michael. The first pair were prominent figures in the third, and the second pair in the fourth quarter of the twentieth century. The last three had a good deal in common. They were all lifelong bachelors; they were all of a very high intellectual calibre and could easily have been university dons; and for the most part they did not consider themselves to be part of the Salopian establishment, though both Mark and Michael made very substantial contributions to the day-to-day running of the School. Brookie, by contrast, was a devoted family man, a Housemaster and an all-rounder, very much an establishment figure, content to do the bulk of his teaching in the lower forms. But all four were gadflies, stinging their colleagues and pupils out of apathy and complacency. They all had the gift of bringing to life any company of which they were members – they were life-enhancers – and in their chosen social context all of them radiated *bonhomie* and contentment. Most importantly, uninhibited by the restraints of hierarchy, convention and career-building, they exhibited a freedom in the style of their personal lives which enabled them to be fully themselves. They were all men of principle, with a clear idea of what mattered and what did not: any outward appearance of insouciance, light-heartedness and sometimes even of flippancy did not prevent them from staunchly defending and advocating those principles when the occasion demanded it. On a much more trivial note of comparison, bicycles played a significant part in the life-styles of three of them. Kek had three bicycles (since he had generally forgotten where two of them were), and Mark had four; Michael had a tendency to fall off his bicycle, a notable instance of which dangerous habit is recounted below. All made a habit of distributing generous largesse to friends and pupils, with Kek , Mark and Michael in chocolates, and with Brookie in half-crowns.

They were all long-serving members of the Common Room. Both Brookie (1933-69) and Mark (1958-94) served for thirty-six years; Kek (1935-60) for twenty-five, though he continued to teach part-time for another fifteen years, not only at Shrewsbury, but also at the High School and Wellington, until the day before he died, in 1975; Michael (1967-95), who had previously taught at Dulwich, served at Shrewsbury for twenty-eight years, returned for another year after the tragic death of his successor, and continued to teach part-time and to tutor for several years after that. Together their service spanned over forty of the sixty years which are the principal focus of this book

Brookie first came to Shrewsbury as a student teacher in 1932, having graduated at St John's College, Oxford, and on subsequently being appointed to the permanent staff, devoted the whole of his teaching career to the School. Kek ('Mac' to some of his colleagues, 'Kek' to the boys) came to Shrewsbury after taking his degree at Magdalen College, Oxford and subsequent experience of teaching at Gresham's School, Holt, where W.H. Auden was one of his Sixth Form pupils. Mark ('Mort' to some of his colleagues, 'Morty' to the boys) had graduated at Christ Church, Oxford and Michael ('Fred' Hall to the boys) at Trinity College, Cambridge; they were close contemporaries in age, Mark having been born in June 1934 and Michael in August 1935. Mark, like Brookie (whose House Tutor he became), spent the whole of his teaching career at Shrewsbury.

There were further similarities: Mark and Michael were the joint doyens of the noble company of House tutors, both long-serving and devoted to their respective Houses, Mark in Rigg's and Michael in Churchill's, both so firmly loyal and established that they became House 'institutions'. Both remained in the ranks in National Service, Mark declining to seek a commission (Willie Jones commented that 'he never had the least desire to be a leader of men'). Michael was debarred from officer training, it is said, for not having taken Maths O level (the story is credible since it was customary at the time for boys who received fast promotion at high-powered academic schools to 'skip' the humbler qualifications). Michael's explanation that he had been the holder of a Scholarship in Mathematics at Trinity College, Cambridge, that he had subsequently gained a first-class degree in Mathematics and was, in fact, Third Wrangler, was received with incomprehension and cut no ice: an O level was what was required!

Both Kek and Michael had been educated at Manchester Grammar School and they arrived in a traditional boarding school as outsiders. Mark, by contrast, the product successively of Summerfields, Eton and Christ Church, could scarcely have been more of an 'insider' on the basis of educational pedigree, but he preferred to be an outsider in stance and temperament. It is not without significance that, on his first arrival at Shrewsbury, Mark shared a flat with Kek.

Kek, Mark and Michael all had wide cultural interests and all bequeathed a literary legacy, though Kek and Mark each displayed a surprising gap in their range of cultural appreciation, Kek with his professed aversion to music, while Mark claimed a similar aversion to drama. Kek's literary achievement was by far the most substantial and wide-ranging of the three, and, very interestingly, almost unknown at school. Mark's brilliance as a satirical poet was, by contrast, very much in evidence and widely admired; after his retirement he achieved a different kind of distinction in his remarkable collection and translation of *Latinised Hymns*. Michael's principal literary contribution was his volume of memoirs, entitled *Around the World in Forty Years*, and he supplemented this by the regular distribution to his friends of a succession of typed monographs on varied subjects which had caught his interest and which he entitled *Joies de Vivre*.

That both Brookie and Kek have a rightful and prominent place in the roll of Salopian eccentrics is beyond question; but I have written at greater length about Mark and Michael, my own exact contemporaries, than I have about Kek and Brookie in the remainder of this chapter because I knew them better and for twice as long. In their different ways both Mark and Michael were as influential in the day-to-day life of the School as Brookie had been, and while nearly all of their energy and commitment was focused within the School, (with the notable exception of Michael's responsibilities as District Commissioner of Scouts), the sphere of Kek's activity was much wider and its character more independent. Brookie and Kek, Mark and Michael, followed Southwell and White in becoming 'The Two Men' of their respective generations. The attention I have paid to these four masters is substantial because their contributions provide a uniquely valuable insight into the essential atmosphere and nature of the School. All four were powerful influences in preserving that elusive ethos. The finest tribute to all of them is the fact that to this day they are frequently spoken of, by those who knew them, with a smile and with affection, admiration and respect.

Hugh Brooke (RHJB)

Hugh Brooke came to Shrewsbury in 1932, from St John's College, Oxford, with a cricket Blue. After an apprenticeship as a student teacher, known in Shrewsbury in those days as a 'creeper', he was appointed to the staff in 1933. He played a major part in school life, first as extremely successful master in charge of the 1st cricket XI both before and after the Second World War (during which he was absent on military service), and subsequently, from 1947 to 1962, as the much-loved Housemaster of Rigg's. He was ordained in 1959, retired to a country parish in Essex in 1969 and died in 1973.

His colleagues remember a 'wit, philosopher, sportsman, man-about-town, above all a Christian', someone whom it was ' a delight to be with … good fun, refreshing, liberal, inventive', supplying 'a non-stop flow of unlikely anecdotes, idiosyncratic phraseology, scattered fragments of song with a marked predilection for puns, a gadfly in the Common Room'. It might be said of him, like Jack Point, 'Winnow all my folly and you'll find a grain or two of truth among the chaff'. Brookie, like our three other eccentrics, was comfortable in his own skin and exhibited the self-confidence which expresses that condition. A colleague observed, 'He has this in common with the Unjust Judge in the third Gospel, that he regards not man'. It was a comment which might equally have been applied to our other three 'characters'.

Brookie was the life and soul of the bachelor establishment during his sojourn in the New House between 1933 and 1939. It was he who famously appeared clad only in a fig leaf and a fez, both worn correctly, and armed with a ceremonial sword; and it was he who inaugurated 'The Suckers League' as recounted in the chapter on the New House. The anonymous author of the appreciation of Brookie, published upon his retirement in the Salopian Newsletter in 1969, records how one night he 'found himself flattened against the door of Hugh's room playing the role of St Sebastian while his host made practice with his new set of darts'. He also remembers that

he (Brookie) once planned a splendid sherry party to which nasty characters who receive mention in the Bible would be invited. The Unjust Steward (in charge of catering) was to hand round South African sherry. Dives lorded it, Agag cringed, Laban fawned, and so on. Martha, who was, of course, not qualified to attend as a guest, washed up afterwards.

Brookie's fame was not confined to the Site. One of the most famous stories about him relates that, when serving in the KSLI, Hugh was standing on the edge of a cliff, addressing a group of soldiers. After announcing 'I know a quick way down', he slipped, fell over the edge and, as he disappeared from view, was heard to say 'HGB'. He was injured and taken to hospital. After he had recovered sufficiently, there was much interest in that mysterious exclamation, and his visitors asked him what it signified. 'HGB?' he mused … 'HGB?'. 'Ah, yes. HGB … Here goes Brooke.'

One of Brookie's eccentricities was his custom of lavishly dispensing half-crowns to those who had pleased him. On one occasion, while accompanied by the Rigg's Head of House near the Kingsland Post Office, Brookie met one of his own contemporaries. 'Ah, Jenks', he exclaimed with his customary affability, and, presenting his friend with half-a-crown, airily passed on his way. A few minutes later, the senior Riggite came running down the hill, 'Excuse me, sir,' he said, 'Mr Brooke wonders whether you would be kind enough to lend him half-a-crown?'

My own first encounter with Brookie also involved half-a-crown. Arriving at Shrewsbury, like him, as a 'creeper' and from the same Oxford College, I was invited to lunch with Brookie and his monitors on Head Table in Rigg's and was placed opposite the Housemaster. It was, I think, my very first experience of House lunch and I was on my best behaviour and somewhat nervous in the presence of this august senior colleague. His first words to me were as follows: "What's the difference between Noah's Ark and Joan of Arc?" The monitors on either side of me whispered in my ears. 'Say "Don't know"', they advised. "Don't know," I duly replied. "One was made of wood and the other was Maid of Orleans," Brookie explained triumphantly. "Laugh," the monitors prompted. I duly laughed and Brookie pushed a half-crown towards me across the table.

Brookie created a notably happy, unorthodox, enthusiastic and successful community around him in Rigg's. It is as unsurprising as it is significant that he invited a similarly unorthodox young colleague – another of our four eccentrics, Mark Mortimer, - to be his House Tutor. Brookie himself was a man of great, if often transient enthusiasms, and it was said that Rigg's functioned on a three-year cycle of such enthusiasms, Cups, Culture and Christianity. (When gardening became another enthusiasm, it was alleged that Compost became a fourth 'C'!). He liked both to encourage commitment in sport but, at the same time, to profess detachment from the results: he would wander round the boundary or stand on the touchline during crucial House Matches and, pointing at the clouds, would airily announce to bystanders that the results were "all written up there." Rigg's flourished mightily in cricket and rowing, but Brookie also held art exhibitions and encouraged drama. On a second visit to Rigg's, when I attended House Dix (at a time when this assembly invariably consisted of a hymn and some prayers), Brookie, having announced the number of the hymn, added the rubric, 'Verse three to be sung by all those who haven't had a bath for a week.' However, concealed behind this flippant veneer was a deep concern for individuals, which in turn created a compassionate environment, in many respects ahead of its time. Brookie was concerned that Riggites should have the confidence to be themselves; and many of his charges, some of them later very prominent in public life, have paid warm tributes to his success in this respect.

When Brookie retired, Donald Wright saluted him as 'an incomparable Form Master'. Brookie's first principle in the classroom was 'Never be a bore' and his method 'a triumphantly successful unorthodoxy', whose refreshing liveliness managed to get generations of less academically able and inclined Salopians to take an interest in French irregular verbs and to surmount the challenges of School Certificate, then known as 'the ticket'. At one stage Brookie kept a miniature set of traffic lights on his desk. When the light shone green, merriment ruled, when it turned to amber, a more sober and attentive response was expected. When red appeared, focused attention and hard grind were required. In the classroom, as in the House, the happiness of his pupils was one of Brookie's principal concerns, and he was second to none in encouraging boys of whatever ability or potential.

The Revd Frank McCarthy Willis-Bund, speaking at Brookie's memorial service in 1973, identified the two contrasting aspects of Brookie's personality in which while 'exercising his delightful social qualities, he guarded from public view the serious and devout inner man'. One element in the latter was Brookie's deep Christian faith and commitment. This, too, was lightly worn and never paraded. Brookie had been a Lay Reader for several years, but this ministry had been exercised in country parishes rather than in the School Chapel. When, in 1958, Brookie announced his intention to be ordained, this caused surprise to those who did not know him well. It also involved a term's absence from Rigg's, while Brookie received the necessary, but much accelerated training at theological college. Such, however, was the influence of his personality and the security and acceptance of the regime which he had established, that he was able safely to leave it in the care of his House Tutor at the time, Mark Mortimer's predecessor, Richard Holmes. On Brookie's return, Salopians were exposed to a typically idiosyncratic performance in the pulpit, characterised by highly unorthodox examples of scriptural exegesis and, to the delight of his audience, strictly limited to eight minutes. One example of Brookie's preaching, delivered to a well-heeled congregation in a country parish, was based on the story of the Rich Young Man. Brookie's message was: if you want to know what Jesus really thought about rich people, just look around you! No wonder that Bertie Fowler summed up the impact of Brookie's clerical career in the memorable statement: 'Too many Brookes spoil the cloth.' Yet at Great Canford, in Essex, where Brookie spent the last four years of his life as Rector, he quickly earned the same response of affection and respect he had elicited at Shrewsbury.

Two of Brookie's leading characteristics were shrewdness and courage. He was a careful listener with a penetrating gaze. Willis-Bund remarks that 'it was *you* and *your thoughts* to which his whole attention was given'. It was this disposition which enabled him to become such an effective pastoral schoolmaster and informed his vocation to become a priest. Brookie's courage was demonstrated in his self-command, in a life which contained prolonged physical suffering, of injury and illness. The sustained patience and the reticence with which he responded amounted to a particular brand of courage, which Willis-Bund identifies as the virtue of Fortitude.

In August 2003 thirty-four Riggites, together with Michael Charlesworth, who had been Acting Housemaster of Rigg's in 1976, met to remember Brookie. On that occasion Michael noted and properly emphasised the great debt that was owed to Brookie's wife Dorothy, who bore the brunt of the domestic side of the House and supported him in all his eccentricities and enthusiasms. As Willis-Bund again observes, there can be no doubt that Brookie's wife Dorothy and their children David, Carol and Sally provided the security which enabled him to play his part on the Salopian scene with his characteristic brightness of spirit and happiness of heart. An appropriate tribute to Dorothy was contained in the adapted version of the *Carmen* which was offered as a Grace before the 2003 dinner by the Venerable C. Hewetson:

> Rex Hugh Brookie, te canamus
> Pium Housemagistrum
> Nec alumni sileamus
> Uxorem Dorotheam
> Mente nunc edamus grata
> Dulcissimam hanc cenam
> So may all that Riggite laughter
> Resonat Sabrinam.

Frank McEachran (FMcE)

In my appraisal of Kek, I defer to Laurence Le Quesne, who knew him well for many years, who had also shared a flat with him, and who has played a crucial role in preserving his work and honouring his memory. Anyone who wishes to learn about Kek can do no better than read Laurence's introduction to *A Cauldron of Spells*, an anthology in whose selection and production Laurence played a leading part. Here he provides the best introduction, not only to Kek's thinking and writing, but also the deepest insight into his character. I acknowledge the considerable debt which the following brief sketch owes to what I have learned from him about Kek.

Kek came to Shrewsbury as a teacher of modern languages, but his preference was always for the literary rather than the strictly linguistic aspect of the subject. He was happiest when employed in so-called 'minority time', in which he had the freedom needed to communicate his enthusiasm for what came to be known as 'Spells'. He defined a 'Spell' as 'concentrated poetry of sound or sense' and Richard Brain provided a slightly extended definition of Spells as 'those fragments of verse or prose that concentrated meaning and verbal rhythm and sound'.

Kek's teaching method was as follows: he circulated typewritten screeds of such 'Spells', and encouraged his pupils to learn them by heart. He then persuaded them, in turn, to stand upon a chair surrounded by a magic circle of three rings, and declaim their chosen passage. A variation from this individual recitation was an invitation to the whole class to participate in a general incantation of the spell. The three rings, within which the speaker might not accept food or drink, were a reference to Coleridge's stanza in *Kubla Khan*:

> Weave a circle round him thrice
> And close your eyes with holy dread
> For he on honey dew hath fed
> And drunk the milk of paradise.

Kek was neither an organiser nor a disciplinarian by temperament, and when his colleagues asked him how he responded when the proceedings, predictably in a group of ebullient Sixth Formers, got somewhat out of hand, he was wont to reply, 'Oh, I just go away: they soon calm down'.

Mary Beard, now Professor of Classics at Cambridge, was a pupil at Shrewsbury High School during Kek's time . Writing in the *Times Educational Supplement* in February 2014, she remembers that 'He went around Shrewsbury ... teaching his stuff – Italian language, English and Philosophy' and comments:

A teacher like Frank McEachran would never be allowed in Britain's education system today ... he was completely, in modern terms, 'off-message'. There were no 'learning objectives' for him ... He inspired us all to consider that the intellectual life had a point to it ... he made us think that there was something out there that was bigger than our world, where people talked and debated ... by opening up possibilities beyond what we had imagined he gave us the confidence to go on and do something more. There was also a sense that this was fun. There were no assessment criteria: it was just interesting.

Paul Foot records that his first reaction to Kek's teaching was contemptuous; he thought it mad, but he soon became an admirer and indeed came to the conclusion that it was Kek who was truly sane.

There can be no doubt that Kek's method, unusual and unorthodox as it was, stimulated an awareness and appreciation of poetry, and of literature more generally, in successive generations of Salopians: and the recitation of Spells became a regular feature of the post-prandial proceedings at Old Salopian gatherings. This was not the only way in which Kek sought to widen Salopian horizons. He anticipated the provision of a school bookshop by instituting the *Kek Shelf*, on which he placed a selection of books which he thought boys ought to read and might like to borrow, and he convened and presided over a masters' discussion group, *The Friday Club*, whose consideration of a variety of educational, literary and philosophical topics ranged far beyond the usual parochial concerns, and which he always opened with the formulaic words, "Well, since there are no minutes ..."

Kek was also famed for his end-of-term reports, highly idiosyncratic, handwritten in a spidery script, often confined to one corner of the allotted report sheet. His most common brief was to teach Divinity to Sixth Formers and he often took the opportunity to try to capture the essence of a boy's character in a brief comment, a process in some ways analogous to a Spell. One such (complete) report on a whole term's work was as follows: 'He still looks rather like a tadpole, but no doubt, like all tadpoles, he will eventually turn into a butterfly (sic)'.

The character of the ageing and chaotic schoolmaster, Hector, in Alan Bennett's play *The History Boys* owes much to what Bennett learned about Kek from his Salopian friends who had been Kek's pupils. In an article in *The Salopian*, Peter Fanning surveys the encounter between the old educational methods and the shock of the new, 'in which the love of learning greets the face of modern technology'. In *The History Boys* Hector is contrasted with and confronted by a young colleague of the mill-board examination-technique, curriculum-specific and results-oriented generation of schoolmasters, who considered Hector's contribution useless and responded to it with scorn. At a deeper level, therefore, the play addresses the question of where true values in education are to be found.

Spells became so popular that there was a widespread demand that they should be given more permanent form: *Spells* was succeeded by *More Spells;* and subsequently *A Cauldron of Spells* was produced to include the greater part of the content of both books, in a new arrangement.

Many of the Spells were drawn from Scripture, from Shakespeare and from Dante, and the whole collection spanned eleven languages. The very short selection of Spells which follows may introduce them to, and whet the appetite of, those readers who have not met them before.

When the breadfruit fall
And the penguin call
And the sound is the sound of the sea
Under the bam
Under the boo
Under the bamboo tree

Über allen Gipfeln ist Ruh'
In allen Wipfeln
Spürest du kaum einen Hauch
Die Vögelein schweigen im Walde
Warte nur: balde ruhest du auch.

Bare ruined choirs, where late the sweet birds sang

And, perhaps the most famous of all, Hitler's proud boast:

Niemand hat je gesagt ich wäre feig gewesen

Of which Kek used to say that if it was recited by a group of teenage boys together, it conveyed a terrifying impression of the hynoptic power exercised over the young by the Nazi movement.

Kek's impact on his pupils is commemorated not only in these volumes of spells, but was also celebrated in an annual dinner in his memory, a tradition which was sustained from his death in 1975 until the centenary of his birth, in the year 2000. Quite recently a new school prize, the McEachran prize, has been instituted, which continues the tradition of the public recitation of Spells. A more permanent and tangible tribute is provided by the plaque affixed to the wall on a staircase in the Main School Building, on which there is an engraving depicting Kek and an inscription from Nietzsche 'We must have chaos within us to give birth to a dancing star'.

Kek is distinguished from our other three eccentrics by the fact that his literary contributions were so considerable, both in range and substance, that they might well have launched him into a completely different career. Although this aspect of Kek's activities is not relevant to the particular theme of this chapter, it requires a mention, albeit of the very briefest kind, if a balanced picture of his achievement is to be presented. A full bibliography of Kek's writings has been compiled by John Bridgen and is reproduced in *A Cauldron of Spells*. In addition to numerous articles, it includes several books, of which *The Civilized Man* and *Freedom the Only End* are perhaps the best known. As the latter title suggests, Kek was convinced that freedom was the only legitimate end of human activity; and he believed that great literature, enshrined most powerfully in Greek tragedy, the Bible, Shakespeare and Dante, expressed basic values of civilization from which modern society had diverted its attention, to its very great danger and impoverishment. Laurence's estimate was that Kek 'was one of the very small minority who genuinely have something to say to the world, a polymath of extraordinarily wide interests and reading'.

Kek had other idiosyncracies, of course, apart from his unconventional teaching methods; these were physical, social and ideological. The former included the wearing of his Moser's scarf, the possession of his three bicycles and his habit of dispensing Mars bars to all and sundry. His opening gambits in conversation could be alarming 'What do you think of the African mind? 'Are you in the dome? (of the Headmaster's consciousness) and, to a newly arrived colleague, after Kek had appraised him, in the Masters' Bar, for a few minutes. 'You are not an academic, you are not a sportsman, and you are not a 'good chap', so why are you here?' (As it happened, Kek, on this occasion, was wrong on all three counts.) And finally, his professed dislike of music, which he asserted had no meaning at all, and which he considered was (together with organised religion and organised games – the emphasis is on the adjectives) – one of the three forces which erode the human spirit.

Alan Laurie reminds us that

Kek was not Mr Chips. It would be a pity if Old Salopians who never knew him came to accept this pigeonhole for him as the truth. He often spoke about 'the Truth' in a gnomic way and it was very important to him ... Kek was deadly serious when talking about the political and economic lessons of the twentieth century. He believed with passion that there was a better way for the world to go. He believed that there were reasons for much of humanity's social and economic disorder and that reason could apply appropriate remedies. It is a message of hope and we need it more than ever.

But in the specifically Salopian context, the definitive assessment, once more, is provided by Laurence Le Quesne, who saw Kek as

a teacher of genius, able to communicate with anyone, a good man, a gentle man and generous man. Not the best, or the wisest, but the most remarkable, the free-est man I have ever known ... he neither offered nor sought intimacy ... what he was, above all, was a goad, an inspirer and kicker of young imaginations into life.

Perhaps one of Kek's own Spells should provide the last word:

I'm not a man, I'm dynamite.

Mark Mortimer (MM)

Mark Mortimer spent the whole of his teaching career – thirty-six years – at Shrewsbury, joining the staff in 1958 and retiring in 1994. The appearance, which he was happy to cultivate, was of a light-hearted gadfly, who took nothing very seriously. This is how many Salopians will remember him, but it does not begin to do justice to the reality of a hard-working, reliable and committed colleague who made a substantial but deliberately unobtrusive contribution to many aspects of Salopian life, in the classroom, as the designer of the school timetable, as a House tutor, and as a pillar of the Hunt; faithful and willing, too, as an official on the athletics track and as a cricket umpire. Exterior light-heartedness therefore concealed a meticulous devotion to duty and a willingness to take on menial tasks, quite out of the limelight.

The members of the Classical Faculty at Shrewsbury had a well established connection with their colleagues at Christ Church, Oxford, and Mark's distinguished performance as an undergraduate there had been noted and closely monitored. Accordingly, after he had completed his National Service, he was appointed to join a department which had a long and famous tradition of the highest academic standards, and was still acknowledged to be the leading department in the School. Though he taught Classics to every age-group, Mark was probably most at home when teaching the Classical Fifth, and its successors as the top stream of the Fifth Form. He also taught the lowest (seventh) Mathematics set in the Third Form, and liked to claim that he was responsible for the attainment of the worst mathematician in the School. For many years he was also in charge of the Thursday afternoon activities of the Third Form, and he liked to keep a kindly eye on those newcomers who were having difficulty in adjusting to their first experience of boarding school. He was responsible for the construction of the school timetable, a task which became increasingly complex as both options and numbers rapidly grew. On one occasion visiting Inspectors specially commended the subtle manner in which he had managed to achieve maximum flexibility within its complicated structure.

Beyond the classroom, Mark was a devoted House tutor of Rigg's, where he spent 101 terms, supporting six Housemasters in turn, providing an invaluable element of stability in difficult times, and making himself readily available to assist hundreds of Riggites with their Top Schools. Willie Jones records Mark's devoted allegiance to the Hunt, and the vital, but characteristically unobtrusive part he played, not least by going out on the days before the traditional Hunt runs were due to take place, to ensure that no new fences had been erected or other hazards had appeared, which might block the prescribed routes. Generations of Salopians will have memories of Mark brandishing his clapper-board to start the track events in athletics, or presiding at the wicket in the humblest of cricket leagues.

One institution about which Mark was deadly serious was Amnesty International. He liked to say that he considered that he was overpaid, and he both made and solicited contributions to the charity, devoted the proceeds of *Mort*, the anthology of his poems published in 1997, to that purpose and lent his Morris Minor to all and sundry, on the condition that it should be returned with a full tank and a contribution to Amnesty.

On the fly-leaf of *Mort*, under the heading *A Good Cause*, Mark wrote:

> Myself I've never felt restrained
> from writing what I wanted;
> and that's a freedom which we tend,
> I think, to take for granted.
>
> But in the world are others who
> have lost it, or could lose it.
> This book may cost a bob or two
> but AMNESTY will use it.

That Mark was an independent free spirit was very evident, from his earliest days in the Common Room, and he was often (some colleagues would say unreasonably and excessively) a thorn in the side of authority. On the occasion which took place on the Kingsland House lawn when Donald Wright, as the Headmaster-elect, was introduced to the members of the Common Room, Mark chose to wear a wildly inappropriate tie. It was largely (but not entirely) concealed beneath a V-necked sweater, and his younger colleagues took great delight in repeatedly flicking it out into full view, to the bemusement of the guest of honour. When it was decided that the whole school would attend a Eucharist in the newly consecrated Coventry Cathedral, Mark declined to attend. By coincidence, on the previous evening, a visit by the Balliol Players, a famously satirical group, had been scheduled, Mark's younger brother Edward being a member of the cast. Mark's refusal was highlighted when a pseudo-Shakespearean scene was included in the programme, in which an imposing royal figure appeared, issuing the command, "Set on towards Coventry!", whereupon a breathless messenger rushed on to the stage with the appalling news, "Young Mortimer doth refuse to go!"

When the precinct around the Moser Building was established, it was decided, in the interests of safety, that it should be closed to cyclists, who would be required to use the longer route along the newly constructed road. Mark did not consider that his cycling across the precinct constituted any danger and he persisted in the habit. When he was summoned to explain himself, a heated confrontation with the Headmaster ensued, which resulted in a compromise, namely that Mark would only cycle across the precinct when he was in a hurry!

Mark's open and obvious amusement at the repeated use, in a gathering of parents at the conclusion of the New Boys' service, of the analogy of a triangle to emphasise the importance of keeping the relationships between school, parents and pupils harmoniously together, (a perfectly valid point in itself), resulted in colleagues being required to leave the Chapel immediately upon the conclusion of the service, so that they would not acquire further ammunition by hearing the analogy again. Mark responded by sending invitations (typically by simply drawing a triangle and a question mark on a scrap of waste paper) to invite colleagues to repair to a 'Triangle Sunday' party, where, as Willie Jones records, 'he would dispense large doses of Gordon's with lashings of effervescent wit'.

More serious was the occasion upon which Mark, now vastly amused by the new nomenclature identifying colleagues, subjects, sets and rooms (impenetrable to the uninitiated – e.g. MM, LL1 in Cl3), mischievously proposed that the abbreviations should be extended to comments on half-term reports, such as DQW (doing quite well) and CDB (could do better), and placed a notice advocating this on the Common Room notice board. When this was taken seriously by novice colleagues, resulting in a number of totally incomprehensible documents, the further consequence was a decree by the Headmaster that it was time that Mark took a sabbatical, a sentence which was only quashed when the Headmaster resigned before it was due to take effect. It is certainly true that Mark lived most dangerously when attempting to show that Wright was wrong.

The main channel for Mark's satirical wit was, of course, to be found in his poems, and Salopians owe a great debt of gratitude to Philip Lapage, who collected and arranged a selection, and to Richard Hudson, who published the resulting volume, entitled *Mort*. Mark hit a wide selection of targets, which included anything that was pompous or pretentious, foolish or inconsistent in Salopian life. His brilliant and penetrating shafts were almost invariably acclaimed with affection rather than received with resentment. Most of his verses were of superb quality. Willie Jones salutes him as 'a metrist of inimitable skill and unfailing memorability of phrase'; while Anthony Bowen considers that 'Mark's verses live for their form' and likens him to Ovid 'who had a somewhat satirical wit and wholly perfect form'. He relates how Gunner Mortimer, unsurprisingly, was once found chuckling in the NAAFI over a volume of Ovid's poems!

One example of Mark's skill is to be found in the words which he put into the mouth of Louis, the headmaster's dog, who was sentenced to castration after he bit a master, Mike Partridge:

> A eunuch I'm condemned to be,
> a gun without a cartridge,
> It seems a drastic penalty
> for having mauled a Partridge.

Mark's poems, like so much else in his opinions and character, have an enigmatic quality. Although Mark makes a clear statement of intention -

> My verse is a game that I play
> one in which (let me put it this way)
>   my ambition has been
>   To say what I mean
> but never to mean what I say.

Willie Jones has his doubts:

The lightness of tone never quite belies the seriousness of the intent – but what the intent may be is never, at least to me, absolutely clear.

Prominent among Mark's targets were the Boat Club and School Drama. Here he imagines a sponsored row from Shrewsbury to Bristol by members of the RSSBC:

> On, on they row, with blistered bums
> And undiminished rating
> Until at last the moment comes
> For which we've all been waiting.
>
> And thousands watch from either shore
> As brother meets with brother;
> And one colossal Severn Bore
> Is swallowed by the other.

As for the theatre:

> Arriving at the Ashton T
> the other evening (silly me)
> I might have made a swift retreat
> on finding someone in my seat.
> Some demon took my wits away:
> I turfed him out – and saw the play.
> It's true. I could have gone to bed
> or watched TV, but chose instead
> an evening of pretentious trash,
> Of V-ll-g- Voice and L-ghtn-ng Flash
> and music played ffff …
> I left disgruntled, bored and deaf
> And more convinced than ever it's
> the truth that DRAMA IS THE PITS.

(The deleted characters refer to two boys who took leading parts in that particular production.)

Mark was consistent in this view. When referring to an acclaimed production of *The Beggar's Opera* he was accustomed to substitute Uproar for the last word in the title and his substitution for the second word can easily be imagined!

To what extent, if any, did Mark really mean what he said? Another enigmatic area was religion. His wit was often peppered with scriptural allusions and he was assiduous in his attendance at Chapel, as one might expect from one who had spent his youth in College Chapels, whose father had been a professor in the Oxford Divinity School and later became a senior diocesan bishop, but Mark was never known to express a clear religious opinion. (When sending his trunk home from the railway station at the end of term, as one did in those days, he was vastly amused when, having asked that it should be sent to 'The Palace, Exeter', the clerk enquired whether that was a cinema or a dance hall!)

The habit, deeply ingrained by his ecclesiastical background, meant that Mark would attend even the most voluntary and unadvertised services:

> It's an atheist age (ichabod),
> with the courts of the Lord little trod:
> last Saturday's prayer
> saw nobody there
> but me and the Chaplain and God.

But he had strong views about what should happen during these services, a dislike of excessive preaching, especially at anti-social hours, and an irreverent approach to liturgical innovations.

> Cursed be the parson, who to spite his flock
> insists on preaching at the eight o'clock.
> Dyspeptic and on homilies force-fed,
> the angry sheep puke up – or stop in bed.

If there had been a sermon at Mattins and any of the clergy then ventured to approach the chancel step at Evensong, clearly intending to 'say a few words', Mark would rise from his pew, bow to the altar and depart.

When the ancient custom of exchanging 'a sign of peace' was reintroduced in the new liturgy and I obediently turned round to the pew behind in order to offer one, my neighbour anticipated me, saying 'Good morning, my name is Mortimer, do you come here often?'

Mark expressed a strong aversion to the Papacy and the Catholic tradition (how genuine could this really have been?), and on the occasion, five years ago, when substantial ecumenical progress had made it possible to invite a Catholic Cardinal to preach to the assembled school on the occasion of its annual visit to St Mary's, colleagues who remembered Mark, stunned by the colossal irony, could hardly believe their ears when His Eminence, having dutifully searched for a Salopian reference to illustrate his remarks, and having by chance read Mark's obituary in the *Times*, took the theme of sainthood and ventured to suggest that its subject revealed some of the characteristics of a modern saint.

There are many examples of Mark's idiosyncracies: the upturned cereal bowls at breakfast, (for which he had another description), upon which he used to rest his copy of the *Daily Mail;* his habit of wearing two or three sweaters even in the middle of summer; the spurious, shocking pink 'Leander' socks he donned when officiating on the river. There, he was in his element as starter of the annual race, in eights, between the Masters and the Praepostors. Having given careful and elaborate instructions to both crews on the exact verbal formula he intended to use, he then proceeded to substitute a much shorter and cruder version at the crucial moment, for which his colleagues were prepared, but their opponents were not. He frequently appeared on formal occasions, when he was required to wear his suit, with blue plimsolls on his feet and his trousers tucked into his socks. He was generally not at ease on such occasions, and would, whenever possible, stand somewhat apart from the milling crowd. Once, when he had done so, and retreated, with his charged glass, to a corner of the Alington Hall, at the reception after prize-giving, a boy's mother, seeing his isolation, and misled by Mark's perennially youthful appearance, approached him and kindly enquired what prize he had won. It was his fifty-fourth birthday.

Mark delighted in using military terminology, with its characteristic inversion of descriptive adjectives. A typical example occurs in his account of the kit with which he was supplied in order to compete in a regimental athletics meeting during his National Service. He wrote:

> They issued shorts
> a pair, extremely loose, of
> what I suppose were "Drawers Sports
> Ranks Other, For The Use Of."

At the dining table he was generally equipped with a torch and a whistle, the former used, in subdued light, more closely to examine the food which had been served, and the latter to draw attention to any solecisms or deficiencies which might occur during the meal.

Not infrequently, I was myself the target of Mark's devastating wit. On one occasion, returning in a group of rather noisy young colleagues, along a road which was thickly populated by Day Boy families, (I was their Housemaster at the time), and having failed to restrain their ebullience, I noticed a police car, parked at an intersection ahead. Thinking it prudent to dissociate myself from the others, I turned right and walked by myself for fifty yards before crossing over to the other side and rejoining them, only to be greeted by Mark with the single word "Levite!" (Luke 10.32). After I had taken my doctorate, he would always introduce me to guests as 'My senior medical adviser'; and my copy of his collected poems is thus inscribed.

Peter Hughes remarks that Mark was a creature of habit and that he never sought wider horizons. Travel was narrowly circumscribed: he only once went abroad; he would not accompany the Hunt to away matches; Exeter-Oxford-Shrewsbury-Cumbria was his invariable axis. He occupied the same cramped and crudely furnished flat, pervaded by a slight smell of escaping gas, virtually throughout his time at Shrewsbury. Visitors encountered a domestic panorama of washing, drying on clothes horses, together with empty Mars Bar boxes and empty bottles of gin, whose contents had been lavished on pupils and colleagues respectively. Yet Mark always seemed deeply content.

In one of his poems, *Opting Out*, Mark accuses himself of wasted talent.

> Around the age of twenty-five
> (it's quite a common story)
> this former scholar ceased to strive
> for intellectual glory.
> an artist too, until he took
> a similar decision,
> he nowadays prefers to look
> and not record the vision.

A bachelor and disinclined
to swell the population
or sacrifice his peace of mind
in wanton procreation
he means to live and hopes to die
by passion untormented
a pig from Epicurus' sty
ingloriously contented.

And only on the Judgement Day
found wanting in the balance,
will he discover what's to pay
for burying his talents.

Mark had been a painter of considerable promise, and was a very competent musician, a flautist in the Orchestra and a member of Concert Choir. But few could doubt that his supreme talent was as a poet. That his field was much infinitely wider than that of Salopian satire was evident when, in retirement, he produced his volume of *Latinised Hymns*, in which he translated over three hundred well-known hymns into Latin with rhyme and identical metre, enabling them to be sung to the original tune. It was a formidable achievement; and Mark's final illness was brightened when, having sent a copy to Dr Rowan Williams, then still Archbishop of Canterbury, he received a careful and substantial reply, commenting as expertly as one would expect, and with profound admiration, on the quality of the translations and hailing him as the worthy son of a distinguished father. Indeed Mark has a strong claim to be considered the finest composer of Latin verses the country has produced in his generation. Many of his poems were written both in Latin and in English. Latin was sometimes the original version, and it is a great pity that the decline in the teaching of Latin in schools restricts the number of people who are able to appreciate the comparison, and the facility with which Mark moves from one language to another. It was very moving – and entirely appropriate – that one of his Latin hymn versions was sung at his funeral in Newton Reigny.

It seems equally appropriate to conclude this chapter by returning to the subject of verse. There was one topic in his poetry in which Mark showed a deep and serious interest: and that was the school *Carmen*. This was composed by Dr Alington in 1911, as Mark records, during the course of a single morning. Mark admired it greatly, deeply deplored its falling into disuse, wrote many comments and versions in the same metre, (thereby exactly reversing the procedure followed in *Latinised* hymns) and provided a valuable translation into English. All of the following verses conform to that original metre.

Of Alington:

Inspiration found the Master
            at his breakfast seated;
Luncheon – few could labour faster-
            saw the work completed;
Shrewsbury's Song, which we inherit.
            marvel of invention,
one which might be thought to merit
more of our attention.

And the Carmen translated into English:

To King Edward from the loyal
            sons of his foundation
hymns are due, and to his royal
            Sister salutation.
Let us, friends, acknowledge proudly
            king and queen as founders,
and with 'Hail Sabrina!' loudly
            fill the fields around us.
Floreat Salopia!

Next be praise to those accorded
            who were here before us,
one who crowned a life much lauded
            with a death more glorious,
and another (ever splendid
            his renown) who teaches
humankind from whence descended
            theirs and every species.
Floreat Salopia!

Others mourn headmasters plundered
            almost ere they've seen them:
we boast three who spanned a hundred
            years and more between them.
In their day Salopian learning
            (all must know the story)
set both Cam and Isis burning
            with Sabrina's glory.
Floreat Salopia.!

Scholars long by cramps vexatious
            cabin'd and frustrated

from their town to fields more spacious
        finally migrated.
Sites may change, but not ambition:
        ours has never faltered;
and our forebears' high tradition
        we maintain unaltered.
Floreat Salopia!

On our hill, to serve our Mother
        fame through art we'll give her,
fame in learning, as we love her,
        fame on field and river.
praise on praise be hers, and never
        may we fail to seek it,
praise that shall be heard wherever
        British tongues can speak it.
Floreat Salopia!

(For readers who may wish to study Mark's accomplished technique more closely, I have placed the Latin original and Mark's English translation side by side in an Appendix).

At the dinner celebrating Mark's sixtieth birthday and consequent retirement, Anthony Bowen and David Allcock sought to honour the poet in verses of their own. Appropriately Anthony provided both a Latin and an English version, of which the latter follows:

Assist me, Muse, as I embark
upon propemptic praise of Mark.
For thirty-something years, well nigh,
MM has cast a beady eye
on boys and masters at the Schools
behaving variously like mules,
chiding in chief all jumped-up jacks
in office with well-versed attacks
of wit and grace and elegance
and deftly-turned intelligence:
a second Epicurus he
for Puritanic modesty.
and first for sober-headedness
sharing with the bachelors' mess.
Of Shrewsbury's conscience he the prick
is now also the inner tick.

Farewell, most cherishable man.
At least these slender verses scan,
But whether they are up to mark
I leave to others. Up, to Mark!

David Allcock added his contribution:

We salute a young man we call 'Mort'
Along with the thousands he taught.
From him – Lim'ricks pour,
We clamour for more,
As we honour the friend we call 'Mort'

We all have a friend we call 'Mark'
Who thought it would be a good lark
To be quite perverse
In sharp pointed verse
To keep the School up to the mark.

He roams the Salopian hills,
His verses evaporate ills.
We pray that M.M.
Will continue to *pen*
And provoke us with humorous thrills.

We think Morty's poems very clever
But company soon he will sever.
As Mortification's
A pleasing sensation,
We hope it continues for ever.

(David appended a rubric: Bicycle clips and trainers will be worn; whistles shall be blown at random intervals.)

Ten years later, at a private family gathering to celebrate Mark's 70th birthday, in June 2004, his younger brother Edward read some verses, entirely worthy of, and no less brilliant, than those of his elder sibling:

Today we celebrate, with solemn toast,
An elder bro, of whom we proudly boast
That in the space of seven short decades
He mastered many unexpected trades:
Fast bowler, poet, landscapist and gunner,
Then flautist, pedagogue, long-distance runner.
All this must now be set out in large print
To fill a truly Marcan Septuagint-
In which there will be plenty to include
That would by some be deemed a trifle rude,
Were it not veiled, as Gibbon might have sung,
In decent darkness of a learned tongue.
But none need be offended by scatology
When it's demurely shrouded in philology.

So let us don our rosiest-tinted specs
To look back on these annos LXX
And pray that yet more glorious than them
Are those still rolling on towards MM.

It was typical of Mark that he was accustomed to respond to any of the richly deserved tributes which were paid to him by saying that he found their subject unrecognizable. A long-established tradition in the Common Room is that when any of its members are leaving, such tributes and responses are arranged in ascending order of the seniority of the recipient. In 1994 Mark's speech was eagerly awaited, but to the immense disappointment of everyone present, the meeting was cut short, just as he rose to his feet, by the sound of the school bell, summoning everyone to the end-of-term assembly. 'Whatever I would have said', Mark interjected, 'consider it said.'

Willie Jones, in a superb article in *The Salopian* No 146 (Summer 2010) attempts to describe and evaluate the enigma that was Mark. They were friends for many years, and even after they both left Shrewsbury, Willie for Japan and Mark for Cumbria, they maintained a regular correspondence. But Willie, perhaps of all his friends the one most likely to be able to provide the definitive appraisal of Mark, concludes that he was unwilling to express what he really thought about God and man. Though ever ready to comment with his brilliant and light-hearted wit on the vagaries and absurdities of the Salopian scene, Mark was extremely reticent about himself. Even to his closest friends he remained 'something of a puzzle, even perhaps a paradox'.

Michael Hall (FMH)

Michael Hall played a major part in Salopian affairs for a over a quarter of a century as Head of Mathematics and Head of Basic Year (more precisely for twenty-six years in Basic Year, of which he served as Head of the organisation for twenty, and twenty-nine years as Head of Mathematics). Educated at Manchester Grammar School and having taught previously at Dulwich College, he was initially a little suspicious of public schools and particularly boarding schools; and he made an assurance that there was no longer any corporal punishment or private fagging by boys at Shrewsbury a condition of accepting his appointment. Both in the classroom and on expeditions he came into contact with all levels of the School, but because of the much more public nature of Basic Year and the fact that every member of the School had been involved in it for a whole year, more Salopians came to associate him and remember him in connection with the latter rather than the former sphere.

However, this assessment of his balance of activities was seriously inaccurate and greatly irritated Michael. He was always quite clear and absolutely insistent that his main priority and responsibility lay in the classroom. His colleagues and pupils, together with the distinguished record of his department during his tenure, all testify to the fact that he was a superb Head of Mathematics. Donald Wright, in his foreword to Michael's memoirs, noted that in the eight years after Michael's appointment the number of sixth-form mathematicians grew from fifty to over one hundred. Michael gathered round him a team of talented and devoted mathematicians, whom he both consulted and co-ordinated meticulously. A first-class mathematician himself, he retained a lifelong devotion to his Cambridge college, Trinity; and he had sampled, but rejected, a career in mathematical research. While at Shrewsbury he produced and published a fine course in Abstract Algebra.

A second danger in assessing Michael's contribution at Shrewsbury is to allow reminiscences about his colourful and eccentric character to obscure the very firm principles upon which his vocation as a schoolmaster was based and his total devotion to it. The stories about him are legion, and many of them are extremely humorous, but behind them lies his absolute commitment to Churchill's as House Tutor, where he was resident for many years, a period commensurate in length with the two responsibilities already mentioned, a commitment which continued even after retirement and which was appropriately commemorated in 2012, on the initiative of Richard Hudson, the current housemaster, by the installation of a commemorative window at the boys' entrance to the house. A second area in which Michael showed equal commitment was as a Sixth Form tutor. He was a very popular choice and he took immense care in advising his tutees, monitoring their progress and their university applications, writing their reports, both internal and external, and meeting their parents, many of whom were astonished by the thoroughness of the appraisals they had received from him, which in turn revealed how well he knew and how much he cared about their sons. Since he often had more than half-a-dozen tutees from each of the Upper and Lower Sixth this imposed a very significant and additional pastoral and administrative load upon him, which he willingly accepted.

His interests and his expertise ranged far beyond the confines of Mathematics and Fieldcraft. He was a connoisseur and enthusiastic collector of wine and amassed an impressive 'cellar' which he kept in a shed, adapted for that purpose, behind his house. With typical generosity he bequeathed the contents to his colleagues in the Common Room. He held regular wine-tastings, and his enthusiasm led at least one of his tutees later to pursue a career in the wine trade. He insisted upon, but did not on every occasion meticulously observe, the precept that one must not 'swig', an injunction upon which Mark Mortimer made a typically satirical comment in verse:

> When Hall instructs us not to SWIG
>   his aim is rather off
> He might as well dissuade a pig
>   from emptying its trough.

Michael was an 'opera buff', with an encyclopaedic knowledge of operatic plots and characters, especially those of Mozart and Verdi and, not surprisingly for a mathematician, was also a great admirer of Bach. On one occasion, when I accompanied him to the Opera in Vienna, he applauded so long and enthusiastically at the conclusion of the performance, that the auditorium had emptied, and the principals and orchestra had gone home, but the spear-carriers and the fan-bearers felt in duty bound to respond, in the umpteenth curtain-call, to the distant sound of clapping from 'the gods'.

Michael continued to demonstrate and share the breadth of his interests during his retirement. He regularly circulated a series of typed commentaries, each headed *Joie de Vivre* to his circle of friends. The topics included *Ten favourite buildings*, with reasons for his choice; *The Three Greatest Mathematicians*, justifying his inclusion of Gauss with Archimedes and Newton; *Scary Frontier Crossings* – he had experienced many, on one occasion having been suspiciously sniffed and ferociously pursued by an Alsatian guard-dog from a railway platform upon which he had ventured, back to his compartment; and *Media Mirth*, a selection of articles in the press which had caused him to chuckle.

Michael was hospitable and generous to a fault. His door was always open to an endless procession of joyful guests (and he insisted on the importance of having a front door of good quality). Colleagues and other friends, tutees and Basic Year Instructors eagerly presented themselves at that front door, forming an endless procession of would-be diners. All were required to wash up and sign the visitors' book before they departed. Adult guests were exhorted to 'come early and have a drink before supper'. The longest interval which I can remember between arrival for the pre-prandial drink and the appearance of the first course on the table was four and a quarter hours, from which it will appear that although Michael was an expert cook, his timing and the logistics of the meal were not always impeccable. The invitation often was to 'a very simple supper', but that description did not preclude the appearance of six, seven or even eight courses, and some of these banquets became legendary. Selby Martin kept the menu for a dinner Michael gave in 1995. It consisted of: Olives, Seafood Platter, Poached Salmon, Roast fillet of beef Lace Baskets 'avec les deux glaces de la maison', les fruits tropicaux, Chantilly garnie, and cheese: and Selby comments that it was 'a menu which would have strained the abilities of Gordon Ramsay himself'. On the occasion of the Queen's Golden Jubilee in 2002 Michael invited forty guests to a buffet luncheon in his garden, during which he proposed four toasts, to the Queen herself, to the Duke of Edinburgh, to the Prince of Wales and to the School Catering Manager, the last of whom was about to retire. The inclusiveness of that recognition was typical of Michael.

It was also typical of Michael's kindness and thoughtfulness; and he was as sensitive as he was kind. For many years he recognized the friendship which a group of Matrons had displayed towards his widowed Mother, by taking them annually to the dramatic production at the Ludlow Festival. He was a devoted son to her, never failing to send her a sequence of postcards from every stage of his far-flung travels, even though the famed illegibility of his handwriting meant that the pride and delight with which she received them were clouded by inability to decipher their content. Indeed, he was a great man for postcards, dispatching them on every occasion (and there were many) on which he thought it appropriate to express appreciation. There were, however, occasional lapses in that characteristic sensitivity. As Michael served coffee to his mixed company of guests after one of his magnificent repasts, the handle came off the coffee cup as he handed it to one of the seated lady guests, and the whole contents fell into her lap forming a small pool in her skirt. Appalled, Michael rushed into the kitchen and returned with a dishcloth. 'It hasn't gone on the sofa, has it?', he enquired with breathless anxiety.

He was an indefatigable traveller. In addition to his enterprises in Basic Year, he led trips in the summer holidays, accompanied by colleagues and boys, almost every year. Starting with a series of Alpine trips, he ventured further afield to Turkey (a favourite, visited several times), Syria, Jordan, Egypt and South India, Eastern Europe and the Baltic States, Mount Kenya and the Karakorum Himalayas, Borneo, the Guyanas and the Caribbean. Donald Wright, in his preface to *Around the World in Forty Years,* noted that Michael, 'soaked to the skin, celebrated his sixtieth birthday with a colleague and thirteen Salopians in the Guyanan jungle at the foot of the Kaieteur Falls, twice as high, 825 feet, as the Victoria Falls'.

For many years, an association with Aiglon College enabled him to lead a skiing party to Villars in Switzerland in the Christmas holidays. The number of those participating grew, like Topsy, until finally it exceeded sixty, eventually including not only his colleagues and pupils, but members of their families too. On one notable occasion, he persevered with his plans, although warned at Dover that there was a general rail strike in France, and that no trains were running there. Miraculously, he did in fact manage to find a couple of trains that were still in service and also discovered viable sleeping accommodation for his party in an empty train in the sidings of the Gare du Nord; but the full extent of his leadership qualities was demonstrated when, finding that the Paris Metro was running, but that the turnstiles were closed, he issued the *quasi* -Napoleonic command: "We're going over". All sixty-six of us did; and astonishingly we completed our journey, arriving at our destination only seven hours late.

Upon retirement, when he felt that he was no longer qualified to take school trips, he joined in a series of less adventurous and certainly more civilised Easter trips with colleagues, to Austria, Slovakia, Poland, Switzerland, the Czech Republic, the Harz mountains, Spain and Portugal. But the spirit of adventure never left him: during the week in which he died, in February 2005, he was preparing to set off on a Tall Ships expedition.

One of Michael's idiosyncrasies was his marked predilection for cats. A notice beside that hospitable front door warned the visitor to 'Beware of the Cat'. He always kept one cat and sometimes two. The most famous of his cats was called Atatürk, after the Turkish nationalist leader. Atatürk not only featured as the name of a desirable prize in Basic Year, but also, to the mystification of the candidates, in mathematical problems which Michael set in the Entrance Scholarship papers. His cats had to adapt to the necessity of frequent trips to the cattery, the inevitable consequence of Michael's regular absences; he took immense trouble to retrieve them, if they strayed; and when he acquired two cats, they did not get along. But these experiences did not destroy Michael's devotion to cats. On several occasions he demonstrated the extent of his devotion by dressing up as a cat himself, having hired a cat suit to appear in some stage production or as a candidate in a balloon debate.

Michael's Land Rover, PER 65, one of the 1955 long wheelbase series, was also a renowned feature of his entourage, a vehicle in which hundreds of Salopians must have travelled. Its 25th and 33rd birthdays were accordingly celebrated with due ceremony. It was decorated with bunting, and libations were both poured over the vehicle and consumed by its occupants, while its owner drove round the Site, continuously sounding its horn. On one of these occasions Michael chose to drive along the narrow path immediately beside the windows of the Pentagon, in which, at the same time, a Housemasters' meeting happened to be taking place. Unknown to Michael and his guests, the senators happened to be discussing the perils of excessive alcoholic consumption, but several masters who were his passengers, already somewhat embarrassed by the exuberance of the celebration, realising where they were going, and with their future careers in mind, quickly discarded their charged glasses and are said to have prostrated themselves, out of sight, on the floor of PER 65.

Mark Mortimer's opinion of the vehicle was unfavourable:

Fr-d's vehicle, so we are told,
is a third of a century old.
and it isn't what I'd
recommend for a ride
being crowded and bumpy and cold.

Michael could be entirely un-selfconscious, even on the most public and most formal occasions. Charged with firing the shotgun (in the days before it fell victim to Health and Safety Regulations) marking the five-minute, two-minute and one-minute lead-up to the start of each division of bumpers, and arriving rather late on one occasion, he fired it immediately beneath Kingsland Bridge, causing great consternation among the crowds assembled upon it to witness the races. On another occasion, after the races had finished, the Mayor and the Headmaster, who were formally dressed, were approached by a local press photographer. Michael was photographed with them, wearing shorts and a T-shirt on which the figure of an orang-outang had been printed. On yet another occasion, having fallen dramatically off his bicycle and been consigned to hospital, he announced in a staff meeting, on his return, that he was holding a sweepstake on the number of stitches he had subsequently required; colleagues were invited to record their guess on a piece of paper which he duly circulated, and Michael kept interrupting the proceedings with whispered injunctions to 'keep passing it round.' At the conclusion of the Heads of Faculties Meeting at the beginning of the Michaelmas Term, he was accustomed to offer refreshments in the form of exotic food and drink, the former not entirely prepossessing at first sight, which he had purchased in equally exotic locations, during his summer travels. Only the more adventurous remained to sample them: the wiser heads fled precipitately.

Michael is remembered for his speech mannerisms, which are regularly repeated even to this day. 'Micky Mouse' was a derisive expression, used as an adjective to describe any organisation or arrangement which he considered was not up to standard. He was also meticulous in preserving the distinction between a supposition or hypothesis on the one hand and an established fact on the other. Frequently he would begin a statement with the words, 'I suspect ...' but conclude it with an almost agonised admission: 'I suspect ... but I'm afraid I don't *know*'. On one notable occasion, however, when one of his pupils had spectacularly distinguished himself in the Mathematics examinations, he announced triumphantly to the Headmaster and his fellow Heads of Faculties, 'I expected him to do better than I expected.'

In retirement, in 2000, Michael collected the statistics of his activities in his forty years of schoolmastering. Although he introduced them as some 'useless and inconsequential data', he proudly recorded them as follows:

Number of periods taught:	35,000
Number of Preps (Dulwich) and Top Schools (Shrewsbury) set and usually marked (1 unit is Top Schools for a whole set)	15,000
Number of different boys taught (many for 2 or more years)	1,600
Number of duty nights in Churchill's	2,100
Number of House swimming sessions taken	1,000
Number of Extra Lessons taken	12
Number of KH duties undertaken	200
Number of penals set (when it was allowed) (record was 130 in one bedroom)	Lots:
Number of boys encouraged in 'Benjies'	15,000
Number of boys encouraged in 'The Tucks'	15,000
Number of boys involved in Basic Year	3,500
Number of boys taken skiing	1,000
Number of boys taken abroad on 'Hall's Tours'	300
Number of different mountains climbed with boys	About 100
Number of years (sic) spent under canvas	About 4

Also in retirement, for a period of about ten years, Michael came to relish an annual tradition of a week, spent in the company of two or three friends, in the comfort of a Devon hotel, between the conclusion of the Michaelmas Term and the approach of Christmas. One of my last memories of him, only two months before his death, and very poignant in retrospect, is seeing him, cocktail in hand (remarkably he claimed he had never encountered a cocktail until he went there) reading a memoir of the Revd Canon F.A. Simpson, of Trinity College, Cambridge, entitled *The Last Eccentric*.

In his address at Michael's memorial service, Selby Martin referred to a letter which Michael had written, at the end of his last term, and addressed 'To my loved relatives and best friends at Shrewsbury School', in which he wrote:

Above all I have been allowed to do my part in bringing up to manhood some of the next generation and, I hope, giving them a sense of the true values, with a mixture of fun thrown in. A schoolmaster reaps his reward only after many years, when his charges mature and are doing their bit for the World, and fulfilling themselves. I am beginning now to see this, as I keep in touch with boys that I have known, and this gives me huge satisfaction.

It is a touching valediction and an eloquent expression of the spirit in which Michael pursued his vocation.

Michael was a 'larger than life' character who richly deserved the widespread respect and affection in which he was held. I consider it appropriate that the final tribute to him in this chapter, should be that recorded by Donald Wright, who appointed him, recognised his outstanding qualities, and gave him unfailing support as he developed them to their full potential:

His attitudes, intrepid and generous, have been without self-seeking. What has mattered most to him, and not only in high mountains and other wonderful places, is the extra dimension.

CHAPTER THIRTEEN

SALOPIAN SLANG, SATIRE AND MOTTO

One of the characteristic features of many traditional public schools was the development and use of a private language, the school slang. Its very existence indicated that this was a place set apart and new members of the school community, both pupils and, to a lesser extent, teachers, had to make a deliberate effort to learn this new language if they were to understand and cope efficiently with everyday conversations and occurrences. In some schools this private language was very extensive – the Winchester *Notions* provide the prime example. Shrewsbury too, at the beginning of the period with which we are concerned, had well over a hundred such slang expressions. One of the signs that such schools were abandoning their isolation and opening up to the outside world was the gradual decline of this school slang. Only about a dozen examples of the traditional slang have survived these changes, but around this hard core a peripheral collection of ephemeral expressions is constantly being renewed. Several attempts have been made, in the *Salopian Newsletter*, to investigate and record Salopian slang. A preliminary list was included in edition No 101 in 1987; helpful additional comment was provided by Anthony Jones in 1990 (No 106); a more comprehensive list was collated by Michael Charlesworth and Colin Leach in 1997, together with a subsequent brief addendum; and still more recent slang was explained in 2007 (No 141) by Chris Jamieson. I acknowledge my debt to all these contributors. However, I have not found any discussion which treats the slang vocabulary by topics. I hope that such an approach helps to convey the atmosphere of the place, and accordingly that it what I have attempted to do in the following paragraphs.

Two elements of the Salopian School slang are constant: the first is the unique and elaborate vocabulary of the Royal Shrewsbury School Hunt. This is fully described in the appropriate chapter. The second generally stable element is the collection of names ascribed to school buildings and locations. Of course, it is debatable whether some of the following examples should be considered proper names or genuine slang, nor have all of them been simultaneously in use, but my criterion has been to include those which would require explanation to a visitor. A current Salopian walking from Severn Hill or Ridgemount towards the *Main School Bs* (Bs being the customary Salopian abbreviation for 'buildings'), would first have to climb *The S-bend* from the Lower to the Upper Common. (The clump of trees outside Oldham's, *The Oasis*, has been removed and the massive *Science Bs* have taken its place.) He would pass *The Gallows*, the lamp-post outside Oldham's Hall, and enter the *Moser Precinct*, with the *Lyle Bs* on the right. On the left he might notice the figures of *Philomathes* and *Polymathes*, representing the lover of learning and the educated man, or the 'novice' and the 'finished' Salopian, set into the wall of the Moser Bs. He might see Sixth Formers emerging, after morning break, from *Quod*, their common room, on the right. He would pass *Oliver's Egg*, originally an egg-shaped area of grass, but now a brick-enclosed pond. If he had attended Chapel earlier that morning, he would no longer have referred to it as the *Dix barn*, nor, when he looked towards the transept would he have realised that it once accommodated *The Hen Coop*, the area to which ladies visiting chapel were customarily confined. Emerging from Chapel, he would see *The Masters' Garden*, and he might have time to walk 'behind' the Main School Building to glance at the magnificent view over the town from *The Queen's Terrace*, inaugurated in 1952. Then walking past the façade of the School Building, *Castor and Pollux*, the two trees on the lawn and *Romulus and Remus*, the two lamps which flanked the clock tower, familiar to Salopians of previous generations, having all been removed, he would turn right, passing the *Darwin Statue*, cross *The Drum*, continue up *Central* towards *The Alibin*. (Alternatively he might, of course, having passed the Masters' Garden, have turned right immediately and have taken the parallel route up *The Lane* leading towards Ingram's. But he would neither have called or recognised the route as such, as the hedge alongside it has long since been removed.) He would then turn left, walking past the hexagonal building known as *The Pentagon*, added to the Alington Hall in 1968. Turning right again, he would rejoin the alternative route and stand in front of *The Crush Hall*, formerly illuminated by its exterior lamp, *Apollo*. If no assembly requires his attention, he might glance over at the *Moss Gates* and *The Kennedy Bs*, observe *Philip Sidney* on his memorial plinth but turn right in search of refreshment end enter The School Shop, *The Grot Shop*. Skirting the reconstituted *Pier* on his right, Ingram's on his left and then *Senior* (the 1st XI football pitch) on his right again, perhaps remembering (if he was sufficiently senior in the School) that the new Emma Darwin Hall had once contained *T.C.* (the former Sixth Form Club), he might find time for a little music practice in *The Maidment*, before walking down to *K.H.* (Kingsland Hall) for a well-deserved lunch.

The words formerly used to describe people, activities in the classroom, conduct, sanctions, rewards and privileges, emotions, dismissive remarks, sporting and military activities, school routine and traditions, might generally be acknowledged to fall within a narrower definition of 'slang'. The new boy (a term now frowned upon as discriminatory and mildly pejorative) at Shrewsbury would discover a world in which he was a *doul* (or 'slave') liable to be called upon to answer *doul calls* and required to run errands and perform menial duties for the monitors. Not until he became a *two-year old* would he be released from such servitude, and for the first year he would be referred to as *a new scum*. He would be in awe of *praepostors* (school prefects), he would be expected to listen to the announcements of *Hall Constables* at tea, who would traditionally end their proclamations with the words, 'God save the Queen and down with the Radicals' and then prepare his work *(Top Schools)* diligently for the *Brushers* (masters) who taught him. He would begin to refer to Day Boys as *skytes* (barbarians) and learn that the handyman in each house was called a *John*. He would compete, both in the classroom and on the sports field, with the experts, the so-called *tweaks*.

In the classroom he might find it difficult to understand, *grip on to* the harder concepts. If he did particularly well he might be awarded an *alpha-tail*, a high commendation. *Gats* (lots of) *bumf* (paper) would be required. There would be many *slips* (short tests). He would occasionally be *shipped* (punished for unsatisfactory work) by being given *penals* (a common word for a sheet of paper on which lines were to be written out); more seriously, he might be given a *blue penal* (only his Housemaster kept a supply of those, so this would involve an unpleasant interview). There would be *Top Schools*, set work to be completed in the House, each evening. He would be in trouble if he *cabbed* (cheated) or if he *paved* (wrote translations in) his texts. His best recourse would be to *sap* (work hard); he might indeed be *wrecked for work*, or *stiff for sap*, finding that there was too much to do. For lighter relief he might be encouraged by one of the *brushers* to learn a *Spell*, a short passage of poetry, and stand on a chair to recite it.

A number of slang words describe social conduct. *to bag* and later *to grip*, *to tox* (a verb thought to be of Liverpudlian origin), *to lift* and *to finger* all describe petty and usually temporary pilfering; *to rot* is to tease, *to scale on* is to make sarcastic comments about people or situations, *to ram off* is to cut appointments and obligations. *To mill* is to rag about; *to sell* is to sneak; *to grease* or *groize* is to ingratiate oneself. *Lift*, as a noun, is cheek, and *to be lifty* is to be cheeky. *To reduce* is to cause someone to weep.

Sanctions for breaches of discipline included *Extra Lesson* (now called *SD)* which involved an interview with the Headmaster, *biffing*, being beaten with a light mini-cricket bat; being *Headroomed*, being beaten or slippered by the House Monitors and being *Postored* (much more serious), being caned by the Praepostors. The final sanction was *to be bunked* or *to be ruxed* – that is, to be expelled (one might, much less seriously, also be *ruxed out of the room* for misbehaviour in class). Another sanction was to send a boy to *stand on Doctor's grass*, outside the Headmaster's study, with the attendant risk that the Headmaster might be prompted to enquire the cause of this apparition. Rewards included being sent to the Housemaster or Headmaster to show up good work, a *Merit Extra* (long defunct), and among the privileges *Long Lie* (permission to remain in bed during First Lesson) and *First Day* (permission to leave early at the end of term), both now similarly long defunct. Sporting successes might be celebrated by a feast, or *Slay*, particularly after success on the river, and often held in a bedroom.

A whole range of emotions and feelings was expressed in Salopian slang. *He was black* conveyed that someone had exhibited furious anger or displeasure; *blitched* meant sleepy; *bushed* indicated loss of temper, *braced* pleasurable satisfaction, *stirred* being physically hurt and to *wazz* (a very common expression) meant to be nervous.

Adolescents are notorious for making hurtful and dismissive remarks. Among them were the following slang versions: *Face off*, would mean 'Get lost', (or its riper equivalent), to someone who was 'in your face' with a similar injunction, *Tag off* meaning 'you're not wanted in our group'. *Bush off* meant 'hold on to your temper', and, most commonly heard of all *Spec off*, was addressed to someone who was expressing unrealistic aspirations. An unpleasant and unpopular person might be described as a *grimmer*, *a loather* or, more recently, as an *eesh*.

Apart from the distinctive vocabulary of the Hunt, the following expressions might be heard in sporting activity: *to tow*, referred to running in general; *to tub* meant to boat on the river. One might *ruxed* out of a team; a fixture might be cancelled or *scragged*; an exhortation to make a final effort, especially in running, might be delivered in the phrase, *Bring it in*. Most notorious and potentially embarrassing was the word *erection*, denoting an informal soccer practice. One can imagine the stunned perplexity of the master of a visiting XI, who, descending from his coach on arrival, was greeted by the School Captain of Football, who politely enquired whether he would like one before lunch! In the days when the CCF was compulsory, it, too, attracted its little group of slang terms, *Beano* being a bayonet, *Corps Fugs* denoting military uniform and *Corps saps* being a description of military enthusiasts.

And then there are the distinctive Salopian institutions: the *Colour Exam* (distinctive but not exclusive) in which new boys were tested not only on house colours, but also on a much wider range of conventional school lore; the *Fasti* (again distinctive but not exclusive), the word used to describe the termly calendar; *Brown Book*, the School register of the current term or year, which in our period has successively been black, grey, brown, orange and blue; *lock-ups*, after which one might not leave the house without signing a book; *swills*, obligatory cold showers in the earlier days; and *capping*, the gesture required to acknowledge a master, when approaching or passing him, performed by placing a cupped hand behind the ear in order to raise the already non-existent boater (which used to be known as a *basher*) and now itself, as a practice, entirely defunct.

In the 1980s another small group of slang words came into common use: *grots* for sweets; *brats* for new boys, and *brat bash* for the practice of teasing them; *to veg* to describe those who were glued to the television; *zogs* were computer buffs, and together with *spods* the word was also used to describe those who were considered oddballs, weirdos or freaks.

After the turn of the century slang became sophisticated and added new targets to those with which it had formerly been concerned. The sophistication lay in the importance of the pronunciation (or equally often in the mispronunciation of the word) which could be used to express a meaning which was the opposite. Traditional themes were retained: *scrowl* described a pilferer; *gimp* described an excessively hard worker; but a little group of slang words concerned with lying became prominent, *yoi*, *boosh* and *waff*. More attention was paid to a person's physical appearance: a *barry* was a remarkably tall person, who might be greeted with cries of '*Waay*', while a distinctly stocky individual was a '*chode*'. Other new slang words included *lead*, used to describe a poor joke or a person notorious for his addiction to them; *beef* referred to a person or thing that was unimportant or trivial. An *HSR* (Hot Sausage Roll), was a favourite order in the *Grot Shop* sometimes eclipsing *Shop teas*, which had been commonly awarded by masters as a recognition of a boy's good performance in competitive sport or in Basic Year while finally *Schweff*, a term unlikely to have found prominence in the Shrewsbury of the 1950s, has come to mean someone who actively pursues members of the opposite sex.

While adolescents retain their linguistic inventiveness, new slang expressions tend to be rather more ephemeral and the overall use of slang is in decline, a process which the arrival of girls has tended to accelerate.

Satire

If slang provides the vocabulary in which Salopians traditionally express themselves, this expression has not uncommonly been couched in a satirical vein, so much so that a propensity to gentle satire might possibly be identified as a Salopian characteristic. Throughout the period with which this book is concerned, there has been a strong satirical streak in Salopian domestic literature. Its origins are usually attributed to the remarkable coincidence that four boys with an interest in and talent for satire, happened to come to the same school at the same time, and to develop lasting friendships. When they reached the Sixth Form their views and talents found expression in *The Salopian*, the School's official magazine. They found an ally in Laurence Le Quesne, then a young master, who protected them from the fulminations of his colleagues and encouraged 'the breeze of originality' which then began to ruffle its pages. Considerable significance has been attributed to their association; perhaps rather greater than the participants might own. Alex Went notes that this collaboration was

an early example of that intellectual give-and-take between pupil and teacher, which would come to be the mainstay of the educational philosophy of succeeding generations

and Laurence's future wife Mary, then still his fiancée, was warned that she was about to marry 'the man who was responsible for the 1960s'! Laurence is careful to point out that this was a breeze of anarchy not of protest; all four fitted well and participated fully in school life. Their satire was not aimed and delivered with deadly or hostile conviction:

they found it possible to be comfortable and happy within the school establishment, even though they enjoyed taking the mickey out of it and tweaking its nose occasionally: they were gamins, not demonstrators

but he recognises that *The Salopian* of the mid-fifties was in its way the incubator of the *Private Eye* to come; and it was principally their association in *Private Eye* which linked the four in later years.

Richard Ingrams (1950-55) and Willie Rushton (1950-56) were successive Heads of House in Churchill's. Ingrams was later to edit *Private Eye*, to contribute both to *That Was The Week That Was* and to *I'm Sorry I haven't a Clue*. Later he edited *The Oldie*. Willie Rushton, who was an immensely talented cartoonist and also contributed to *Private Eye* and *That Was The Week That Was*, was said by contemporaries to have 'highly developed antennae for the absurdity of the human scene'. His cartoon of two Old Salopian fathers, with their families, meeting again on Speech Day, has entered Salopian legend. Among Ingrams' and Rushton's targets were earnestness, strenuousness and pretentiousness; to this end they founded *The Pseuds Club*, whose members sported a black tie on which a beta minus was embroidered. The Club had no functions, but the tie made a statement. It proclaimed the principle that one shouldn't be seen to strive too much. Christopher Booker was in Ridgemount (1951-56). With Ingrams and Rushton he co-founded and subsequently contributed scripts for *That Was The Week That Was* and for *Not so much a Programme*. He continues to be a regular contributor to *The Sunday Telegraph* and *The Spectator*. Paul Foot was in School House (1951-56). Laurence Le Quesne, who knew him well, noted that Foot demonstrated a streak of radicalism and a moral intensity that was absent, during their schooldays, from the attitudes of his three contemporaries. Foot was a praepostor but also a strong opponent of corporal punishment in the School. Later, he was a contributor to the *Daily Mirror* for many years.

Whilst at Shrewsbury, the group also published *The Wallopian*, which they described as a 'scurrilous lampoon' of the Salopian scene. It still has its successor today, rather less tastefully entitled *The Falopian*, with a shadowy editorial team drawn from the ranks of the School's intelligentsia, appearing, in true *Samizdad* style, at irregular intervals. Satire has been kept alive and well in the Common Room, most prominently by Mark Mortimer, whose poems have been collated and edited by Philip Lapage in a book published until the title *Mort*. One of Mark's subjects, appropriately enough, was *Private Eye*, and at one stage copies were being sold weekly, in the Masters' Garden, as the boys came out of morning chapel. Mark's tongue-in-cheek response to the practice was as follows:

     Pluck it Out

Through Chapel doors flung open wide
       Their orisons complete
The scholars come, well fortified
       Life's challenges to meet.

Yet see them all, as they emerge,
       run on with outstretched hands,
To where, upon the grassy verge,
       (Alas!) the Tempter stands;

Who there purveys to young and old
       Corruption, filth and lies,
Exchanging for ill-gotten gold
       His evil merchandise.

Vile peddler! Was it not enough
       To hawk such filth around,
That you must even flog the stuff
       On Consecrated Ground?

It was followed, the week after, by an answer to the question, 'But please, Sir, what is *Private Eye?*'

A pornographic magazine,
So tasteless, cheap and lewd,
Salacious, blasphemous, obscene,
Wet, tedious and crude,

Obnoxious, prejudiced, unfair,
Malicious, vile and cruel,
That one is forced to wonder where
Its authors went to school.

But it seems that the Salopian Satirists were not ashamed of their School and their schooldays. Willie Rushton accepted the Presidency of the Old Salopian Club and both he and Richard Ingrams returned to the School on official occasions, Rushton to open the new Art School in June 1976 and Ingrams in June 2001, when the editors of the broadsheet *Public Nose* were introduced to him. Ingrams was photographed with them, holding a copy of their latest edition; the boys brandished copies of that week's *Private Eye*. Credit all round but particularly to the Salopian regime in the 1950s, often portrayed as the last redoubt of the die-hard traditionalists, which allowed the satirical tradition to burgeon, survive and ultimately to flourish.

The School Motto: Intus si recte, ne labora

T.P. Mannix (M 1934-39) inaugurated a learned discussion in *The Salopian Newsletter* in 1998, on the obscure origin and meaning of the School motto, which, he confessed, continued to trouble him. Applying strict parsing and analysis, he failed to discover a satisfactory translation and wondered whether, if the phrase were subjected to the tenets of Kennedy's *Revised Latin Primer*, it would not in fact be translatable.

Professor Colin Leach (O 1945-51) agreed that *ne labora* was bad Latin, although there was an example in Vergil of a similar usage. He suggested that, taken together with *recte*, it appeared to be 'a sadly crude translation of a Greek proverb'. He suggested that the translation 'If you are all right in your heart, there's no need to worry' might serve. He has heard of other contexts in which the motto has been used and he suspects that it may not have been adopted for the exclusive use of the School.

Mark Mortimer (Master 1958-94) was sure that *ne labora* means 'don't worry'. He would settle for 'All's well, if all be well within'. In characteristic vein Mark added that for a school motto, the implication that there was 'no need to clean your shoes or fasten your collar' had always struck him as pleasingly subversive. However, he too was puzzled about the origin.

Frank Allen (O 1933-39) offered a contemporary political interpretation: 'If your gut feelings (*intus*) are right-wing (*recte*), join New Labour (*ne labora*).

Charles Bird (S 1967-71) pointed out that the motto was probably adopted at the time of the Reformation and may constitute a theological message applied to the Faith versus Works controversy. *Intus si recte* - 'If your heart's all right' (faith) -*ne labora* - 'don't worry about what you do' (works) - the Protestant view; but if the motto was first displayed on the old school building in the town, Bird also supplied an ingenious suggestion that it could deliver precisely the opposite theological message 'If what's going on inside (the building) is all right, *ne labora*- then don't fix it', that is, adhere to the established religion, Catholicism). It's an intriguing suggestion, as the School Charter was granted in February 1552 at exactly the time when the radical Protestants were in the ascendant and had the young king Edward VI's favour; but within eighteen months he had been succeeded by his half-sister Mary who was determined to restore her realm to its traditional Catholic allegiance. Charles Bird concluded, 'All in all a good, because an impenetrably ambiguous motto'.

CHAPTER FOURTEEN

SUPPORT STAFF

Although, in any description of a school, the spotlight generally and understandably falls upon the teaching staff, no school can achieve its potential without the full support of the financial, administrative, catering, domestic and grounds staff, who together provide the context in which the teaching and learning which produce an all-round education can take place. In this respect Shrewsbury has been exceptionally fortunate in recruiting and retaining men and women who have appreciated and assimilated the ethos of the School and have been happy to serve it tirelessly with loyalty and dedication. The following selection of only a few of these people is inevitably invidious, but has been made to demonstrate the range and quality of such contributions.

The deliberations and decisions of the Governing Body, though they generally take place 'behind the scenes', play a vital role in shaping the development and ensuring the continued success of the School. Its activity is not merely the support but the foundation of all the School's activities. Policy is determined, or at least carefully considered and endorsed by its members. Questions of expansion or retrenchment, financial provision, fees and salaries, buildings, the purchase and sale of land and property, political developments affecting the School, marketing, and crucially the appointment of headmasters to execute these policies, all fall to them. During the last sixty years Sir Offley Wakeman, Duncan Norman, Sir Fred Pritchard, Dr. Walter Hamilton, Sir Peter Swinnerton-Dyer, Sir David Harrison, Sir David Lees, Richard Burbidge, and the current chairman, Matthew Collins, have presided over this body. Many of its decisions, such as the introduction of Central Feeding and the admission of girls have had extremely significant long-term implications for the School. The examination of how decisions such as these have come to be made over the last sixty years, recorded in the Governors' Minutes, would require a substantial, separate study. I have therefore confined my attention to the two occasions on which the Governors were brought into direct and immediate contact with the daily business of the Site, the first in 1959 when several influential members of the Common Room agreed to approach the Chairman on a matter of concern, and the second in 2005, when a decision of the Governing Body evoked a rapid and vigorous response, not only from staff and pupils, but from parents and Old Salopians also. I have referred to these occasions in their appropriate place in the chapters devoted to the Headmasters at those times.

Fund-raising, with the focus both on bursaries and capital projects, has been another vital element, conspicuous throughout our period, in securing the prosperity and enabling the development of the School. In earlier years this was achieved by means of a series of Appeals for specific purposes, the first of which was the Fourth Centenary Appeal of 1952, conducted by Jimmy Street. Since then both members of the Common Room and professional fund-raisers have been involved, Michael Charlesworth, Adrian Struvé, Mike Eagar and Nick Bevan being among the former, and R.N. Watkins-Pitchford, Brigadier D.D. Zvegintzov, Ian Edwards, Marek Kwiatkowski and Paul Virgo among the latter. The two most significant developments in the methods of fund-raising occurred in 1965 when the Friends of Shrewsbury was established by Trust Deed under the chairmanship of Lord Coleraine (OS), and in 1991 when this organization was re-shaped as The Foundation, shifting the focus from the financing of individual projects to a continuous accumulation and a more flexible allocation of funds. Ian Edwards set up Shrewsbury's full-time fundraising office in the early nineties. Since then the Foundation has experienced steady growth, attracting an impressive donor base, which continues to support its efforts to the present day. Both The Friends and the Foundation have benefited from a strong core of Chairman and Trustees, who have worked steadfastly on the School's behalf. The current Chairman of the Foundation is Peter Worth (OS) and John Rolfe has been the longest-standing Director to date. At the time of writing the institution is celebrating the Golden Jubilee of its original inception and it is in the middle of the most ambitious phase of the School's fund-raising history, with a £10,000,000 campaign. On Old Salopian Day in October 2015 the opening of the new nineteen-classroom Academic block, to be named Hodgson Hall, will mark a key stage in its continuing development.

In turning from corporate to individual contributions by the support staff, I have decided to select and focus upon only one person from each of a number of areas in which loyal service has been given to the School, in order to contain the material within a manageable compass. I stress that any choice in this area must be invidious, and I hope both that this element will be reduced by observing this restriction, and that the individuals chosen may serve as the representative of the others who have performed a similar role. Also, to be consistent with my declared intention, stated in the foreword, 'to focus on the visible, daily life of the School', I have taken this factor, together with length of service, into account when making my choice.

Together with the Headmaster, the Bursar provides a permanent link between the Governing Body and the day-to-day running of the School. During the sixty years with which this study is primarily concerned there have been eight bursars. B.L.H. Alder (1947-58), B.M. Edwards (1958-64), M.M. Jones (1965-73), J.T. Dixon (1973-75), R. Harrison (1975-85), D.J. Crompton (1985-96), I.P. Somervaille (1996-2002) and S.J. Dowson (2003-2010). The current Bursar is M.J. Ware. An interregnum in the Bursary has occurred twice during these years. Mary Taylor served as Acting Bursar in 1965, and Michael Charlesworth in 1973. 'Micky' Jones, together with Kirkpatrick ('Pat') Young provided Donald Wright with the means to effect his transformation of the School and the debt which is owed to them by the Salopian community is incalculable. Mary Taylor served the School tirelessly for sixty years, with faultless efficiency and a shrewd understanding of people, but few of those who remember him will contest my selection of Wing Commander Ron Harrison to represent the Bursars.

Wing Commander Ron Harrison

It was clear that Micky Jones' tenure as Bursar would be a hard act to follow, but the new Headmaster, Eric Anderson, knew the very man. Both Eric Anderson and Ron Harrison came to Shrewsbury from Abingdon, where Ron had instantly established his reputation by perceiving the urgent and imperative need to insure the main buildings against storm damage. Eleven days later a high wind blew the bell tower through the Chapel roof.

Anderson identified three of the qualities required in a great Bursar in the address he gave at Ron's memorial service, and what follows is heavily indebted to the insights provided then by one who knew Ron best. Foresight, as in the case just related, was one of those qualities; practical wisdom and unflappability were two others. Ron was richly endowed with all of these, but he also possessed other invaluable qualities: encyclopaedic knowledge, a delight in solving problems and profound humanity being prominent among them. Excellent personal relationships proved to be a crucial element in his success; and it was a personal friendship combined with identity of policy and intention between the Headmaster and the Bursar which formed the bedrock of their joint achievement. Anderson considered his association with Ron Harrison 'one of the best working partnerships of my life.'

On his arrival in 1976 Ron faced financial problems no less daunting than, but different from those of his predecessor, for their source was no longer internal (these had already been tackled) but external. His first task was to take stock. He considered that

the school had just gone through what was probably the most shattering years in its financial history.

He then defined his role:

My job was to support the academic staff in their aims by providing good facilities ... I also saw myself as a window-dresser in support of sales.

When Ron retired, the anonymous colleague who wrote an appreciation in the *Salopian Newsletter* indicated how effective Ron had been in fulfilling those two stated objectives:

few bursars in Shrewsbury's history have done more to make good the basic appearance of the Site ... and he kept a keen eye on the aesthetic appearance of the school.

Ron's knowledge was both practical and humane. Sir Eric again records that 'There was nothing he did not know something about'. This knowledge encompassed not only the specifically professional equipment of a Bursar, financial acumen, knowledge about roofs and foundations, turf and fertilisers, mastery of insurance schemes, and of health and safety regulations, but extended to gastronomic and even to medical matters. He had his own recipe for Pimm's, and was in his element when he presided over the termly 'Happy Hour' which he instituted in the Masters' Bar. His genial bonhomie and the pleasure which he so obviously took in the company and conviviality of his colleagues remain a glowing memory among those who participated in them. Of course he knew what brand of whisky would be required when a certain royal visitor came to lunch in Kingsland Hall.

Far from any tendency to avoid or shelve problems, Ron positively revelled in solving them. Those who visited his office on business were struck not only by the nature of the welcome but also by the outcome of the discussion. Like many a professional man at the top of his game, Ron gave the deceptive but encouraging impression of being at leisure, with nothing else to do and no pressures to which to respond, other than to pay full attention to the matter his visitor had introduced. There would be a period of silence, while the visitor's heart sank as he reflected on the intractability of the issue he had raised, the financial expense likely to ensue and the all too obvious futility of his visit. Ron's eyes would roll characteristically towards the ceiling; then, nine times out of ten, would follow the totally unexpected response, in far less common usage then than now, and with much heavier significance: 'No problem'.

Ron's personal qualities and his considerate man-management elicited a warm response throughout the Salopian community. Simon Langdale, Eric's successor as Headmaster, recorded that Ron

achieved the impossible by being, for nearly ten years, both an immensely successful Bursar of the School and at the same time extraordinarily well liked.

Another colleague made the same assessment in different words, quoting from a memorial tablet in Christ Church, Oxford. Ron 'deserved and obtained the approbation of the whole society'. His advice was eagerly sought and greatly valued in matters which went far beyond the bounds of his responsibilities; he was punctilious in acknowledging and appreciating the work of his subordinates, and in expressing his thanks. He was kind, humane and had a great capacity for friendship. He knew what made others happy and delighted in seeing them so. When, towards the end of his tenure, he became seriously ill, the extent to which that appreciation was reciprocated became fully apparent.

When Ron reviewed his time as Bursar, he asked himself, 'What has Shrewsbury taught me?' and he identified three points: a greater tolerance than he had known before; the necessity for a school to have good men who are prepared to stay and set standards; and the sheer dedication of the teaching staff.

The final words about Ron must be left to Eric Anderson:

There are not many people of whom it can be said that they are the best at their job of anyone in the country. Ron was one of those rare people.

Gerry Sturges

I have chosen Gerry Sturges to represent the contribution of the Support Staff to Salopian activities on the river. Gerry was the School Boatman for thirty-four years, during which he transformed the standards in the Boat House, not only in terms of the quality of the craft he produced and in the imagination with which he constructed them, but also in the manner in which they were stored and handled. Recruited by Peter Gladstone, on the recommendation of George Harris, the Christ Church boatman, Gerry came to Shrewsbury in 1954 to find the equipment in the Boat House in very poor repair, and the fixed-seat House fours and tub pairs all clinker-built. Among the notorious boats he inherited were *The Upside-Down banana boat*, the *Dumb Blonde* and

Twisted Jane! The improvement which followed was dramatic, rapid and sustained. A fourth bay and a workshop were constructed in 1956 and Gerry set to work to build a whole fleet of shell house fours and sculling boats.

His imagination as a designer was demonstrated in the construction of the *Decalogue*, a double-hulled coaching boat, an enterprise in which he was assisted by Peter Gladstone and Roger Blomfield, and which received national attention. Gerry built one of the first short-stern boats in the country. He was the first, too, to design a 'front-loader' pair, in which the cox was placed in front of bow. He also built *Shrewsbury*, a lightweight clinker eight and the *Yarra*, one of the most famous of the School's expanding fleet of eights.

Gerry's skills in quickly repairing damage to boats in emergencies were legendary, not least on the occasion when the trailer was involved in a road accident on the way to Henley and both boat and oars were seriously damaged. But the crew appeared at the start on time and in good shape. He accompanied the 1st VIII far and wide, both in the UK and on trips abroad, where his dignified demeanour and smart appearance caused him, on more than one occasion, to be mistaken for the Headmaster! Gerry's long tenure as School Boatman inaugurated a new era in the history of the RSSBC.

Ken Spiby

The visible legacy of the work of Ken Spiby is to be found everywhere on the Site. Ken matches Gerry Sturges not only in length of service but also in the transformative effect he had upon the sports with which he was concerned. Few sights were more fearful than that of Ken approaching, on the warpath, in defence of his beloved grounds. The accolades bestowed upon him by my colleagues successively in charge of both football and cricket speak for themselves, and they were reinforced by the admiration expressed by generations of visiting coaches. Since they cover two of the School's major sports, I have considered it more appropriate to record them in each of the relevant sections of the book, to both of which I refer the reader. Ken was urged on more than one occasion to apply his exceptional skills on more famous, if not more beautiful turf, but his loyalty to Shrewsbury was total. It is said that on one occasion he posed as a visiting grandfather at another school in order to make sure that the standards of the groundsman there , who had applied for a job at Shrewsbury, were up to the mark. . The finest tribute to him is expressed in the cricket section by Stephen Holroyd: 'his guardianship was more a labour of love than a job of work'.

Mike Stone

Mike Stone played a major and indispensable part in the inauguration and establishment of Central Feeding in Kingsland Hall in 1969. He was appointed Head Chef three months before the Hall was opened and immediately drew attention to the fact that the new equipment which was being installed would only produce two hundred meals at a time, when the number of boys in the school alone (without taking the teaching and support staff into account) was approximately 580. He supervised the provision of three meals a day for the Salopian community for over thirty-three years. He always did the School proud on formal occasions or when a celebration was arranged, triumphantly meeting the challenge when Her Majesty Queen Elizabeth the Queen Mother came to lunch during his first few weeks in the post. He produced fine menus for a whole series of lunches and dinners for Old Salopian gatherings and for Common Room Guest Nights; and he built the reputation of Kingsland Hall as a desirable venue for social occasions for the wider civic community. He worked with six Bursars, moved from franchise to independent management and vice versa, and calculated that he had cycled approximately 35,000 miles between his home and Kingsland Hall in the discharge of his duties. He retired, with universal appreciation and acclamation of his sterling contribution, in June 2002.

Malcolm Brewster

If Mike Stone provided the direction and inspiration in the 'engine room' of Kingsland Hall, Malcolm Brewster, for a substantial but rather shorter time, performed the same function 'on deck'. He joined the School in the early 1980s and soon established himself as an 'institution'. With a friendly, easy and cheery manner, closely in touch both with the teaching staff and the boys, he was the first port of call for anyone who wanted to hear the news circulating 'on the grapevine'. He became the visible face of Salopian hospitality, equally adept in ensuring that good humour was maintained and customer satisfaction registered on occasions ranging from Governors' dinners to potentially turbulent boys' tea after seventh lesson in winter. It was rightly observed that he 'knew how to keep the punters happy'. Spotted, in his russet jacket, presiding over the Salopian refreshment tent at the National Schools' Regatta, he achieved even wider fame when he was described in the *Daily Express* as Ted Maidment's butler! When *The Prince Rupert* beckoned with a tempting opportunity, he was, appropriately enough, dined out by the members of the Common Room and granted Common Room rights.

To conclude this chapter I offer a miscellany of unsung heroes and heroines who contribute so much to the character and the harmonious functioning of the School. A richly deserved tribute must be paid to the graciousness and discretion of *Mrs Jane Gibbs*, the Headmaster's Personal Assistant and Principal Secretary. Four Headmasters have much cause to be grateful for her support over more than twenty-five years. The warmth of her personality is immediately conveyed even over the telephone and she has given many hundreds of enquirers an extremely favourable first impression of the School, strongly reinforced by her welcome when they subsequently visited.

Honourable mention must be made of **Ernest Hartshorne**, who served the School for nearly fifty years (1916-65). As School Porter after 1932 he tirelessly brought round the Headmaster's messages to every classroom. Having first been appointed by Sawyer, he served five Headmasters; and David Bevan, in his address at Ernie's funeral, remembered that he was 'Hardy's tireless messenger, Sir John Wolfenden's chauffeur, Peterson's friend and Wright's counsellor' and when Hardy revived boxing, Ernie *was often in the gym coaching and taking punishment from eager boys less than half his age and more than twice his size ..... Wonderfully gifted with boys, his relations were friendly, natural but never familiar; he was treated with a warm affection and respect. He was the perfect natural disciplinarian and it would never have occurred to anyone to take the slightest liberty with him.*

Ernie's finest hour surely occurred when he held an umbrella over Her Majesty the Queen during her visit in 1952.

Mr Lycett, of Adnitt and Naunton Ltd, supplied the School's stationery for many years. He was always most anxious to help, and on one occasion, having being asked to supply some waste paper to help ignite a bonfire in front of Kingsland House for some celebration, duly obliged with his usual alacrity. It was the week before the Entrance Scholarship examination and it was windy. The paper blew around and it was noticed that some of the sheets had print on them. Some curious Salopians picked them up, only to discover that they were the discarded proofs of the impending Entrance Scholarship papers. 'My brother's taking the Scholarship next week,' exclaimed one excited bystander who was already safely in the School. Remedial action was quickly taken.

The irrepressible **Steve Wareing,** the current Senior Caretaker, stands in the line of loyal and colourful characters reaching back to Ernie Hartshorne. When Steve is on duty humour is never far away. For twenty-two years he has been an unofficial Court Jester in the community, greeting all alike with his cheerful banter and his famous (or notorious) 'post-watershed' jokes, recounted in an accent which has not strayed from its roots in Anfield and the Walton Breck Road; and his loyalty to Liverpool FC is undimmed. Their successes, particularly against Everton or Manchester United, are celebrated with raucous glee, sending rival supporters into hiding until the time comes for revenge. Somehow he always has a ready riposte. He is an obliging professional and an experienced ex-soldier. It is not all cut-and-thrust with Steve: in quieter mood he is a shrewd observer and a sympathetic listener. In the best tradition of jesting, behind the wit lies wisdom.

Then there are the devoted staff of the Sanatorium; the patient staff of Kingsland Hall, who manfully shoulder the burden of providing three thousand meals a day, not to mention the unremitting sequence of special occasions required to cater for every kind of visitor; the laundry staff, the faithful – and tolerant- army of cleaners, the groundsmen and boatmen who equally faithfully maintain Ken Spiby's and Gerry Sturges' exacting standards; the technicians and laboratory assistants, who make everything work, the administrators, unseen by many though they may be, who carefully ensure that the School is compliant with the avalanche of requirements which are imposed upon it.

And finally, but far from least, there are the matrons, generally unsung, always indispensable, typically dedicated, sometimes eccentric (one matron was reputed to put unattached plugs into the sockets of her sitting room to prevent the electricity leaking out during the night), not infrequently formidable, occasionally militant, and at times heroic (Peter Gladstone's House matron during his bachelor days qualifies for that description). Shrewsbury could not do without them or any other members of the support staff: they all play a vital part in turning a school into a community.

CHAPTER FIFTEEN

ACADEMIC CHANGES

The context in which a Salopian of the 1950s approached his academic work was very different from that which pertains today. Extra-curricular distractions were few and far between. Sporting fixtures with other schools were available only for the athletic élite; drama, music and art were pursued by a small minority; organized expeditions away from school were limited, for the great majority, to visits to Shrewsbury House in Everton, to Rovers' camps and (after 1960), to Talargerwyn; leave down town was strictly limited and was a matter of privilege for the senior boys; Top Schools' time in the evening was absolutely sacrosanct; access to a television set was rare; mobile phones and the vast array of technological gadgets in which teenagers of today seem to be almost permanently absorbed had not been invented. Whereas a Sixth Former in 2015 is likely to be found having a meal 'down town' on a Saturday evening, a Sixth Former in 1950 was likely to be found writing an essay in his study.

The academic profile of the School in the 1950s, too, was very different. Sixty years ago a much smaller proportion of Salopians reached 'A' level and far fewer went on to university after leaving school. The speed at which different individuals moved up the School also varied greatly. It was possible to take one, two, three or even four years to reach 'O' level. Some members of the School completed their secondary education at Shrewsbury never having reached the Sixth Form at all. This situation had interesting social consequences: for while a House monitor might well still be toiling towards 'O' level, a fourteen-year-old in the same House might be about to enter the Classical Sixth. At the start of the period Classics still reigned supreme. The ablest boys were placed on arrival in the Classical Fifth. On entering the Sixth Form one year later, their academic diet consisted almost entirely of Latin, Greek and Ancient History, with a couple of lessons of Divinity, and perhaps one other 'minority' subject added to provide an element of variety. The Sixth Form was constructed on the basis of 'Sides': the Classics, Modern, History, Mathematics, Science (and temporarily the General) Sides. Each of them had considerable latitude to prescribe the number of teaching periods which they felt their subject required. This meant, of course, that it was impossible to produce a fully integrated timetable (particularly on the Arts Side), although at the end of the 1950s the scientists were taking steps towards some degree of integration. Even on the Science Side there were complications, Botany and Zoology temporarily attracting A level candidates. Elsewhere English struggled to escape from its subordinate relationship to History; and Geography was very much a poor relation. A colleague who was at the centre of academic affairs for the first twenty-five years with which we are concerned considers that in the late 1950s the academic 'pecking order' was: Classics, Mathematics, History, Science and Modern Languages (the humble position of the last of these being explained by the fact that able linguists tended to study Classics). In the lower part of the School the 'form master principle' prevailed and persisted for another twenty years. The designated colleague generally taught his form English, History, Divinity and one foreign language (though the combination varied a little). Mathematics and the Sciences were setted. More generally, throughout the School, external examinations occurred much less frequently than they do today, syllabuses offered considerable latitude and a master had much greater freedom to convey his own academic enthusiasms.

When Donald Wright became headmaster in 1963, one of his earliest moves was to consult two eminent HMIs and invite them to consider the situation; and he followed this initiative up by private discussions with colleagues who played a leading role, both in the Arts and in the Sciences. He was keen to introduce a 'block system', in which subjects would be distributed in three or four blocks of eight periods, so that a new Sixth Former could choose freely between them, though, of course, boys were advised that certain combinations of subject were more coherent and complementary and more likely to advance their future academic prospects. Most boys chose three such subjects, fewer chose either two or four. Some subjects also appeared in more than one block, in order to produce greater flexibility of choice. Arnold Hagger was appointed Second Master and charged with implementing this crucial change. A supremely methodical person, he described the problem facing him as 'putting the curriculum into *diaeta* in order to produce a time-table'. The Headmaster was also keen to abolish the so-called 'First Lesson', a teaching period which took place at 7.45 am, before breakfast. He wanted to establish subject centres, to encourage team teaching, to put an end to the Classical Fifth and generally to curb what many of his colleagues thought was the too rapid promotion of highly intelligent boys. While Classics and Mathematics lent themselves quite successfully to that existing practice, it was argued that in other subjects, English, History and the Sciences among them, greater intellectual maturity was needed if a boy was to make the fullest use of his abilities in the Sixth Form. Donald also supported, and Salopian masters greatly contributed to another important initiative: the development, adoption and implementation of the SMP, the Schools Mathematics Project.

Moves towards the present situation in which all Salopians move up the school at the same rate came only gradually; but by 1980 both the fastest and the slowest progress had been eliminated, and all boys took the main group of their 'O' levels either after two or after three years (though even then there was some provision for boys to take one or two subjects a year earlier than the others). The practice of admitting a substantial minority of entrants to the school in the Lent, and a lesser number in the Summer terms, also slowly petered out and the loss of numbers caused by the exclusion of the least able applicants was more than compensated for by the rapidly increasing number of dayboys drawn from local professional, and particularly from medical and legal families.

In the sixties and seventies the focus had been on the internal reorganisation of academic affairs: in the eighties there was an increase in government intervention and prescription, which has been continuous and unrelenting ever since. The decade began with the publication of the National Curriculum, to which Independent Schools were not, theoretically, bound to subscribe, although they found it prudent, in practice, to do so. The introduction of a new 16+ examination, the General Certificate of Secondary Education (GCSE) to replace 'O' level was announced, and much of the attention of Simon Langdale and of his Director of Studies, Lyndon Duffield, was directed towards the implementation of the former, and preparation for the latter of these two initiatives. The first GCSE courses were started in September 1986, and the first GCSE examinations took place in the summer of 1988. This involved a shift in emphasis, at this level, from the acquisition of knowledge *per se*, and also a reduction in the volume of material to be studied, to a concern with methods of study and greater opportunity for a pupil's own critical appraisal. These developments were accompanied by more restrictive syllabuses, with more elaborate systems of grading performances and equally elaborate and prescriptive assessment objectives. Coursework began to play a greater role; this brought its own problems both in terms of validating the authenticity and independence of the work submitted and also of the ensuing moderation. There were problems, too, arising from the allocation of pupils' time between those subjects which involved coursework and those which did not and from the increased demands of marking and administration placed upon their teachers.

This system, as newly established, ran through the nineties without major alteration, but superimposed upon it were the requirements of OFSTED and the pressures of the League Tables. Ted Maidment and his Director of Studies, Richard Auger, had to respond to these additional challenges. Auger's meticulous preparation for the first full-scale OFSTED inspection of a boys' Independent School, which took place in 1994, ensured a triumph. The institution of League Tables had focused parents' attention on examination results to an unprecedented degree; and in an article in the October 1993 edition of the *Salopian Newsletter* Ted Maidment warned that there were serious doubts about the League Tables as a yardstick of a school's success, even of its academic success, and pointed out that the position of a school in the tables continues to depend on the selectivity of its intake. He continued:

Shrewsbury is more selective academically than most boarding schools. We take a fair number of scholars, a majority of average boys, and a few who are below-average academically, but who, for all sorts of reasons, deserve to be here. We cannot be (and would not wish to be) as exclusive in our academic entry as many of the famous City Day Schools. A boarding school has a range of broader and deeper aims. In any case, there is so much more to education than the purely academic. The most important achievements of a school cannot be measured.

While in the 1990s the School was responding to these external pressures, the internal pressures resulting from a desire to provide an academic diet which was both compliant with external requirements, but also desirable and sufficiently nourishing were just as intense. A judicious balance had to be kept between 'core' and 'optional' subjects; and the range of the latter was ever-increasing. How they were all to be contained within the compass of a weekly timetable was a subject of recurrent debate. Were 32 periods of 40 minutes preferable to 36 periods of 35 minutes? Would a 37th period have to be added? Or would a fortnightly timetable have to be followed in order to accommodate all the desirable choices?

In 1994 a third-form entrant studied English, French, Classics, Mathematics, History, Geography, Divinity, Drama, Physics, Chemistry, Biology, Art, Music, Design and Technology, Information Technology and Physical Education. In their second term some boys managed to add either Greek or German.

The GCSE courses began in the Fourth Form. English Language and Literature, French, Mathematics, Physics, Chemistry and Biology were the core subjects. To these boys could add three more, of which one would normally be either History or Geography:

the other optional subjects included Latin, Greek and Classical Civilisation, German, Spanish, Divinity, Art, Music and Design.

In the Sixth Form twenty-one different A level courses were being studied: Latin, Greek, Ancient History, English, History, Divinity, French, German, Spanish, Russian, Geography, Business Studies, Mathematics, Further Mathematics, Physics, Chemistry, Biology, Art, History of Art, Music and Design. Italian and Japanese could also be studied in 'minority time', and a General Studies programme was in operation.

The very extensive range of these academic options, at all levels of the School, has been maintained and slightly increased during the last twenty years.

By the end of the nineties the principal focus was once more upon examinations and the government's decision to make all A level courses modular from September 2000 and to introduce a new tier of examinations. The courses were to consist of six modules: the first three modules were to comprise an AS level award, which could be self-standing, and which would be examined at the end of the Lower Sixth Year. The other three modules were to be set at Upper Sixth level and the final examination would be called A2. All six modules would have to be completed to attain an A level, but any module could be repeated. The first decade of the twenty-first century thus became 'The Age of Examinations'.

It had fallen to Richard Auger to respond to and implement this avalanche of government requirements. Already in 1994 he had commented, 'Never has it been more important in this era of value-added and league tables to hand on an independence of aim and of judgment'. It is well-known that developments in education tend to proceed in cycles and it is striking how closely he echoes the concern of Inspectors who had visited the School, just over forty years previously in 1953, before all the changes which we have been considering had begun to take place. They had written:

Shrewsbury rightly values its past standard of scholarship and its tradition of sound learning: yet the observer cannot help being struck by the degree to which masters and boys are conscious of external examinations both in the Fifth and Sixth Forms. External examinations must have their necessary place, but that place is subordinate to a school's own sense of standards and its own inherited ideals of work. No external prop or stimulus, no external assessment for internal purposes ought to be needed in a school which prides itself on its own ideals, on its power to achieve and to evaluate its achievement.

Plus ça change!

The crucial and exacting role of Director of Studies, more recently entitled Deputy Head (Academic), has been discharged, during the last decade, by Martin Cropper; and the following appraisal of the current academic situation of the school, which concludes this chapter, is based upon two discussions which I had with him in the summer of 2014.

The most significant changes during his tenure have included increased pressure to gain qualifications, stronger competition for university places and the greater volume of assessment by examination, caused by the introduction of the modular system and the opportunity for re-takes which it has allowed. The introduction, in the Lower Sixth, of another tier of examinations has had different effects in different subjects. In the essay-based subjects a degree of intellectual maturity has been required at that stage, together with sophisticated examination skills and techniques, which many pupils do not acquire securely until they reach Upper Sixth level. In general, however, examinations have been a satisfactory measure of academic ability and have resulted in satisfactory qualifications.

Cropper considers that the Academic League Tables initially stimulated competitiveness and had a positive effect; but that with the steady proliferation of different qualifications they are now attempting to measure the unmeasurable, nor do they shed any light on the crucial question of the extent to which Shrewsbury and similar Independent Schools are achieving their aim of providing a balanced all-round education in which academic achievement is only one, though a vitally important and indispensable component of what the schools hope to offer. They mislead as much as they enlighten: and it is for this reason that many of these schools, including Shrewsbury, no longer take part.

New examination subjects at A level have also been introduced in the School. Economics (as distinct from Business Studies) was in fact reintroduced as it had already been a part of the curriculum in the 1960s. Theatre Studies and Physical Education were also added. There have been new means of assessment; and the current trend favours a return to linear syllabuses. Pre-U courses have recently been introduced to provide an alternative to A level. They provide more scope for the candidate to demonstrate his ability and also the opportunity to encounter a greater breadth of material. Both teachers and pupils are able to have a deeper involvement with their subject, and since the courses are examined only at the end of two years, examination pressure is thereby considerably reduced. This option generally suits abler and more organised students better, though the alternative A level courses remain open, except in French. At present pre-U courses are offered in French, Physics and History and the three Distinction grades available to the best candidates stretch the ability and sharpen the aspiration of the high-flyers. A D3 grade corresponds to an A grade at A level and a D2 to an A*. A D1 is prized as a mark of real distinction. The number of these grades awarded is, of course, partly dependent upon the restricted range of subjects currently offering a pre-U syllabus, but in August 2014 fifty results ranging across the three distinction grades have been awarded, and Cropper has no doubt that the introduction of the pre-U courses has been a great success.

Two other new means of assessment have been introduced. The EPQ (Extended Project Qualification) provides an opportunity for a member of the Lower Sixth to submit a dissertation on an academic area of his choice. It is designed to develop skills which will prove advantageous at university, but a good performance would also boost AS results. Participation is voluntary. GPR (Global Perspectives) is a pre-U version of EPQ and provides an opportunity to develop similar research skills.

So far as subject choices in the Sixth Form are concerned, the number of students opting for courses in Mathematics and the Sciences has grown. Between 70 and 80 pupils enter the School at this level each year and the trend in choices is noticeable both in boy and girl entrants, and both in British and in Overseas students. Apart from this, there has been remarkably little change in the distribution of choices across the wide spectrum of subjects available; and the admission of girls has made little difference in this respect. There has been no decline in Modern Languages, and Classics is booming. Cropper does not consider that the curriculum is too specialised; indeed he feels that it is very well balanced in the

Lower School; and in the Sixth Form some broadening is available in the Complementary Studies programme. This programme is flexible, offering courses which vary from year to year, some of which last only for one term, others for the full two years in the Sixth Form. The subjects available are those suggested by colleagues who have offered to take part and who have a particular academic interest which they wish to share. The programme is not very different from its predecessor, General Studies.

The academic qualification for admission to the School at 13+ is an average mark of 55% across the whole range of Common Entrance papers. This pass mark has recently been strictly enforced, but it is not a particularly demanding requirement in itself; some comparable schools have a higher pass mark, and the 55% level still makes it possible to admit middle-ranking academics, all-rounders who will make a valuable contribution outside the classroom. Great emphasis has been placed on the requirement that members of the school should achieve at least five B grades at GCSE to qualify for entrance to the Sixth Form.

The Entrance Scholarship examinations at 13+ now usually attract between 25 and 30 candidates, compared with 40 fifteen years ago. This is partly due to the somewhat fragile situation of the Preparatory Schools and in particular to the fact that only a few Preparatory Schools nowadays have a dedicated 'scholarship' stream. Many Preparatory Schools in metropolitan areas now tend to send some of their ablest pupils, at the age of 11+, to the well established Grammar Schools, not only in cities such as Birmingham and Manchester, but in towns like Stockport and Macclesfield also. However, the academic quality of candidates who enter for the Shrewsbury scholarship has changed very little, and the School continues to attract candidates of outstanding ability.

Potential Sixth Form entrants pay a 48-hour visit to Shrewsbury. They take examination papers in four subjects and take part in two interviews. There is no shortage of applicants. In order to qualify for a place, Sixth form entrants are required to achieve a minimum of three A grades and three B grades in their GCSE results. Overall, therefore, it is more difficult to qualify for entrance at 16+ than it is at 13+, as the successful entrants correspond in ability to the top four streams of the current six-form entry in the Lower School. Eight scholarships are awarded to candidates on the basis of their overall performance in examination and interview.

It is now considered 'par for the course' for about a dozen Sixth Form candidates to receive conditional offers of places at Oxford and Cambridge colleges. This is certainly a lower expectation than would have been entertained fifteen or twenty years ago. Oxbridge is now much more accessible both to applicants from maintained schools and to students from abroad than was the case then. But the Director of Studies has not discerned any systematic bias against candidates from Independent Schools. He has, however, noticed that Shrewsbury's performance in this area has been much more consistent than that of some of our competitors.

Cropper considers that in recent years there has been a better performance in the middle and lower ranges of ability in the School. There has been a more purposeful attitude academically. The examination culture has tightened up the approach overall, and although this may have slowed down the most able pupils to some degree, the most recent changes in educational policy may have begun to remedy this. The admission of girls has contributed to the number of motivated and intelligent Sixth Formers, but has not in itself resulted in a 'step change' in results. The appointment of teaching staff to monitor the academic performance of each of the successive age-groups in the Third Form, the Middle School (comprising the GCSE years in the Fourth and Fifth Forms) and the Sixth Form, has also made a valuable contribution; but the principal factor in improved results in the Sixth Form has been the higher entrance hurdle at 16+, both for boys and girls.

The School, through the agency of the Salopian Club, continues its long-established tradition of conferring its highest academic accolade by the award of the Sidney Gold Medal. It was first introduced in 1838 for the best Classical Scholar subsequently going on to Oxford or Cambridge, and particularly for distinguished work in the field of Latin and Greek Prose Composition. The practice of conferring the award was interrupted after 1854, but was revived in 1899. Between 1940 and 1960 fifteen such medals were awarded; between 1960 and 1980, mainly as a result of the decline in the prominence of Classics, only four. Since 1980 the award has been available to Sixth Formers from all academic faculties, but the Club has insisted that an award should be made only to pupils who are truly outstanding. The current procedure is that Heads of Faculties submit the names of any pupils whom they consider to be worthy of the award to the Director of Studies, who advises the Headmaster on the final nomination to be made to the Salopian Club. The nomination, during the last decade, has been well spread between the Faculties, with Mathematics, Science and Modern Languages being well represented, and the overall standard recently has been high enough to justify an annual award. A list of the winners of the Sidney Gold Medal since 1950 is provided in an Appendix.

This survey of the current academic situation demonstrates the very extensive and challenging role of the Deputy Head (Academic) ranging, as it does, over the supervision of the Heads of Faculty, compliance with government directives, changes in educational policy, the maintenance of academic records and statistics, and the appraisal and introduction of new syllabuses and examinations and of new forms of assessment. It is an immense and unremitting task of macro-management to which Martin Cropper had devoted himself unsparingly and over which he has a truly impressive command. The most recent development in the academic sphere is an initiative to reinforce his achievement by the appointment of a Director of Teaching and Learning, whose task will be one of micro-management, to supervise and encourage best practice in the classroom. The responsibility for the administration of staff appointments has also been transferred to another member of the Senior Leadership team.

The strictly academic status and activity of the School during the last sixty years has had to withstand a whole series of challenges, both philosophical and practical, externally from the prescriptive pressures of government intervention and internally from the pressures exerted by the very desirable and ever-expanding range of extra-curricular activity. It will always be difficult to achieve and maintain a proper balance, but certainly no effort is being spared to do so; and the present situation suggests that the School is not far from achieving a positive, productive and judicious compromise between the competing claims.

CHAPTER SIXTEEN

ADMINISTRATIVE CHANGES

Some of the most significant and far-reaching changes at Shrewsbury have been in the administrative sphere, so great that they have constituted an administrative revolution. The main stimulus has been the relentless succession of government directives during the last twenty years: a steady trickle during the first of the last two decades has become a deluge during the second. Mike Tonks, the Second Master, recently reported that 'in the last four years I have written or revised in excess of forty policy documents, all of which help to ensure that we comply with externally imposed 'standards.' Each organisation or procedure is identified by its own acronym, the ISI (the Independent Schools' Inspectorate), PICs (Pre-Inspection Commentaries), PIPs (Pre-Inspection Paperwork), SEF (Self-Evaluation Forms), NMS (National Minimum Standards), the requirements of OFSTED (the Office for Standards in Education), the recommendations of the HMC (Headmasters' and Headmistresses' Conference), and beyond the strictly educational requirements, the CSCI (the Commission for Social Care Inspection), Section 87C of the Children Act (dealing with its implications for Education), Health and Safety legislation and Criminal Record checks. Among all these administrative requirements, the Child Protection measures stand out as having had a demonstrably positive and beneficial effect, not only in responding to the problems of individuals, but also in maintaining an awareness of the standards of consideration and sensitivity required in a healthy community.

Four examples of the impact of external pressures upon the School occurred, in as many years, in the first half of the 1990s. In 1991 the first 'League Table' of A level results was produced. On the 14th October of the same year The Children Act became law and a school liaison officer was appointed. In 1992 the first formal inspection of the School under the provisions of the Act took place, and in 1994 OFSTED selected Shrewsbury as the guinea-pig for its first inspection of a boys' Independent School, despatching a full team which spent several days examining every aspect of Salopian life.

Legal requirements and marketing pressures have led to a dramatic expansion in the numbers of the administrative staff. The 'Blue Book', (Brown Book's lineal descendant, (see next paragraph) listed 6 members of the Headmaster's Office, 11 in the Bursary and 7 other Administrative staff in Michaelmas Term 2014. Other external pressures have led to the appointment of 6 administrators in the Admissions Office and Marketing Office and 4 in the Development Office. A more general point is that when the staff of the general services department, the library and the sports facilities department are added, together with 9 technicians and 6 members of the IT department, the total represents a very significant change in the balance and nature of the Salopian community as a whole during the course of the last six decades. Although the component categories were very similar sixty years ago they do not correspond exactly. However, the point is illustrated by the fact that the Brown Book of Michaelmas Term 1954 lists 43 full-time members of the Common Room with 5 administrative staff in a school of 522 boys: in the Michaelmas Term 2014 there are 123 members of the Common Room and over 60 administrative staff (excluding those members of the Common Room who also have administrative roles) in a school of 764 boys and girls.

'Brown Book' was the name given to the current school register, which was produced throughout the sixty years between 1950 and 2010. Although the colour of the book's cover changed from time to time, it continued to be known as 'Brown Book' until the last decade, when references to it finally had to recognize that its colour was actually blue! In its heyday Brown Book was a mine of information, containing a list of the members of the Governing Body, of the teaching staff in order of appointment, of School Officers and of teaching sets. There was a full, alphabetical School list, giving a boy's house, academic position in the School, membership of different forms and sets, birthday, term of arrival and initial form placing. This was followed by a full list of the members of each house, the houses being placed in the order in which they were first established. The *Carmen*, the School song, occupied one page. For many years, the usefulness of Brown Book was greatly increased by the inclusion of the *Fasti* (or School Calendar) for the particular term. For all these years the Brown Book was the first 'port of call' for researchers, being both comprehensive and readily accessible, though of course it shared the disadvantages of all printed documents, of giving permanency to mistakes and of being unable to register changes: the incorporation of the *Fasti* compounded the latter difficulty. Inconsistency in production caused a further problem. Until 1973 the Brown Book was produced termly: then, for the next twenty years, twice a year, one book covering the Michaelmas Term and the other the Lent and Summer Terms. This new arrangement made the inclusion of the *Fasti* in Brown Book impossible. Inconsistency in the listing of the members of the teaching staff in Brown Book also presents difficulties for researchers. The long-established custom of listing them in order of appointment made changes, arrivals and departures easy to identify: the change to alphabetical order, introduced as an experiment a decade ago, quickly discarded and recently reintroduced, has obscured the chronological context. A further change in the production of Brown Book in 1998, in which it was only produced annually, lasted for seven years. This opened up the possibility that an individual boy's name, or at least his assumption of a new responsibility, might be omitted from the record entirely. In 2005 the traditional pattern of a Brown Book for each term was resumed. However, since then data protection regulations have gradually reduced the content – and hence the usefulness – of Brown Book, and the preference for electronic records has increasingly prevailed. At the time of writing Brown Book *aka* Blue Book has been reduced to a drastically attenuated form. The School Register , which preserved a record of the date of entry to the School and the date of leaving of all Salopians since 1798, together with the briefest outline of their school record and subsequent career, if known, has ceased to exist. The third and latest edition was produced as far back as 1975.

Another important consequence of the outside pressures referred to earlier has been the need to create, delegate and distribute responsibilities among the senior members of the teaching staff. In 1960 the convention was that if the Headmaster was away from the School the senior master by appointment deputised for him during his absence. This convention scarcely ever came into effect, for the then headmaster, Jack Peterson, was generally content to confine his activities to the Salopian stage. Donald Wright, by contrast, was keen to respond to developments outside the School. The crucial academic changes which he inaugurated seemed to require the specific appointment of a senior colleague to implement them. Accordingly Arnold Hagger was appointed Second Master to do so. Donald also decided that the position of Senior Master should be validated by an official appointment rather than acquired by mere length of service in the Common Room. David Bevan was the first such appointee. In the ensuing years there was some inconsistency in the way in which the titles of Senior Master and Second Master were used. But the general principle, namely that one senior colleague was the Headmaster's deputy and the other his principal administrator, was consistent. Eventually the colleague with the latter responsibility became known as the Director of Studies. This degree of delegation persisted for roughly forty years. But in clear response to the administrative deluge, a more elaborate Senior Management Team (called the Senior Leadership Team since 2012) has been developed during the last decade. In the Summer Term of 2005 it was composed of the Senior Master, the Second Master and the Director of Studies. Later that year there were two further additions, the Head of Careers and the Director of Staff Training, together with the Registrar. In 2009 a Director of Communications and Marketing, the Bursar and a Director of Finance were added. The Director of the Foundation was added in 2011. The Senior Leadership team since the Michaelmas Term of 2014 comprises the Headmaster, the Second Master, the Deputy Head (Academic), the Deputy Head (Pastoral), the Deputy Head (Staffing), the Bursar, the Director of Admissions and the Director of the Foundation. There is further delegation and definition of responsibilities among the senior members of the staff. In addition to the post of Director of Music (long established) four other specific posts have recently been created: the Director of Drama (a surprisingly late addition), the Director of Sport, the Director of Activities and the Director of Teaching and Learning.

Academic changes have been fully discussed in a separate chapter but they resulted in a number of administrative changes in the organisation of the school day. The last 'First Lesson', the single teaching period before breakfast, took place on 7th July 1967. It was claimed at the time that this was a tradition which had lasted for more than four centuries. In the first seventeen years of our period, 'Second Lesson' had begun, after Chapel, at 9.50 am and had consisted of two further teaching periods. After a morning break a single, fourth period, followed. Morning school was over by 12.30 pm. Since breakfast (at 8.30 am) had been comparatively late, lunch did not take place until 1.45 pm. The gap of 75 minutes between the conclusion of the fourth period and the start of lunch was known as 'After 12' and was used for a variety of purposes, both academic and sporting, in which Fives was a major element. Afternoon school, then known as 'Third Lesson', has until very recently followed a consistent pattern, with two teaching periods following in the early afternoon in the summer and in the late afternoon in the winter. Since 1967 the two breaks which occurred before lunch have been replaced by one, with three lessons before the break and two afterwards, as a rule. The change was controversial at the time, opposition being most vocal from the Fives lobby, widely supported by many colleagues who appreciated the leisurely feeling caused by the frequent breaks in the teaching day, which resulted in there never being more than two consecutive teaching periods at a time. But the argument that 7.45 am was not a time at which teaching was at its most effective and that it was an intolerable time for the rapidly growing number of Day Boys to be required to arrive at school won the day.

In 1977 the school day was further rearranged, so that an hour after lunch was freed from academic or sporting commitment. An earlier start in the morning, with the first lesson beginning at 9.00 rather than 9.15 am was needed to make this possible, and in 1982 'Societies Hour', with priority accorded to music, was finally established after lunch on Mondays. In the Michaelmas Term of 2014, with the aim of reinforcing the academic element in Salopian activity, a third period was added to Monday afternoon, and a six period morning (with an early start at 8.30) was introduced on Thursdays. In a further adjustment in September 2015 the third period on Monday afternoon will be abolished and Wednesday, like Thursday, will become a six-period morning.

The changes in the daily routine have been matched by changes in the timing and in the integrity of terms. In the 1950s school terms were unbroken. The Michaelmas Term did not begin until the third week in September and the Summer Term continued until the end of July. Now the academic year begins and ends approximately a month earlier, principally as a result of the timing and proliferation of external examinations. There was a distinctly nostalgic quality in the comment in the editorial of the *Salopian Newsletter* reviewing the Summer Term of 1987: 'We shall not see its like again. The new examination system will ensure that'. Michaelmas Term 1988 spanned five calendar months, from August to December: the summer holidays which followed in 1989 were ten weeks long. Clearly the long-established sequence and proportion of school term and holiday were becoming unbalanced. In 1991 Shrewsbury pioneered an attempt to restore that balance, by extending the Summer Term for three weeks after the conclusion of the Summer examinations, but subsequently reverted to the traditional practice of ending the term soon after the external examinations were finished. The idealised notion of long, lazy summer days on the cricket field and the river has been replaced by the harsh reality of an almost unbroken series of external examinations involving the top three years of the school, which begins almost as soon as the Summer Term has started; and the opportunity for members of the Lower Sixth to work at a more leisurely pace and to take a wider view has disappeared with it. However the forthcoming return to linear exams will, once again, free the Lower Sixth from this treadmill.

The Salopian who came to school in September in the 1950s would be unlikely to leave Shrewsbury, (except for matches and expeditions under the auspices of the School) until the Christmas holidays. The first weekend Exeat was introduced in the Michaelmas Term of 1962. Since then both the length and the frequency of these Exeats have grown. The current situation is that each term is effectively divided into four quarters. There is a week-long Exeat in the middle of the Lent and Summer Terms, and a two-week Exeat in the middle of the Michaelmas Term. On either side of these Exeats, there are so-called 'Coach Weekends' some of them lasting from Saturday lunchtime to Sunday evening: and 'Extended Coach Weekends', stretching from Friday lunchtime to Sunday evening or from Saturday lunchtime to Monday evening. This development, common to many similar schools, caters for the desire of parents to keep in closer touch, and it has a reciprocal relationship with the shrinking catchment area of these institutions. Parents increasingly show preference for schools which are in easy reach and favour those which, by the provision of such Exeats, allow them to take full advantage of this proximity.

Speech Day used to be the principal, indeed perhaps the only occasion, on which parents were encouraged to appear on the Site. Both the time and the nature of the occasion have had a chequered history over the last sixty years during which it has sometimes occurred at the middle and sometimes at the end of term, once occurring on a Thursday rather than a Saturday and on Friday between 2005 and 2010. In the 1950s Speech Day was the centre of a weekend celebration, in the middle of the Summer term, stretching from Friday lunchtime until Sunday morning chapel. It started with a ceremonial parade of the Shrewsbury School CCF, inspected by a visiting senior officer. Prizes were distributed in the Alington Hall on the Saturday by a distinguished guest and speeches were delivered. Chapel services, usually with an equally distinguished visiting preacher, occurred on the Sunday morning, after which boys were allowed to go out with their parents for the remainder of Sunday, but there was no formal Exeat. Term resumed as normal on the Monday morning. This pattern lasted until the 1970s, though the CCF parade was discontinued earlier. Subsequently a longer Exeat was introduced after Speech Day. Later still Speech Day and Prize Giving became separate occasions, the latter being transferred, with the visit of the distinguished guest, to a date in the second half of the Summer Term, while the main focus on Speech Day itself was the Headmaster's Address to Parents. In the summer terms of 2013, 2014 and 2015 all the component features and participants of Speech Day celebrations were united in a most successful initiative in which distinguished guests, governors, parents, teachers and pupils were all assembled, at the end of term, in a large marquee on the Top Common. Speeches were made and prizes were presented. This gathering of the whole Salopian community is greatly to be applauded.

CHAPTER SEVENTEEN

SOCIAL CHANGES

Schoolboys are notoriously conservative: they tend to prefer familiar circumstances and relationships and are suspicious of change. This is particularly true of Sixth Formers, the 'senior citizens' of the school society. The members of each successive Upper Sixth customarily observe that life was much tougher for them when they were Third Formers than it is for Third Formers now, and that the latter are much cheekier than they would have ever dared to be when they were their age. Long gone are the days of 'new scums', and even the term 'new boy' is now discouraged. The thirteen-year-old Salopian has his own respectable status as a 'Third Former': Sixth Formers are no longer demi-gods, but simply *primi inter pares*.

The demolition of the hierarchy, the decline of privileges and the relaxation of boundaries which gained momentum in the 1960s have all been fully discussed in the chapter on 'The Public School Revolution'. The greater accessibility and informality of Housemasters, the widespread use of Christian names both in the Common Room and between the boys and girls and also by members of the staff when speaking to their pupils have all helped to create a friendly and co-operative atmosphere and to recognise and promote individuality. The introduction of the Children Act and the appointment of a master to supervise its implementation reinforce this recognition of the interests of the individual and are an important element in the pastoral structure of the School. But the elaborate tutorial system is, perhaps, the most powerful element in the very extensive provision of pastoral care.

The system originated in the 1960s, when increasing specialisation in academic subjects, a greater range of subject choices and, most of all, the availability of new combinations of subjects in a boy's academic programme, made it increasingly difficult, first in the Sixth Form and then in the Lower School, for a Form Master to preside effectively over an individual's general progress. Tutoring in the Sixth Form emerged originally as an administrative expedient, but it soon developed a more personal character. Form Mastering in the Lower School survived into the 1980s, but in 1989 personal tutoring was introduced in the Fifth and Fourth Forms also, and it finally spread to the Third Form in 1990.

A Sixth Former may choose his tutor; more junior boys are allocated to a tutor by their Housemaster. The Sixth Form tutorial system is school-based; in the junior part of the school it is house-based. At all levels of the School the tutor's responsibility may simply be described as being to befriend the tutee, in a challenging rather than an indulgent sense, to look after his or her welfare as an individual, and to encourage the pupil both to make the very best use of the opportunities available and to develop his or her potential. The principle is that every member of the teaching staff (with very few exceptions) should serve as a Lower School tutor in a house-based team. In house tutorial meetings there is an excellent opportunity for the pooling of ideas and the sharing of problems.

This is a far cry from the situation in the 1950s when the House was the Housemaster's castle and unchallenged admission was granted to only one colleague, the single House

Tutor (a generation further back it was not unknown for the House Tutor, even in the absence of the Housemaster, to be confined to the 'Private Side' of the House).

Nowadays it is normal for each member of the team of House Tutors to take charge of routine matters on his weekly 'duty night'. On designated weekends, the Housemaster may declare himself to be 'off duty' and delegate his responsibility to one of his tutors, usually the nominated Assistant Housemaster. The fact that the boys and girls are accustomed to meeting half-a-dozen members of the Common Room on a regular basis, in informal circumstances, in their own House, has had a profound effect upon the social relationships in the School. The idea that discipline was best maintained not by the monitor's cane but by private discussions of aspirations and problems between individual members of their House and their Housemaster – considered a dangerous and potentially subversive innovation in the early 1960s – is now an established orthodoxy. It is taken for granted that a pupil's happiness is a vital condition for the achievement of full potential at school. As already noted, the work of the colleagues responsible for the School's adherence to the provisions of the Children Act has been crucial in safeguarding the happiness of individual pupils. A great debt of gratitude is owed to these colleagues, foremost among whom is Dr Chris Minns, who has discharged this responsibility for sixteen years.

What the Housemaster loses in autonomy, however, he gains in support and perspective. His tutor provides each individual boy with a second member of the staff, to whom he can easily and legitimately turn for advice in addition to, or as an alternative to his Housemaster. Clearly the responsibilities of the Housemaster and his House Tutors now considerably overlap and reinforce each other; perhaps it is fair to say that whereas the focus of the Housemaster's concern must be the community for which he is responsible and the place of the individual in it, the Tutor's starting point is the welfare of the individual and the furtherance of his happy and active participation in the community: a fine but significant distinction between the two complementary roles, which are, in any case, by no means mutually exclusive. Writing in the *Salopian Newsletter* in 1990, just as the tutorial system had been completed, I commented,

> *It is surely appropriate that at a time when the influence of mass media, popular culture and group pressure can only too easily obscure the importance and inhibit the development of personal values, our school should seek to place renewed emphasis on individual care, to provide stimulation of individual aspiration and excellence, and to affirm the central place which personal example, standards and relationships should occupy in a tradition such as ours.*

Two other institutions, both introduced in the 1960s, have had a significant effect upon the social milieu. Although House allegiance remains strong, the provision of Central Feeding in Kingsland Hall has greatly facilitated the development of friendships between boys and girls and their contemporaries in different houses. The fact that much of the training in Basic Year, which for thirty years after its inception was compulsory for all Fourth Formers, was in small groups formed on an alphabetical, rather than a House basis, had a similarly powerful effect. The shared activities and relationships experienced then ensured that each boy knew members of other Houses well for his remaining three years in the School.

The provision of better facilities for the members of the Sixth Form has been another important social development during the last forty years. It was a response not only to the recognition in wider society that pupils of Sixth Form age were more appropriately regarded as young adults rather than as schoolchildren, but also to the need for better study facilities at a time when the results of proliferating external examinations were becoming crucial factors in determining the future prospects of a cohort of students nearly all of whom were intending to proceed to university. Both social and academic factors thus directed a sharper focus upon the Sixth Form. The opportunity to meet Sixth Formers' academic needs was provided by the establishment of central feeding: the vacated domestic quarters of the boarding houses were now available for conversion to bedsits for Sixth Formers; at the same time the disciplinary powers and supervision which the House Monitors had formerly exercised had been largely superseded by the routine presence of members of the teaching staff.

The standard of accommodation in the Houses has improved out of all recognition during the course of the last sixty years, by a continuous programme of refurbishments and extensions to the Houses in rotation. The bedsits in the girls' Houses have *en suite* facilities. At the beginning of the period, however, all boys, even the Head of School, slept in dormitory-like bedrooms. There were a few individual studies for very senior boys and the monitors enjoyed some private comfort in 'Headroom', a room specially set aside for them, but the great majority spent most of the day in cramped private studies, arranged in a row, in the older Houses on either side of long stone corridors. One Housemaster's wife used to remark that they reminded her of pictures of Pentonville Prison! Typically, there was a hierarchy of occupants in these studies too, comprising one Fifth Former, a Fourth Former and a Third Former, and when in the House boys spent most of the day either in their studies or in the Hall, the latter providing the only area in which they could congregate.

In the first twenty years of our period, all meals were taken in the House. This placed great pressure on the Housemasters' wives, which their successors have not had to experience, and particularly so if the house cook happened to be ill and they had to prepare the meals for fifty or sixty hungry boys themselves. The Housemasters' wives of that time are prominent among the unsung heroines of the Salopian story. In the days when fees were paid directly to the Housemasters and budgeting was still in their hands, expenditure on food effectively came out of a Housemaster's own pocket. Bachelors, it was rumoured, could afford to be more generous and the boys in their houses fed well, but there is a well-known story of a Housemaster's wife visiting the butcher's and ordering 'two pounds of best steak and twenty pounds of boys' meat'!

Ablutions were performed in Spartan conditions; sometimes only two or three baths were available for the whole House and evening 'bath rotas' were common. The whole provision particularly shocked the series of American ESU scholars who spent a year or more at Shrewsbury in the nineteen-sixties, who felt that it was like being transported back to the nineteenth century. Most of them regarded their sojourn – in retrospect if not always at the time - as providing an invaluable educational experience, from which they profited enormously overall but several of them remember the facilities with masochistic nostalgia. One such transatlantic Salopian recounted that the food was poor. Everyone lost weight and had to supplement House fare with regular visits to the School Shop. His Housemaster had confided in him that his budget for house meals was seven shillings and sixpence (then equivalent to one dollar) per boy per week. There were two house baths, for the use of 55 boys. A cold bath was taken before the 7.45 am first lesson. The weather being exceptionally cold that winter, it was decreed that boys might be excused if ice had formed upon the surface of the water. In the afternoon all the boys came in for a hot bath, after games. The condition of the water when the latecomers arrived can easily be imagined. Our correspondent's habit was to put his finger into the bath water. If he could not see his finger tip, he decided that he would be cleaner if he stayed out of the bath than if he got into it! Unimaginable to his pampered Salopian successors as it may be, the story lends colour to the well-known assertion about the traditional Public School, 'If an Englishman can survive his education, he can survive anything'.

By the middle of the 1960s provision was being made for a small number of senior boys, individually, or sometimes in pairs, who felt stifled and confined in the conditions of the traditional boarding house and whose attitudes unsettled the others, to lodge in the private houses of members of the staff or with other friends of the School as 'outboarders'. This expedient was gradually extended and a small colony of senior boys, under the supervision of a bachelor master, was established in the buildings surrounding the courtyard of Kingsland House, in the years immediately before their demolition to make way for Kingsland Hall.

Soon afterwards it was decided that there should be a central location, beyond the individual houses, where all Sixth Formers could socialise and which might serve as another bridge between childhood and adulthood, between school and university. Accordingly a Sixth Form Club, named *The Seventy Club*, after the year of its inception, was formed in No 40 The Schools. The location was cramped and the facilities were extremely limited: for two years it was little more than a place in which members of the Sixth Form might call in for a 'legitimate' drink. It was modelled on a similar club recently opened at Charterhouse. The Club had a licence, granted by the local magistrates, which allowed 17-year-olds to consume prescribed alcoholic drinks, provided they were doing so as recorded members of a legally constituted society, with supervision by named members of the Common Room, with an elected committee and an agreed framework.

The Club really 'took off' two years later, in 1972, when it moved to premises adjacent to Tudor Court, which now provided its new name. It flourished under the leadership of Chris Etherington as Warden, with Simon Baxter as Steward. A Club room was constructed, with five bedsits for members of the Upper Sixth on an upper floor. An active committee of boys grew in responsibility in monitoring behaviour, in allocating duties and in careful accounting of bar sales. The Club was open to members before tea on weekdays, and there were social evenings every Saturday in which 'temporary members' could take part and girls could be entertained. Dances took place twice a term. The Upper Sixth 'residents' varied both in character and in academic performance, from those who were anxious to part with their Housemaster on the one hand, to scholars who were determined to secure their place at Oxbridge on the other. This new accommodation, freed from the tyranny of bells, provided another transition between school and university life. Chris Etherington commented:

*Donald Wright and Micky Jones gave flesh to a Governors' decision to build a Sixth Form
Club properly and not just in some poor bachelor's front room. In my judgment that made the
School a better place.*

The Sixth Form Club still flourishes, but it is now located in the Moser Precinct, above
the former baths, and is called 'Quod'. It is now the accepted venue for social occasions of
many kinds, but sometimes the gathering is too numerous to stage an occasion there, and
it is an interesting speculation what the thoughts of Moss, Alington, Sawyer and Hardy
might be if they could really look down from their portraits to see Salopians of both sexes
parade along the cat-walk during the annual fashion show in the Alington Hall!

Access to the town has become much easier over the years for all Salopians. The
ending of the requirement to wear School dress in the town, in the 1980s, also allowed
members of the School to merge more easily into the general public. Sixth Formers were
generally only required to sign a book outside the Housemaster's study if they wished to
go 'down town' out of lesson time and before 6.00 pm on weekdays. More junior members
of the School might be required to obtain verbal permission from the Housemaster or one
of the House Tutors as well. On Saturday evenings Sixth Formers were permitted 'to go
down town for a meal', though it was expected that any alcoholic consumption should not
infringe the law of the land. In practice the permission was variously construed as allowing
the consumption of steak and chips and half a pint of beer on the one hand to several pints
of beer with a packet of crisps on the other.

Whereas expeditions further afield had at one time been restricted to 'away matches',
visits to the Club in Liverpool and weekend visits to Talargerwyn, now they became as
commonplace as they were varied. Coaches and minibuses left for Art trips to Glasgow, field
trips to Durham, concerts in Birmingham and London, lectures at universities and choral
evensongs at Cathedrals. The movement was reciprocal: the ever-increasing prominence
of drama, music and the fine arts in the School during recent decades, and the very high
standards achieved in all of them, has meant that local residents have been only too eager
to throng the Site to attend the plays, concerts and exhibitions which have been staged.

Even before the official advent of girls in 2008, the previous fifty years had seen
a steadily increasing female presence on the Site. Ladies were admitted to the Concert
Choir in 1951 and girls in 1960; girls from the High School were keen to take part in
School and House plays: the days of boy Ophelias and Lady Macbeths were numbered.
The next logical step was that female parts in plays should only be taken by boys if a
markedly comic effect was intended. However, a female presence in the Common Room
and the classroom was slow to develop, though there had always been an exception, on
the part-time staff, for native speakers of foreign languages and for teachers of musical
instruments, Mlle Larguier being a conspicuous example of the former group and Miss
Goliah of the latter. However, the presumption of male exclusivity was slow to die: in the
earlier part of our period ladies were confined to the south transept, popularly known as 'the
hen coop', during services in Chapel and the installation of the first ladies' lavatory on the
Site was a portentous indication of things to come. The first full-time female member of
the teaching staff was appointed in 1979. The subsequent increase in the numbers of female
colleagues is described in the chapter on the Common Room. In 1968 the Editor of the

Salopian Newsletter wrote, 'We read of girls at Marlborough; how soon will they be here?' The answer was to be 'Forty years on'. Although a handful of local girls was admitted to work with the 'seventh term' Upper Sixth in the early 1980s, as part of their preparation for the Oxbridge scholarship examinations, it was only, in each case, for a period of a few weeks in the Michaelmas Term. The whole situation was, of course, transformed by the admission of girls as full members of the Sixth Form in 2008 and a further major development has been the inauguration of full co-education, from the age of thirteen, in September 2014.

Two members of the Senior Leadership Team were contemplating the consequences of the imminent arrival of girls in 2008. Sara Hankin, the first Housemistress of a girls' boarding house, observed,

I think the School felt it was ripe for change … I think we would be doing the students a disservice if we continued to be single sex between 16 and 18. Life at that age is much more natural together

Peter Fanning wondered how the change would affect the boys

Certainly some will find themselves challenged in their habits of work. Some may be resentful, some perhaps will find a comb and spend more time in daily grooming. Social life for one or two will no doubt have a different meaning. But for the vast majority, the change may be more subtle - learning to live with the opposite sex may lead to an easier, more accommodating attitude to life, something that prepares the boys for life at university.

Inevitably there were some teething problems as a school which had been for boys only for over 450 years adapted itself to co-education, even if only in the Sixth Form. There are few more conservative animals than adolescents, and attitudes took a while to change, often making life uncomfortable for girls in the first two years. Seven years on, no current pupil can remember a time when there were no girls in the School. They have established themselves securely and have participated wholeheartedly in every aspect of boarding school life and few would argue that co-education has not greatly enriched the Sixth Form.

Yet another major change in the social context has been the development of Sixth Form entry to the School. In effect this has meant that the proportion of Sixth Formers has grown from two-fifths to one half of the total roll. This, together with the increasing importance and frequency of examinations, has led to a perceptible growth in seriousness in the approach to academic work throughout the School, but it has also meant that the much briefer sojourn at Shrewsbury of these Sixth Form entrants has made it more difficult for them to absorb and transmit the distinctive ethos of the school and to form a lifelong allegiance to it. The background of the entrants to the School is much more varied at all levels, the monopoly of British preparatory school boys having been decisively and irrevocably broken. While the School has lost the uniformity of background and experience among its pupils which was a major element in reinforcing its sense of community, it has gained great cultural enrichment from the recruitment of a substantial minority of international pupils. Currently these constitute slightly less than 20% of the total roll and include students from Germany, Russia, France, Italy, Spain, Austria, Lithuania, Poland, Bulgaria, Norway and

Ukraine; from the USA , Canada, the Cayman Islands and Chile; from Armenia, Bahrein, Saudi Arabia, Afghanistan, India and Mauritius; from China, Hong Kong, Taiwan, Japan, Korea, Burma and Thailand; from Singapore, Malaysia and Brunei; from Kenya, South Africa, Swaziland and Nigeria; from Australia and New Zealand. A week in the School calendar was set aside, in February 2015, to celebrate this international diversity.

One final characteristic of social change is that there is a much wider range of opportunity, nowadays, for the opinions of pupils to be expressed and taken into account. Traditionally, the Praepostors have provided one such channel of opinion. Their role as intermediaries between the Headmaster and the members of the School has long been generally accepted. Basil Oldham noted that they are

a kind of senate or representatives of the School in relationship to the Headmaster ...If a favour is asked for the School, or a remonstrance is wished to be respectfully made, they address themselves through the Head Boy to him. This representative character of the praepostors, in which they made on several occasions compacts with the Headmaster on behalf of the School, is what apparently impressed the (Clarendon) Commissioners as differentiating the system at Shrewsbury from what had been reported to them from other schools.

The Praepostors continue to meet the Headmaster or his deputy at fixed times every week. Since 2005 this opportunity to express opinion through representatives has been extended by the establishment of a School Council, to which each House sends a delegate. Initially all age-groups in the School were represented in one meeting, to which they had sent elected representatives. However, in order to give more junior members greater confidence to express their opinions, two separate Councils, senior and junior, were set up and it was discovered that nomination of the members by Housemasters, rather than elections, led to more positive discussions. The Senior Council is attended by the Head of the Sixth Form and the Junior Council by the Heads of the Middle School and the Third Form. The meetings are held fortnightly, minutes are taken and forwarded to the Headmaster. Discussions have ranged over a wide area: health and the environment, blood donorship, the quality of school meals, the conditions of leave-out, opportunities for socialising and changes in the timetable. A more informal vehicle for the expression of opinion is the publication of *Public Nose*, an occasional broadsheet , edited and produced by pupils, to comment on contemporary Salopian affairs. School Firsts, as the name implies, were originally awarded to those who had earned their colours in the first teams of the major sports, though similar precedence was conferred on those who had won awards at Oxford or Cambridge. Gradually the distinction was extended to those who had made a major contribution in music and drama, and then to others who had been similarly prominent in social service, as technicians or who in any other way had given notable service to the School. Now a committee meets at the end of term to discuss the likely candidates and to make the awards. Here again the *vox populi* makes itself heard.

CHAPTER EIGHTEEN

MUSIC

Just as it has had six headmasters, Shrewsbury has had six Directors of Music in the last sixty years: John Stainer (1950-58), Standish Lester (1959-76), John Yarnley (1976-79), Colin Edmundson (1979-82), Andrew Auster (1982-89) and John Moore (1989 on). Two of these, Stan Lester and John Moore, have been long-term occupants of the position, and it was in the second half of this period that the dramatic transformation in the range and status of music at Shrewsbury took place.

John Stainer and Stan Lester managed to maintain a high quality of performance with much more limited resources than are available at the present day. The focus was very much on the Concert Choir and the Chapel Choir and they took immediate personal charge across the whole range of musical activity. Ladies were first admitted to the Concert Choir in 1951 and High School girls in 1960. Stainer produced a fine musical score for the 1952 production of the *Masque*. *Trial by Jury* was staged in 1957, the first time, it was then claimed, that Salopians had tackled a Gilbert and Sullivan opera. There were regular performances of oratorios, and both choral and instrumental inter-house competitions took place annually. Much attention was paid to congregational singing in Chapel. Stainer recorded that about 120 boys learned a musical instrument (some, of course, learned two) and he considered that

the musical life of the School depend[ed] almost entirely on the voluntary effort and enthusiasm of the boys, and therein surely [lay] its great value.

During Stan Lester's time as Director, the School's music took huge strides towards its present very high standard of achievement. He was organist and choirmaster, conductor of the Orchestra and Concert Choir, and a meticulous teacher of the piano and organ. On his retirement in 1976, the author of his appreciation in the *Newsletter* suggested that 'many a Salopian will remember for life the left foot *ostinato* during choir practice or the withering glower at a missed entry during an orchestral rehearsal.' Richard Hudson, a trombonist in his orchestra as a schoolboy, calls him the most terrifying conductor he ever worked with. Lester expected and obtained high standards from his pupils and from all those who performed under his baton, but while quick to identify such deficiencies, and forthright in castigating them, he had the gift of making the performance come right on the night. The repertoire ranged from *Belshazzar's Feast* to the Verdi *Requiem*, Lester's conducting of the latter perhaps being the peak of his Salopian career. Large-scale oratorios became an annual event.

Lester could certainly be forbidding and on several occasions I experienced that myself. As a no more than adequate organist, I used then to play for some chapel services, also providing the concluding voluntary. On one occasion he greeted me as I came out of the transept door at the end of the service with the words. 'I never knew it sounded like that' and on another, with a dead-pan expression. 'I've just received a telegram from the Royal College of Organists: they want you to accept an Honorary Fellowship!' More serious perhaps was the occasion when he had persuaded me to play the xylophone in an orchestral piece. The arrangement was that he would 'look at me' twenty-three bars before I came in; but his glare was so compelling when he did so, that involuntarily I began to play at once! However, his obituarist in the *Salopian Newsletter* observes that 'humour was never far away from those who braved the acerbic tongue and discovered the twinkling eye'. Stan Lester fully deserved both the widespread admiration and genuine affection which he earned.

John Yarnley and Colin Edmundson were each at Shrewsbury for only three years, but they both diligently maintained and nourished their musical heritage. They were succeeded by Andrew Auster, who served as Director of Music for seven years – a comparatively brief but very significant tenure. Upon his departure in 1989 to take up a headmastership, I wrote,

We shall not see his like again, nor will music at Shrewsbury ever be quite the same. Andrew, with his supreme talent as an impresario, certainly put Shrewsbury on the musical map, and the scale and flamboyance of his productions will long be remembered: the Big Band performing with fire-eaters and belly-dancers at The Buttermarket; African drummers from Wolverhampton massed on the stage of the Alington Hall to invest the performance of The African Sanctus with ethnic authenticity; the pay-your-money and sing-along performance of the Messiah at St Chad's, recorded for broadcasting by Radio Shropshire; the coachloads of performers being transported to Birmingham Town Hall to perform The Dream of Gerontius; the Chapel Choir trying not to hurry down the aisle at the end of the Carol Service, but very conscious that on Central there was a minibus waiting to speed some of its members down the M6 to Birmingham Airport to catch a plane for a choir tour in Paris – an objective which a timed trial run on the previous day had suggested was just feasible; skiing and singing mixed in equal proportions amid the fjords of Norway; broadcasts of the first performance of Alex Clarke's Rock Requiem, most invitingly and quite accurately advertised as a World Première. The audacious panorama steadily unfolded and the above is only a glimpse. The sceptics repeatedly claimed that this time Andrew's latest daring enterprise could not possibly succeed, and invariably he confounded them.

No enterprise was too ambitious for Andrew, and like a Pied Piper he had the knack of persuading others to follow where he led. In the Community Choir, the Big Band, the Subscription Concerts, the vastly expanded choral and instrumental competitions, and the extremely popular Singing Weekends, he left convincing proof that never before had so many boys in the School played some part in making music, nor so many visitors from near at hand and far away been drawn into Salopian musical activity.

If Andrew Auster set a challenging precedent and opened up an expanding horizon by drawing the wider world to the School to hear and make music, it is during John Moore's quarter of a century in charge that the high quality of Shrewsbury's music has created a reciprocal echo far beyond the confines of the School, as it has become one of the most distinguished elements in the School's reputation, both in the United Kingdom and abroad. There has been a vast expansion in the range of options open to musicians, a strengthening of the strictly academic element in the subject, particular attention to the teaching of singing, and above all an emphasis on the provision of opportunities for pupils to perform in public – and even to conduct the full school orchestra as Stephen Wood did in *Rio Grande*. Not a week in term goes by without pupils being given the chance to perform either as a soloist or in a group. A key feature of these recent decades is that even the largest-scale performances are almost entirely 'home-made': there is very little (and often no) participation or reinforcement by professional players from outside the School. Another aspect of Salopian music is the frequency with which compositions and arrangements by Salopians are themselves performed. Reference has already been made to Alex Clarke's *Rock Requiem*. This was followed by Anthony Merryweather's opera *Troy*, Richard Fitzhugh's *Requiem* and the five-movement *Darwin Cantata* composed by a group of Salopian musicians, Chris Cox, Stephen Craigen, Sam Grainger and Philipp Legner. At a less ambitious level, smaller-scale compositions and arrangements, not least for the House Singing Competition, are commonplace, as are pupil-run ensembles.

Yet the full-time teaching staff of the Music Department has not been extended at all. There remains a nucleus of four: the Director of Music, an Assistant Director of Music (a new appointment) who is also the Director of Chapel Music, the Head of Strings and the Head of Academic Music, though a fifth colleague has effective oversight of the teaching of wind instruments. The dramatic expansion which has taken place has been among visiting musical staff, a list of whom first appeared in Brown Book in 1985. Now there are nearly thirty and Moore's policy and objective has been to provide a specialist teacher for each and every instrument. Provision is now made not only for all the traditional orchestral instruments, strings, woodwind and brass, but also for the saxophone, now played by vast numbers, for bagpipes, tuba, percussion and drumkit, for three styles of guitar-playing, classical, rock and jazz, for the jazz piano and for the organ. On the classical piano the standard of performance has been raised beyond recognition by Peter Bradley-Fulgoni. And veterans of Chris Etherington's pioneering jazz band will be delighted to know that jazz musicians are as well catered for as their classical contemporaries. The range and quantity of musical prizes now awarded at Speech Day pays eloquent tribute to the quality and versatility of the individual musicians concerned.

Though a succession of organists had been appointed in the first half of these sixty years, to work with the Director of Music in Chapel, Denny Lyster was the first master specifically appointed to take charge of Chapel Music as a distinct and defined responsibility; but with boys' voices breaking earlier and earlier, the top line in the choir was increasingly struggling. Richard Dacey tackled the problem by recruiting boys from Kingsland Grange to reinforce the choir. In the last two decades, under the stewardship of Chris Argent, Simon Dearsley and Kathryn Burningham, the size, quality and reputation of the choir have all grown. The Carol Services have provided the best opportunity for the choir to show its paces; and their popularity has meant that the number of such services in December has been increased, first to two and then to three, to meet the demand for tickets. The admission of girls to the School in 2008 solved the problem of the top line; the choir now has sixty members, and under the current Director of Chapel Music, Alex Mason, himself a former Cathedral Organist and latterly Director of Music at St David's Cathedral, the choir is flourishing as never before. Basil Oldham states that the first school choir was formed in 1864, so last year marked its 150th anniversary.

The current chaplain, the Revd Gary Dobbie, has reinforced the musical element in Chapel services, introducing the performance of one or more pieces of music in many of the weekday and Sunday services. However, one prominent feature of the fifties and sixties, the weekly Congregational Practice on Fridays, lapsed in the restless days of the seventies, despite occasional attempts to revive it. This practice had been useful in extending the repertoire of hymns, and also in allowing full congregational participation in the Canticles, which Johnson had done so much to promote in the 1940s. One echo of this practice is to be found in the recently reintroduced and very brief, but also very moving participation of the congregation in the *Libera Me* from the Fauré *Requiem* in the Remembrance Day service.

During the last two decades the choir has been extremely fortunate in being able to rely on the very considerable expertise, at the organ, of Dr John Godwin. Though recently retired as Head of Classics, he still continues to play for Chapel Services. The choir has maintained its tradition of visiting a series of cathedrals to sing Evensong, the range of its excursions extending to Chester, Hereford, Lichfield, Worcester and Gloucester, to York Minster, Southwell Minster and, in 2013, to St George's Chapel, Windsor.

More generally, the music department has developed and maintained close links with cathedral choir schools; many cathedral choristers have come on to Shrewsbury on scholarships and the number of music scholarships awarded each year rarely falls below ten, with the result that, at any one time, there are between forty and fifty music scholars in the School. Scholarships have also been awarded to students from overseas. The standard of all aspects of music has been greatly enhanced by these students, recruited from areas ranging from Bulgaria to Bangkok. The link with Shrewsbury International School in Bangkok is particularly close, with regular visits each way and joint performances by the two school orchestras. In 2013 a Salopian musical was even exported and performed in the Bangkok school.

Indeed, Salopians now regularly take their music further afield. Between 1998 and 2009 they travelled, each February, to present a full orchestral concert in London at St John's, Smith Square. More recently there has been a series of similar concerts in Birmingham Town Hall, their scale and popularity indicated by the long procession of coaches required to transport both performers and audiences to and fro. Most recently the School's musicians have appeared at other venues in London, including Cadogan Hall and Wigmore Hall.

One major and renowned development has been the production and presentation of School musicals, again many of them 'home grown'. The production of *Guys and Dolls* (1993) started the tradition. Then came *Jekyll* (1995), the first musical produced by the inspirational trio of Alex Went (who wrote 'the book'), John Moore (who composed the music) and Peter Fanning (who directed the resulting performance). This was followed by *The Time Machine* (1997), then a second production of *Jekyll* (1999), followed by The *Lost Domain* (2000) and *The Bubble* (2002). Sondberg's *Into the Woods* was presented in 2004. Other subsequent productions are mentioned in the chapter on Drama. The original team was subsequently augmented by the inclusion of Peter Hankin and Julian Roach. A traditional sequence of performances was developed: the musical was 'tried out' in the Ashton Theatre in Shrewsbury in November; it was then taken to the Edinburgh *Fringe* in the following August; and finally (but not invariably) presented in London in the January of the following year. The productions consistently received favourable reviews in Edinburgh: *Jekyll* even received a coveted *Fringe First.* The most recent original musicals by Peter Fanning and John Moore include *What You Will* and *Harry*, both modern versions of Shakespearean plays. In conjunction with Helen Brown, the newly appointed Director of Drama, a production based on *Great Expectations* is planned for Michaelmas 2015, words by Peter Fanning, music by John Moore and direction by Helen Brown.

These performances alternated with tours abroad, usually in the summer. Indeed, it came to be accepted that the musicians would be away in August, if not in Edinburgh, then even further afield. TMusical groups of varied composition, including the full orchestra and the Big Band, have travelled frequently abroad, several times to Prague and to Paris and on other occasions to the Rhineland, the South of France and Austria, and even further afield to Boston USA and to Bangkok. In 2013 choristers and musicians sang and played in Austria.

The Subscription Concerts, inaugurated nearly fifty years ago, have developed into an ambitious programme which now takes place under the new title of Salopian Musical Activities. Both the Alington Hall and the Maidment Building have, in effect, become the concert halls for the locality. Among the singers who have performed there are three world-famous groups which have included an Old Salopian member, Richard Eteson in *The Swingle Singers*, Patrick Craig in *The Tallis Scholars* and Bruce Russell in *The King's Singers*. Distinguished soloists have included John Ogden, John Lill, Peter Donohoe and Nikolai Demidenko: and visiting orchestras have included the Hallé, the Royal Liverpool Philharmonic, the BBC Philharmonic and the Orchestra of the Age of Enlightenment. As will be clear from the above list, Salopian musicians have also performed before a much wider audience, and at least two of them, Fergus Macleod and Stephen Wood, have mounted the conductor's rostrum and are well on the way towards professional conducting careers.

Meanwhile there were significant changes on the domestic musical scene, of which by far the most important was the inauguration of the Maidment Building, by His Royal Highness the Prince of Wales, in February 2001. His visit has been fully described in the chapter on Celebrations. The new building not only provided an auditorium in which vocal and instrumental solos could be performed, together with chamber music and small-scale orchestral works, but also accommodated a generous provision of practice rooms.

In choral music the focus shifted from the Concert Choir, which steadily declined in the nineties, to the Community Choir, to the Chapel Choir, directed by Alex Mason and to the Chamber Choir directed by Dympna Nightingale; both these last two groups, being smaller, aspiring to reach an even higher standard of performance. The inter-house Instrumental Competition also fell into disuse, but the inter-house Singing Competition, comprising both a unison and a part song performed by every house, replaced it and has flourished exceedingly. This now constitutes one of the major musical events of the year, providing the prelude to the Michaelmas half-term Exeat, the competition between houses for the top prizes every bit as fierce as in sporting competitions. In November, though on a school rather than a house basis, the St Cecilia Concerts give the instrumentalists their turn.

In 1999 the Bursar, Derek Crompton, suggested that the principal musical entertainment at the end of the summer term should be held in the open air, turning the event, in practice, into a Promenade Concert. This has proved to be a most successful initiative, attracting large audiences, well furnished with their picnics. It has been 'rained off' twice, most spectacularly in the deluge of 2012; but the most recent concerts, shielded in an 'open' marquee, have been a spectacular success.

The current pattern of musical occasions is now well established: the House Singing Competition in October, the St Cecilia Concerts in November, the Carol Services in December, a major orchestral performance (often an 'away' fixture) in March, an opera at the start of the summer term and a promenade concert at its close. The musical calendar (it will be observed) steps gingerly through the minefield of examinations. Salopians seem to get busier and busier as the range of examinations and of sporting and other extra-curricular activities continues to expand. Fifty or sixty years ago it was comparatively easy to assemble the necessary forces for a major concert; there was then much less time pressure and competition for slots in the *Fasti*. In spite of all this, the quality of the music and musicians which Shrewsbury produces continues markedly to rise. A new generation of Salopians is attracting notice on a wider stage, and the indications are that this development is not only likely to continue, but to be further reinforced. Among them the name of Galin Ganchev (M 2010-2015) will certainly appear. His performance, in March 2015, as the soloist in Rachmaninov's Third Piano Concerto, followed a series of dazzling solo recitals and was appropriately hailed by the Director of Music as 'a landmark moment in Shrewsbury School's musical life'.

In a wider perspective, Public Schools, occupying a middle position between the state schools on the one hand and the specialist music schools on the other, play a crucial role in training the country's musicians, and in so doing make an invaluable contribution to the cultural heritage of the nation. In this, Shrewsbury plays a full and widely acknowledged part. That this is so owes much to the energy and stamina, enthusiasm and devotion which the current Director of Music John Moore has invested in Salopian music during his long and distinguished tenure.

CHAPTER NINETEEN

SCHOOL DRAMA

The status of drama and the quality of dramatic productions have changed out of all recognition during the last sixty years. In 1950, and for many years thereafter, the Alington Hall was the only venue in which it was possible to stage a major production; though individual houses produced their own plays on improvised stages within the house, very often after Bump Supper, which was then a very much more prestigious occasion. Another traditional institution was the School House Slay, held at the end of the Michaelmas Term, whose main theme was to satirise members of the Common Room; there was great pressure on the 'brushers' to attend, to discover what was in store for them, and many did so with considerable apprehension. There were also staff revues from time to time, perhaps the most famous being *A Yank at Shrewsbury*, directed by Rodney Hoare, which recorded the adventures of Hiram P Knickerbocker, a fictional American exchange student. There were some memorable staff performances, some of which elicited uproarious applause from the contemporary Salopian audience. On one occasion Russell Hope Simpson, the senior master (also the horticultural architect of the magnificent Masters' Garden, which he could be seen cultivating with skill and devotion evening after evening) drew enthusiastic applause simply by walking across the stage, shod in green wellies and pushing a wheelbarrow, with a puzzled smile playing about his lips, uncertain why he had been asked to do this, and bemused by his rapturous reception. Similar acclaim was received by Patrick Childs ('P.C.'), perceived by some as a rather austere figure and a firm disciplinarian, who appeared on the stage in helmet and tunic, dressed as a police constable, and when Selby Martin, known for his devoted patronage of the Bee-Keeping Society, rushed across the stage, pursued by a swarm of bees. The tradition of staff revues was preserved, intermittently, right up to the last decade but has now sadly lapsed, at least in its original form, another casualty of the increasing curricular and extra-curricular demands placed on teachers in the modern Shrewsbury.

The most important of these special occasions was, of course, *The Masque*, written by Paul Dehn with music composed by John Stainer, and directed by Arnold Hagger in 1952 to mark the Fourth Centenary of the foundation of the School, an enterprise on which Michael Charlesworth commented

Seldom can any work have been written which better caught the atmosphere of the time or more suitably matched the occasion. In the intermingling of sentiment, sharp wit and studied understatement, Paul caught what I believe is a very Salopian characteristic.

The presentation, a decade later, of *1066 and All That*, by the staff of the History Faculty and the members of the History Sixth, at that time over a hundred in number, was another exceptional event upon the Alington Hall stage.

But in the normal course of events The Speech Day Play, directed in turn by George Simmons, Arnold Hagger, Willie Jones, Anthony Bowen and Tom Wheare, was the main (and often the sole) production of the year. The back-stage facilities were extremely limited and the acoustics extremely poor. Many experiments were adopted in an attempt to overcome the latter problem; a temporary stage was erected, lengthways, along the inside wall of the hall; on several occasions performances were staged at the other end of the hall, beneath the gallery, as in the case of Willie Jones' *An Elizabethan Evening* and *A Victorian Evening*; nor did the limited facilities preclude ambitious productions, such as Willie Jones' *Othello* (in which he himself took the title role) and Anthony Bowen's *The Beggar's Opera* and *Macbeth*.

Drama at the School made distinct progress during the 1970s. Housemasters were beginning to appreciate the considerable value of house plays in strengthening their House communities and were keen to encourage the activity. A new venue for small-scale productions was provided in E4, an English classroom on the first floor of the Main School Building. From time to time the main hall of the new Art School was pressed into service. Day Boys took ambitious advantage of the rapid growth in their numbers by staging a succession of Shakespearean plays requiring a large cast, *Henry V, Hamlet, Julius Caesar* and *Richard II*, although the Headmaster's warning to the Mayor, as he greeted him on the stage of the Alington Hall on the morning after the final performance of *Julius Caesar*, that he had seen the chief citizen being murdered on that very spot the previous evening, contained an interesting ambiguity. Day Boys' subsequent performance of *The Mikado* perhaps constituted the best of their dramatic efforts. Meanwhile Tom Wheare's production of *The Importance of Being Earnest*, with Michael Charlesworth and Michael Ling as the two butlers, reached a more sophisticated level. There was no doubt that productions in general were becoming more professional, yet the traditional features evoked by the term 'school play', of boys taking female roles, of lines not learned, of scenery falling down, of actors repeating the lines of a sequence of several pages in a 'loop', and of faulty timing, (knocks on the door occurring after rather than before the actor on stage calling out 'Who's that?'), were not entirely absent. A wind of change was certainly blowing through the wider world of drama in the 1970s; workshop theatre and community theatre were coming to the fore and Shrewsbury's competitor schools were also taking much more notice of the activity and beginning to fund purpose-built school theatres.

The breakthrough occurred in the first half of the 1980s. It was marked by the virtually simultaneous arrival of Robin Case and Peter Fanning. Robin was specifically appointed to produce plays. Peter was recruited to be Head of the English Faculty, and although this involved no specific obligation to involve himself similarly in play production, he had, after leaving Cambridge, been the manager of his own theatre company and brought invaluable experience in and enthusiasm for dramatic productions with him. Both also brought to Shrewsbury an awareness of higher standards and new techniques in such enterprises which were current outside the School.

However, without the provision of the Ashton Theatre in 1984, a project which was nurtured and vigorously supported by Simon Langdale, the enthusiasm and ability of these two new colleagues would have been severely cramped and confined. The adaptation of the former gymnasium to become a theatre was therefore the crucial enabling factor, for it had been extremely difficult (if not impossible) to produce drama of the highest quality and sophistication in the Alington Hall. It was both ironic and significant that a building originally provided by H.H.Hardy, as Headmaster, in 1938, to promote his enthusiasm for PT, should be officially re-opened, in its new form, by Robert Hardy, the Headmaster's son and himself a distinguished actor, to provide the launching pad for a veritable explosion of dramatic activity. With its infinitely better acoustics, proper provision for the technical aspects of production – sound, lighting, recording and special effects – adequate space for changing and the storage of scenery and properties, flexible arrangement of the seating, greater comfort for the audience, and, above all, a space which enabled the audience to be 'drawn in' to the action, for the first time, productions of much greater technical expertise and sophistication were made possible exactly at a time when two members of staff had been appointed well qualified to take full advantage of the new facilities.

It is not surprising that one of the consequences of this should be that many more people wanted to produce plays. Houses were keen to take advantage of this vastly improved provision and it soon became customary for every house to produce a play each year. Boys began to produce and even to write not only their own plays, but also their own musicals. As the proliferation of examinations made the production of a senior School Play impossible in the summer, the major school production was consequently moved to the Michaelmas Term. The competition between the Houses for the use of the theatre in the Lent Term (and particularly for those occasions in the School *Fasti* which were likely to attract a sizeable audience) became intense, and a House Play was being produced there practically every weekend during those ten weeks.

It fell to Robin Case to preside over the launch of this crucially important dramatic development and he did so with total dedication and super-abundant energy. Keen, as he was, on community theatre, he began with several large-scale ventures, even before the Ashton Theatre was provided. *Tamburlaine the Great* and *Nicholas Nickleby* were produced in the Alington Hall, *Nicholas Nickleby* and *Move over Mr Moss,* a great pageant to mark the centenary of the migration of the School to Kingsland in 1882, was staged in front of, in, on top of and down the facade of the Main School Building, requiring all the techniques of *son et lumière* to entertain an audience in the open air. It was a considerable risk and challenge, a monumental achievement and a resounding success. *Tin-Pan Alley* was Robin's first show in the new theatre. At one stage Robin was producing three plays a year. Peter Broad, during his few years at Shrewsbury, was also a member of this team of professional producers, contributing a memorable performance of *Gotcha*.

Behind the scenes Gilbert Roscoe (well experienced with the Pembroke Players) was teaching the boys how to manage the lighting and, together with John Massey, trained a nucleus of technicians who made a major contribution to school life in this way. Their role has subsequently been shared with 'Gap' students and more recently with post-graduate technicians.

Meanwhile Peter Fanning had directed *A Comedy of Errors*, with Peter Broad. Peter and Robin combined to present *Twelfth Night* both at Penshurst Place and in Zutphen. Peter also went on to stage productions of *Hamlet*, *The Duchess of Malfi*, and much later, a very moving presentation of *Racing Demon*. At the same time, at the beginning of the 1990s, and by a very happy coincidence, the Music Department felt ready to spread its wings, under its new Head of Faculty, John Moore. The result was a whole succession of musicals, inaugurated and sustained by Peter and John. *Oh, What a Lovely War, Guys and*

Dolls and *West Side Story* led the way. But at John Moore's suggestion, and in the second stage, they began to write, compose and present a series of 'home-grown' musicals of the very highest quality which have done much to spread and enhance the reputation of the School.

Peter Fanning, John Moore and Alex Went presented *Jekyll* in 1994, a musical adapted from Robert Louis Stevenson's novel *Doctor Jekyll and Mr Hyde*; *The Time Machine* followed in 1996, and *The Lost Domain* in 1999. All these were subsequently presented in Edinburgh, where *Jekyll* won a Fringe First Award; it is still, at the time of writing, the only School production to have won this accolade. *The Lost Domain* was also subsequently performed at the Linbury Studio Theatre, at the Royal Opera House in Covent Garden. A regular pattern developed of the production of a new musical every other year (in the alternate years Alex Went produced a series of Shakespearean plays) as the principal dramatic enterprise of the School. Since then the company has appeared regularly at the Edinburgh Fringe with specially written musicals, including other original shows, such as *The Bubble, Frankenstein, Harry,* and *What You Will*, each of which was subsequently staged in London theatres. Most recently, in 2013, *The Bubble* was revived at Shrewsbury International School, Bangkok, *Jekyll* is currently in repertory with Varna Children's Opera, Bulgaria, and *The Lost Domain* was revived at the Edinburgh Fringe in August 2014. The company aims to present new writing of quality, carefully framed for the voices and talents of a youthful cast. The enterprise has been informed by a careful appraisal and adoption of methods and trends in the professional theatre and facilitated by the growth and increasing sophistication of IT.

The ambition of the venture and the strong community feeling which it engenders has attracted a nucleus of supporters whose devoted participation has been indispensable. Peter Fanning and John Moore have been assisted by Alex Went, who did much of the writing of the earlier productions to which important contributions were also made by Peter Hankin and Julian Roach. The mantle of Gilbert Roscoe and his technicians has been passed on to Alex Davies, who, assisted by James Brown (OS) and Al Wager (OS), was Technical Director of the most recent production in Edinburgh. Invaluable assistance has been provided by Sara Hankin as an expert choreographer; in the supervision of the wardrobe by Jane Fanning and Philippa Moore; and successively by Michael Clarkson, James Marshall and Toby Perceval as administrators of a large cast, moving to a series of different locations. The August 2014 production was the twelfth occasion upon which John Moore and Peter Fanning have collaborated at the Edinburgh Fringe.

It is a story of remarkable achievement. Peter notes the equally remarkable fact that a Director of Drama was not appointed until 2008. He emphasises that the production of high-quality drama requires an adequate (which in practice means a very considerable) amount of time, with a dedicated cast which is available at times of day when its members are not exhausted by their legitimate and necessary commitment to other forms of activity, both academic and extra-curricular. In the early 1980s Top School time was ring-fenced. Gradually time in Societies' Hour became available, gaps in the daily routine (such as Thursday afternoons after CCF) were exploited; time on Sundays was invaluable and eventually not only has sufficient flexibility been developed to allow time on weekday evenings for rehearsal, especially when a production is imminent, but drama has been included as a curriculum subject. Peter claims, along with the sports coaches and other colleagues who preside over major extra-curricular commitments, that participation in a major team effort (such as a play) can positively help members of the cast and crew to manage their time more efficiently. Confidence and self-discipline are nurtured in this community activity, with its definable and immensely rewarding outcome. He has been delighted by the wholehearted response of the members of his cast and crew, and astounded by their capacity to grow, relating that 'they are trusting and will go the extra mile-and-a-half'. At House level the time and commitment required to produce a play which reaches the high standards now generally expected are such that it has recently been thought prudent to reduce the participation from each house from a yearly to a two-yearly appearance on the stage.

That Salopian drama at top level now attracts enthusiastic audiences not only in its own Ashton Theatre but in other venues as varied and far-flung as Edinburgh, London, Zutphen, Varna, and Bangkok evokes an interesting historical parallel, for Shrewsbury School had been established for less than thirty years, when the first Queen Elizabeth set out from London, hoping to see one of Thomas Ashton's plays!

CHAPTER TWENTY

VISUAL ARTS

It is clear that the successive Heads of Art at Shrewsbury have experienced considerable contentment and fulfilment in their role, for there have only been three during the last three-quarters of a century. Arthur Broadbent (1939-1969), John Alford (1969-1989) and Philip Woolley (1989-2014). Together they have created a calm and civilised oasis at the hub of frenzied and competitive Salopian activity.

Seventy-five years ago, Art was still very much a peripheral subject, and its cramped and improvised location, on the top floor of the School Building at the School House end, reflected its comparatively humble status. Art's shaky position was further weakened by Arthur's absence during the war, in which, equipped with a commission, paints and a motorbike, he travelled all over the country, advising the military authorities on camouflage, and designing and installing fake 'cities' in remote areas on the Pennines for the *Luftwaffe* to bomb! But on his return to school, Arthur's gentleness and sincerity attracted many Salopians to the Art Room. Such was his placid and tolerant nature that Russell Hope Simpson averred that 'it would be quite impossible to make Arthur lose his temper.'

Arthur made the very best use of the limited facilities and resources available to him, offering not only drawing and painting, but also adding bookbinding, typography and a model railway to the range of available options, and, having built a kiln himself, introduced ceramics (then called pottery) too. Arthur was a talented painter, and particularly a potter. Although, unlike his two successors whose own distinguished paintings have been regularly exhibited, Arthur did not mount exhibitions of his own work, though his designs for the *Masque*, staged in 1952, were considered outstanding. He also contributed fine murals to the churches of St Timothy and St Ambrose in Everton, which parties from the School had renovated in an area near to Shrewsbury House, the School club. It was characteristic of Arthur that, when he heard that both churches had subsequently been demolished, he merely laughed. He used his extensive travels in Europe to amass a considerable collection of fine-quality slides still used at the School to illustrate the history of art and architecture.

In 1955 the teaching of Art was moved to No 6 the Schools on Ashton Road and a second colleague, Christopher Pemberton, was appointed to help to exploit the extended facilities. The provision of many separate rooms naturally assisted and encouraged a further proliferation of activities. John Alford succeeded Christopher Pemberton as an assistant to Arthur in 1958 and at about the same time Art and Art History became serious examination subjects. It was already clear that the subject was 'taking off'. John succeeded Arthur Broadbent as Head of Art in 1969 and in 1974 Arthur Morgan was appointed to assist him. It was at this time, in the late sixties and early seventies, when Shrewsbury was not entirely unfamiliar with the rumblings of student unrest, that the Art Buildings provided a refuge for those who still felt alienated and unappreciated during the last years of the traditional public school; and the sympathetic reception they received there did much to head off trouble and to divert their energies into more positive channels. In this the Art School exercised a valuable social function: it was partly as a result of the availability of this hospitable sanctuary that student dissent at Shrewsbury was much less in evidence than in many other similar schools.

But when John and his wife Jean offered, with characteristic generosity, to take some of the potential rebels as outboarders, matters were not always so straightforward. John remembers that

they did get oil paint all over the bedclothes, eat flower decorations at table, find girlfriends at an earlier age than most and, while making movies on the top floor, had been known to set fire to the furniture. They were unpredictable and frequently alarming, but never dull.

During John's time in charge, the importance of creative work, not just for the few, but for the school as a whole, was increasingly recognised. Successive headmasters increased the Art teaching staff and successive bursars improved the facilities. Although the move to No 6 had brought many improvements, there were still problems of timetable, budget and staffing to be overcome. Yet again the appointment of an assistant was quickly followed by the provision of vastly superior facilities for the teaching of Art. The completion of the New Science Buildings had freed the Old Darwin building. This was adapted to become the Art School, duly opened, in characteristically flamboyant style, by Willie Rushton, on 4th June 1976. Leonard Baart had made the best possible use of the money allotted for the conversion of the building, and at the same time John Alford defined the three aims which he considered that Art should fulfil: to encourage an individual's creativity; to teach the necessary skills; and to impart an appreciation of our heritage in the visual arts. The new facilities greatly enhanced the opportunity to achieve these aims. This was surely the most important event in the teaching of the subject during the last sixty years and provided the launching pad for developments both in range and quality of the work produced which have enabled Art to establish the prestigious position it now occupies in the School. Speech Day exhibitions in the Art School, ever since, have never failed to win the admiration of all who viewed them. Art trips to galleries both at home and abroad became a regular feature of the termly *Fastis* and the quality of the work produced by Art students made it possible to stage a regular series of one-man exhibitions, which included sculpture and ceramics as well as painting. Arthur Morgan, who left Shrewsbury in 1980 to become Director of Art at Winchester, remembers that visitors were impressed by the scale and the scope of the new building and recalls that 'nearly every major city boasting a good gallery has entertained shock troops of aesthetic Salopians on Field Days.' One poster in the Art School advertised visits to London, Paris, Florence and Venice: 'Join the Art School and see the world' was not an idle cliché.

Arthur Morgan bequeathed an impressive outline of the opportunities available in the greatly improved facilities of the new location. The first year course in the Art School in 1980 offered a basic introduction to all areas of activity and the time available was shared with the Craft Centre. At the end of the first year the pupil had to choose between the two locations. In the Art School a two-year course to 'O' level followed. The examination consisted of a practical studio examination, as well as a paper on the Italian Renaissance. After this a candidate could pursue an Art and/or a History of Art course to 'A' level; in this there were three areas of study, Painting, Graphics and Ceramics, each supported by drawing. All studio work was undertaken in free afternoons and evenings, which left the formal school time-table free for other subjects, so offering Art to all. Drama constantly drew upon the Art School's resources.

Morgan noted that in the four years since 1976 Salopians had taken up careers in Graphic Design, Interior Design, Fashion, Ceramics and Theatre/TV Design, not to mention the steady and consistent exodus of painters and designers. His valedictory message emphasised the vital role played by Art in nurturing skills and imagination and its place in a wider educational context:

If we look at the future of this country, there is no doubt that a creative discipline will have a greater role to play. Industry is crying out for a revival in energy and direction, and this in effect suggests a creative, practical outlook. In its broadest sense I interpret Industry to mean designing, manufacturing, marketing: and without this we have no wealth and no civilized society

and he quotes, with approval, the remark of Sir Alex Smith, then Director of Manchester Polytechnic: 'If I were a dictator in education, I would ordain that every child, in every school, every year, should design something and make it'.

Courses in History of Art attracted the allegiance and enthusiasm of many Salopians, and writing in 1985, Alford endorsed the lifelong value of their choice:

Works of art reveal the priorities of society with great clarity to those who really learn to look ... they provide abiding pleasure ... it is worth remembering that from the age of about twenty-four, with the best three-quarters of their lives to come, both academic work and sport soon lose their charm for the majority.

He was also able to report that:

this year there are ten Sixth Formers who are intending to read History of Art at university – neither they, nor any of their contemporaries, knew that such a subject existed when they arrived at the School.

and in that same year a member of the first History of Art 'A' level group was appointed Director of the Ashmolean.

This was the situation in the last decade of John Alford's long and distinguished tenure in the Art School. When Philip Woolley took over from Alford in 1989, he records that "I inherited a wonderful Art building and a respected subject". In a generous tribute to his predecessor, Woolley commented on the series of magnificent exhibitions of his own paintings which John Alford has mounted in Shropshire and elsewhere, in which there is 'the indelible sign of every brushmark having been torn from the soul'. *Cognoscenti* who are fortunate enough to acquire these paintings 'will have the changing light of Shropshire forever on their walls'. Indeed, John's magnificent paintings are prized possessions in dozens of local homes. Meanwhile, in the new Art School, the quality of the work in ceramics, in particular, has developed out of all recognition under the leadership of Philip's wife, Victoria Dark-Woolley, who has also been most generous in her contributions to the Art work in Chapel, as described in the appropriate chapter. The Art School has been updated and its facilities further expanded, most significantly by the installation of four new mezzanine floors. This has made it possible for all year groups to have their own dedicated space and for all Sixth Formers to have their own studios. The staffing of the Art Faculty has been doubled, from three to six, plus a technician; and with the addition of a Photography course to those already existing, Art, Art History and Ceramics, four 'A' level subjects are now on offer. Currently there are nearly 100 candidates taking examinations in these options, either at 'A' level or at GCSE. One notable feature of recent years has been the regular series of one-man exhibitions by current pupils, which has vividly displayed the range and quality of individual talent.

Philip was very fortunate in having the assistance of Caroline Pringle, who made a major contribution to the work of the Art School during her thirteen years at Shrewsbury. Energetic and resourceful, she taught drawing and painting, as well as some print making and sculpture, at all levels of the school, and also History of Art to A level in the Sixth Form. Among her many imaginative projects was the preservation of crabs and lobsters. She led painting expeditions to Nesscliffe and was generous in furnishing extra evening classes in which she never failed to communicate her enthusiasm for the subject to her pupils.

The Art School, through the Salopians who studied there during the last seventy-five years has nurtured and encouraged a galaxy of talent, which has provided the wider Art world with some of its most famous figures, the Director of the National Gallery, the Surveyor of the Queen's Pictures, the Director of the Courtauld Institute among them, together with Professors of Fine Art both at home and abroad. On the domestic scene, particularly in the field of architecture, Salopians have made a distinguished contribution both in the town and at the School. Their affection for the Art School and their allegiance to it was demonstrated when they gathered, on Saturday, October 9th 2010, to celebrate John Alford's eightieth birthday with an Old Salopian Art exhibition.

CHAPTER TWENTY-ONE

CRAFT, DESIGN AND TECHNOLOGY

In the first two decades of our period Salopians had to content themselves with the facilities of the Carpenter's shop, first in the Moser Precinct and then in the old farm buildings, but this was superseded in the latter location by a purpose-built Craft Centre which came into operation in Michaelmas Term 1969. It was used, in parallel with the Art School, by boys in the Lower School, for two periods a week, as part of the official curriculum. Twenty Sixth Formers used it for their own projects on Thursday afternoon, and it was open to all in free time.

The Craft Centre quickly established its reputation in the 1970s, not least by the successful participation of Salopians in the BP build-a-car competition, under the supervision of Ted Barber and Grant Butchard. The challenge was to design a small car for two adults with their luggage. 600 schools participated, and 27 were represented in the finals, in which Shrewsbury came fourth. In the second competition a smaller car, the *Pygmy*, came third. Its potential for use as an invalid car was widely noted: and the *Invashrew* was developed for that purpose and completed on 29th September 1978. This was placed second. It appeared on TV, was exhibited in the Motor Show and won the 16-17 age group in the 'Young Engineer of Britain' competition. Three years later, in 1981, five entries from Shrewsbury reached the final; they included the *Invashrew II,* a kettle *Tiltezee*, designed to reduce the risks, for the elderly, involved in boiling a kettle of water, an automatic windscreen-washer bottle-filler which collected rainwater to fill the bottle, a light-bulb extractor to enable a person in a wheelchair to change a bulb in a ceiling, and the *Inva-Retro,* a wheelchair which enabled its occupant to be tilted backwards, primarily intended for use in a dental surgery. It won the Young Engineer for Britain competition in 1981 and gained much publicity when Sir Douglas Bader was photographed sitting in it.

Salopian inventiveness faced a new challenge when, in 1984, members of the Lower Sixth were invited to design and make a spire for a new church in Bayston Hill. Each boy produced a scale model of his suggested design, and the Church Building Committee made the final choice. The finished article was like two canoes moulded together and was made of fibreglass. A fortnight after installation it was struck by lightning, but a lightning conductor had been attached, and since then the spire has survived extremes of heat and cold, and several gales. Adrian Struvé, who was closely connected with the enterprise, wondered whether any other school could claim to have a-spired to such an achievement!

Meanwhile the new syllabuses of Craft, Design and Technology had brought these skills firmly into the academic orbit. CDT took all that was good and worthwhile from traditional woodwork and added a whole new dimension of technological problem-solving. The aim was 'to develop the crucial skills of problem-solving, planning, technological understanding and innovation needed in a rapidly developing technological society.' All Third Form pupils studied CDT for two periods a week. Subsequently they could opt for either or both of two GCSE courses, CDT Technology or CDT Design and Realisation. A level Design and Technology attracted about fifteen candidates a year, and here again the emphasis was on problem-solving in a technological environment. The course description was forbiddingly challenging: 'boys are expected to develop a sound understanding of the economics of commercial production, the relationship between designer, manufacturer and consumer, the environmental impact of technological and manufacturing activities and of relevant government legislation, as well as in-depth knowledge of materials and manufacturing processes'. The implementation of this programme, the provision of the necessary facilities and the full integration of CDT into the school curriculum was the remarkable achievement of David Nickolaus and Trevor Kidson.

In recent years the spirit of inventiveness inspired by the *Invashrew* has been applied, by Third and Fourth Formers, under the supervision of John Holloway, to the design and racing of electric cars. Problems of materials, gearing and aerodynamics have all had to be solved. Young Salopians have raced their cars at Mallory Park, Darley Moor, Castle Combe, Aintree and Silverstone in the Greenpower 24 competition, and the mention of 'pit-stops' is engagingly reminiscent of Formula One! Shrewsbury's team has recently won the prize for the 'Best Engineered Car' for the second year running in the North-West heat; and as John Holloway remarked in 2013, 'For a 14-year-old to build a racing car from scratch and race it on a professional track is the stuff of dreams'.

Now, in 2014, the impressive scope of the activity in the Department may be described as 'problem-solving in a man-made world'. Kevin Lloyd, the current Head of CDT, reports that there is even more strongly focused emphasis on Design and Technology and very much less upon traditional Craft. The process starts with the investigation of a specific problem, followed by the modelling of an idea or concept, initially upon a computer but then realised in a three-dimensional trial model, followed either by a return to the computer or by further testing, and finally by working in the actual materials. Of all these stages, meticulous initial planning is the most crucial.

All members of the Lower School have some instruction in Design and Technology, which still alternates with Art in a two-period allocation in the Third Form year. Fourth and Fifth Formers may follow a course to GCSE, for which 60% of the marks are assigned to a portfolio and 40% to a written paper. Currently 72 members of the School are taking this course. In the Sixth Form, the elements of the 'A' level course are similar (thirteen members of the Lower Sixth and nine of the Upper Sixth are taking it, with the number of girls growing each year), but the range of materials and processes is broader, and the whole emphasis is placed upon guiding the Sixth Former to find his own area of interest. Possible choices (not yet actual choices in every case) span engineering, electronic product design, consumer product design, interior design, furniture design, fashion design, textiles and jewellery.

Salopians of the 1960s will remember the carpenter's bench and the traditional craft machines; they might well be bemused, should they enter the Design centre nowadays, when they find themselves confronted by the panoply of computer-aided manufacture, laser cutters, thermal image transfers, 3D printers and computer numerical controls together with the objects, reminiscent of a science fiction scenario, which they have produced. But there is yet more to come. Projected staff development will bring a sharper focus on robotics and on business and marketing; and the planned move to the Lyle Building will place Design in immediate proximity to Physics, Information Technology and Art, the three subjects to which it is most closely allied, and establish it firmly as the most contemporary of all subject choices.

CHAPTER TWENTY-TWO

SPORT: INTRODUCTION

Basil Oldham observes that 'in some schools… athletic distinction has often tended to develop idolisation. This does not seem ever to have been a characteristic of Shrewsbury'. He quotes the words of a master, bred at another school, 'Shrewsbury never produces little tin gods' and he concludes that 'the School's traditional dislike of 'lift' – that is, the assumption of airs and self-importance - does seem to have preserved it from the excessive worship of athletic (or any other) success, and all but a few of the most eminent athletes have been the most unassuming, if also the most influential of boys'. Shrewsbury has produced some very distinguished sportsmen during the last few years and my own experience suggests that Oldham's evaluation still remains true.

One of the really significant developments in the last sixty years has been the vast expansion in the provision and variety of sporting activity. The current situation is certainly worlds away from that in the School's earliest days, when Thomas Ashton recognised only 'shooting in the long-bow, running, wrestling, leaping and chess-play' as permitted recreational pastimes. . Even a comparison in much more recent times, between the School *Fasti* for any term in the 1950s with the corresponding term in the last decade, would demonstrate, at a glance, the dramatic scale of the change. In the 1950s, most competitive sport was House-based. Inter-school fixtures were rare and confined to the first, and occasionally the second teams in the over-16 age-groups. Fixtures for more junior boys were rarer still. A clear distinction was made between the five 'major' sports – football, cricket, rowing, fives and the Hunt, and other sports, such as swimming, tennis and athletics, for which rather limited provision was also made.

One of the most important features of the succeeding decades has been the steady increase in the provision of inter-school fixtures, at every level of the School. The number of matches arranged for school football teams provides the most notable example: whereas, in the Lent and Summer Terms, rowing and cricket, fives and rugby all claim the allegiance of a considerable proportion of boys, most boys play soccer at some level in the autumn. In the Michaelmas Term of 2014 seven senior football teams were fielded. The 1st XI had 22 matches, the 2nd XI 19, the 3rd and 4th XIs 17 each: the 5th XI 11, the 6th XI 5 and the 7th XI 2. Junior teams were fielded at Under 16, Under 15 and Under 14 level. Four teams were fielded at Under 16 level: the A team had 14 matches, the B team 13, the C team 3 and the D team 2. Three teams were fielded at Under 15 level: the A team had 15 matches, the B team 16 and the C team 6. Four teams were fielded at Under 14 level: the A team had 14 matches, the B team 12, the C team and the D team 5 each.

Other sports have witnessed a similar expansion, while not catering for as great a number of participants. All this has meant that there has been considerable and ever increasing competition for the time and individuals available. In the earlier years the competing claims were arbitrated by the Sports Committee; and the skilled diplomacy of Martin Knox, as Chairman, was required in order to arrive at an acceptable consensus, week by week. Much more recently the whole spectrum of sporting activity has been co-ordinated under the supervision of the Director of Sport. At the same time, while an increasing number of boys took part in school teams, there was some feeling that those who were not quickly selected for these teams were being neglected; and all the while the numbers in the School were steadily and significantly growing.

Improved facilities were required to respond not only to growing numbers but also to the intensity of competition. Squash courts, a new gymnasium, and new changing rooms, a weight-training room, the all-weather surface and adjacent extra tennis courts were all provided, albeit at the cost of the athletics track. Later came the Cardus cricket centre and a new swimming pool. The Fives Courts were renovated and expanded. Extra bays were added in the Boat House, the adjacent 'Cottage' was restored and the Yale Building with its Ergo Hall was inaugurated.

The introduction of a new position on the staff – Director of Sport – in 2005 brought with it central supervision, administration and monitoring of sport and the formulation of a clear policy to provide a sufficient range of sporting activity for everyone to be able to find a sport in which he – and later she – would wish to participate. Greater attention was to be paid to those who were not regularly selected for established school teams. Still more fixtures have been provided for this purpose: and the number of less expert players participating has grown.

A degree of obligation to take part in sport, at all levels of the School, has been defined. 'To do changes', has indeed been a consistent feature of the last sixty years, but for the greater part of this time the focus was on the junior boys. Checking that the obligation was fulfilled was left, in the first instance, to the monitors, whose commitment and efficiency were variable. Now there is consistent, centralised checking that everyone fulfils his or her obligation to complete four sessions of sport each week in the Lower School, and latterly, two sessions of sport per week in the Sixth Form also. Rowing, Fives, The Hunt and Fencing have particularly profited from this arrangement. Also the number of training sessions in swimming has risen from one to five each week.

There are persistent problems, however. Shrewsbury's geographical position makes it difficult to arrange appropriate fixtures with independent schools; the proliferation of external examinations has severely restricted the opportunities for participation in organised sport, particularly in the Summer Term – the days when First House Cricket was played in two leagues, with unlimited overs, are long gone! The place of, and provision for Rugby in the sporting programme has been a much debated issue. To these difficulties more recent, specific problems have been added. Among our traditional opponents, Bradfield and Repton are the only corresponding independent boarding schools which can still put out a full range of teams. Some traditional Grammar School opponents, though willing to play on Saturday mornings, are now unwilling to accept a fixture for Saturday afternoons. Local day schools and local Shropshire League teams now figure regularly in the fixture list. The standard of performance on the football field in northern and midland preparatory schools also appears to be declining.

Speculation about the future suggests that if the number of boys in the school continues to fall appreciably as a consequence of full co-education, it might be necessary to reduce the number of sporting options available. The traditional sporting profile of the Salopian has been that of a gentleman amateur, but recently there has been a marked growth in professionalism. All the Salopian traditional sports are well on the path towards national reputation and representation; although fives players are much less numerous in the country as a whole, the sport has broken out of the monopoly which schools (rather than clubs) - and particularly independent schools – used to maintain. Here, too, Shrewsbury has consolidated and enhanced a leading position during the last decade. The School is in the exceptional position of providing a full sporting programme for rowing as well as for football, cricket, rugby and cross-country running.

Girls' sport inevitably made a shaky start in 2008, when the intake was restricted to the Sixth Form and confined to one House, but in 2014, with the admission of younger girls also to the School, it has visibly begun to gain momentum. Full development will, of course, only be possible after a full generation of girls has passed through the School, but as readers will see from the account provided in the appropriate section, the present situation is more than encouraging. Another welcome development has been the institution of Sports' Awards, now in their third year, which has not only served as a stimulus to individual aspiration, but has also prompted the welcome return of two Salopians prominent in sports administration, Tim Lamb (SH 1966-1971), formerly Chief Executive of the English Cricket Board and Richard Bevan (DB 1974-1978) Chief Executive of the League Managers' Association to preside over the ceremony. Most recently, in April 2015, the Guest of Honour was another Old Salopian and prominent local sportsman, Tony Barker (DB 1968-1973). Girls have already won their fair share of these awards.

I have given substantial consideration, in the chapters which follow, only to the five 'traditional' sports, the Hunt, the Boat Club, football, cricket and fives, seeking to place them all in their historical context. I have included rugby, polo, mountain-biking, diving and girls' sports (and sailing in the 'Wider World' section) on the grounds of novelty or change of status, but a Salopian in 2015 might also choose to take part in athletics, badminton, beagles, track-cycling, equestrian skills, fencing, golf, hockey, basketball, martial arts, shooting, netball, squash, swimming, tennis, trampolining – or yoga!

CHAPTER TWENTY-THREE

THE ROYAL SHREWSBURY SCHOOL HUNT

Of all Salopian sports the Royal Shrewsbury School Hunt (the Cross-Country team) is the most historic and the most distinctive. Many of its institutions and much of its ritual are peculiar to Shrewsbury. The Captain of Running is known as the *Huntsman* and the ritual is based upon the pursuit of an imaginary fox. The Huntsman therefore wears a jersey of hunting pink, together with red stockings and a black cap upon which crossed golden whips are embroidered; he carries a whip and, in a leather holder, a hunting horn which he takes out to sound from time to time. His Vice-Captains are called *Whips*, Senior and Junior, each with specific roles, and they too carry such implements on the runs. These whips themselves are ancient objects and have traditional names. Members of the School team are called *Gentlemen of the Runs* and carry batons. The runners, of course, are called *Hounds* and together they form a *Pack*. At the start of a run, the participants are *coupled up*, that is, counted in pairs and said to '*throw off*'. At various stages in the run the leaders pause to allow the remainder to catch up. Styled *all-ups*, these pauses are another distinctive feature of Shrewsbury cross-country running. The end of an all-up may be signalled by another shout of *Gently forward* ! It is therefore only the last stage of the run which is actually a competitive race, and this '*run in*' is started by a traditional formula; *All hounds who wish may run in: run up and run well*' or by an alternative modern version *All hounds who run, run hard and run well: and may the devil take the hindmost*. The winner of the race is said to *kill*; 'Gentlemen' have not always been allowed to compete on the same terms as the *Hounds* and sometimes the result has identified a *Killing Gentleman* and a *Killing Hound*.

Shrewsbury had an organised system of cross-country running earlier than any other school, and as a closed club, it has a strong claim to be the oldest cross-country club in the world. The first recorded Huntsman is known to have entered the School in 1819; there is further evidence of the existence of the Hunt in 1824, and an account of a run which took place in 1831 has been preserved.

In the very earliest years there was no central organisation; cross-country running depended upon private initiative and there was fierce rivalry between the different *packs*. The discipline was lax, with negligible regard for the School rules. Basil Oldham cites a letter of L.W. Denman (1834-39), in which he tells how, after a run, the members of the Hunt used to go to the Dog and Partridge Inn 'to take a glass of ale and smoke a pipe, while stops for sherry and other drinks in the middle of a run were common' and on one occasion 'two magnificent bowls of punch and as much beer as we could drink were provided, after which the run was continued'. About 1840 the Hunts were unified and the *Hound Books* provide an unbroken record of the School Runs since 1842. Dr Kennedy, the Headmaster at that time, strongly opposed the Hunt; its activities were saved by the mediation of the Praepostors; and it was legalised after the imposition of certain restrictions.

The routes taken by the runs are also traditional (though, again, this was not so in the earliest days, when they were sometimes marked out by pages torn from Dr Kennedy's *Latin Primer*). Most of the runs in the nineteenth century, when the School was still located in the centre of the town, were to the north. After the move to Kingsland in 1882 they changed direction to the south. The length of the runs increases steadily from three to ten miles, and each run has its own specific name; the Bog, the Bicton, the Horton, the Redhill, the Shelton, the Bomere Pool, the Cruckton, The Hookagate, The Ley Grange, the Long, the Longden and so forth. For several years there was a tradition, now lapsed, of naming a Run after the previous year's Huntsman. Most of the changes which have occurred to the routes of the runs have been occasioned by new fences, new roads and increased motor traffic.

Willie Jones (Master 1959-77) and Mark Mortimer (Master 1958-94) in effect had joint charge of the Hunt for most of the sixties and seventies. Both wrote verses about the indelible impression of companionship and of freedom that the activity made upon them. Willie succeeded Adrian Struvé in the Michaelmas Term of 1961, left the School in 1978, and for over thirty years has lived in Japan, and is now a professor occupying his own personal chair in the University of Sapporo.

Willie wrote:

And so, for nearly eighteen years,
I ran through Shropshire countryside,
About its farms, beside its meres,
Up bracken hill, down woodland ride,
By meadow gate and hedgerow stile,
No better pastime to beguile
The afternoons of days that spun
From sweet September's mellow sun
To dull December's frost and snow,
With views from ridge-tops of the hills
That mark the boundary with Wales
Where dark clouds masked the sunset's glow,
Until I tore a tendon sheath
And buildings shrouded Bicton Heath.

In his poem *One Last Toll Of Fancy's Knell* (revised in 2012), Willie records the reconnaissance of the runs and devotes a stanza to each of them, two examples of which are given below:

When boys might play till dark
Or five o'clock school or tea,
Either I would call for Mark
or Mark would call for me:
and leaving behind all traces
of tasks we had left undone,
with the sun upon our faces
we would set our course and run ...

We began with *The Bog,* a run
to start the new term on its toes:
an 'Indian Summer' sun,
a lingering summer rose,
the haws like droplets of blood,
in a balmy September heat
the stubble a golden flood
as we crossed it on delicate feet

and later in the year:

The air grew chill for *The Cruckton,*
as wheel-ruts filled with rain,
and oaks turned black and sodden
and furrows swam with grain,
until up from Hanwood climbing
for a hilltop farm we strode,
and raced home in the darkening
down the length of the Longden Road.

The most famous of all these runs is *The Tucks,* so called because it was originally run across the fields of Farmer Tuck on the day of Shrewsbury Races in order to ensure that the boys attended the former rather than the latter event! Traditionally the Tucks had begun and ended on the School Site, but the danger of a horde of five hundred boys charging across the inner by-pass at the end of Kennedy Road was as apparent as the disciplinary problems attendant on the same horde assembling in some ploughed field to wait for the laggards to arrive at an all-up. As a result, The Tucks was temporarily suspended: but after a brief hiatus, the run was resurrected. The start and the finish were moved to Meole Brace; all-ups were abolished in the specific case of The Tucks, and a 'wave system' was adopted at the start, by which House Captains of Running select 'seeded' runners to form the first wave. Two other waves follow, in turn, after a short interval. After a period in which members of the Upper Sixth were excused, the whole school, boys and girls, now once again takes part; and over the years many members of the Common Room have joined in. The record for participation in the race is thought to be held by a senior (now retired) member of the staff who has completed over fifty Tucks runs (though in recent years 'complete' rather than 'compete' and 'participate' rather than 'run' are more accurate descriptions of his performance!).

Understandably, and particularly as it existed before its reform, The Tucks was not Willie Jones' favourite run:

The Tucks was another affair,
the school *en masse,* in a rout
for which I did never much care,
when a gent might behave like a lout:

> simply all-licensed jesting and games
> in comical hat-wear and togs
> that upset young mothers with prams
> and terrified slumbering dogs.

In his poem *It's happening at last* Mark Mortimer deplored the disruption of the traditional Hunt runs caused by the exigencies of modern transport and planning; the poem's seriousness of tone is in marked contrast to the generally light and satirical note evident in other examples of his verse quoted elsewhere in this book:

> Where many a bosky by-way
> explored the countryside,
> appears a three-lane highway,
> obscenely straight and wide,
>
> and secret, rustic places
> the Hunt meandered through
> in rarely witnessed races
> are opened up to view.
>
> It had to be; so be it:
> I'm thankful that a man
> who'd surely weep to see it
> is safely in Japan.

The distinctive terminology of the procedures of the Hunt and the equally distinctive names of the runs could lead to unintended and highly unfortunate misunderstandings by the uninitiated. The story is told of the Housemaster, delighted by the performance of one of his new boys, who sent the following telegram to the boy's parents: 'Nigel killed on The Bog. Congratulations!'

Most of the 'domestic' runs occur during the Michaelmas Term. The 'New Boys' Race (now the 'Third Form Race') used to go off the Site during the 1960s. Girls took part in it for the first time in Michaelmas Term 2014. Most recently, however, it has been confined to the Site and the Quarry and the 2014 race followed the 'Benjy' course. The 'Benjy' (generally reputed to be named after Benjamin Hall Kennedy) constitutes the staple of junior running in the earlier part of the school year. Starting on 'The Drum' in front of the School Building, the route is up Central, along Ashton Road, round the Top Common, down Oldham's Gap to the river, up Port Hill Road to the gate, past Severn Hill and Ridgemount, then left to the path at the top of the School bank, back on to the Site, past Chapel and so back to The Drum. For many years inter-House Benjys were a prominent feature of the weekly sports programme for members of the Third and Fourth Form. There were five consecutive races, at fifteen or twenty-minute intervals, on one afternoon each week, between pairs of Houses in a weekly league. This arrangement made it very easy to spot running talent and enabled serious runners to join in for up to five trials, providing excellent, regular training for them. There was keen competition for the Benjy trophy, but the arrangement ended, in the last decade, when the opportunity to participate in a wider range of sports was offered to junior boys.

Steeplechases and Athletics also fell originally under the authority of the Huntsman and were regarded as integral parts of the Hunt, though in Steeplechases Shrewsbury was not as obviously pioneering as in the other two aspects. Complete records for Senior Steeplechases have been kept since 1845 and for Junior Steeplechases since 1856. Just as the terminology for Cross-Country Running was taken from fox-hunting, the terminology for Steeplechases was taken from horse-racing. The competitors were called *horses* and were accompanied to the start and were also *run in* to the finish by their *owners*. Racing cards were issued to spectators, featuring names such as *Mr. K.S. Tamburlaine's P.Q. Othello*. Until the nineteen-forties Steeplechases bore all the less desirable marks of the traditional, hierarchical Public School. *Horses* had to fight their way through hedges between points marked at each extent by *douls,* who for this purpose were described as *sticks.* Protective clothing and gloves were worn, and if the hedges proved too thick, recourse was taken to diving over the hedges, or *belly-hedging.* Carbolic baths were prescribed at the end of the race, and the winner required not only considerable ability as a runner but also considerable moral strength, or 'guts'. Though this ordeal did not survive into our period, the obstacle element, though much attenuated, did, as did the tradition of *horses* and *owners*, which lasted into the 1970s. *Owners* traditionally assembled as many house and school colours as they could and were swathed in these as they accompanied their assigned competitor. In recent years both horses and owners have faded from the scene and the obstacles have been removed, though the name of the race survives. Steeplechases are now a relay race between House teams composed of one member of each year-group in the School – in effect an inter-House cross-country competition.

Two new 'domestic' races have recently been introduced on a Sunday in the Summer Term. One is *The Quarter-Mile Challenge,* held round a rectangular course from the middle of Central down to the Drum, then left and left again up the parallel road, round the Alington Hall and back to the starting-point. The other race, even shorter, is *The Sidney-Darwin Dash* down Central between their two statues. In 2014 and 2015 most members of the School came to watch these races which took place immediately after morning Chapel. Both staff and pupils have figured prominently in the recently instituted Shrewsbury Marathon and Half-Marathon races held in June. A Preparatory Schools' Cross-Country Championship, which is now in its fourth year, is held on the Site in October, and in 2014 this attracted about 200 entrants, boys and girls, drawn from ten different schools. Another recent and exciting innovation has been the invitation in 2012 and 2014 respectively to the distinguished runners Sentayu Eshetu from Ethiopia and the Olympic Gold Medallist and five-time world Cross-Country Champion John Ngugi to spend a week in Shrewsbury as Coaches-in-Residence.

Competition in cross-country running against other schools occurs mainly in the Lent Term. Shrewsbury has maintained a distinguished record throughout the last hundred years. In the *Blue Book* of 1944 it is recorded that 'The School's running record is extremely high, only six Cross-Country races having been lost since 1909'; and Basil Oldham, writing in 1952, states that 'of the sixty-three Cross-Country runs that have taken place against other schools, Shrewsbury has won fifty-three, drawn one and lost nine'. Nowadays the competition is always strong, but Shrewsbury continues to be well in contention. The strongest opposition currently comes from The Judd School, St Albans School, Skinners Tunbridge Wells, R.G.S. Newcastle on Tyne, Bradford Grammar School, Winchester and Sedbergh.

The big races, which often attract more than forty schools, are the ones to win. Among these was the Rugeley meeting, with its course on Cannock Chase, in which the RSSH has won several team and individual victories. Subsequently the Shrewsbury team has competed in the Midland and Northern Independent Schools' Championship (MANIS), where it has repeated its earlier successes. These competitions have had two formats, cross-country team races and cross-country relays. The latter have usually attracted the best running schools in the area and there have been frequent wins for the RSSH at Loughborough, Worcester and Lichfield, sometimes with more than one team in the top three. The two races which always attract a large number of schools from all over the country are the Knole Run at Sevenoaks and the King Henry VIII relay at Coventry. The RSSH team has never managed to win at Sevenoaks, but came second or third several times and has had the individual winner twice. There were few years in which the RSSH was not in the top ten.

Athletics at Shrewsbury started in 1840, nine years earlier than at any other school. The name given at Shrewsbury to the Mile Event, the Derby, dates from the same year. Originally the whole terminology of the programme cards, in Athletics also, was taken from horse-racing and Athletics remained under the Huntsman's control until the first Captain of Athletics was appointed in 1950. In annual competition against Cheltenham between 1919 and 1932 Shrewsbury won twelve times and drew once. In 1920 and 1921 Shrewsbury won the Challenge Trophy at the Public Schools' Sports at Stamford Bridge. A fixture with Malvern started in 1933. Other school fixtures have been with Repton, Wrekin, Lancing, Gordonstoun, St Edward's and Manchester Grammar School.

An Athletics track was provided in front of the old Sanatorium in 1956, but this was turned into an all-weather pitch in 1998. During the four decades which intervened Athletics had a prominent place in the Salopian sporting calendar, with a full programme of matches against other schools. Domestic Athletics took place in the Lent Term. Every boy was encouraged to take place in the Athletics Standards Competition, and subsequently in the Athletics competition proper, which together dominated the last three weeks of term. An army of heroic colleagues fired guns, waved flags, manipulated tape-measures and peered at stop-watches, often, notoriously, in conditions of biting wind and sometimes falling snow.

Since 1998, however, Salopian athletes have had to travel to other venues to train and compete, but the appointment of an enthusiastic and efficient master-in-charge and the re-introduction of an annual inter-house athletics competition at the Shrewsbury College's London Road ground, which all members of the School attend, has given Salopian Athletics a new and vigorous lease of life. Salopians owe much to the succession of dedicated masters, Adrian Struvé, Willie Jones, Mark Mortimer, Bob Parker, Michael Barratt, Tim Foulger, Peter Middleton and Ian Howarth who have preserved and nurtured this most historic and traditional of Salopian sports.

The Old Salopian Hunt was founded by Adrian Struvé, Nigel Miller and Ian Fraser.

There is an annual race against the School, which is held towards the end of the Michaelmas Term. Old Salopians also participate in the Thames Hare and Hound Alumni race. Salopians associated with the Hunt may take up life membership, which Mark Mortimer liked to say was actually 'forever'. He is still toasted in 'Gin and Tonic' before the start of every committee meeting and those present nostalgically associate his memory with that of Michael Hall, a devoted participant, supporter and Treasurer of the Hunt, who, over many years, used to supply the meeting with a characteristically generous prescription of that beverage.

The devotion which so many members of the Hunt feel towards their traditional sport is perhaps expressed in the concluding verses of Willie Jones' *One Last Toll*, the penultimate verse in the form in which it was originally composed in 1988 and 1989, and the last verse added in 2012.

> From Michael's mass to Christ's
> come sun, come rain, come snow
> we kept our yearly trysts,
> now decades long ago,
> while time runs ever faster
> and does not seem to mind
> that ends come nearer quicker
> while youth drops far behind:
>
> Our youth, that is: today's
> young runners hasten on,
> although those ancient ways
> are now un-trodden, gone;
> the eager hounds still quicken
> to the Huntsman's melody,
> but now I'm fifty-seven,
> Mark rising fifty-three
>
> *Envoi*
> So, on they press, the years,
> my tally now four score,
> but Mark, who had no peers,
> is dead at seventy-four:
> the knell of closing time
> has stilled Mark's hymnody,
> and my regretful rhyme
> must be his threnody.

CHAPTER TWENTY-FOUR

THE ROYAL SHREWSBURY
SCHOOL BOAT CLUB

Rowing first became an official school activity in Dr Kennedy's time. His predecessor, Dr Butler, had prohibited it, but Kennedy lifted the ban in 1839 and in that year the first of many regattas was held. However, rowing was still an informal affair, and the earliest existing Regatta card dates from 1854. Inter-school races started in 1864 and the Boat Club proper was inaugurated in 1866. The following year, 1867, was the first active year of the Club: Bumping Races were instituted and continuous records of the results have been kept from the very start. On several occasions the competition extended over six days. Silver Challenge Oars and Knock-Out Sculling Races were also organised on an inter-house basis.

Dr Alington strongly supported the Club and in 1912 the 1st VIII made its first appearance at Henley. The Headmaster liked to say that this was one of the principal achievements of his time at Shrewsbury. Between 1909 and 1939 the Crew was coached by the legendary 'Kitch' (A.E. Kitchin, Master 1909-43); during his period in charge the 1st VIII won the Elsenham Cup in 1919 at the 'Peace Regatta', and the crew subsequently won the Ladies' Challenge Plate twice, in 1924 and 1932. The 2nd VIII won the Public Schools Challenge Vase at Marlow Regatta in 1938 and 1939 and also in 1949 and 1962.

Kitchin coached the 1st VIII from 1910 to 1940 and he laid the foundation of Shrewsbury's reputation as a rowing school. Between them Stacy Colman (1940-47) and Mike Powell (1947-52) covered the forties. Peter Gladstone (1952-65) dominated the fifties and the early sixties, recording three victories in the Princess Elizabeth Cup at Henley in 1955, 1960 and 1961. Roger Blomfield (1965-68) and David Christie (1968-73) shared the next eight years, although Roger's profound influence on the RSSBC as a whole was to extend over several more decades. Nick Bevan (1973-88) coached the 1st VIII over a span of fifteen years, with a break of one year (1978-79) in which Peter Owen was in charge. Gordon Woods then coached the 1st VIII for a year. Mike Partridge (1988-97) served for nine years overall, though Steve Fox coached the VIII throughout 1996 and in the Lent and Summer Terms of 1998, during Mike Partridge's absence and after his departure. Bill Sayer's tenure covered four years (1998 -2002), Martin Orviss' three (2002-04). Todd Jesdale then took charge for eight years overall (2004-07 and 2009-12) with a break of two years in which Nick Henderson (2007-09) in tandem with Philip Lapage coached the 1st VIII. Athol Hundermark has been in charge of the 1st VIII since 2013. Few would, I think, disagree that, on the basis of achievement and length of service combined, Peter Gladstone, Roger Blomfield and Nick Bevan take pride of place, as worthy successors to the legendary 'Kitch' in the generation before. Although Todd Jesdale's tenure was comparatively brief, his triumphant success at Henley in 2007 earns him an honoured place in this distinguished company of rowing coaches.

Russell Hope Simpson, David Bevan, Frank Hadland, Alan Laurie, Rex Connell, David Gee, Simon Baxter, Stuart Guise, Wally Marsh, Andy Powell, Peter Owen, Philip Lapage, Peter Twelves, Gordon Woods, Steve Fox, Gavin Williams, Martin Worster, Tim

Whitehead, Paul Manser and Rob Wilson have all played a prominent part on the river during the last sixty years. Clare Wilson did much to establish girls' rowing.

The coaches have been marvellously supported by a series of skilled and dedicated boatmen including Dickens (who, it seems, was only ever known by his surname), Gerry Sturges, David Jarvis, Ian Turner, Keith Brown and currently Andy Clark. A separate article on Gerry Sturges can be found in the Support Staff section.

There has been a revolution in equipment. Clinker boats have been replaced by shells; carbonfibre, fibreglass and composite materials have been used to supplement or replace wood in boat-building and Gerry Sturges made several fibreglass sculling boats. The construction of the 'Decalogue', in which the coach could literally 'walk the plank' between the rows of oarsman on either side, thus enabling him to correct and improve individual technique, caused a considerable stir in the rowing world. Two Decalogues were produced during this period, both built by Gerry Sturges. The first Decalogue was made of wood, and introduced by Peter Gladstone. When the first Decalogue came to the end of its natural life, Gerry built its successor out of fibreglass donated by Miles Duncan and named after Miles' father. This remained in use until it was superseded by the eight-seater rowing tank.

During these last sixty years fixed seats have been replaced by slides and fixed pins by gates. The shape of the blades has changed frequently: 'pencils' have been replaced by 'spoons', 'bats', 'spades' and 'cleavers'. Dan Rowland (Rt 1958-60), an ESU scholar from the USA, was persuaded by Peter Gladstone to remain at Shrewsbury for a second year, to serve as Captain of Boats. The impact Gladstone made not only through his personality, but also as a result of the specific introduction of new blades, was so memorable that Dan recalled it in a speech, on 3rd May 2012, marking his retirement as Professor of History in the University of Kentucky. He recalled what difficulty the crew had in adjusting to the shape of the new blades Gladstone had adopted (Shrewsbury were only the second crew to do so) and to the new method he had devised for 'taking the catch' with them: it was so difficult, Dan claimed, that it was not until the semi-final at Henley that the crew finally mastered the technique; but also so effective that the crew won the 1960 final by three and a half lengths - setting up a record which lasted for five years – without even feeling tired after the race! The surviving members of this 1960 crew, assisted by two substitutes, and with Dan Rowland as stroke, rowed past the enclosures at Henley in the tea interval, fifty-five years later, on Saturday 4th July 2015.

Gerry Sturges built a clinker VIII, *Shrewsbury*, reversing the current trend. This was in the days of 'restricted boats', which had to be made to certain dimensions, and Gerry cut everything down to the absolute minimum, including bevelling the edges of the wood so finely that it raced as fast as a shell; the boat then weighed the same as a shell eight, much lighter than the conventional clinker restricted boat. It was therefore much quicker off the start, giving its crew the edge right from the beginning of the race, with younger crews often making a significant difference to the outcome. Steve Fox remembers that a Shrewsbury crew was the last to use a home-made wooden VIII at Henley Royal Regatta. The *Mike Partridge* reached the semi-finals in 1997, having been specially made down to weight by Dave Jarvis.

The School 'Boathouse' was originally just a roof, with no sides. After the inauguration of the RSSBC in the 1860s, more substantial provision was progressively made. In 1921 the

Pugh Boathouse, with its three bays, was constructed and opened. The plaque, in memory of John Edwin Pugh, who died of wounds the day after the signing of the armistice which concluded the First World War, constitutes one of the most moving inscriptions in the School. An additional bay was added to the Boathouse during the 1950s, and in 2012 a new Boathouse was built on the site of its 1860s predecessor. The project was instigated and driven by Nick Randall (O 1972-76), Captain of Sabrina Club and a member of the 1st VIII (1976), with the assistance of John Rolfe, Director of the Shrewsbury School Foundation. It was funded by the generosity of Mark Yale, the Lywood family and many Sabrina members. This new Yale Boathouse provided two bays to house twenty rowing eights, with a gym and ergo room above capable of housing forty ergo machines.

An initiative by Peter Gladstone enabled a workshop to be built in the 1950s adjacent to and downriver from the Pugh Boathouse. Subsequently he installed a rowing tank, to accommodate one oarsman, behind the ferryman's cottage. Roger Blomfield was able to provide a new rowing tank, funded by the generous donations of Alan Palgrave Brown and Sabrina members. It was designed by Bill Sayer to accommodate either eight oarsmen or four scullers.

Meanwhile, as part of the New Boathouse project of 2012, Martin Slocock and Peter Bowring, again supported by Sabrina Club members, funded a complete refurbishment of the Clubroom in the Pugh Boathouse. Nick Randall spent six years researching records and collecting over 100 photographs to decorate the room, and the magnificent result provides an impressive and comprehensive archive of the members and achievements of the RSSBC. He has provided a similar record in 'the Shrewsbury Room' in the Leander Club.

Domestic rowing has continued on the familiar basis of Bumpers, Challenge Oars (Junior and Senior) and Sculling competitions. These competitions were inaugurated in a similar format 150 years ago. During our period the four divisions in Bumpers have been reduced to three. Physical contact between the boats in Bumping has been prohibited (pursuing crews have to be content with achieving a prescribed overlap) and the starting gun has been replaced by a klaxon. During the last five or six years, girls have taken part in all competitions, both domestic and external. One notable feature of the Summer Term is the Novice IVs competition in which crews have to launch their boats under the exacting eye of members of the 1st VIII, impressively arrayed in their 1st VIII blazers and white flannels, each equipped with a mill-board and a mark sheet, who assess the novices' skill in the technique and synchronisation of their boat handling and the cleanliness of their kit.

Further afield the RSSBC continues to play a prominent role in the North of England Head of the River Race at Chester and in the Schools' Head of the River Race on the Tideway, both of which occur during the Lent Term. At Chester, where the 1st VIII competes against Senior Clubs and Universities, as well as other schools, the crew has won the race in 1968 and on seven subsequent occasions, including 2011, 2012 and 2015, and has frequently been runner-up. In the Summer, crews at all age levels, and of both sexes, compete at a wide variety of regattas, in Eights, Fours, Pairs, Quads, Double and Single Sculls and Octuples.

The main focus of the rowing calendar is, of course, on Henley Royal Regatta. Here the RSSBC has recorded 14 victories including its first in 1919. Since then Shrewsbury and Eton have hotly contested the lead, drawing level in 2013 with fourteen victories each.

In 1919 the 1st VIII won the Elsenham Cup outright (Sandy Irvine's name is one of those engraved on the cup), but subsequently the School re-presented it to the National Schools Regatta for a new competition as the trophy for Second Eights. Shrewsbury have been the winners on eleven occasions and runners-up on nine. Shrewsbury has won the West Cup (for Third Eights) thirteen times since 1947, the most recent victory being in 2011. The competition for Third VIIIs and Colts, first held at Godstow, moved to Pangbourne in 1963 and then to Holme Pierrepont, to be merged into the National Schools Regatta, when it was inaugurated there in 1973.

The principal competition at Henley for the 1st VIII in the earlier period was the Ladies Plate, which the Shrewsbury crew won in 1924, in which they were runners-up in 1931, and victorious again in 1932. Since 1946 the target has been the Princess Elizabeth Cup, which Shrewsbury has won in 1955, 1960, 1961 and 2007, having also reached the final in 1947 and 1957. The 2007 race, in which Shrewsbury beat Brentwood School, Canada by one foot, was voted Race of the Year by USA Rowing News. Nick Henderson records the unbearable tension of the last two minutes of the race:

'At the mile marker, Shrewsbury have drawn level'. Raucous cheering sounded in the Stewards' Enclosure, at that news: for it wasn't just Shrewsbury parents who were cheering for the RSSBC, it was Eton and Radley and Abingdon – it was all the crews Shrewsbury had raced and beaten [who] now simply wanted (the PE Cup) to stay on this side of the Atlantic. Tensions tightened like a violin string as Brentwood and the RSSBC battled in the last minute. Shrewsbury stroke Richard Putnam felt his vision going – his consciousness leaving - but he didn't care, so long as he was able to raise the stroke cadence when he needed to. Shrewsbury took it through the roof in the last ten strokes, moving from three feet down to level and possibly ahead in those last ten cursed strokes, where the stream factored against them most heavily of all. The silence was oppressive in the two minutes in which the Stewards reviewed the photo finish and made their ultimate declaration. Mothers wept, fathers cursed – and many crossed their fingers.

'And the winner of the Princess Elizabeth Cup, by a margin of one foot ... Shrewsbury School.'

That was the apogee of the RSSBC's achievement during the last half-century. But the participation of Shrewsbury and of many other schools in the Princess Elizabeth Cup was interrupted, between 1974 and 1988, by the requirements of the examination timetable. The Special Race for Schools was introduced in the fifteen-year interim. Shrewsbury won that race seven times and were finalists on another four occasions.

Athol Hundermark, the present coach of the 1st VIII, places great emphasis on a scientific approach to coaching. Telemetry and rowperfect machines are used to give the coaching team much more information about individual performance and boat speed, and great attention is given to conditioning in the gym. In recent years ergometers have played a significant part in training. More recently still, Hundermark has given greater priority to weights. Since 2012 the membership of the Boat Club has grown rapidly every year. This summer (2015) there will be eight school boys' VIIIs taking part in external competition, four senior VIIIs, 1st 2nd, 3rd and 4th, and two crews at both Under 16 and Under 15 level, with Under 14 crews and girls' crews in addition. This has put considerable pressure on available equipment. However, thanks to some significant and generous help from Old Salopians and from parents, it has been possible to purchase two new Empacher, carbon rigged VIIIs, the best that money can buy.

This year has seen the arrival of 13-year-old girls in the RSSBC. Although this has placed further pressure on equipment and staffing, there is the prospect of the continued progress of these oarswomen, across the whole age-range, during the course of the next few years.

In the past few years both boys and girls in the 'Top Squad' have made an annual trip, during the autumn Exeat, to race in the Head of the Charles River Race in the USA. This is the largest 'Head' in the world. In December 2014 the RSSBC is probably the largest school Boat Club in the country and it is hoped that recent developments will prove to be the catalyst for some strong performances in the years ahead.

The composition of the Oxford and Cambridge Boat Race crews has changed dramatically in recent years. At the beginning of our period they were manned almost exclusively by undergraduates drawn from schools similar to our own. Currently, however, the crews are recruited largely from international post-graduates who have already gained rowing honours abroad. On the domestic scene, in that earlier period, Etonians have dominated the crews, but Salopians have been a clear second, with Radleians and Wykehamists in third and fourth place.

Members of the RSSBC have played a prominent part in representing Great Britain. J.G.H. Lander rowed in the Coxless Fours in the 1928 Olympics in Amsterdam: Jack Wilson in the Coxless Pairs Olympics at Henley in 1948, where both won Gold Medals. (They both also won the Ladies Challenge Plate at Henley in Salopian crews, Lander in 1924 and Wilson in 1932.) In 1964 the 1st VIII, coached by Peter Gladstone, came third in international competition. In 1968 a coxless four, coached by Roger Blomfield, came 3rd and a coxed pair 7th. However, in 1976 and thereafter, individual school crews, other than pairs, were no longer selected, but many Salopian oarsmen have been invited to join a composite GB squad. A notable example was Adrian Cassidy's participation in 1989, in which he won gold in the coxless fours.

The 1st VIII has toured abroad on several occasions in the last fifty years, travelling with Roger Blomfield to the USA in 1966, with Nick Bevan to Australia in 1974 and to South Africa in 1978, with Mike Partridge to Australia in 1993 and with Todd Jesdale to the USA in 2010 and 2012. The School's performance in all its traditional major sports has done much to enhance Shrewsbury's reputation, but perhaps it is fair to comment that the status of Henley as the premier international regatta places the achievement of our oarsmen under a world-wide spotlight.

CHAPTER TWENTY-FIVE

FOOTBALL

School football, before the last quarter of the nineteenth century, was a rough and tumble affair. Dr Butler had denounced the sport as 'fit only for butcher boys'. But even before Dr Kennedy 'legalised' it, Shrewsbury, like many other similar schools had developed its own distinctive version of the game. The Salopian version was called *douling*, possibly because at that time it was the only sport which was compulsory ('doul' being the Greek word for 'slave' adopted in Salopian slang to describe junior boys); and douls and others who failed to take part were routinely punished with a 'kicking'. Unlimited numbers could take part in 'douling'. The numbers involved on the opposing sides did not need to be equal;a goal could be kicked at any height and the rule that no player might wilfully stand between the ball and the opponent's goal made forward passing impossible. There was no prescribed kit: trousers were tucked into socks and the mud was scraped off clothing afterwards. Though keenly contested between all groups in the School, douling was little more than a brawl. Obviously the differences in their respective rules made competitions between schools impossible, although in the third quarter of the century, in a series of meetings in Cambridge, Salopians played a prominent part in attempts to draw up a common code.

The adoption of this code in the season of 1876-77 was marked by a match against Uppingham. This landmark year heralded a series of fixtures, under the rules of Association Football. The Liverpool Ramblers match was inaugurated in 1883, there was a major expansion of the fixture list in 1887, and during the 1890s, a golden decade for amateur football, the first match against Repton in 1894 and against Malvern in 1896 began a series, in each case, which was to be continued for a hundred years, but from which Malvern has recently withdrawn. The Corinthian Casuals also became regular opponents. W.J. Oakley and G.B. Raikes, as Old Salopians, became England Internationals. Meanwhile, after the School's move to Kingsland in 1882, A.H. Gilkes (Master 1873-85) exerted a key influence on the development of the game, initiating coaching and finding the funds to effect a levelling of the Top Common to provide pitches, an operation which he supervised himself.

A decline in the standard of Salopian football during the first decade of the twentieth century was reversed by the appointment of Dick Sale (Master 1912-49) as coach; but the fixture list was significantly restricted during the First World War. By the 1920s the 1st XI was playing a dozen matches each Michaelmas Term, Charterhouse (first match in 1922), Handsworth Old Boys, Shrewsbury Amateurs, a variety of Oxford and Cambridge colleges and the Oxford Centaurs having been added to the fixture list; later the Bradfield fixture (first played in 1934) became a further long-standing tradition.In 1924 Shrewsbury won all their inter-school matches. Alan Phillips (Master 1925-65) took over the 1st XI in 1929. Although it was considered that most of the 1st XI sides of the 1930s were only of average quality, one highlight of the decade was a 10-1 victory over Charterhouse in 1938. In the inter-war years 'Senior', the 1st XI pitch, was renowned for its mud – a factor which placed Salopian teams at a considerable disadvantage when they encountered much lighter conditions in away matches – and which was immortalised by the despairing cry of the supporter of a visiting team 'Get it down the deep end, Repton!' One distinctive feature of the thirties was the 1st XI's tour of élite schools in Nazi Germany in 1937. The trip, which had been organised by Herr Kraenzli, who had briefly been an Assistant Master at Shrewsbury, took place in a militaristic and ceremonial environment and the Salopians emerged victorious overall from the encounters on the pitch.

Tom Taylor took charge of the 1st XI in 1943 and he was succeeded as Master-in-Charge by Robin Moulsdale in 1952. Robin points out, in his chapter in *Shrewsbury School Football* that most Public Schools of comparable size play rugger, and that Shrewsbury's situation as a school in which both football and rowing are major sports is paralleled, among schools of comparable size, only by Westminster. He records that in the mid-forties H.R.S. Rhys and J.B. Pugh were the outstanding players. In 1943 Shrewsbury beat Bradfield 8-1; and in 1946 Robin himself was Captain of the XI. Summarising the period he remarks that the successful sides of the early and mid-forties were followed by weaker sides from 1949-51; after that there were good results until 1957, when a poor run, interrupted by a very good side in 1959, culminated in eight successive defeats in 1961. During this period Highgate had been added to the list of School opponents; and Shrewsbury were victorious in the first two matches in 1955 and 1956. By 1960 Bolton School, Manchester Grammar School and Wolverhampton Grammar School had joined the fixture list and by the end of the decade the 1st XI was playing eight of the strongest sides in the country.

Tactically very little had changed during the previous two decades. Robin Moulsdale records that there was very little gym work and few training runs. Strength and speed continued to be more valuable than ball skills. But the signs of better things to come, and the means to effect them, were heralded by the arrival of Ken Spiby as Head Groundsman in 1957. Hitching a lift in a helicopter from a visiting General, he detected hitherto unsuspected drains on the Common and cleaned them out. His enterprise was absolutely crucial to future development. Soon afterwards, lighter, plastic-covered balls became available. Meanwhile a football cage had been provided to facilitate coaching, in which George Hart had played an enthusiastic part. And in 1962, with the appointment of Robin Trimby as coach of the 1st XI, Salopian football acquired the services of a man supremely qualified to take full advantage of the new techniques and the new situation. Indeed his tenure is regarded as effecting a transformation in Salopian football and ushering in the modern age.

During those twenty years (1962-81), a wide-ranging collection of changes made the game much more skilful, much faster and more competitive. There were changes in tactics and formation: the 2-3-5 formation of 1962, with its full-backs, half-backs and inside forwards had become 4-4-2 by 1982, with full-backs attacking, wingers tackling back and Salopians heading the ball properly. Pre-season training was introduced and during term-time training became much harder and more consistent. The fixture list grew from eight to ten matches in 1962, to fifteen or more in 1981, and as Shrewsbury increased the number of 1st XI matches against Northern Grammar Schools, the result was probably the toughest fixture list in the country. Links were also forged with Wolverhampton Wanderers and with Shrewsbury Town, and overseas tours for the 1st XI began. Although the navy blue strip and the Maltese Cross were retained, school shirts and shorts had become lighter and a manager for the 1st XI was introduced. Benches were provided for supporters, and although the compulsion for all members of the School to attend the principal inter-school matches ended in the 1960s, these matches still attracted a large number of enthusiastic masters and boys. All the school fixtures between 1962 and 1981 remained 'friendlies', although Shrewsbury did enter the annual Public School Six-a-Side competition, performed well in it and won the trophy in 1976.

One of the features of the whole period between 1950 and 2010 has been the greater attention to and provision for the other school football teams and the steady expansion of their fixture lists. All this was particularly notable during Robin Trimby's time in charge. In 1962 the School had fielded 1st and 2nd XIs, and the Under 15 and Under 16 XIs also played a few inter-school matches; but by 1981 there were approximately 10 school teams, including the 3rd and 4th XIs, together with A, B and C sides for each of the under-16 year groups. The current provision is fully detailed in the first chapter of the sports section. This expansion was made possible by the greater involvement of members of staff in providing the necessary management and coaching. Robin Moulsdale had only had three or four colleagues supporting him; Robin Trimby had ten, either coaching, or else refereeing and organising boys' football. Richard Raven, David Morland, Barry Pitt and Peter Morris were prominent among them. By 1981 there were also two staff teams, recruited every week, to play against the House First Leagues' sides in turn. These popular and highly competitive matches attracted many spectators, and Robin considers that one or two of his colleagues would certainly have been red-carded, if they had played today. On a day-by-day basis, of course, it was the inter-House Leagues, 1st, 2nd, Under 16 A and Under 16 B Leagues which constituted the 'bread and butter 'of Shrewsbury School football. Robin fully recognised the vital importance of these encounters in promoting the sport and was keen to encourage them. The Referees Society, founded originally by Michael Tupper, provided a chance for boys who were not ball-players, but who were sufficiently interested in the game, to acquire the necessary training and qualifications and to take control of and referee the weekly League Matches – and occasionally School matches. They contributed a great deal to the maintenance and smooth running of these numerous inter-House games. School football has had many unsung heroes behind the scenes, among whom the most devoted and invaluable was Martin Knox.

Robin has happy memories of the Peter Thwaites side of 1964, which was the first Shrewsbury side to defeat all five traditional Public School opponents, and all of whose members were reunited, fifty years on, at a gathering at the School on 29th November, 2014: happy memories, too, of Richard Lloyd's 1976 Six-a-Side team which won the Public Schools' Tournament. He considers that Tony Barker's 1972 side, which won eleven of their thirteen games and remained undefeated in the other two, was probably the strongest team of all, but John Rowlinson in 1966, Stuart Jones in 1968, Will Tutton in 1971, Jimmy Burns in 1977, David Arthur in 1980 and Peter Wozencroft in 1981 all captained very successful sides,playing attractive football. Between 1967 and 1981, 15 Salopians were selected to play in the national Public Schools XI, and Will Tutton captained the team on a tour of Uganda in 1972. Robin remembers with pride the respect accorded to Shrewsbury School soccer wherever the team played.

Mark Dickson took over from Robin Trimby as Master-in-charge of football and coach of the 1st XI in 1981, and served for 24 years. The 1980s produced several more successful teams, Steve Dala being the outstanding player of the decade and the 1985 XI, which also included the players who won the Public Schools Six-a-Side trophy for the second time, being the outstanding team. The 1980s also witnessed a further substantial increase in the number of School teams: by the end of the decade Shrewsbury was fielding twelve such teams, of different ages and standards, during the Michaelmas, Term. From 1983 a pre-season tour on the continent became a regular feature of the 1st XI's programme.

Mark was fully supported by Martin Knox, Julian Walton and David Smith in the eighties and by Bob Kendall, Paul Pridgeon and Stephen Holroyd in the nineties, in the coaching and management of these proliferating teams. Martin Knox, indeed, gave thirty years of devoted service to Salopian football and to Salopian sport generally, and Paul Pridgeon's arrival gave a valuable boost to coaching skills. Mark also, like his predecessor, was keenly aware that although the School teams stole the limelight, the real heart of Salopian football lay in the House leagues. Even 'B' leagues, humble though its position in the hierarchy may be, is played with passion, excitement and enthusiasm. The importance of these House league matches, in terms not only of fun and enjoyment, but of their wider educational value, is not to be underestimated.

The performance of the 1st XI of 1992 inaugurated a period of sustained success. Most of its members remained at school in 1993, and in that year the team was victorious over Repton, Malvern, Charterhouse and Bradfield, all its principal Public School opponents that year. The 1990s also witnessed Shrewsbury's entry into cup football, initially for the Shropshire County Cup, victory in which was the necessary qualification for participation in the English Schools' cup competition. Both footballing and social horizons were expanded by the experience. There were several memorable occasions when a large contingent from the School assembled to cheer on their team under the lights of Shrewsbury Town's old Gay Meadow stadium.

Even more thrilling and challenging were Shrewsbury's experiences in the English Schools' competition. In the 1990s Shrewsbury reached the quarter-finals twice and in 2001 the team came within touching distance of the Schools' Cup Final. In 1992-3 the Boodle and Dunthorne's ISFA Cup competition (now the Boodle's competition) was inaugurated, sponsored by Old Salopians Nicholas and Michael Wainwright. This quickly became recognised as the 'Champions' League' of Independent Schools' football. On 20th March, 2000 twenty coachloads of Salopian fans – almost the entire school – travelled to Leicester City's old Filbert Street stadium, to watch their team defeat Charterhouse 1-0. BBC Shropshire broadcast live updates from the ground. Cup football, on occasions like this, can attract huge crowds, not only of Salopians, but also of interested outsiders. But, quite apart from these exceptional occasions, Mark Dickson points out that Shrewsbury has always benefited from its close ties with, and loyal support from, 'the long lines of families from the Manchester and Liverpool commuter belts, who have played football for Liverpool Ramblers, had season tickets at Old Trafford or Anfield and sent their children to Shrewsbury School to play football.'

Robin Trimby, writing in the *Salopian Newsletter* in June 2006, shortly after Dickson's retirement from the School, comments on Mark's astonishingly single-minded and long-serving commitment to the game at Shrewsbury and beyond. He notes that Dickson, was the driving force behind the inauguration of the Boodle and Dunthorne Competition and that his team's victory in the competition in 2000, the pinnacle of his coaching career, was a richly deserved and entirely appropriate reward. He applauds Dickson's introduction of the hugely successful annual Prep Schools' competition at Shrewsbury. He records that his teams, competing against the best 600 footballing schools in England, have reached the last sixteen of the ESFA competition four times, the last eight in 2005-6, and the last four in 2001, in addition to winning the Shropshire County Cup on six occasions; and he notes that in his last season in charge, Dickson guided his 1st XI to the brink of the ESFA semi-finals with fourteen victories and only a single defeat, completing one of the most successful of his twenty-four years at the helm. Dickson was also noted for his calm and civilised manner on the touch-line.

It was this blend of meticulous organisation, of detailed preparation of tactics, coaching and fitness, combined with an insistence upon self-discipline, playing the game the right way and maintaining high standards that Mark will be remembered for, quite as much as his splendid record of results.

Dickson himself makes an eloquent defence of the value of extra-curricular activities, cultural as well as sporting, recently threatened by the emphasis on academic League Tables, arguing that 'it is having time for these activities which particularly distinguishes boarding education from the day schools'. He argues that employers want people who can work as a team, who are determined, well organised and who can get on with others, who don't give up, who are good characters and entertaining personalities. These crucial additional qualities are particularly developed in extra-curricular activity, be it on the sports field, or in the school play or orchestra... 'indeed', he claims, 'some leading headmasters are to-day increasingly of the opinion that, as on-line educational packages become ever more sophisticated in the coming years, the old concept of education of the whole man will become ever more crucial to the revival of boarding education. *Mens sana in corpore sano:* neglect extra-curricular activity at your peril!'

Mark Lascelles took over from Mark Dickson in 2006 and records that he realised that 'following the Alex Ferguson of Shrewsbury was never going to be easy', but he was blessed with an outstanding group of players during his three years in charge. Huge support for the school team was very much in evidence. The installation of irrigation across the whole of the Top Common improved the quality of the playing surfaces out of all recognition and a number of pitches on the Lower Common were also relaid.

The fixture list contained the traditional overnight stays in matches against Eton and Charterhouse, block fixtures against the northern Grammar Schools and other fixtures against King's Chester, Repton and Malvern, although Malvern subsequently gave up playing football in the Autumn term. Pre-season tours were popular; during one such tour in Spain, at Villareal and Barcelona Football Clubs, Salopians were coached by professionals and enjoyed games against the academy teams.

The following three seasons proved the most successful for many years, only seven or eight games being lost during that period, and they are well remembered for the attractive and exciting brand of football the sides produced. Will Hughes improved the fitness and conditioning of all the players and his attention to detail in training made a real difference.

The Boodles Independent Schools' Cup, the brainchild of Mark Dickson, was incredibly difficult to win, since it attracted so many schools that were well coached and well organised. This period saw a disappointing defeat in the quarter-finals on penalties against Charterhouse and earlier exits against other schools such as Brentwood and Leeds Grammar School.

The English Schools' Cup Competition, with over 600 entries, allowed Shrewsbury to play against other schools it would not normally encounter. Between 2005 and 2009 (that is, including Mark Dickson's last year in charge) the 1st XI reached the quarter finals three times and was desperately unlucky not to progress further on each occasion. This competition certainly toughened the teams up and became a real highlight of the season. By this time football was really flourishing, with seven teams put out in the Sixth Form, and at times thirteen other teams in the junior part of the School.

Steve Biggins succeeded Mark Lascelles as Master-in-charge of football in 2009 and he has served in that capacity for six seasons. He brought with him extensive experience, both as a professional footballer himself, and subsequently as a coach of preparatory School football for over twenty years. It was a mixed blessing that, in his first year in charge, the 1st XI, cheered on by 750 Salopian and Old Salopian supporters at the MK Dons Stadium in Milton Keynes, in March 2010, defeated Repton and reached the pinnacle of Independent School football, by winning the Boodles ISFA Cup for the second time. Roy Chatterjee became the first player to score a hat-trick in a Boodles Cup final, and the 3-0 winning margin was the largest in ISFA Cup Final history. However, nothing daunted by the scale of that achievement, successive 1st XIs since then have maintained Shrewsbury's position as one of the leading Independent School teams, both in inter-school and in cup matches; and the 2012/2013 team reached the semi-final of the Boodles Cup. In these cup competitions Shrewsbury's opponents, even in the earlier rounds, often look upon the encounter as their own 'final'! Indeed, that often proves to be the case.

Surprised, when he first took over, by the sheer extent of the School's participation in football, Steve has taken particular care to monitor the progress of individuals, in successive age groups, from preparatory school to university, and to maintain personal links to ensure consistency in coaching methods. Coaching DVDs are circulated and, at the top level videos are made and the heart-rate of the players is monitored during training sessions (a far cry indeed from the conditions and standards which pertained when the game was first played on Kingsland!). Although the fixture lists for the top teams in each age group have remained consistent, more fixtures for the 'B', 'C' and 'D' teams have been introduced during the last six years, and professional coaches have been recruited to improve the performance of School teams at every level. Overall, and year by year, school football becomes steadily more competitive and itself more professional. Many schools, and particularly maintained schools, are closely associated with the football academies of professional clubs. Although the School now offers a limited number of Sports Scholarships, only two of these, so far, have been awarded to football players. The institution of the Alex Wilson Scholarship, however, not only offers the promise of the recruitment of talented local footballers in the future, but more generally bears testimony to Salopians' enthusiasm for the game and affection for the player after whom it is named. As a postscript it may be added that on 29th November 2014, the members of the victorious team of 1964, all fit and well, met to celebrate their Golden Anniversary and to watch their successors play Repton. As he hands over to his own successor, there can be no doubt that Steve Biggins leaves Salopian football well prepared, not only at top level, but – equally important – in depth, to meet the ever more exacting challenges that it will surely face.

CHAPTER TWENTY-SIX

CRICKET

Basil Oldham in his *History of Shrewsbury School* has comparatively little to say about the historical antecedents of Salopian cricket, but this is simply because the origins of the sport, in contrast to those of the Hunt and the Boat Club, had little to distinguish them from those in other schools. However, in one particular instance, it was the Captain of Cricket, Spencer Phillips, who, in a famous correspondence in 1866, asserted Shrewsbury's new status as one of the great Public Schools. He wrote, as follows, to the Captain of the Westminster X1, to arrange a fixture:

Sir,
I write to ask if a match between Westminster and Shrewsbury can be arranged for this season? The most convenient day would be any day in the week beginning June 17th. We shall be happy to play on any ground which you may select.

He received the following reply:

Sir,
The Captain of the Westminster Eleven is sorry to disappoint Shrewsbury, but Westminster plays no Schools except Public Schools, and the general feeling of the school quite coincides with that of the Committee of the Public Schools Club, who issue this list of public schools – Charterhouse, Eton, Harrow, Rugby, Westminster and Winchester.

This elicited a crushing retort from the Shrewsbury Captain:

Sir,
I cannot allow your answer to my first letter to pass unnoticed. I have only to say that a school, which we have Camden's authority for stating was the most important school in England at a time when Westminister was unknown, which Her Majesty has included in the list of Public Schools by the Royal Commission, and which, according the report of the commissioners, is more distinctly public than any other school, cannot be deprived of its rights as a Public School by the assertions of a Westminster boy, or by the dictum of the self-styled Public Schools Club. I regret to find from your letter that the Captain of the Westminster Eleven has yet to learn the first lesson of a true public school education, the behaviour due from one gentleman to another.

Cricket has always enjoyed its reputation as a gentleman's game and of all the Salopian sports it is the most closely associated with the beauty of the Site. Neville Cardus famously referred to its green expanse as 'the most beautiful playing fields in the world'. Martin Knox suspects that, having been translated from the smoke of Manchester to 'the rich open air of England', Cardus may have been indulging in hyperbole, and this suspicion is reinforced by Cardus' later reminiscence that 'to have been at Shrewsbury in those days and known cricket there, is to have lived in a heaven here below'. If Cardus was captivated by the beauty of the grounds in 1914, he would have been even more delighted by their superb condition a century later. Their enhancement is principally due to Ken Spiby, Head Groundsman for more than forty years. Paul Nichols writes that 'No-one who played cricket in that era will have failed to appreciate how much he did to make Senior the best School Cricket Ground in Shropshire, if not in England'. Spiby's removal of 'The Pier', which jutted out at 90 degrees in front of the School Shop and the two elms framing it which, *after* he had removed them, he claimed were riddled with Dutch Elm disease, created a perfectly round field and a clear view from the pavilion to the scorebox. Spiby enjoyed legendary status among his work colleagues and cricketers, who shared Stephen Holroyd's appreciation that his guardianship was more an act of love than a job of work. For many years Laurence Le Quesne presided at the wicket – a familiar sight in his white coat. He loved the game and found enormous fascination in its history ;and Salopian cricketers owe him a great debt of gratitude for his loyalty and devotion.

What is certain is that Shrewsbury cricket has never enjoyed greater success and prestige than it does, at the moment of writing, in 2014. Cricket had flourished under Hugh Brooke and declined somewhat thereafter. Writing fifty years ago, in 1964, Geoffrey Phillips, then the master-in-charge, stated that 'cricketing Old Salopians... have been worried about the lack of success of the 1st X1 in the last ten years', but Phillips, assisted by Robin Moulsdale and Robin Trimby, began to raise the general standard during the second half of the sixties. Mike Eagar comments that at that time 'they had no professional assistance, but the other key teams, the junior teams, were run by other outstanding schoolmasters, including Martin Knox and Michael Ling, who produced a steady supply of players of 1st XI standard for the successive masters-in-charge to work with'.

Paul Nichols remembers Phil Bryan (R 1963-68), a slow, left hand 'wrist-spin'bowler, who played for the 1st X1 from the age of fourteen, who told him that he had forgotten how many times he had taken eight wickets, but could remember taking all ten in a 1st House match! But all the cricketers of the time could remember the best post-war XI the School produced - in 1970 - of which Paul was himself a member, later captaining the side. Pride of place in that team is universally assigned to Nick Pocock as Captain, whom Mike Eagar described as the best schoolboy batsman he had ever seen, and who subsequently captained Hampshire; and to Tim Lamb, who opened the bowling, gained his 'Blue' at Oxford, had a long career playing for Middlesex and Northamptonshire and subsequently became Chief Executive of the English Cricket Board. The 1970 XI recorded the remarkable achievement of capturing 108 out of the 110 schoolboy wickets of the opposition. Among other outstanding players at this time were Paul Blackburn, an exceptional wicketkeeper, and Richard Boys-Stones, who had the rare gift of being able to swing the ball in both directions – and under control.

An observer of Mike Eagar's time as master-in-charge of cricket remembers that 'his fiery temperament and extraordinary cricketing insight made for exciting times. To play for him was to be inspired and tested to the limit and it was a loss to the game that he moved on to housemastering and to a headmastership'. 1st XI cricket changed substantially from the 1970s onwards. Shrewsbury played Wrekin, Ellesmere and Denstone with 1st XI sides, which meant that there was far more inter-schoolboy cricket and fewer problems caused by facing too many experienced and older club cricketers; it was also morale-boosting for the inexperienced young members of the XI. Cricket festivals started in the late sixties: being placed in the calendar at the beginning of the summer holidays they provided a marvellous mixture of freedom, adventure and competition. Turning his attention to House level, Mike produced a plan which has survived for forty years, for league cricket to be played at more levels, with eight rather than eleven players a side. No one then had time to stand around bored, uncalled upon to contribute, because there were two batsmen, a third padded up ready to go in, two umpires and a scorer. As there were no boundaries, fielders and batsmen alike had to take a lot of exercise.

Noel Darrah, who succeeded Mike, was a quieter type, but just as competitive, his mild exterior concealing inner steel. He gave back to the Captain of Cricket powers that had existed in his time at school, but which had since been eroded. This policy had its hazards, but one outstanding all-round sportsman more than earned the responsibility. Richard Lloyd, in the first team for four years, a leading batsman, a left-arm spinner, and a right-arm medium pacer, dominated the sporting scene, winter and summer, for he was Captain of football and rugby, too, yet a more modest figure about the school it would be hard to imagine. In his time arrogance went out of fashion. Neil Crawford came to the School when only twelve, but he looked seventeen at least, and played like it. He was ahead of his time in that he hit the ball hard and high at every opportunity, contrary to the then current orthodoxy. At fourteen, playing against Wroxeter CC 1st XI, he hit the ball out of the ground five times; in a House match he twice cleared the Alington Hall on his way to 196 and in a festival game against Charterhouse, he made a century before lunch! He made it to his Blue as a bowler! It seems that Salopian batsmen have always tended to be more aggressive than their opponents. This feature persists to this day and may in some measure account for their success in T20 competitions.

Mark Williams took over at the end of the 1970s, and our correspondent remarks that

> the English language does not have words adequate to describe his enthusiasm for cricket... he assumed the same commitment in others and would have organised fixtures seven days a week, if he could.

In the summer he would play cricket on every available day; and Mike Hughes (SH 1975-80) records that he once took an overnight train, having played in Scotland, to make it to a match on the South Coast the following morning!

> He was even known to organise two matches for the same day, a situation which could only be resolved by the two visiting sides playing each other ... He was a highly successful coach – and a very generous and sporting opponent. He had some very good players in his teams and he gave them every encouragement, as well as making them earn their places.

Rupert Marsh, who took 169 wickets in under three seasons, was a leg-spinner of class, who mastered the art of combining flight with testing pace and was also an outstanding batsman. Ian Hutchinson, an elegant batsman, made it to county level. Mark Williams also made a crucial contribution to Salopian Fives, which is recorded in the appropriate chapter.

The shrewd Joe Williams maintained these standards on the cricket field before he took over a House and he was succeeded by Stephen Holroyd, who had played in the Durham University XI with Julian Pettegree, one of the outstanding Salopian cricketers of the early 1980s. Stephen may be credited with laying the foundations of modern Shrewsbury cricket. He inherited strength and, characteristically, he sought to develop it further. He persuaded the School to appoint a professional for the first time in many years, the first step towards challenging the domination of Millfield. Until that time Salopians had rarely looked beyond Club Cricket. It was Paul Pridgeon, the new professional, who opened up the route to Worcester, and it was Stephen Holroyd whose vision was fulfilled with the opening of the new indoor cricket school. He had been instrumental in securing funding for this project which has played such an important part in recent developments.

The changes in these years in many ways reflected the revolution in the first-class game. Limited overs cricket was introduced at 1st XI level. Shrewsbury cricketers benefited from the experience of overseas tours for the first time and from exposure to more variations of the game. But whilst a number of excellent players emerged to play first class, professional and university cricket, technical progess was held back by a suffocating fixture list and limited indoor Winter facilities. It was an era when, on Wednesdays and Saturdays, matches between schools whose reputation was at stake laboured towards dull draws, with coaches, masters-in-charge and captains reluctant to take risks with declarations and tactics and with docile pitches contributing to stalemate. Salopian coaches and players set out to be more positive and aggressive in play and strategy based on an understanding that, whilst some games might be lost, many more would be won. An inevitable corollary to this was the advent of the one-day limited overs format. There was huge opposition to this; and 'the unbeaten season' still enjoyed holy grail status. Shrewsbury, along with a small group of similarly minded schools, took a different approach. Stephen Holroyd, with John Claughton of Eton and Guy Waller of Radley, met to devise an end-of-season festival designed to prove that competitive limited overs matches deserved a place in the canon of public schools cricket. With the blessing of the retiring Warden of Radley, the Silk trophy was born and proved to be a wonderful tournament, with some of the country's finest young players locking horns and enjoying the competition in a format which replicated the changing shape of the professional game.

Four players stand out during Stephen Holroyd's time in charge. Duncan Bowett was an all-rounder of immense natural ability, being both a fast-medium bowler and a hard-hitting middle-order batsman, who dominated school cricket. Patrick Trimby (son of Robin) was a thinking cricketer: studiously academic by nature, the art of leg-spin bowling (including a well-disguised googly) and captaincy suited him well. He gained his Blue at Oxford and enjoyed a spell in the professional game with Warwickshire. Scott Ellis was a supremely gifted all-rounder whose century during the second Silk Trophy competition at Eton in 1992 displayed awesome power and belligerence, but it was as a genuinely hostile opening bowler that he caught the eye of the professional scouts at Worcestershire. Ian McCarter brought both aggression and determination to the 1st XI's play. Like Bowett and Ellis he was equally effective with both bat and ball and had a transforming impact on Shrewsbury cricket.

Mark Lascelles was in charge of cricket between 1997 and 2003. He shared Stephen

Holroyd's ambition to see Shrewsbury at the very top and was relentless in pressing for higher standards in every aspect of the game. Overseas tours were a part of this process, not least in providing targets for which to aim. He inherited a two-day game against Uppingham and block fixtures against Malvern, Oundle and Repton. The Silk Trophy developed as a three-day festival of 50-overs cricket in which Radley, Eton and Shrewsbury, together with an overseas touring side, took part. Radley was later replaced by Oundle. Games against county age-groups, such as Shropshire, Staffordshire, Warwickshire, Worcestershire and Lancashire, were added to the fixture list. There had been earlier cricket tours to Barbados, but touring really began in earnest during Lascelles' tenure, to Barbados again in 1997 and then to South Africa (2000) Australia (2002), Sri Lanka (2004) and Western Australia (2006).

It was a time when the introduction of the AS level examination further restricted the cricket programme. Particularly during the last decade, the combination of an expanding fixture list for School teams, a shrinking Summer Term and the 'deregulation' of other sports has had a marked effect on House cricket. Gone are the days when every 1st House side played at least four matches lasting all afternoon: no longer will it be possible for there to be three centuries in the First House final, two on the losing side! Even more remarkably, Dominic Burrows once scored 203 out of 230 for Ingram's. They lost, too! Under-16 House has given way to Under-15 House and Second House is no more.

But there have been more positive developments. The vast cricket square was reduced in size and relaid with Surrey loam. The game was hugely well resourced, not only in financial terms by the school management, but in human terms by the dedication of staff coaches and ground staff alike. Lascelles considers that overall this was not a vintage period for Salopian cricket: although the teams did bowl and field exceptionally well, they lacked depth in batting. However, his enthusiasm and competitiveness had laid the foundation for the remarkable development in standard and achievement which was to follow during the course of the next decade.

Andy Barnard, a well-known local cricketer, with an appetite for the game that challenges Mark Williams, took over in 2003. He highlights, among other factors which have contributed to the great success of the most recent years, the crucial role played by Paul Pridgeon, the cricket professional, to whom Lascelles, Holroyd and Barnard himself all pay the warmest tribute. Paul's contribution, both in introducing technical changes and improvements, and by instilling a professional approach and a winning mentality, cannot be overstated. He has devoted many hours to coaching individuals, James Taylor, as the first Old Salopian to play Test cricket, being foremost among them. James was selected for the 1st XI when only in the Third Form. Perhaps the most striking of his achievements while at school came in 2005, when he led the Under 15s to victory in the Lord's Taverners' trophy at Trent Bridge, now his cricketing home. Opening the batting in every match, he was never out and therefore can claim to have been on the field for every minute of playing time in six matches. Passing five hundred runs he fittingly hit a six in the final over, to give Shrewsbury success at last after three previous unsuccessful finals. He went on to play for Nottinghamshire and later for England. The intensity of Ross Stephen's approach as a visiting coach, who brought with him wide connections in the world of cricket and an Australian will-to-win, also played a valuable part in nurturing and developing several very successful cricketing careers. The number of Salopians attached to first class counties in the past five years is greater than in the preceding forty.

The importance of these personal contributions was matched, in terms of facilities, by the provision of the Neville Cardus Centre in 2005. It was the launch-pad which enabled enthusiastic cricketers, both coaches and players, to hone their skills and develop their full potential. Its very presence attracted cricket-minded boys, particularly Sixth Form entrants. The thousands of hours of indoor use which were now available produced a step-change in quality. Quality cricketers required quality surfaces upon which to play. On Chance's, the square was enlarged some years ago and a new pavilion was built to replace its thatched predecessor, destroyed by fire. The pitch behind the Senior scorebox, known as Ground 5, has been re-sited, with a much larger boundary, and a maintained square has been developed on the Craig pitch. In an effort to reproduce match-day conditions, élite teams now practise in 'cages' wheeled out onto the Senior wicket. The drainage and irrigation of the outfields has been a major project of recent years. At the same time a number of pitches have been relaid, drains added, new topsoils applied and the pitches meticulously levelled, resulting in two outstanding squares, three of good club standard and one semi-permanent square, which is improving year by year.

Achievement on these squares was enhanced by the expansion of the Sixth Form and in particular by the generous provision of the Cassidy Sports Scholarships, which have attracted six talented cricketers to the School since 2005. Barnard has continued and further developed the tradition of overseas tours which Lascelles had bequeathed, believing not only that they constituted an important factor in developing a team spirit, but also that they had their own distinctive educational value. In recent years membership of these tours has been extended not only to members of the 1st XI squad but to the Under 15 squad also. In 2010 over fifty cricketers took part in the tour of Dubai and Australia, the 2012 tour to South Africa was also very well subscribed, as was the most recent tour in December 2014 to Dubai and South Africa.

Barnard believes that the establishment of strong personal relationships with other clubs and teams has also been a significant factor in bringing success. Potential links were carefully researched by Paul Pridgeon and Will Hughes, and by Barnard himself, whose local knowledge has proved invaluable. The close connection with Shrewsbury Cricket Club has been the most important of these links; the SCC has frequently provided an extension of the cricketer's experience at school. Close links have been forged with County Cricket Clubs, most notably with Worcestershire but also with Warwickshire, Northamptonshire and Glamorgan. A significant exchange has been established with clubs in Perth, Western Australia. Annual Under 11 and Under 12 County Cricket Festivals take place at the School during July and August, together with an annual pre-season festival for Millfield School, Worksop College and Worcestershire County Cricket Academy. As we have noted, the School had already been competing in the Lord's Taverners Cricketer Trophy for the Under 15s for several years, but national competition has only recently begun for other age groups.

All these factors have reinforced each other; and the results speak for themselves. 2013 was an 'annus mirabilis' for Shrewsbury's cricket teams. Three school XIs won national championships for their age-level. The Under 18 team won the 20:20 competition; and at Under 17 the XI shared the 40 over championship, while the Under 15 XI shared the 20:20 competition. For good measure the 1st XI won the Silk Trophy in the same year.

Individual achievements included 1st Class Cricket contracts for James Taylor (Leicestershire/Nottinghamshire), Joe Leach (Worcestershire), David Lloyd (Glamorgan), Alex Blofield (Worcestershire), Stephen Leach (Worcestershire), Ruaidhri Smith (Glamorgan) and Edward Barnard (Worcestershire), while Ben Williams captained the Oxford University XI in 2012, Ian Massey captained the Cambridge University XI in 2007 and Alistair Pollock is captain in 2015. At the pinnacle of achievement during the last decade have been the four Salopians who have won international honours and who provide a spur to the aspiration of their successors. James Taylor has been Captain of the England Limited Overs Squad and has played for England in the World Cup in 2015: he has also played in two Test Matches against South Africa. Edward Barnard has represented England, first at Under 17 level, when he scored a century in his debut, and subsequently at Under 19 level at the World Cup in Dubai; and Ruaidhri Smith has represented Scotland in the same age-group. George Panayi has subsequently represented England at Under 17 level. The emphasis which has recently been placed on individual coaching programmes, personal development during the years at school and critical observation of individual performances in matches, helps to explain the fact that one cohort of cricketers won 51 of their 56 matches while at Shrewsbury. And after surveying the galaxy of talent which has distinguished Salopian cricket during the last decade, one should not forget the generosity of benefactors and the devoted services of coaches and groundsmen, who have provided the context which has, arguably, made Shrewsbury the premier location for schoolboy cricket in the land.

CHAPTER TWENTY-SEVEN

FIVES

Fives has for long been a major sport upon the Salopian scene. As early as 1798 it is recorded that Shrewsbury had two courts for 'bat fives', but the game as it is now played originated at Eton, where it was first developed upon the Chapel steps. Subsequently different versions of the game were developed at Rugby and Winchester. Shrewsbury adopted Eton Fives, probably with Uppingham acting as the intermediary, where Thring, as Headmaster, had established and encouraged the sport. The links between Shrewsbury and Eton were very close throughout the twentieth century, and their association and competition in the fives court did much to strengthen them.

At Shrewsbury, too, the game has owed much to the influence of two of its Headmasters, Cyril Alington and Jack Peterson, both of whom did much to reinforce the links between Shrewsbury and Eton. Alington was a fives enthusiast; Jack Peterson was a superb fives player, as will appear below. Fives profited enormously, too, from the devotion of a whole series of masters-in-charge. F.T. Prior (Master 1891-1933) did much to establish the game at Shrewsbury; and Alan and Geoffrey Phillips, Robin Moulsdale, Alister Barthlomew, P.J. Knowles (the joint author of the recently published *History of Eton Fives*), Mark Williams, Michael Charlesworth, Richard Raven, Noel Darrah, Robin Field, Simon Baxter, Mark Lascelles, Chris Conway, Andy Barnard and Seb Cooley nurtured the sport, honing the skills and extending the participation. Recently Fives has benefited from the appointment of professional coaches, such as G.D.P. Williams and M.P. Hughes. Torin Morgan and Matthew Barrett have also made an important contribution to the coaching team.

The generous provision of Courts has been another important factor in the prominence of Fives. By 1900 there were six courts; subsequently it was reported in the *Salopian* that 'only four courts were roofed in 1908. They were all roofed in 1911, and court No 10, previously fitted as a lavatory, was added in 1912'. A century later the School now has fourteen courts, which were refurbished and re-roofed in 2010 owing to the generosity of Peter Worth OS, a school governor and himself a distinguished fives player. Having an unusually large number of courts has enabled Shrewsbury regularly to host the Public Schools and Northern Championships and also to provide facilities for a flourishing group of local players, the Monday Club. Another favourable circumstance, which, for many years, helped to consolidate fives' prominent position in the School's sporting programme, was the arrangement of the School timetable. 'After twelve' was a period of an hour and a quarter, after morning lessons and before lunch, in which games could be played, providing a length of time which was ideal for fives practice.

Fives was originally a public school game, and the participating schools were few; but it rapidly expanded, first within and then beyond the orbit of these schools, eventually to attract national participation. School matches developed in the early twentieth century. Shrewsbury's first inter-school fixture had been against Uppingham in 1897. Soon Shrewsbury, Eton, Uppingham, Harrow, Highgate and Charterhouse were in regular competition and these six schools formed the nucleus. Between the First and Second World

War the *Times* was reporting the results of twenty-one schools. The first Public School Competition was held in 1928, the first Junior Competition in 1930 and the first Under 14 competition in 1974.

Among the many distinguished Salopian Fives players, mention must be made of John Stewart Stephenson, and of A.T. Barber, who, partnered by Desmond Backhouse, won the Kinnaird Cup in 1934 and 1936. Jack Peterson, when a boy at Shrewsbury, was in the school fives team for four years. At Oxford he won his half-blue for fives in three successive years. Together with his partner, Charles Sheepshanks, he won the Kinnaird Cup three times, twice during the 1930s and on the last occasion when he was forty-eight years of age, in 1950, and just about to return to Shrewsbury as Headmaster. The Worth family produced fine fives players in three generations, R St J Worth, who had played fives with Peterson, his son Peter Worth who won the Schools' Championship with Nick Pocock in 1970, and his grandson Rex, who matched his father's achievement in 2007. Robin Moulsdale gained his half-blue at Cambridge in 1951. With A.R. Kittermaster he was a finalist in the Kinnaird Cup in 1950, 1951 and 1952 and won the trophy in 1954, 1955 and 1956. Geoffrey Phillips was a Kinnaird Finalist in 1954. Ed Taylor was a finalist in 1998 and again, with Ian Hutchinson, in 2000.

Salopian fives (and cricket) owe a great deal to the enormous enthusiasm of Mark Williams, who joined the Common Room in 1977 and made a major contribution to both sports. What follows is an edited version of an appreciation provided by Mike Hughes (SH 1976-1981), who had been one of Mark Williams' earliest Captains of fives at Shrewsbury and was later to share the coaching of fives with him at Eton.

He thought nothing of driving down to London after sport on Saturday, playing two fixtures and returning on Sunday night; and he brought the same energy and commitment to coaching the players and getting them to matches or tournaments that he had applied to his own game. He single-handedly kick-started the sport into vigorous life and within a few years had built an infrastructure which enabled the game to develop further. He persuaded some of the better cricketers in the school of the merits of the game and soon the number of players involved and the quality of play improved enormously. The standard achieved was particularly helped by the introduction of regular matches of the top school pairs against Robin Moulsdale and Mark Williams himself. He always encouraged a dynamic and attacking game, in which it was great fun to participate. He introduced the 'Fives Tour' to London allowing the School to fulfil all its London fixtures in a condensed three or four day period. His lasting legacy is that fives regained its traditional status as the major sport of the Lent Term, and that Shrewsbury School (and indeed the Old Salopian Fives Club) re-emerged as a force to be reckoned with. He produced three pairs who reached the final of the Schools' Fives Championship, T.J.C. Anderson and D.J. Saunders in 1981, R.J.P. Burton and J.M. Eaton in 1982 and J.M. Eaton with D.J. Pollock in 1984. He subsequently coached the game both at Harrow and at Eton, and while at Shrewsbury coached Mark Lascelles (SH 1982-87), who was to be one of his successors in charge of fives at the School.

Another indication of the Salopian enthusiasm for the game occurred in 1989 when four Lower Sixth Formers, Craig Webster and Mike Wycherley (both Rb), with Stuart Parker and Robbie Lonsdale (both SH) completed 37 hours of actual play in order to take the previous record for Marathon Fives Playing from Uppingham. The rules allowed them a five-minute break per hour, which had to be added on to the playing time. This meant that they had to be on court for 40 hours overall. They began to play at midnight on the Tuesday before Speech Day and, encouraged by a large crowd, triumphed at 4 pm on Speech Day itself.

Mark Lascelles, who took charge of the sport in 1993, noticed that fives at that time was a preferred sport for those who might otherwise have turned out on the rugby field. Eton, Harrow, Highgate and Wolverhampton Grammar School were the dominant forces then, but over the years, as fives struggled on in so many schools, Wolverhampton Grammar disappeared off the fives map altogether and Harrow found it difficult to put out teams with any depth. St Olave's, in Kent, under the inspired coaching of Howard Wiseman, rapidly became a force to be reckoned with. Shrewsbury was certainly the strongest school in depth and won the newly introduced Williams Teams' Cup on numerous occasions and more often than any other school. The difficulties of maintaining fixture lists was very evident and many a Salopian spent every other Saturday on the road to Eton to play any number of schools.

Andy Barnard, who took over from Mark Lascelles in 2003, built upon his success. Lascelles had battled for a good budget for fives, a sport in which travel to compete in other locations was absolutely necessary if Shrewsbury was to maintain its prestigious position. Barnard was helped, on the domestic scene, by structural changes, including re-roofing, refurbishment and new lighting in the courts. The sport grew markedly in popularity and in these years Shrewsbury gradually began to overtake its strongest opponents, Highgate. The contribution of outside coaches, including many from the Monday Club, was an important factor in assuring the School's continued domination of the sport. The arrival of Seb Cooley to take charge in 2011 provided a further boost to Salopian aspiration. Cooley now has the distinction, with his partner, of winning the Kinnaird Cup in the last five consecutive years.

One notable feature of the last six years has been the participation of girls. This opened a new chapter in the history of Salopian fives and established it as one of the few Salopian sports which can be played in mixed teams, offering both competitive strength and social interest. A.S. Brett and J. Tse won the Schools' Mixed Nationals in 2011; and the arrival of girls in the Third Form presents a chance for them to take up a sport which is new both to them and to the boys. That fives has been a popular sport with the girls since their arrival is thanks, in no small part, to the enthusiasm and expertise of Chris Conway and Andy Barnard. Andy, who has been in charge of girls' fives ever since they arrived, reports that

It is the most rewarding job, as the girls constantly strive to attain the same levels as the boys, despite their natural differences. They have had a very positive and influential impact on Fives at Shrewsbury and have proved to be great performers. Alice Walker, our first girls' captain, went on to captain Cambridge and until recently has been heavily involved in the development of Ladies Fives as a member of the Eton Fives Association. Rosie Parr will become Captain of Oxford next year.

The achievement of the Sixth Form girls has been fully matched by new arrivals in the Lower School and on 8th March 2015 Nina Lange and Tilly Reynolds, both Third Formers, won the Under 15 Girls' Fives National Trophy, an achievement which is not only a 'first' for the School, but a most encouraging portent for the future. Tilly Reynolds and Sophia Breese won an all-Salopian final in the Ladies' Festival competition of the Schools' Nationals, beating Lizzie Ware and Phoebe Wasdell. Nina Lange played with Daniel Humes in our top pair in the Under 14 Beginners' Tournament (open to competitors of both sexes), beating pairs from Eton in both semis and final. In the light of all these successes Andy Barnard was rightly nominated for the award of EFA Coach of the Year.

Throughout our period many members of the Common Room have been attracted to the sport, often, as House Tutors, playing in a 'Fives ladder' or a knock-out competition organised in the House with which they were associated. 'After 12s' and Thursday afternoons were the favoured times for these encounters and colleagues were quick to realise that such participation provided an excellent means of getting to know their pupils outside the classroom. On Thursday afternoons it was commonplace for a master to invite his partner and opponents home for tea after the match. In the 1980s a staff team would play one of the Houses in a fixture which could attract as many as nine pairs, with drinks or supper thereafter in the House concerned. In this way fives has played an important part in strengthening social relationships in the community; and after a lapse of some years an annual staff-versus-school fixture was reintroduced in 2012. Inter-House competitions remain the competitive focus of the domestic fives calendar and are played at all levels: there are Under 14 and Under 16 House leagues, a senior knockout competition and a mixed competition. These are all played during the Lent Term.

The new century has witnessed a golden era in Salopian fives, as a quick glance over the dates recorded below will confirm. Salopians have been prominent and strong competitors in the Public Schools Championship ever since it was first instituted, and the last decade has been outstandingly successful. In the last forty-three years Salopians have been in the final sixteen times, in 1970, 1981, 1982, 1984, 1995, 1996, 2000, 2002, 2004, 2005, 2006, 2007, 2008, 2011, 2012 and 2013, eight of these appearances being in the last decade. On five of these occasions they won the competition. The victory of Peter Worth and Nick Pocock in 1970 has already been mentioned. The remaining four victories have all been recorded in the last nine years. T.W.P. Cox and T.D.Gerrard won in 2004, A.T. Parker and R.St J. Worth in 2007, J.G. Hudson-Williams and G.Thomasson in 2011 and J.G. Hudson-Williams again, with H.G. Lewis in 2012. 2012 was a truly outstanding year for Shrewsbury in which all four finalists were Salopians! The return of Salopian fives to this strength in the last decade or so was in no small part due to an increased fixture-list against the major fives-playing schools in the south. The introduction of new competitions for the Under 14 beginners in 1990 and the C.M.B. Williams teams competition in 1993 allowed Salopians to develop their game.

In the 25 years of beginners' competition to date, Shrewsbury has been in the final 20 times, winning fifteen times and providing all four finalists on seven occasions: 1996,1998, 2003,2006,2007, 2008 and 2011. This strength has been converted into winning the full Under 16 competition five times: in 2005 (A.T. Parker and A.St J. Worth), 2010 (J.G. Hudson-Williams and S.G. Welti), 2011 (G.D. Williams and W.H. Miller), 2013 (G.P.G. Lewis and T.C. Breese) and 2014 (T.C. Breese and G.D. Panayi). Tom Breese is the only player to date to have won the Under 16 tournament twice, having been a beginner at Under 14. The record in the Williams Cup has been similarly impressive: Shrewsbury have

Laurence Jeffcoate (Ch 2009-2014) playing Mozart with John Moore and the School Orchestra in the Cadogan Hall, London.

Galin Ganchev (M 2010-2015) one of Shrewsbury's finest ever pianists.

The House Singing Competition 2007. Churchill's Hall's Unison Song. The Competition, in October, is one of the most popular musical events of the year. Mike Webb (S 2003-2008) wrote at the time. 'Every boy sings and every boy counts ... What a thrill, to give your all, to know your housemates are too, to be buoyed up together on a glorious wave of sound!. (And, incidentally, what a formative experience for a new boy in his first, nervous weeks!)'

Drama and Musicals

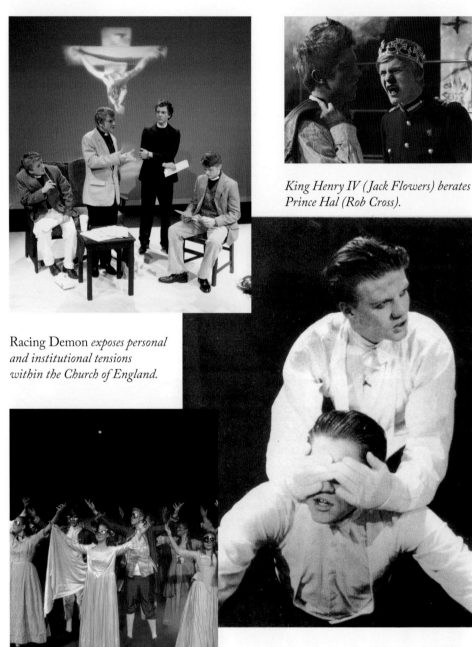

King Henry IV (Jack Flowers) berates
Prince Hal (Rob Cross).

Racing Demon *exposes personal
and institutional tensions
within the Church of England.*

Dr Jekyll and Mr Hyde (Andrew Harper and
Christopher Chaney). Jekyll! *was the first of the
series of original musicals produced by the School.
When it was presented in Edinburgh it was
awarded a 'Fringe First'.*

'Welcome to the ball'. *The cast in the 2014
revival of* The Lost Domain *one of the
most popular musicals by Moore, Went
and Fanning.*

All eyes are on Cyrano de Bergerac (Harry Al-Adwani)

Harry! *'a tuneful, cerebral, witty, moving re-working of* Hamlet.*'

'Are you keen to join the army?' Sam Ansloos attempts to recruit in The Lost Domain.

Royal Shrewsbury School Hunt
The RSSH in Kenya

The Touring party.

Running on the Kamariny Track.

Competitors in the English Schools' championships.

The Tucks in 2013.

Charlie Tait-Harris (S), the winner of the Tucks in 2014, is presented with the trophy by John Ngugi, Olympic Gold Medallist and Coach-in-Residence that October.

Royal Shrewsbury School Boat Club

The Yale Boat House.

The Club Room, which has been fully restored and its records meticulously retrieved, collated and exhibited by Nick Randall OS (O 1972-1976), Captain of Sabrina Club.

The scene at Bumpers 2013.

Their coach, Todd Jesdale, gives a final word of encouragement to the 2007 1st VIII as they take to the water for the final.

The 1960 1st VIII, having adjusted to their new oars, establish a clear lead to win the final of the Princess Elizabeth Club.

The 2007 crew on their way to their victory over Brentwood School Canada, by a margin of one foot.

Football

A perfect day. A dream come true.

Cup final team (1-2-4-1-2):
Laurie Briggs; Charlie Marlow (capt.);
Richard Bainbridge; Ross Gardner;
James Elcock; Matthew Jones; Sam
Kemp; Rob Champion; Andy McLaren;
Tom Evans; Ben Chapman.

Substitutes: Charlie Stockbridge (for
Jones); Tom Wainwright (for McLaren)

Substitute not used: Tom Walling

CHARTERHOUSE

SHREWSBURY

DUNTHORNE
CUP WINNERS 2000

*The winners and the
memorable electronic
scoreboard*

The Shrewsbury 1st XI of 1999–2000 celebrate their victory in the Boodle and Dunthorne Cup.

*The 1st XI lift the ISFA Boodles Cup following their 3–0 victory against Repton in 2010, matching
the achievement of their predecessors a decade earlier.*

Will Waterworth in action against QEGS Blackburn.

Sam Bryan, scorer of 39 goals in 42 matches.

The changing face of Salopian football. The Under 15A team of 2014 with Nina Lange (3rd from left back row)

James Taylor (R 2003–2008), Captain of Notts CCC and Captain of the England Limited Overs Squad 2015, who has played two Test Matches against South Africa and has also played for England in the World Cup 2015.

Shrewsbury School
1st XI Cricket 2013

T.E.H. Harvey-Scholes (Scorer), A.E. Fisher, H.C. Blofield, J.D. Carrasco, J.S.S. Doyle, M.A. Gregson
G.P.G. Lewis, T.B. Milligan-Manby, E.J. Pollock, E.G. Barnard, C.E. Farquhar, C.M.J. Kidson, W.G. Cook

The 2013 1st XI, winners of the HMC T20 and also the Silk trophy, chosen to represent a whole series of recent outstanding 1st XIs because that year witnessed the finest performance on record of school cricket teams as a whole.

The Cricket Centre interior.

Alex Wilson (Rb 2003–2008) in typically aggressive form. An outstanding all-round sportsman, in whose memory a sports scholarship has been instituted.

Cricket on the Common.

Fives

The Fives Courts, generously restored by Peter Worth. (M 1965–1970) The remarkable success of recent teams is recorded on the newly installed Honours Boards (above).

Facing the camera, Jesse Mattinson (Rb): back to camera Josh Himsworth (Ch).

Winners of the Under 14 National Schools' Beginners Final. Nina Lange (G) and Dan Humes (I). Nina also appears in the photograph of the U15 A football team.

The Schools' Open National Championships. The winners in an all–Salopian Final 2012, Jack Hudson-Williams (PH left) and Henry Lewis (I rt). The cup was presented by Richard Barber (OS).

The Salopian contingent at an away match at Eton, pictured in the original Chapel court, where it all began.

A ruck in a match against King Henry VIII Coventry.

The 1st XV of Lent Term 2014 after experiencing 'one of Shrewsbury's best rugby days to date'.

In action against Bishop Vasey's.

*Sam Hill (Rb)
reaches for the ball
at a line-out against
Bishop Vasey's.*

Other Sports

Professional downhill racer Joe Smith demonstrates a severe drop on a track called 'The Wobbler' near Bala, North Wales, on Field Day 2013.

Ed Chapman at Llandegla mountain-bike centre, North Wales, demonstrates an 'all weather' commitment.

The divers take the plunge at Stoney Cove.

Polo against Uppingham (2007)

Sailing

Cross–Channel sailing March 2004. Destination Honfleur.

Warmer climes and calmer seas. The Ionian Sea summer 2004.

Girls' Sports: Netball

Netball: *Netball in Spain. August 2012.*

Girls' Sports: Hockey

Hockey: *1st XI Hockey Team 2013–2014*

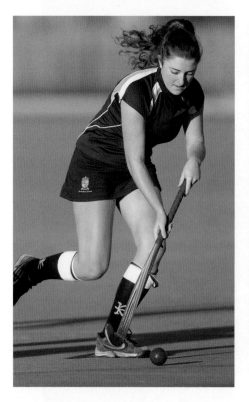

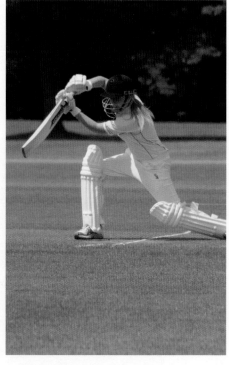

Eliza Wood, Captain of Hockey 2013.

Cricket: *Joanna Cull, a pioneer of girls' cricket at Shrewsbury.*

Girls' Sports

Cross Country: *Mrs Kait Weston with the winners of the Midland and Northern Independent Schools Cross-Country Championships in Sedbergh, March 2014.*

Fives: *The Ladies Festival Winners. Tilly Reynolds and Sophia Breese (centre) flanked by Runners Up Phoebe Wadsell and Lizzy Ware.*

Rowing: *Competing at the Fours Head.*

Outdoor Activities

A Rovers/CCF winter mountaineering expedition, Cairngorm Mountains, February 2015.

The approach to Lochnagar: Rovers/CCF Winter Mountaineering. Cairngorm Mountains. February 2015.

*The Third Form on a Bronze level Duke of Edinburgh Award expedition.
Long Mynd June 2014.*

Sea-Kayak training for the D of E Gold level Award. North Wales 2015.

Outdoor Activities

Mutual congratulations on completion of the D of E Gold level Great Glen Sea Kayak expedition. Summer 2013. Sam Ansloos (G) and Katie Williams (EDH).

Royal Marine cadets and staff, 'tired but happy' on completion of the endurance course in the Sir Steuart Pringle competition, CTCRM Lympstone.

A brief pause on the Stiperstones, School Sponsored Walk, September 2011.

Fancy dress on the School Sponsored Walk, September 2011.

Adam Booth, (PH 1995–2000) who reached the summit of Everest on 13th May 2013, the second Salopian known to have done so. Julian Thompson (SH 1989–1994) preceded him on 30th May 2005. The outcome of Sandy Irvine's attempt in 1924 is still unknown.

Talargerwyn

Talargerwyn, at the start of its association with school in the early 1960s.

A Third Form group from Churchill's is introduced to Talargerwyn.

Members of Emma Darwin Hall visit Talargerwyn.

Other Activities: Blue Chairs

The Blue Chairs on parade.

The Blue Chairs visit the Blue Mosque.

The Blue Chairs in Venice.

Other Activities

Bee-keeping. A summer hive inspection to check the brood.

*Viewing the solar eclipse
20th March 2015.*

*Robin Field (Master 1986–2007) and members of the
Salopian Ventures team display their wares.*

Other Activities

Medic Malawi Mapping out the foundations for the Eye Surgery (2012)

The surgery is complete and the signwriters hold the plaque aloft.

Other Activities

Huw Peach (Master 1991 on) and members of the Model United Nations team, pictured at Manchester Grammar School, where they won the prize for best delegation.

Max Yale (S) addresses the gathering at the School Hustings in the Ashton Theatre, prior to the General Election of 2015.

The colourful assembly of delegates, with their flags, on Central, during the International Young Physicists tournament in July 2014.

been winners ten times in sixteen finals. In 2014, sixteen pairs represented the School at the Under 14 National Championships (there have been more than twenty pairs in some years) and over ten senior pairs are regularly entered for the Schools' Open Competition.

Clearly this very impressive performance, both at senior and junior level, needed to be properly recorded, and in September 2013, honours boards detailing Salopian victories and appearances in the finals of the various Schools' competitions were installed at the courts and unveiled by Robin Moulsdale.

Further afield, at the universities, in addition to Jack Peterson, A.R. Kittermaster and Robin Moulsdale, Peter Nichols, R.F. Griffiths and R.St J. Worth all won half-blues for fives at Cambridge and Alice Walker won her half-blue at Oxford in 2011. Indeed Salopians have regularly been in Varsity sides: the 2014 Varsity match saw three Salopians, J. Flowers and F. Collings for Oxford and R. Griffiths for Cambridge in the top three pairs; the Ladies' Varsity matches the tally: A. Walker, H. Pritchard and L. Rands all playing for Oxford's top six. Salopians also distinguished themselves in the wider competition of the Kinnaird Cup, winning the trophy in 1934 and 1936, in 1954, 1955 and 1956 and producing finalists in 1950, 1951, 1952, 1954, 1959, 1998 and 2000. Salopians have been prominent not only on the Fives court, but also in its administration. Jack Peterson, A.T. Barber, Desmond Backhouse, Richard Barber, and Peter Worth having all been chairmen of the EFA.

An effort has been made in the last few years to strengthen the links between the School team and the Old Salopian Fives Club, thus ensuring that the latter gains full advantage from the strength of the School team, rather than losing track of players when they go to university. There have been regular fixtures between the OSFC and the School, often taking the form of a 'North vs South' fixture, in which Old Salopians and present members of the School form mixed teams. The Monday Club, previously mentioned, comprises Shrewsbury-based Old Salopians and others who play almost every Monday of the year. They are regularly joined by members of the School and of the Common Room during term time and often provide players for Ramblers matches against the School.

From all this it will be clear that Salopian fives in 2015 is flourishing exceedingly, in attainment, provision and participation alike, both at the School and in the links which it has forged outside with the other participants in the sport.

CHAPTER TWENTY-EIGHT

OTHER SPORTS

The total number of school sports in which a Salopian may currently take part is nearer thirty than twenty. Many of these sports, such as tennis and swimming, are long established; many are flourishing, and all deserve a mention. Any selection is bound to involve an arbitrary element. However, in order to avoid a extensive catalogue, which might become tedious and which would certainly prove disproportionate to other elements in the book, I have regretfully decided to adhere to the criteria of selection stated in the preface.

Rugby

The story of rugby at Shrewsbury, during the last century, and particularly during the last fifty years, has been one of a slow, tenacious and ultimately successful struggle for recognition. The 1944 Blue Book records that rugby was introduced in the Lent Term, soon after the First World War, chiefly to provide attractive exercise for those not involved in School rowing. It was generally played on a House League basis. A seven-a-side, knock-out House competition was inaugurated in 1940 and some inter-school matches were started in 1942.

Rugby has always had difficulty in establishing itself in a School in which soccer, rowing and cross-country running have long been recognised as the major winter sports. Its situation had changed little by 1965, when Michael Maloney observed that

by the time you have taken out the natural footballers, the natural ball-players, the fast men and the big men, you have not all that much out of which to build a match-winning First XV.

The rugby 'season' was confined to the first seven weeks of the Lent Term, but the opportunities available during that time were often restricted by adverse weather conditions. The School fielded a 1st XV, with a fixture list of seven matches, and a 2nd XV with four. There was an inter-house seven-a-side, and also an inter-house Under 16 competition. The introduction of the latter, two years previously, had been somewhat controversial: it involved an unwelcome element of compulsion, but it also provided a basis on which to build a higher standard of senior rugby for the future. Michael acknowledged that the match record of the School XVs had been poor, but he was confident that there was both the potential and the spirit for greater success in the future.

When Chris Etherington took charge of the sport in 1970, he realised that to make rugby a part of a Salopian's education – the only reason for having it – the school programme would have to expand a bit, though there was very little 'give' in the sporting Fasti of the Lent Term. The Houses used the sport to soak up amateur energy. These games were often risible, and the risks of injury were great. The promotion of rugby in the School 'was a forlorn flag to fly.' However, the 1970s were blessed with a series of dry, clement winters and the potential hostility of rival colleagues evolved into thoughtful helpfulness. The School Top

Squad contained some outstanding players, many of them Day Boys; in the 1972 season, the 1st XV lost only one match and a standard had been reached for future teams to emulate. A hooped jersey and the establishment of a 1st XV pitch on the Upper Common both helped to enhance rugby's image.

The 1st XV needed a junior infrastructure, requiring the introduction of Under 15 and Under 14 fixtures. The application of much diplomatic skill in the meetings of the Sports Committee would be needed to achieve this, and Chris remembers that he got his knuckles rapped once or twice; but by the end of the 1970s an accepted seven-week structure was in place, with two senior (occasionally three) and three junior teams, each with enough fixtures to make serious training worthwhile. The coaches, Richard Auger, David Lang, Guy Marsden, David Morland and Hugh Newhouse were 'schoolmasters first, rugby men second and heroes to a man'. When Alister Bartholomew succeeded Chris he instituted the Half-Term tour (Edinburgh 1980, Lancashire 1981) and new coaches included Lawrence Edbrooke, Chris Conway, Jonathan Peat and Andrew Auster. All but the 1st XV matches took place on the Lower Common – on Chance's, Craig, old Track and the absurdly muddy Upper Kingsland; and in bad weather negotiations with Ken Spiby were as delicate as those with 'rival' coaches! At House level there were 1st, A and B Leagues every week, and one incontrovertible sign of the higher status of the sport was that two successive headmasters were among the indefatigable colleagues who refereed them; and on Tuesday afternoons the weekly Staff v. Combined Houses matches took place, restricted to twenty minutes each way, to preserve both breath and dignity!

When Duncan Kirkby joined the staff in 1986, rugby was still played exclusively in the Lent Term. There were two senior XVs and A and B teams at Under 16, Under 15 and Under 14 levels, with the junior teams restricted to four matches. Rugby still had to struggle against the long-established sports in order to achieve adequate provision, but further rugby pitches had been established on the top common, with designated pitches on the lower common in addition: the Headmaster, Ted Maidment, was keen that rugby should be given its fair share of facilities and fixtures.

Kirkby took over from Joe Williams as Master-in-charge of rugby in 1989 and has presided over a period in which there has been much more junior rugby and an increased number of fixtures. Since 2010 rugby has also been played in the Michaelmas Term. Currently there are more sports than ever competing for the limited time available, but there is greater integration between the sports, and the views of those in charge of sports are less entrenched.

The question of safety on the rugby pitch has become prominent, both in the national press and at the HMC, as boys have become heavier and physically more developed. Great care is taken nowadays with physical and technical preparation for participation in the sport. Those currently involved in coaching the sport consider that rugby is not a suitable game for boys to be compelled to play: the contemporary view is a far cry from the opinion of a Salopian rugby coach of fifty years ago who expressed the attitudes of the traditional public school when he wrote:

> *some of us are so old-fashioned as to believe that it is quite good for most boys, bad for very few boys and very good for some boys to lie at the bottom of a loose maul and be energetically 'heeled' by both sides indiscriminately!*

In 2014 'domestic' rugby is confined to House senior and junior sevens only. Much of the external opposition comes from Midland Day Schools, such as King Edward's Birmingham, King Henry VIII School Coventry and Adams Grammar School. There has been a long-standing fixture against Old Swinford Hospital. The introduction of the game in our Michaelmas Term has made it possible to establish fixtures with schools in which rugby is the principal winter sport, such as Stowe and Stonyhurst; and the extent to which rugby has progressed both in status and provision is powerfully demonstrated by the fact that on the very day on which this section has been composed, in the middle of the Michaelmas Term 2014, the 1st XV has an away match against – Rugby itself! Rugby tours have been made by Senior teams to Valencia and Venice and twice to Ireland and to Canada. A tour to Argentina is planned for 2015. Junior teams have established a regular tour to Dorset.

There have been more participants in rugby during these early years of the twenty-first century than ever before. External coaches, such as Shaun Perry, have effected an enormous improvement in standard. Some Old Salopians, such as John Henry Carter (Rt) and Tom Dhillon (O) have played at the highest professional level. To give the last word to Chris Etherington:

It's safe to say that Shrewsbury rugby has become accepted and respectable. With the onset of the Kirkby era (Father and Sons) Rugby has gone from strength to strength. Coverage in The Salopian *has grown broader and the formation of Old Salopian teams has reflected the solidity of the plant. I think that the School's only English International, Hal Sever (Rt 1923-28) would have been proud to see the present strength of it.*

Polo

Polo may seem to be an unusual element in the wide range of Salopian extra-curricular activity, Shrewsbury being far away from the recognised centres of the sport, with the closest polo club – the only one within comparatively easy reach – being in Chester. The recent availability of polo at Shrewsbury is due to the appointment of Mr Jim Sheppe to the staff in 2003; he came to Shrewsbury from Marlborough, where he had previously been in charge of the polo team. Since then Salopian polo players have made their mark and have gained a certain amount of respect on the circuit, recording some particularly strong performances by individuals, some of whom have won awards, in competition with schools, mainly in the south, where teams have been long established. Participation in the sport requires a very considerable amount of time and effort. The best training facilities are at Long Dole in Birdlip; and those who wish to participate must be prepared to give up most of Sunday (the only day in the week in which other school commitments leave an opportunity to travel), to make the ninety-mile journey each way. Polo ponies can be hired for training and competition. The sport has attracted Salopians from every level of the School, including complete novices, and those who already have considerable experience, and it is, of course, available to girls as well as boys. As in most 'minority' sports, both participation and performance have varied but, at its most flourishing, the Salopian Polo Club has had over a dozen members during the last decade and its fortunes have owed a great deal to the wholehearted support of some loyal families: the Smyth-Osbournes and the Heywoods being among the most prominent. The arrival of polo provides a welcome and challenging opportunity upon the Salopian scene.

Diving

Diving has been a School activity for at least a quarter of a century. In 1989 Andrew Powell and Peter Scales led an expedition to Eilat on the Red Sea for a two-week expedition. The aims were to complete the training for the British Sub-Aqua Club Ocean and Sports Diver (BSAC) qualification and to carry out survey work on the reefs around Eilat. Underwater photography was an important aspect of the expedition. A second expedition, to Gozo, followed in 1991. In 1992 a party of 31, containing some members of 'Dive 5', a local club which assists the School in all its open water training expeditions, returned to Eilat, to enable Sports Divers to become Sports Leaders. At Easter 1996 a diving expedition to Kenya was combined with a safari expedition. The tradition is maintained to this day. About twenty Salopians each year take part in the training, which is open to Fifth and Sixth Formers. It begins in the swimming pool at School as a Thursday afternoon activity and is then continued at Stoney Cove in Leicestershire. The BSAC qualifications are still the aim and the course has a theoretical as well as a practical component. During the October Exeat of 2014 a group of nine divers travelled to the Egyptian resort of Sharm-el-Sheikh, to take advantage of the warmer and clearer water.

Mountain-Biking

Mountain-biking is an adventure sport and a Thursday afternoon activity. Its antecedents certainly reach back into the 1990s, but it became firmly established after Paul Kaye, who has a qualification in mountain-bike leadership, took charge in 2004. The average number of participants is about a dozen. These were originally drawn from the Upper School, but at present all age-groups other than the youngest, the Third Form, are represented.

Mountain-biking is essentially off-road cycling and the countryside environment is an important part of its attraction. It can involve competitive, timed orienteering exercises, which require racing between check-points, arrival at each of which produces a prescribed number of points, simpler races over a fixed course, or endurance and cross-country biking; Paul enjoys them all. However, the boys soon converted him to their own preference for down-hill cycling and it is on this that the activity now focuses.

The necessary equipment includes a downhill bike with full suspension and a full-face crash helmet; knee pads, elbow pads, gloves, neck braces and spine-protectors also come in useful. Most boys have their own bikes, but a budget from the School has produced a small 'pool' of bikes which boys can borrow. Paul submits a 'risk assessment' for every outing and parental consent is obtained before boys are allowed to join. He reports that there have been fewer injuries than in conventional 'contact' sports.

The training takes place on established tracks. These tracks, like ski-runs, are graded according to difficulty. Paul goes ahead of boys who have not experienced a particular track and 'talks them over the course'. Style and technique are all-important. The challenge is to cycle over unpredictable terrain and rough ground at speed. This requires quick reactions, good balance and correct body position, all of which are particularly important when 'cornering'. Every corner is different and requires a different response. The mountain-biker may encounter obstacles, may have to deal with sudden drops of anything up to ten feet, or may have to jump the bike across a gap, either horizontally or upwards. Nesscliffe, Ercall woods and Eastridge woods are among the nearer locations. If time permits, the group travels further afield to Llangollen, Moelfre or the Revolution Bike Park at Llangynog. Sometimes they receive 'uplifts' from local farmers, who pile boys and bikes on to a trailer and haul them up, by tractor, to the start of the run. They also travel further afield in North or in South Wales, and have had trips to Scotland and to the Portes de Soleil in the French Alps. On Field Days the group receives technical advice and expert training from World Cup Mountain Bikers such as Matt Simmonds and Joe Smith. The group has appeared in national motor-biking magazines and websites.

The difficulty of integrating the School 'Fasti' with external races means that any participation in the latter has to be arranged individually. Enthusiasm for the sport has led some of those who have experienced it at school to continue to pursue it at university and beyond. The reader will have observed that throughout this section I have referred only to boys. But already one girl has been a member of the Club. Subsequently she has crossed the Atlantic and maintains her enthusiasm for the sport in Whistler, Canada, the mecca of mountain-biking.

Girls' Sport

Girls' sport is now in its seventh year at Shrewsbury, well established but still in the development stage. It started with only a few Sixth Form girls in one house. This meant, of course, that there could be no inter-house sport; there was considerable difficulty in forming a full team for fixtures against other schools, and the standard of the teams assembled inevitably varied from match to match and year to year, much more so than in the boys' sports where there was greater continuity in the progression through each successive year group. This, in turn, made the formulation and completion of a training programme equally difficult. Now, however, the girls are able to participate in a wide range of sports including hockey, netball, lacrosse, tennis, the Hunt, athletics, fives and rowing, with swimming, badminton and cricket on a more individual basis, and with yoga as an option for those disinclined to take part in team sports. Hockey is played in the Michaelmas Term and netball in the Lent Term. There is already an extensive fixture list against King's Chester, Wrekin, Moreton Hall, Shrewsbury High School, Oswestry and Newcastle-under-Lyme. Junior teams include Rugby and Repton among their opponents. Fives, the Hunt, rowing and cricket (the latter sport thanks to the facilities of the Cardus Centre) are available all year.

The girls are obliged to play sport on exactly the same basis as the boys, taking four changes a week in the junior forms, and two in the Sixth Form. Third Form girls also take part in the timetabled 'Curriculum Games' in which they are introduced to each sport in turn. The willingness of girls who are Sixth Form entrants to take part in this regime varies and often depends upon the requirements, if any, their previous school imposed. On the other hand, the reputation already established by Shrewsbury when a single-sex school, the excellent facilities available and the offer of sports scholarships seem to be powerful inducements in causing girls' families to apply. Any initial disdain held by the boys for the girls' attainment on the sports field quickly evaporated; the girls have proved themselves to be equally 'sporty' and have earned equality of respect.

Girls have gained their fair share of recognition during the last two years in the recently inaugurated annual Sports Awards. These have acknowledged contributions both in promoting a sport and also high standards of personal attainment in it. The arrival of girls in the Lower School, and particularly in their significant numbers in the Third Form, signals the beginning of the second stage in the development of girls' sport at Shrewsbury. They have already begun to make their mark: one of the girls, already noted in the appropriate section, is the principal striker for the under 15 A football XI, and the girls' junior hockey team has, in its first season, won each of its nine games. There is an opportunity now steadily to establish continuity between the ascending age-groups and to produce strength in depth. The process of integration will not be fully completed for another five years, but the future looks more than promising, perhaps nowhere more so than on the fives' court, where the girls' achievement is recorded in the appropriate chapter.

CHAPTER TWENTY-NINE

OUTDOOR PURSUITS

Until the fourth decade of the twentieth century, experience of the wider countryside, beyond the school grounds, had for most Salopians been limited to Hunt runs and CCF Field Days, supplemented by their own individual initiative on bicycle rides on Sundays and whole holidays. In the 1930s, however, a number of newly-appointed members of the Common Room, most notably Patrick Childs and Roger Wilson, seem to have been attracted to the School by the opportunities for hill-walking and climbing offered by its proximity to North Wales. In his article in No. 153 of the Salopian Mark Twells points out that 'almost uniquely among Public Schools, (and certainly among the original schools of the 1868 Act of Parliament) it could take pupils into the hills'.

This opportunity was seized and developed when, in 1934, the Rovers was formed in response to a national appeal for the training of Scoutmasters. Praepostors were encouraged to become its earliest members, in order to invest the group with the necessary prestige. Roger Wilson, later Bishop of Wakefield and subsequently of Chichester, together with Patrick Childs and Jim Pitts-Tucker, were the first staff members to be involved. Soon afterwards a Junior Troop was founded; but by 1937 the initial impetus had been lost, and on returning from a sabbatical in Australia, Patrick Childs realised that in order for the group to survive, more challenging activities would be required in order to maintain interest.

Speaking at a dinner on 25th November 1989 held, somewhat belatedly, to celebrate the Golden Jubilee of the Rovers, Patrick Childs identified three stages in its development. Having started as a Scoutmasters' Training Corps, it had subsequently become a group of Rover Scouts and had finally turned into a straightforward mountaineering and camping club for senior boys.

An important factor in the revival of the Rovers was the recruitment of Charles Evans, a renowned and expert climber. He was later to be a leading member of the 1953 Everest expedition. Salopians were finally to reach the summit half a century later. The Rovers were fully re-established by camps in Ireland in 1937 and 1939 and in the Cairngorms in 1938. In 1937 they crossed the Kerry Hills and in 1939 their location (at Macgillycuddy's Reeks) was so remote that they returned to England unaware that the Second World War had broken out!

The war interrupted the activities of the Rovers, but at the request of the then Headmaster, Jack Wolfenden (1944-50), the group was revived in 1946, with expeditions to the Cairngorms and to Skye; and its leadership was to be reinforced by the arrival of Lawrence Edbrooke, who became a pillar of the institution, taking over the leadership from Patrick Childs in 1965. In the 1950s and 1960s the Rovers enjoyed a period of popularity and stability, with a regular programme of seven or eight weekends a year camping in North Wales, and an annual expedition of ten days in the Highlands in the summer. Technical rock climbing was established during this period, and Robin Brooke-Smith, who, as a boy in the School, was a member of the Rovers at this time, reported that *the emphasis in the Rovers [was] on mountaineering in all its aspects, and we aim[ed] to develop all skills of mountaincraft from efficient living in mountain camps to hill-walking, rock climbing and snow and ice work.*

Impressed by accounts of the successful Rover camps, Wolfenden's successor as Headmaster, Jack Peterson (1950-63) indicated to Patrick Childs that he would like to go with the group one weekend. Patrick decided to take him to the Parson's Nose on Snowdon.

I tied him to Charles Evans, to make sure there was a good engine on the front, and I tied myself on the end of the rope for two reasons: first, I wanted to see how he would cope with it; secondly, I thought that if the worst came to the worst and he fell off, it would be a good idea if I fell off too. I didn't relish the prospect of having to say on Monday morning "By the way, I am afraid we dropped the Headmaster off a cliff in North Wales yesterday". In the event, he skipped up it like a chamois.

The leasing of Talargerwyn in 1959, an initiative which Jack Peterson enthusiastically supported, and its subsequent purchase in 1991 meant that a minibus packed with Salopians set off along the A5 on most weekends during term. Talargerwyn's attractiveness lay not only in its location as a base for mountain-walking , but in the then very rare opportunity which it offered Salopians to get away from school for a weekend. Now such opportunities are commonplace, and the variety and range of expeditions are manifold. For many years Talargerwyn served two other purposes: as a location for prolonged and uninterrupted periods of academic study, in seminar style; and as a venue for House groups – especially groups of new boys – to promote social bonding in informal surroundings. Both these uses have become less frequent in recent years, though some Housemasters still make a point of taking their Third Formers there at the beginning of their school career.

In the late 1960s, Basic Year appeared on the outdoor scene and dominated it for the next quarter of a century, throughout the tenure of Michael Hall as Master-in-charge. This became such a prominent feature of Salopian life that an earlier chapter is devoted to the subject.

The 1990s was a decade of significant change in the organisation of Outdoor Pursuits, marked not only by Michael Hall's retirement in 1995, but by funding issues with the CCF, the tighter controls imposed by Health and Safety legislation and by the rapid development of technical and support facilities. One of the principal consequences of the legislation was that more staff had to be provided to supervise fewer pupils in any circumstances in which an attendant risk might be perceived (whereas six members of staff had previously run schemes for 120 boys, the current provision is four members of staff for sixteen pupils); supervision by senior boys alone is no longer considered adequate. Schemes and circumstances which had been commonplace and routine for many years, and which had occurred without significant misadventure, were now deemed to be too risky; careful risk assessments had to be made and filed for each operation.

Another result of these changes, reinforced by the development of new techniques and resources, was that the pyramidal structure of Salopian outdoor pursuits was given a further emphasis, with basic instruction and experience for the many; and highly specialised, much more ambitious enterprises, requiring a high degree of technical proficiency, for the keener and more committed pupils. The Rovers also widened the sphere of their operations in the 1990s, when Bob Parker, Robin Brooke-Smith (by then a master) and Martin Hansen were among the leaders. Trevor Kidson, Graham Barnes, Mark Twells, Stuart Cowper and Michael Hall joined the Rovers, while Angus Jamieson filled an important role as Medical Officer. The prelude to this new phase occurred in 1989, when Rovers climbed four of the six highest peaks on Mount Kenya, including the highest peak, Batian. The success of this enterprise created such a surge of interest in climbing and mountaineering that subsequent Rover camps were full or oversubscribed. In 1991, in the Karakorum expedition, the peaks of the Lupghar Chain on the north side of the Batura Glacier were the objective. It was claimed that the athletics competition held on the last evening in the area was the highest-ever event in the history of the Royal Shrewsbury School Hunt! Three years later, the 'Over the Sea to Skye' expedition offered an opportunity to combine the skills of sailing and mountaineering. The group sailed from Liverpool, in the ketch *Francis Drake*, to tackle the Cuillin mountains in Skye. The Rovers made trips to Ireland in 1997 and to Spain in 1998; and in 1999 they turned their attention to Arctic Norway, and ascended its highest mountain, Galdhöppigen. Throughout these years, expeditions to the Scottish Highlands, the traditional theatre of the Rovers' operations, alternated with those overseas; among them were camps in Glen Coe in 1988 and in 1992, and trips to Ben Nevis and Ben Arthur in 1997.

At the turn of the new century, with Graham Barnes as the master-in-charge, the focus shifted southwards to the Pyrenees. An expedition had already been launched, in 1998, to climb the Torre de Corredor, the highest peak in the Picos de Europa in northern Spain. In 2000 the aim was to climb the five highest mountains in the Pyrenees. This involved expeditions on both sides of the Franco-Spanish border and brought the Rovers to the highest altitude they had reached for ten years. Another expedition to the Pyrenees took place in 2004. Meanwhile, in 2002, a group of Third and Fourth Formers set out for Italy, to climb in the Apennines. There were also three trips to the French Alps by what was still called 'Basic Year', though the whole of the academic year group was not involved.

The Rovers have been somewhat submerged in this dramatic expansion of outdoor activity. The regular programme of expeditions throughout the year, which was characteristic of the Rovers in their 'classic' phase, is now provided in the much more elaborate and equally challenging requirements of the Duke of Edinburgh scheme, in which the adventurous spirit which motivated the Salopians of those earlier generations lives on. Although the last official Rovers expedition from the School took place in 2001, the tradition of the Rovers has been faithfully maintained, if at a rather less ambitious level, by a group of Old Salopians, co-ordinated by Robin Nugent (PH 1983-88) which meets every summer, at Talargerwyn, or some other suitable base, for a weekend of hill-walking. Plans are currently afoot to revive and reinvigorate the group.

Mount Everest's place in Salopian annals pre-dates all the developments so far described, for of course it was a Salopian, Andrew Irvine (CJB, WHM now S 1916-1921) who, probably as the result of a chance encounter with Noel Odell, a regular member of the early Everest expeditions, and partly on account of his mechanical expertise with primitive oxygen apparatus, was selected as a member of the 1924 attempt. It was he, who with George Mallory, was briefly seen, from the camp below, until cloud obscured the view, as they approached the summit; but the weight of opinion has concluded that they did not reach it. Sir Charles Evans (DB 1932-37) with his partner Tom Bourdillon, the first summit pair in 1953, got within 300 feet of the summit.

Fifty years were to elapse before other Salopians attempted to reach the summit. Murray Campbell (O 1992-1997) led the way in 2002, Richard Taylor (O 1994-1999) as a member of the Irvine-Lovatt expedition, followed in 2004 and reached 8000m on the north side of the mountain: then Jonjo Knott (PH 1989-94), as a member of the British Services Mount Everest West Ridge expedition, reached 8100m in 2006. But at the time of writing only two Salopians are known at the School to have reached the summit: Julian Thompson (SH 1989-94) on 30th May 2005, followed, eight years later, by Adam Booth (PH 1995-2000) on 13th May 2013.

Mark Twells places these achievements in context, pointing out that most of those who attempted to climb Everest prior to 1950 were drawn from British Public Schools; that of the 4,000 or so who have so far reached the summit, two are Old Salopians, and that four Old Salopians since then (and Sandy Irvine before then) have reached the so-called 'Death Zone'.

In recent years there has been a very significant proliferation of outdoor activities, previously more narrowly focused on Basic Year and the Rovers. The name 'Basic Year' is no longer used. In Michael Hall's time it was a strictly civilian organisation, in part funded, with rather questionable legitimacy, from military sources. This connection was severed and subsequent camps have very properly been specifically military. There are now three separate camps in the summer and one camp at Easter. The activities formerly conducted in Basic Year now continue in the 'Outdoor Skills' section of the programme described below.

Membership of the CCF is voluntary. Most of those who join do so in the Fourth Form. There are approximately 100 cadets, made up of 60 recruits and 40 Junior and Senior NCOs. Some Sixth Form girls have joined, both from Shrewsbury and also from Adcote School, with which we have a CCF affiliation. An Honours Board of military achievements has been installed.

The Marine Section of the CCF has regularly taken part in the Sir Steuart Pringle Trophy, an exacting and prestigious competition held at Lympstone, providing a rigorous test of military skills. The School has won the trophy on several occasions and has generally won a high place among the nineteen schools which have such a section.

Other choices available in the Fourth Form are Outdoor skills (the re-branded Basic Year, which now includes a Conservation element) and Sports Leadership. The latter choice is focused on organising rather than simply participating in sporting events, the value of the activity consisting in the requirement to take initiatives. In addition a small group is engaged in mountain-biking.

Many Salopians participate in The Duke of Edinburgh Award Scheme; and the Expedition component, outside the school curriculum, provides an opportunity to take part in an activity formerly available in Basic Year. Originally facilities were only available for the Gold Award. Now members of the School offer themselves as candidates for all three levels, Gold, Silver and Bronze. At each level they are required to develop a skill and to participate both in a sport and in a service activity (uniformed service qualifies for this requirement); all these activities can be pursued in term-time. However, the Expedition requirement, a venture which has to be self-propelled (for example on foot, by canoe or on bicycle), necessarily has to take place in the holidays. Such expeditions have taken place in North Wales, the Peak District and the Shropshire hills, with canoe or sea-kayak expeditions taking place on local canals, in the Great Glen in Scotland and in the warmer climate of the Dalmatian coast of Croatia. Shrewsbury is one of a small number of Independent Schools that is an operating authority for the Award. This means that the School has a lot of opportunity to tailor a programme which is appropriate for both boys and girls.

Thursday afternoon

Extra-curricular activities on Thursday afternoon have been a consistent feature of the last sixty years, but the range of these activities has been greatly expanded. The Third Form have always had their own programme, which in the earlier years included talks on the history of the School, a subject now provided as a course of six short lectures, spread throughout the year, which take place in assemblies before first period early on Tuesday mornings. The Fourth Form originally had a choice between membership of the CCF or of Basic Year, but the latter soon became all-embracing. More senior boys had a wide range of choice, which included participation in Community Service.

Now members of the Third Form follow a 'circus' in the Michaelmas and Lent terms, which includes drama and music, information technology and PSHE (personal, social and health education). In the summer they move outdoors, to take part in 'Outdoor week', for the whole of which they are taken out of the classroom, their last opportunity to do so before their GCSE examination courses begin. Half of the time is spent in camp on the Long Mynd; in the other half of the week Third Formers undertake conservation activities such as dry-stone walling (a 'Salopian' wall, restored by Third Formers, exists on the Welsh borders;) a day is spent practising survival skills, building shelters and making fires; another day is devoted to a military competition. The idea is to develop a service element, always including conservation work, in everybody's programme.

The Fourth Form programme has been described above. Members of the Fifth and Sixth Forms can choose from a wide range of activities: rock climbing, riding, gliding, cooking, drama and sub-aqua, yachtmaster skills (learning to navigate), self-defence, journalism, preparing for SAT tests (entrance to American universities), or Young Enterprise (which sets up and runs entrepreneurial companies). Community Service is another option; and the experience gained in this activity has been found to provide a strong recommendation for anyone subsequently applying for a degree course in medicine. Participation in the scheme as a whole is voluntary for members of the Upper Sixth and only a small minority, usually those who have attained leadership positions in the CCF or other organisations, take part.

The current Director of Activities, Nick David, comments on the past history, present situation and future prospects of 'Activities' as follows:

Activities is the general term denoting non-sporting enterprises of an outdoor and wholesome nature that take place outside the classroom. Traditional hobbies, as well as more cerebral pursuits were provided by our Societies programme, e.g. bee-keeping or the model railways club. Over the years, the Shrewsbury programme has expanded, mainly based on the interests and inclinations of the staff, to include an eclectic range of pursuits, such as publishing, sub-aqua, recycling and more. This development reflected a wish to cater for all tastes as well as to acknowledge the fact that society, and thus the profile of our pupils, has changed.

Specific future possibilities include encouraging pupils to teach reading, languages, or ICT skills, to work on canals or on garden projects for those in need, or to help in youth groups. It has also been suggested that all younger pupils should be expected to join a society. The new programme of 'Outdoor skills' for junior pupils leads to entry-level Outward Bound certification in canoeing, bicycling, navigation and climbing; their seniors can participate in a Young Enterprise Programme, undertake habitat surveys with the Shropshire Wildlife Trust, or participate in Community Drama.

The progressive introduction of co-education, together with a belief that we need to update our provision, have further stimulated this change. Weaknesses in our current system included a lack of vertical progression in a skill or activity. There was too little continuity and persistence, because there was too much choice. There were few qualification-based options. Our level of engagement with the outside world was too narrow in scope. Our aim must be

to deliver a high-quality activities programme that encourages the development of skills, a sense of service to the community and the nurturing of enjoyable and satisfying lifelong pursuits. Activities should inculcate the habit of looking beyond the school boundaries and nurture a greater understanding of others.

CHAPTER THIRTY

SOCIETIES, CONFERENCES AND COMPETITIONS

Societies

The 'Blue Books' of 2014 list more than thirty societies, some traditional and long-standing, others novel and ephemeral, the existence of the latter group depending upon the enthusiasm and commitment of the staff and pupils involved. The academic societies comprise the Astronomical Society, the Bastille (History), the Business Club, the Chinese, French, Spanish and Russian societies, the Classical Society, the Darwin Society (Science), the Da Vinci Society (Art), the Heseltine Society (Politics), the Sidney Society (English), the Medical Society, the Shropshire Geographical Society and the Extended Projects group. The meetings of many of the societies take place on Friday evening, specifically designated for them, and a calendar of these meetings is compiled and published every term.

The Bee-keeping Society, the Christian Forum, the Creative Writing Group, the Debating Society, the Drama Society, the International Young Physicists Group, the Model United Nations team, the Reading Group, the Model Railways Society, the Reeling Society and the Quizzing Group extend the range of options still further. The Anacreontic Society, formed to promote the composition and performance of their own music by its members, made a brief appearance. The Listeners, a long-standing society whose members toured the homes of members of the staff to listen to a programme of recorded music chosen by their hosts, extremely popular in its day, no longer exists.

On Thursday afternoons another range of opportunities bridges the gap between 'societies' and 'activities': community action, community drama, community service, EFL for Science, photography and computer-aided design among them. Cooking and Gastronomy deal respectively with the preparation and the enjoyment of the pleasures of the table; Public Nose is a pupil-produced broadsheet of current affairs. Young Enterprise is a pupil-led commercial company. A recent addition is the Kit-Kat Club for members of the Lower Sixth, following the tradition of its eighteenth-century namesake in encouraging all kinds of aesthetic appreciation, artistic, musical, gastronomic and (yet again) oenological.

The Astronomical Society

The Astronomical Society was securely established when, in the 1970s, Gilbert Roscoe built the dome, together with the robotic controls for the telescope. It is an observing Club and it is open to all members of the School. It has a membership of about twenty, and groups of about twelve in number go out weekly to observe the skies. Members are recruited at the Societies' Fair, or subsequently by word of mouth, and excursions are noted on the School intranet. Although observations can also be made from the school grounds, the lesser light pollution in the countryside makes the short trips out there very much more worthwhile. Members have also joined the Shropshire Astronomical Society at Roddington for an observation. Trips further afield are made, from time to time, to the observatory at Knighton, to the Spaceguard Centre in Powys, to the National Space Centre, to Jodrell Bank and to the Royal Observatory at Greenwich.

Astronomy has recently been introduced as a GCSE subject, and there are eight members of the present class. Their observation skills are tested by a controlled assessment, and other requirements are a knowledge of the geography of the sky, the ability to use a star atlas and an understanding of the formation and the development of the stars. An historical element traces the changes in our view of the universe and includes the discoveries of Copernicus and Galileo. Candidates study the respective accuracy of clocks and sundials, the reasons for the apparent variations in the movement of the sun and learn how to calculate the distance of the stars from their brightness. The course provides an admirable introduction for those whose continued interest encourages them to become amateur astronomers in later life. More advanced researches in Astronomy can be pursued by Sixth Formers as part of an Extended Project.

In addition to the Dome telescope, the School owns two other large, and two smaller telescopes and several sets of binoculars. One of the most exciting observations in recent years was of Venus in 2004. The society occasionally has formal lectures, on subjects such as Astronomical Photography.

One of the notable initiatives of the School's astronomers has been their involvement, in 2007 and 2008, as one of the ten participating schools in the Dill Faulkes Telescope Project. This enabled them to reserve periods of actual (remote) control of a powerful telescope in Hawaii; nearer home they have had a similar opportunity of controlling the National Schools Telescope through the agency of Liverpool's John Moores University. In 2010 the School team made the winning entry in POISE, the Polar Orbiting Ionospheric Scintillation Experiment designing a small instrument, subsequently converted to software, for installation in a satellite, in order to measure the distortion of radio signals in the ionosphere. The results from their experiment will help to ensure more reliable satellite navigation and communication systems.

On 20th March 2015 there was a particularly favourable opportunity to observe a partial eclipse of the sun, during which, at its greatest extent, about 92% of its surface was obscured. The occurrence had been advertised in the School *Fasti* and several groups observed the eclipse from the Site; but the Moser Precinct, where about two hundred people assembled, was the scene of the greatest excitement. Dr Mark Elliot had prepared about ten different methods of observation, including two specialist telescopes with appropriate filters, special high-density spectacles, pin-hole cameras and colanders through which to filter the images. Great interest was shown as the crescent of light moved across the sun's surface and as the variations in temperature which accompanied the process of the eclipse were experienced. Many photographs of the event were taken and posted on the School's intranet.

It is highly appropriate that an astronomical society should exist and should be so active and enterprising in a school which counts the current Astronomer Royal among its former pupils.

The Bee-Keeping Society

The Bee-keeping Society celebrated its 40th anniversary with a dinner in Kingsland House on 7th June 2014, to which all Past Presidents and Secretaries were invited. The society was founded when Selby Martin and David Christie bought some second-hand hives and two stocks of bees, the barest minimum of equipment, which they installed on a bank near Tudor Court. The location was later changed and ended up in Ridgemount orchard, a woodland area, concealed and overgrown, but with nectar sources in neighbouring parks and gardens; it was altogether ideal for bees, who also acted as a deterrent for smokers! Thirty boys joined the society, which became a corporate member of the Shropshire Bee-keepers Association.

Limited funding came from the School Shop profits and the Shop also sold the honey which was produced. At one point there were over twenty hives, with the boys sharing responsibility for their management, producing an average of thirty pounds of honey each year. The School recognises the importance of bee-keeping – the only School activity linked to agriculture.

Instruction was given in David Christie's classroom on Thursday afternoons in the winter; practical experience in colony management was obtained in the summer, and the society flourished. Its progress was greatly assisted by the establishment of a weekly Societies Hour after lunch on Mondays (early afternoon being the best time for the activity), also by the recruitment of other members of the Biology staff, Andrew Powell and Andrew Allott, while Ian Lacey gave talks to the society.

A bee-keeping exhibition on Speech Day proved to be a popular attraction and society members attended summer meetings of the Beekeepers Association. They also took the Junior grade examination of the Association, which involved twenty written questions and a ten-minute interview; but a later additional requirement to keep a diary proved unpopular and the examination was eventually dropped.

The society has had its full share of vicissitudes: threats of prosecution by an angry former Shrewsbury MP if the apiary was not moved; damage caused by inebriates emerging from the Boathouse Inn; badgers knocking over hives; and the scourge of the varroa mites, combined with colony collapse disorder. But there have been highlights, too, among them the selection of Harry Boutflower (S 2008-2013) to join a team of three to represent the UK at the International Meeting of Young Beekeepers near Vienna in August 2011.

The reduction of the time available in Societies' Hour, the rival attraction of computers and the Internet and the increased work needed on the maintenance of hives in holiday time produced problems for the society and its survival has been largely due to Selby Martin's boundless enthusiasm and determination. However, Head of Biology Andrew Allott has taken care to accommodate the activities of the society to the exigencies of the current school curriculum. He finds that it always attracts a group of committed bee-keepers; about twelve is the optimum number. Apart from the management of the hives, they purify wax, make candles, brew mead, make up hive parts, identify different types of pollen, hold tastings of different kinds of honey purchased on their international travels and sell the honey their own bees have produced in support of School charities. Andrew recognises the value of an activity which is entirely non-competitive and which never fails to generate enthusiasm among boys who are genuinely interested in the natural world.

Debating

Debating, having lapsed as an activity for several years, experienced a remarkable resurrection, just over ten years ago, with the vigorous encouragement of the Headmaster, Jeremy Goulding and of Richard Hudson.

A new junior House competition was introduced in the Lent Term of 2002. The Third and Fourth Formers in each House entered a team, and following the success of this initiative a senior competition was introduced in the following Michaelmas Term. This has attracted a huge amount of interest and has greatly exceeded expectations, both in the quality of content and research, and in the standard of the delivery of speeches and of their rebuttal. The dramatic revival was spearheaded by our colleague Dr Alex Craig, and in 2004 Chris Lloyd, then a Sixth Former and a keen debater himself, was able to report that 'from virtual non-existence in 2001 Shrewsbury now boasts a national reputation as a hot-house for debating talent'.

In June 2005 the Debating teams travelled to California and fought off competition from 46 American universities and colleges to take both first and second places, in an all-Salopian final; the other two teams reached the final eight of the competition, the Western States Parliamentary Debating Tournament. They reported, on their return, that 'there was some grumbling from the University students about being beaten by a gang of High School kids'. At the conclusion of their visit it was decided that High Schools would not be allowed to enter the competition in future! At home the teams participated both in the Oxford and in the Cambridge debating competitions; this involved trips to the University Unions, to the regional competitions at Solihull School and also to Concord College.

Alex Craig's pioneering work was strongly reinforced by Alex Thomas and Laura Whittle, and Dr Matthew Clark has recently taken charge. Debates are generally held in Societies' Hour and take place in most weeks of the Michaelmas and Lent Terms. This resurgence in debating is part of the wider picture in which Salopians have shown enthusiasm and increasing proficiency in Public Speaking, for which the European Conferences and the Model United Nations Conferences have provided other platforms and records of success.

The Quiz Society

The Quiz Society, which has been very active in recent years, under the supervision, first of Martin Cropper and then of Dimitri Portier, received a further impetus when Dr Charles Oakley joined the Common Room in 2006. His credentials for taking charge of the team could scarcely be better: he had captained the winning team, from Corpus Christi College Oxford, in *University Challenge* earlier that year and was subsequently invited to set mathematical and scientific questions for the competition. Salopian interest in quizzes was further heightened when the members of a Common Room team acquitted themselves admirably on the television programme *Eggheads*. The Quiz society now has two sessions a week, the juniors meeting on Monday, and the Wednesday meeting open to all age-groups. On average the gatherings number a dozen. In the Lent and Summer terms there is an inter-house competition, also held on a weekly basis. The School team operates in the Michaelmas Term, in which the main focus is on the Schools' Challenge in November, usually held at King Edward's School Birmingham, whose delegates frequently provide the strongest opposition. About eight schools compete in the regional final, producing two teams each. There are two juniors and two seniors in each team. The questions are set centrally, and the procedure for University Challenge is closely followed, with a 'starter for ten', followed with a series of bonus questions for which ten points also (rather than the five allotted in University Challenge) are awarded in the schools' competition. The questions are generally, although not exclusively, academic. Shrewsbury has won the competition once and has come third on another occasion since the turn of the millennium.

Conferences

Challenge of Management

The Challenge of Management conference has been a prominent item on the Salopian *Fasti* for nearly forty years. Its origins in the 1970s lay in a scheme devised by the Industrial Society to offer two-day conferences to schools, in which young industrial managers introduced Sixth Formers to problems and relationships in industry. Shrewsbury, encouraged by its Careers Master, Mike Eagar, was one of the first schools to accept this invitation. His successor, Hugh Ramsbotham, also Head of Business Studies, built strongly upon this initiative, keen to convince Sixth Formers that, even though their career choices might lie in other areas – medicine, law or finance - an introduction to the world of business would still prove extremely relevant and valuable for them.

Accordingly young managers - group leaders - from a wide range of businesses and professions came to Shrewsbury to lead case-study discussions, role-playing exercises and competitive business games. A keynote speech was given by a senior manager; and a senior trade unionist attended the two-day conference. With the support of the Headmaster, Eric Anderson, a special conference was held in the last two days of the holidays to convince members of the Common Room who might otherwise be sceptical of the value of such an intrusion into academic time. On this latter occasion each group was led by the Chief Executive of a major company; members of the academic staff were introduced to some of the far-ranging challenges such senior executives might meet and the skills required to tackle them. The closing speech by John Garnett, the charismatic chairman of the Industrial Society, was described by the School Chaplain, Revd David Allcock, as the most inspiring sermon he had ever heard, while the presence of an Old Salopian who was a *Times* correspondent, led to a full-page article on the conference describing Shrewsbury as a pioneer in this venture.

The subsequent annual Sixth Form conferences thrived. McKinseys provided the Chairmen and key speakers; Old Salopians provided the group leaders. Other schools were invited to join the conferences, particularly in order to enable girls to participate. Members of the academic staff volunteered for work experience in industry in the holidays, while similar work experience – and sponsorships – with industrial companies was offered to Sixth Formers. Further developments included a six-month Gap Industrial Experience – INDEX, based upon the army's Short Service Limited Commission, available to Sixth Formers who had a guaranteed place at university.

The Conferences continue to thrive under the dedicated leadership and meticulous attention of Colm Kealy. The aims, membership and activities of the Conferences have closely followed the original pattern. Currently about 180 members of the Shrewsbury Lower Sixth attend, girls from the High School and from Moreton Hall have been recent visitors and during the last five years Shrewsbury's own Sixth Form girls have of course taken part. In the last couple of years, a delegation from the Colegio San Bartolomé, an Argentinian school linked to Shrewsbury, has also joined during its annual visit. The tradition of the keynote speaker has been maintained. The group leaders, often local businessmen, usually have a link with the School and are recruited each year by personal contacts. They preside over groups of seven or eight students who participate in team-building exercises and in role-play, involving both negotiation with Trade Unions and raising funds for social enterprises. Running an ice-cream business is a typical exercise and an effective team will organise itself so as to include financial, marketing, promotion and business development functions, with a chief executive in overall control. Third Formers volunteer to help to operate the computer programme which runs this business 'game'. Recently, however, the time allotted to the Conference has been confined to one day, rather than the original two. This has been done partly to reduce the intrusion into academic time but also because the visiting speakers and group leaders find it easier to spare a single day in which to devote themselves to the activity.

Salopian Ventures, the related enterprise in which Sixth Formers have run their own company to produce a range of School merchandise, also has a long history, having been inaugurated by Robin Field a quarter of a century ago. During the twenty-one years in which Robin was in charge, he was the inspirational leader, guide and anchor-man of this hugely successful enterprise: the company's total profits reached over £100,000 all of which was passed on to support a range of local charities. Though its products are still available, members of the School no longer actively participate in it. During the last two years over twenty members of the Lower Sixth and the Fifth Form have moved over to *Young Enterprise*, which provides the same kind of experience as Salopian Ventures, but in a much wider context. Over one million young people have spent a year running their own Young Enterprise company since this national programme started in 1963. They register their company, set up a board of directors, carry out market research, develop a product or service, manage finances, promote the company, and then market and sell their product to the public. They also have the option to enter the Young Enterprise Company of the Year Competition.

The academic backing of the Economics and of the Business Studies departments, the well-established Challenge of Management Conferences and the actual experience of running a company, originally within Salopian Ventures and currently in Young Enterprise, have together ensured that the pioneering spirit which first motivated Salopians to breach the barriers between School and Industry is as well-grounded and as vigorous as it ever was.

European Conferences

With the appointment of Mrs Jay Upton as European Liaison Officer in 1990, a greater emphasis in the curriculum naturally fell upon European affairs and in 1993 the first European Conference at Shrewsbury inaugurated a series which continued for over a decade. Twelve delegations, one from each House, consisting of all the members of its Lower Sixth, took part. Each House represented the affairs of one European country, allocated to them by the drawing of names from a hat. A member of the Common Room was also assigned to assist each delegation. Two topics for debate were chosen; and preparation for the debates required a considerable amount of research. The boys were strongly encouraged to approach the appropriate embassy for briefing and several embassies sent delegates to support the teams. The first conference focused on the Common Agricultural policy and on Defence and was attended by representatives from the Belgian, Danish, Irish, Spanish and Netherlands embassies. Each delegation proposed a resolution expressing 'their' country's view on each of the selected topics. One of the twelve resolutions relating to each topic was selected for debate, and each delegation in turn responded with endorsement or criticism. The panel of judges usually included visitors well versed in European affairs. In 1993 Oldham's, representing Ireland, were the winners; their reward was a trip to the European Commission in Brussels.

In 1995 the procedure was modified. Two prizes were awarded, one to the winning House delegation (on this occasion Severn Hill, representing Portugal), and one to the five best individual speakers in the competition, who, again, were allowed to visit the European Commission. Perhaps the most memorable such excursion was that of the group of five who visited St Petersburg in 2002.

As the European Conference developed, Huw Peach further modified the procedure to bring it more closely into line with that of the European parliament itself. In 2005 all members of the Lower Sixth acted as MEPs for the day, as they debated the controversial proposal that Turkey should be admitted to the European Union, and, if so, upon what conditions. The motion was carried, and the Counsellor from the Turkish Embassy who was present remarked that the boys whom he had heard were far more impressive than most European MPs!

In recent years the European Conference has been superseded by the School's still more challenging participation in the Model United Nations organisation, where the combination of debating skill and command of contemporary political issues is put to an even sterner test.

Model United Nations

For over twenty years Shrewsbury has participated in the Model United Nations, an informal association of schools interested in debating topical political and economic issues, based on the structure and procedures of the United Nations itself. The member schools announce and host the competitions which take place on a regional, national and international basis. The School has enjoyed marked success during this period and built a considerable reputation. The organisation is particularly strong in the north-west, where Shrewsbury is acknowledged to be a leading contender. Huw Peach, who joined the staff in 1991, not only initiated Shrewsbury's membership in 1992, but has presided over Salopian fortunes in the competition ever since.

Conferences can last up to three or four days and the venues have been far-flung: among these, Cheadle Hulme, Stockport, Withington and Manchester Grammar School, all in the Manchester area, have been nearest; but Salopian teams have visited Edinburgh in the north, Magdalen College School, Royal Russell School Croydon, Haileybury and Haberdashers' Aske's School in the south, and travel annually to an international conference held at UNESCO in Paris.

In each competition, the School delegation is assigned a country which it represents in debates over a prescribed range of issues. Over the years each delegation acquires its own reputation, and it is a measure of Shrewsbury's success that it has progressed from representing Afghanistan and Eritrea to speaking on behalf of China! The Conference opens with a General Assembly, at which between six hundred and a thousand delegates may assemble, but the main work of the conference takes place in committees in which about forty delegates are engaged. The most prestigious committee is, of course, the Security Council, and it is to this committee that a school tends to assign its best speakers. The agenda for each committee is published beforehand, and it may range widely over such topics as disarmament, human rights, economics, health, ecology, culture and the media.

One of the most admirable and valuable features of the organisation is that it is entirely pupil-based and pupil-driven. The candidates are required to brief themselves on the topics on which they have to speak and the committees are chaired by pupils whose job it is to control the debate and assess the quality of the contributions. Successful participation in the debates requires a whole range of skills and qualities, stamina not least among them, and the contest elicits quite as much commitment and is no less exciting than a hard-fought encounter on the games field!

Interest in the Model United Nations at Shrewsbury has grown markedly over the last two decades. This has been an entirely spontaneous development, sparked by the reports and enthusiasm of those who have already participated, and receiving a further boost from the recruitment of Sixth Form girls. Weekly practices are held at School, where newcomers can try out their skills and decide whether to persevere. The average size of a Salopian delegation is between twelve and fifteen, but when both senior and junior teams have been involved it has on occasion risen to twenty-five. Perhaps the greatest achievement so far occurred in the year when two Salopian MUN teams were simultaneously competing at separate conferences. In Edinburgh the A team won the prize for the best delegation overall, and the B team was voted the best delegation in the General Assembly, while at Stockport, during the same weekend, the latter distinction was also matched by the junior team.

The in-depth research into contemporary issues, the full understanding and ready command of them which are required, the honing of debating techniques, the experience of chairmanship and its own characteristic skills, together with the confidence, quick-wittedness, humour and charisma which are required to win one's case, not only constitute an invaluable element in the general education of those who participate, but also provide a rich treasury of resources upon which to draw later in the wider social and professional sphere.

Competitions

Olympiads

For many years the ablest mathematicians and scientists have been competing in a national competition, aimed predominantly at Sixth Formers, known as the *Olympiad*.

Mathematics

The British Mathematical Olympiad (BMO1) was inaugurated in the 1960s and a second, higher level (BMO2) was added a decade later. Although the competition is accessible to those who are preparing for an A level in Mathematics, the questions in the Olympiad are specifically of a problem-solving nature and require considerable mathematical insight. Candidates have 3½ hours to tackle six fiendish problems in the first round; there are only four (even harder) problems in the second round. On average about 1300 candidates take part nationally at the level of BMO1, and 100-150 of those at BMO2. Of the latter group, twenty participants are selected to spend a few days of intensive mathematical training at Cambridge, and eventually six of these are chosen to represent Britain in the International Mathematical Olympiad.

In recent times, between four and ten Salopian mathematicians have taken part each year in the BMO1. One or two regularly obtain a certificate of distinction for finishing in the top 25%, and every few years the best mathematician in the school does well enough to qualify for the BMO2. One Salopian succeeded in reaching the final twenty in 2002.

Physics

In Round 1 there is a 2½ hour paper, externally marked. The top fifty students receive a Gold Medal; there are also Silver and Bronze medals. Salopians have had a number of successes in recent years, notably in 2013 when one Gold and one Silver medal were awarded. The top fifty students then move on to Round 2, which consists of a 3¼ hour paper. Distinction, Merit and Gold Awards are made. The top fifteen are awarded a Distinction and proceed to Round 3 and to the Oxford Training Camp.

Chemistry

This competition is designed to stimulate the most talented young chemists in the country and is open to all post-sixteen students in the United Kingdom. There are three rounds in the competition at the conclusion of which the UK team is selected to train for, and compete in the International Chemistry Olympiad. A weekly session in the Lower Sixth prepares candidates to take the Cambridge Chemistry Challenge. In the Michaelmas Term of the Upper Sixth between ten and twenty students begin intensive preparation for the more demanding Olympiad itself. Round 1 of the International Chemistry Olympiad takes place in February. There is a two-hour examination which is composed of a series of structured questions based on the core of the A level syllabus, designed to stretch able students by making them apply the principles they have learned to new and often more complex situations than they would meet in their A level course; not only is a very sound base of knowledge and understanding required, but also the ability to think 'outside the box'. Occasionally a student qualifies to enter Round 2. Students who reach a further round are invited to attend a residential camp at Cambridge and to give a presentation at the Royal Society. The highest award is the Roentgenium medal.

Biology

The Biology Olympiad attracts thousands of entrants each year. The first round is a two-hour multiple-choice exam covering a very wide range of topics and some very challenging questions. Medals are awarded on the results of this. Between five and ten Salopians enter in a typical year and most receive a medal, with at least one Gold medal being awarded in most years. Recently this exam has been run on-line, making it a test for the IT department as well as the candidates! The higher scoring gold medallists take part in a second test in school and those who do well are invited to a residential competition involving practical biology, at which the four members of the British team are selected. Several Salopians have attended the residential competition in recent years but the ultimate accolade of a place in the team has so far proved elusive.

International Young Physicists Tournament

One of the most prestigious academic competitions in which Salopians have recently taken part is the International Young Physicists Tournament, sometimes known as the 'Physics World Cup.'

The tournament started in Moscow. It became an international organisation in 1988. Originally it was confined to the Eastern Bloc but slowly spread further and is now completely global. Thirty nations compete, and the tournament attracts 150 students, at pre-university level, in teams of five, all passionate about Physics. Seventeen problems in Advanced Physics are set, one year before each tournament. Three of these national groups compete against each other, in each round. The first group makes a presentation, the second group criticises it, and the third group reviews the performance of the other two. Each national team performs each of these functions in turn, the marks being scaled so that the highest marks are available for the presentation and the fewest for the review.

This system of adjudication results in a series of 'Physics Fights' in which students from opposing teams attempt to tear holes in the solutions which have been proposed. Steve Adams, the Head of Science, reports that, with national reputations at stake, these 'fights' can become very heated indeed.

The problems discussed are based on phenomena which, although they are commonly observed, are difficult to explain. One problem concerns water balloons:

Some students are ineffective in water balloon fights as the balloons they throw rebound without bursting. Investigate the motion, deformation and rebound of a balloon filled with fluid. Under what circumstances does the balloon burst?

Another is called 'Chocolate Hysteresis':

Chocolate appears to be a solid material at room temperature but melts when heated to around body temperature. When cooled down again, it often stays melted even at room temperature. Investigate the temperature range over which chocolate can exist in both melted and solid states and its dependence on relevant parameters.

Preparation for the tournament requires real research and requires an immense amount of work together with the application of a broader range of skills than would be necessary in a written examination. A methodical and meticulous sequence of preliminary investigation and research, a study of the history of the problem, a search for relevant literature, the construction of models, the formulation of theory, the conduct of experiments and the formulation of conclusions is the sequence which needs to be followed.

The three teams who have been awarded the highest marks overall during this process compete in the final, though if, as was the case last year, another team has won all its preliminary rounds, it qualifies as a fourth finalist.

Salopians have participated in the competition since 2003, when their team came 5th out of 22 delegations in Uppsala, Sweden. Subsequently Salopians have been present at the tournaments in Winterthur, Switzerland (2005), Bratislava, Slovakia (2006), Seoul, South Korea (2007), Tianjin, China (2009), Bad Saulgau, Germany (2012) and Taipei, Taiwan (2013). In 2014 the International Competition was held in the United Kingdom for the first time, and Shrewsbury School was chosen as the location.

The Conference took place between 3rd and 9th July. The lion's share of the administration fell to John Balcombe (Master 1986 on), who is a member of the international committee of the IYPT and has been indefatigable in promoting the School's participation in the tournament. That the Conference was held here was a great accolade both for him and for the School. The Salopian team was awarded a bronze medal. 28 national teams took part. Singapore and China reached the final; a strong performance in a competition such as this is very highly regarded in their countries. Poland and Slovakia were the other finalists, Slovakia having made the best presentation. Singapore was the overall winner. About 300 delegates and their supporters had to be accommodated.

The guest of honour was the Astronomer Royal, Lord Rees, Master of Trinity College, Cambridge and himself an Old Salopian.

CHAPTER THIRTY-ONE

CIVIC AND LOCAL

Links with the town

Shrewsbury is a 'town school' and its relationships with the town have generally been close, if not always harmonious. The School was founded on the petition of the local burgesses and for several centuries the civic authorities attempted to preserve their influence over the appointment of the Headmaster and the conduct of the School's affairs. Long disputes over the degree of involvement of the Borough Council in the government of the School, over the provision of free places for Day Boys, over the School's location and over the question of whether the school was primarily a local or a national institution came to a head and to a dramatic resolution in the two decades after 1860. The verdict was enshrined in the Public Schools Act of 1868 and the town decisively lost. Thereafter the School was generally perceived as a member of an élite body of national schools whose status was more elevated and whose concerns were wider than those of the town Grammar School from which it had developed. The move of the School to Kingsland in 1882 seemed to the townspeople to symbolise and emphasise the distance which had been established between town and school and, as Colin Leach remarks, the prominent position of the Main School Building, on its hill across the river, seemed to vaunt the sovereignty of parliament over the will of the local population.

However, even at their weakest point, the links between School and town were maintained. Dayboys, although their numbers have waxed and waned through the School's history, have always constituted a significant part of its population; local dignitaries have continued to serve on its Governing Body and today Shropshire Council nominates two of its members to do so. As the twentieth century progressed, there was a distinct rapprochement between School and town. The School renewed its links with St Mary's Church, in which Salopians had worshipped for the greater part of the School's history, by symbolic annual visits for Sunday Evensong in the middle of the twentieth century and, in the last twenty-five years, during which St. Mary's has become a redundant church, for an annual Sunday morning service. Lord Wolfenden, while Headmaster, inaugurated the custom of the annual state visit of the Mayor and Corporation to the School which now takes place each March. In 1952, during the celebration of the School's Fourth Centenary, the School presented the High Cross, erected at the top of Pride Hill, to the town. The arms of the Borough and of the School are engraved upon it and it bears the Latin inscription, *Municipio dilecto, regia schola Salopiensis, sede non fide mutata* which clearly asserted that although the School's location had changed, its affinity and allegiance to the town had not.

The last sixty years have witnessed the forging of ever closer links between School and town. The predominant factor has been the threefold increase in the number of dayboys in the School, but other important features have included the School's participation in locally-based social service and its involvement in local charities, while, reciprocally, the School has opened its gates to visitors and placed its facilities at their disposal to an unprecedented degree.

Social Service

Social service has taken many forms. In the 1960s Rodney Hoare supervised a flourishing home decoration project, whose participants, having honed their skills, practised them upon the properties of appreciative residents in the town. Cultivating the gardens of elderly householders or simply calling upon the lonely for conversation over a cup of tea became an established practice among the Social Service Group on Thursday afternoons. A much more ambitious enterprise, in school holidays, was the redecoration of two churches in Everton. For many years a group of boys went out, every Sunday afternoon, to spend a few hours with the residents of the Condover School for the Blind. Giles Bell, who was in charge of Social Services in the 1990s, remembers that some of the children there did not merely have impaired sight, but also had significant mental problems. He recalls a group of Downes Syndrome children who played very happily with our boys, but that as time went on the children at Condover became more difficult to communicate with, since the local councils sent only the most seriously incapacitated children there, because it was so expensive. Tea parties for the elderly provided a more cheerful environment where, as in residential hospitals and care homes, the boys would entertain their guests with magic and song. At Christmas, the boys used to go carol singing at nursing homes, although Bell recalls one occasion when some elderly people asked if they could stop! On Field Days, Social Services groups went further afield – to Liverpool, Birmingham and London; one foray to the capital included a visit to the drop-in-centre at St Martin's in the Fields. On all these occasions the boys had eye-opening experiences or were regaled with jaw-dropping life histories. Regularly, over the years, Sixth Formers have gone out to help pupils with reading and writing in local primary schools.

In the last few years initiatives of this kind have been incorporated under the heading of 'Community Action', a programme supervised by the Director of Activities, which seeks to involve Fifth Form, Lower Sixth and Upper Sixth pupils far more directly in community work. This contains some of the well-established elements such as garden work for those in need of assistance and tea parties for the elderly, but also encompasses work in village halls and voluntary organisations, canal restoration, instruction in IT skills for those in need, and closer liaison with the Rural Community Council. A group of Lower Sixth Formers regularly visits a local care home for a couple of hours on Thursday afternoons. Other members of the Lower Sixth have drawn up a programme of music and biology lessons, which they have planned themselves, for primary school children at Woodfield Infants School. They have also acted as classroom assistants, helping with reading, Art, PE and film-making.

If Salopian excursions into the local community are frequent, vigorous and rewarding, the incursions of families and local friends on to the School Site are equally so. Sixty years ago, many parents would visit the School only once a year, on Speech Day; now parents are welcome spectators at any matches and often entertained afterwards for tea; many parents visit the School for the House Singing Competition in October, the Remembrance Service in November and the Carol Services in December; and for School and House plays and concerts. They are specifically invited to the Parents' Meetings, which are held annually for each year group in the School. Prospective parents are invited to the Open Days which are held several times each term.

The well-established football competition for preparatory schools, held at Shrewsbury in September, is extremely well attended, and it has been rivalled in popularity recently by a cross-country competition for a similar age-group in October. Football clubs, including Shrewsbury Town and Manchester United junior teams, have used our playing fields for training, and County Cricket Championships, for junior age-groups, are held here during the summer holidays. More generally, the all-weather surface is used at weekends, even during term-time, for a variety of local teams.

The provision of excellent new sporting facilities during the last decade has done much to attract visitors to the School. The Neville Cardus Cricket Centre, the Gemini Swimming Pool and the School's Sports Hall are hired out to visitors on a regular basis. The Cricket Centre was funded by generous donations from the Palgrave-Brown and the Whelan families, and was inaugurated on 19th October, 2006. Since then the facility has demonstrably had a massive impact, not only upon the standard of our own school cricket teams, but also upon a much wider range of local cricket clubs and training programmes. Cricketers are now able to hone their skills throughout the year; and the results have been dramatic. 2013 was an *Annus Mirabilis* for the School XIs which won the national championships at Under 18 level and shared the championship at both Under 17 and Under 15 levels. Between 1989 and 2006 only one Salopian went on to play county cricket; since 2006, however, eight Salopians have done so and others have played first-class cricket for Oxford and Cambridge as noted in the appropriate chapter. International honours, too, have been won in this latter period by James Taylor, at under-17 and under-19 level by Ed Barnard, at under-17 level by George Panayi and at under-19 level by Ruaidhri Smith.

The Centre has been a magnet for the Shropshire Cricket Board Development squads in the 11-17 age-range who use it for twelve hours a week, and for the English Cricket Board Deaf and Disability Squads who use the facilities once a month during the winter. Its facilities are also used by the joint ECB and Shropshire Emerging Players Pathway, and by a dozen local cricket clubs, at Junior, Youth and Senior level, and they can be booked for individual coaching, too. In the Easter and Summer holidays 'Activate Camps' for Preparatory Schools are based in the Centre. Situated as it is, with easy access at the edge of the Site, the availability of the Centre has done much not only to further the integration of the School into the local community, but also to perform an important service which its charitable status requires.

The Swimming Pool hosts the Shrewsbury Swimming Club, the Shrewsbury Triathlon, Keele University, Shropshire Council, Packwood Preparatory School, Adcote School and local maintained schools such as St George's School, St Giles' School, Pontesbury School and Oakmeadow School. *Starfish* (a private group) and members of the Amateur Swimming Association also use the pool.

The Sports Hall accommodates the Shropshire Netball League, the County Badminton team, Hanwood Football Club, Pengwern Boat Club, the Shropshire Basketball Club and the Crossbar Coaching Squad. The Shrewsbury School Squash and Racquets Club is run jointly by the School's Sports Facilities Department and the Squash Club Committee members.

Even more extensive use of the School's facilities is available to visitors, not only in the Easter and Summer holidays, but also during mid-term Exeats, and over recent years the number of courses taking place at these times has increased dramatically. The basic principle has, however, always been that external use must not interfere with the School's regular activities.

During the October Exeat of 2014 a cricket academy, a canoeing academy, and courses in archery and fencing, lacrosse and netball took place, but it is in the still greater length of time available in the school holidays that the most impressive array of facilities is on offer.

For the summer holidays of 2015 both a residential and a sporting programme have been compiled. *Discovery Summer,* an organisation which provides intensive coaching in English, together with a full range of sports options and local excursions attracting students from all over the world, will once again be at Shrewsbury for several weeks. The School will also host a wide range of musical gatherings: the English Camerata, English Brass, teachers of singing, the Grittleton Chamber Orchestra, the Deansfield Primary School Choir and the International Guitar Federation. The Manchester United Under 16 squad (regular visitors) and the Sportsworld Boys Under 12 football teams will use the soccer pitches. The cricket pitches will be thronged throughout the summer, both by established team members and also by players hoping to develop their skills. The Shrewsbury School Academy and the Flintoff Academy will provide for the latter group: among the former will be festivals for inter-county age-groups, for the Midland Under 15s and Under 12s and for the English Cricket Board's Under 15 girls. There will be a Rowing Camp and a National Lifeguard Course. Day coaching will be provided in Fencing, Archery, Tennis, Squash, Swimming and Trampolining.

If the School ever was an 'ivory tower', it is certain that its doors and windows have now been flung wide open and the portcullis has been fully raised!

Charitable enterprises

The charitable activities of the School have been greatly invigorated, during the last four years, under the direction of Lesley Drew; but she insists that most of the initiative and inspiration has been provided by the Salopian pupils themselves. The student-chaired Charity Committee, with its elected president, secretary and members, meets weekly, but there is an open meeting twice a term, where any suggestions for future objectives are welcomed. Publicity material for assemblies, *Twitter* and poster campaigns are regularly discussed. House charity committees are beginning to emerge along the same lines and several charitable enterprises have been conducted independently by Houses: a fund-raising effort based on *Come, Dine with Me*, a Summer Fair and a DVD of House life are recent examples.

Good publicity is vital in attracting support. Poster campaigns (the locations of the posters being carefully chosen, the School Shop always being included) and frequent use of the School's Intranet are the principal means; projects which involve competition between Houses always help, and it has proved useful to set a target sum and to publish the total amount raised from each particular enterprise.

The range of charitable objectives usually includes both a medical and a local charity. Recently support has been given to brain tumour research and also to *The Ark*, which caters for the homeless in Shrewsbury. The Committee also supported the row across the Atlantic last year by two Old Salopians, Harry Martin-Dreyer and Alex Bland (both Rt 2000-2005) in aid of leukaemia charities. They are the most recent pair in a succession of Salopians including Matthew Mackaness (R 1994-1999) and Charlie Marlow (R 1995-2000) who have tackled this transatlantic challenge in recent decades. Often the choice of charity is made upon the personal initiative of a member of the school, who has experienced or learned of, and been touched by, some area of need, and any charitable appeal is strongly reinforced if it is possible to attract a visitor to the School to come to speak in its support.

The School's support for Shrewsbury House in Everton remains paramount; sixty Lower Sixth students visit Everton each year, for three days at a time, to take part in Social Studies Courses. In between passionate games of football and pool, they see for themselves the impact 'The Shewsy' has on the surrounding community, and their accounts of their experiences upon their return raise awareness in the School as a whole. A group of Shewsy Ambassadors has recently been formed, responsible for organising and hosting the Youth Club's visits to the School. 'The Shewsy' benefits most significantly from the proceeds of the Sponsored Walks, held every five years (the most recent walk in 2011 raised over £50,000 for the Club), but also from a variety of other sources, such as Chapel Collections, collections after House Plays, and the proceeds of termly non-uniform days.

Medic Malawi

Medic Malawi is a charity which has recently received particular attention from the School, and every two years visiting Salopians are able to see for themselves the vital work of this small, dynamic institution in one of the seven poorest countries in the world. It supports a hospital, orphanage and nutrition centre, all of which have been constructed during the last fifteen years. Salopian interest in the venture was initially stimulated by Chris Conway, and Shrewsbury, together with other schools, supports it both by funding and by visits from staff and pupils. The visitors 'muck in' at the orphanage, school and chicken farm. On 14th/15th February 2014 a 'Sports All-Nighter', master-minded by Seb Cooley in aid of Medic Malawi, took place in the Gym. Seb reports that *'battle was to be done with badminton rackets, cricket bats, bicycles, Malawi footballs (composed of plastic bags, rubber-bands and string), a normal football, a basketball, table tennis bats, a netball, four ergos and a volleyball'*. A play list was composed, including *Led Zeppelin, Coldplay, Guns 'n' Roses*, and *Sultans of Swing*. Steve Fox completed a marathon (42,195m) on the ergo and reached his target for completion in three hours, between 2 am and 5am. Later an 'African Ball' raised further funds. The eighteen Salopians and six members of staff, who went out to Malawi in 2012, realised that an Eye Clinic was badly needed and made the provision of such a clinic their primary objective. Subsequently Shrewsbury has raised over £15,000 for that purpose; and their successors, a party of nineteen Salopians and five members of the staff who visited Malawi in 2014, had the infinitely rewarding experience of being able to enter the completed four-roomed clinic which had been Shrewsbury's particular project.

In addition to these two principal charities, individuals, Houses and the Committee support a range of causes, both local and national. There is a huge groundswell of support for charity fund-raising amongst the staff, pupils and Old Salopians, and rarely a week goes by without some event occurring – cookie sales, running Benjies in kilts, rowing the Atlantic, throwing sponges at teachers, Variety Shows, All-Night Sports, Fashion Shows, car-washing, moustache-growing, hot-dog eating … and some things which are still but a twinkle in the Charities Committee's eye: pedalo-racing on the Severn, abseiling down Mary Sidney Hall, an e-mail-free day, inter-House poker. Ideas keep bubbling up.

Blue Chairs: a Salopian Fairy Tale.

The Blue Chairs charity arose from an unlikely coincidence. At the same time that one of the members of School House, Artem Bocharov (2000-2006), was diagnosed with leukaemia, two blue chairs (the standard classroom chairs) went missing from an adjacent schoolroom. The master whose room it was, concerned that all his pupils should be able to sit down, naturally instigated a vigorous search for them, e-mailing the entire staff body in an effort to track the missing chairs. Photographs immediately appeared of the two chairs in the most bizarre and unlikely locations: 'drinking' in a local pub, on the moon, on top of the School Building, abseiling down a cliff. His colleague's concern furnished Giles Bell, Artem's housemaster, with a splendid opportunity to provide us with a characteristic example of his quirky and imaginative humour. He decided to bring the chairs to life and he reported that they had absconded in order to fraternise with their very good friends, the benches on the School House lawn. Photographs were produced to provide evidence of their desertion and other photographs continued to pour in.

On further reflection Giles realised that the general amusement this caused offered a much more significant opportunity, for the Blue Chairs to become the means to establish a charity to support Artem's treatment and that of other leukaemia sufferers. In due course £80,000 was in raised, both in aid of the Queen Elizabeth hospital in Birmingham, where Artem was a patient and from where he eventually emerged to make a full recovery, and also of the Shropshire Blood Trust Fund. Blue Chairs calendars were produced, depicting the said Blue Chairs in a vast range of varied company and diverse environments. A Celebrity Blue Chairs Calendar was also produced, together with a Light-Up Blue Chair Pen. On one occasion the presentation of such a pen as a 'goodwill gift' to a guard at a frontier crossing eased the passage of a Salopian traveller to the other side! The presence of Blue Chairs made a powerful impression on the local community when Giles persuaded the school authorities to sanction an occasion on which every member of the School picked up a blue chair and, leaving morning lessons, walked down town in a procession and deposited it to form serried ranks of Blue Chairs in the middle of the town square as an art installation. This had been in response to an initiative by the organisers of the Shrewsbury Visual Arts Week, who had nominated Blue Chairs as their charity and had requested an appropriate exhibition to advertise it.

Since then Blue Chairs have travelled across the world, in backpacks, in the boots of cars and in the holds of aircraft. In the United Kingdom they have been seen in Leeds, Liverpool and Manchester, they have been climbing (and falling off) the Roaches in Derbyshire, they have been on the golf course at St Andrews and in Trafalgar Square in London. They have strayed abroad, appearing in front of the Arc de Triomphe in Paris, in St Mark's piazza in Venice, and beside the Colosseum in Rome. Still further afield they have travelled to Russia, Uzbekistan, Kazakhstan, Turkey and Nepal. They have even posed for the photographer in front of the Taj Mahal in India. They have been seen in the company of many celebrities, both sportsmen and entertainers; with Joe Hart in front of the Darwin Statue, with Andrew Flintoff and the Test Cricket team at a London dinner, and with Nick Hancock and with Lennie Henry among others. Sadly, I am told that they have now been apprehended and returned to their classroom, but their peregrinations provide a wonderful example not only of Salopian quirkiness and spirit of adventure, but also of what a little imagination can do to promote a charitable enterprise.

Sponsored Walks

Sponsored Walks, in which the whole school has taken part, have been one of the principal means of raising money for charity, and they have been held, at intervals of approximately five years, since 1969. Shrewsbury House in Everton has usually been the major beneficiary. One photograph of the 1973 walk shows the Headmaster in the foreground, with an empty stretch of tarmac behind him reaching back to the hills, with the splendid caption 'Keep Wright on to the end of the road!' The route has varied over the years. The first walk in 1969 was from Llanfyllin to Lake Vyrnwy (14 miles) followed by a clockwise circuit of the lake (another 12 miles).

Nick David, the Director of Activities, who was in charge of the most recent walk, describes the route followed in 2011:

the walk started at the south end of the Long Mynd hill area and headed northwards over the Mynd itself, at that point offering a glimpse across what is regarded as one of the finest views in the United Kingdom – the rolling patchwork of fields towards Bishops Castle, the Stiperstones ridge, and, on a really clear day, Cader Idris on the Welsh coast. After a stiff climb towards the Midlands Gliding Club, perched on the western side, the route drops across the valley to the west and climbs again towards the Stiperstones ridge, ultimately heading down towards the finish point at Pontesbury and the welcome prospect of a KH muffin and transport back to the School.

In recent walks, to complete about 20 miles has been considered 'par for the course' but previously stamina has been tested by optional extensions, to 27, 31 37 and even 43 miles. Still earlier, in 1982, it was recorded that 23 walkers went beyond the 31 mile course, two completing 50 and one completing 51 miles! Competition among the boys and girls to raise sponsorship per mile covered has resulted in some impressive personal contributions and has raised some very substantial sums overall. Some staff and pupils have run over the course, one or two have managed to get away with fancy dress: casualties (mainly caused by blisters) have been very few: nearly everyone has finished. Morale has been raised by a pleasant lunch break at which those participating have been entertained by a brass band.

The statistics and logistics involved are formidable. The number of Longmynd Coaches required to convey the walkers to the start and back from the finish: 16; sponsorship target £50,000; highest individual amount raised: £1,400; flapjacks consumed: 786; average number of footsteps per walker: 36,700; total walk distance: 29 kilometres; staffed checkpoints: 23; quickest running time: 2 hrs 46 mins; total footsteps taken: 29,000,000; total number of walkers: 790.

Quite apart from the pleasure of a break from school routine, the good exercise, the fresh air and the beautiful countryside, the atmosphere of these occasions has always been friendly, convivial and thoroughly enjoyable. These are truly splendid excursions which strongly reinforce our sense of community.

CHAPTER THIRTY-TWO

SHREWSBURY HOUSE, EVERTON: 'THE SHEWSY'

The impetus for the foundation of the Shrewsbury School Mission came from the School itself; its nature was determined by its leaders in Liverpool. Digby Kittermaster founded the boys' club, in an old pub building in 1903, as a Christian institution to promote 'godliness and good learning'. He hoped to involve Salopians in the club as much as possible, not only to provide skills and support, but also, by getting to know and love the regular members of the club, to civilise and refine their character. This aspiration was typical of the motives of several Public Schools at the time who were founding similar School Missions in deprived areas of big cities. But the objective sounds strange both to Salopians and to members of Shrewsbury House nowadays. They have long since learned that the benefit is mutual, and that they have much to learn from each other. The relations between School and Club have always been close; and the relative proximity of Liverpool and Shrewsbury was and remains a vital factor in promoting this close and regular contact.

Kittermaster's successors faithfully nurtured and promoted his aims, and the School's support of the Club in Everton was invaluable, particularly during the years of profound deprivation during the Depression. Characteristically, H.H. Hardy (Headmaster 1932-44) established that support on a more businesslike footing. In 1928, largely due to the initiative and devoted support for over thirty years of an Old Salopian, Barr Adams, an Old Boys' Association was formed and developed, a library was equipped, an interest in classical music was encouraged, and a typewritten news sheet, which commented on local and world affairs, was produced. Barr Adams' positive influence had a life-changing effect on some individuals. During the Second World War his news sheet was published two or three times a week and provided a deeply appreciated means of communication between the soldiers at the front and their families at home. The Club was beginning to be forged into a family, but only a skeleton service could be provided in the Club itself and many of its members had been evacuated.

It fell to the Revd James Hill, also an Old Salopian, who became Missioner in 1944, to build up the Club again. His unaffected Christian faith endeared him to the whole community. This was a time when the early initiatives of the Welfare State had led some to believe that the new system could fully replace the services to the community in disadvantaged areas which had until then been provided by the Public School Missions. Others, however, felt that there was a further spiritual dimension which continued association with the School would help to preserve. This was the view both of David Bevan, who almost single-handedly had maintained that link throughout the Second World War, and of James Hill himself. At the Bishop's invitation James added responsibility for the congregation of St Timothy's Church to that of being Missioner; both he and David resisted the Bishop's plan quietly to close St Tim's, and David secured the services of a party of forty boys and masters, during a week of the Easter holidays of 1949, to renovate the Church completely. Arthur Broadbent's painting of the four evangelists in the walled-up east windows was the crowning glory of this enterprise. The effect of this initiative on the

Everton community was profound, making its connection with Shrewsbury School a reality in the area, though the School was slow to realise this impact. Links between the School and the Club continued much as before, with visits to the School by the Missioners, James Hill, John Turner and David Street. Short weekend visits to the Club by House groups took place in rotation. Another holiday painting party in 1960 to renovate St Ambrose's Church Hall (including another painting, of the coming of the Holy Spirit, by Arthur Broadbent) kept the School's interest and presence in the Everton area alive.

The 1960s were a decade of significant social change and it soon became apparent that a new stimulus was needed to reinvigorate the relationship between the School and the Club. Weekend trips to Liverpool were no longer the only glimpse of the outside world available to Salopians in term-time. Shrewsbury House was no longer simply the recipient of Salopian missionary zeal. From the start it had provided the location and the means for forming valued personal relationships and the widening of horizons on both sides. It was becoming ever clearer that it had something of great value to offer in return. David Street had pioneered the idea of Social Studies courses in Liverpool for Salopian Sixth Formers, but he moved on in 1962 and the idea was temporarily allowed to lapse.

In 1963 three men arrived who were to give huge impetus to David Street's initiative. Donald Wright's first instinct, feeling that the days of Victorian patronage were over, had been to sever the link, but Roger Sainsbury, the new Missioner, was a charismatic and resolute figure, who enthusiastically resurrected the Social Studies courses and not only converted Donald to the cause but secured him as his greatest ally. It was said that the Headmaster never seemed to be quite so much at his ease as when he was visiting Shrewsbury House. Roger's wife Jenny soon opened the Club for girls, further developing the family pattern whose foundations had been laid by Barr Adams. Roger was freed to concentrate on Shrewsbury House when Richard Allen arrived to preside over a team ministry in the area. Richard was a man of wide experience, and although the School never really got to know him, it has been said that if the School learned to be proud once more of its connection with Everton, this was due to Richard Allen. He gave publicity to the Club and he founded a free newspaper, *The Everton Telegraph*, still produced by the Club and personally delivered to every house in the parish. Shrewsbury House soon became one of the best-known youth clubs in the country. The Social Studies courses thrived, were enthusiastically received and made a huge impact, evidenced by the growing number of younger Old Salopians who soon became regular subscribers to the Club. A visit to the Club now, reciprocally, proved to be a life-changing experience for more than one Salopian. This was a period of dynamic progress, tragically checked by the premature and irreplaceable loss of Richard Allen in a car accident, but quickly resumed.

It was apparent to all that the old building in Portland Place, which had housed the Club since its move there from the pub in 1907, could no longer accommodate all the varied activities which were being developed. Donald Wright master-minded a massive fund-raising effort by the whole Salopian community. This funded a new centre, including St Peter's Church (reviving the name of a church destroyed in the Blitz) to replace St Ambrose's and St Timothy's which were demolished (sadly, together with Arthur Broadbent's much-loved art work). Accommodation for visitors had always been available, but now a proper hostel for seven residents was provided, in which many Salopians have subsequently stayed to provide voluntary help in the Club. The new centre was opened by Princess Anne in July 1974. The Rt Revd Stuart Blanch described the opening of the new 'Shewsy' as one of the most important and innovative initiatives in his time as Bishop of Liverpool.

Adrian Struvé comments that:

This link between Shrewsbury School and a thriving, grown-up, battling inner-city community is surely unique and has come about naturally. It is a huge privilege for Shrewsbury School to have that relationship and to have that educational resource to call on at will; and it is a wonderful gift to Everton to be able to count on the moral support of the School as exemplified in its many corporate and individual fund-raising activities. Boys at Shrewsbury can learn much in theory. To see at first-hand how a community led by Christians reacts to the Toxteth riots, to the attempts of the Militant Tendency to destroy the area, to the nationwide report of the fatal stabbing of a young visitor outside the Club door, is quite another thing. The word 'mission' was dropped several years ago. But Kittermaster would rejoice that godliness and good learning are still central to the Club's policy and he would laugh to see how Shrewsbury House is educating Shrewsbury School, for he always said that should happen.

The new centre has provided the location and amenities in which Shrewsbury House has been able to develop further. The original boys' club, to which girls were subsequently admitted, has extended its reach and its appeal from being a Youth Club to become a full-blown community centre, catering for local inhabitants of every age. Particular attention has been paid in recent years to the Junior Club, with the aim of preventing future teenage problems before they occur. Julian Charley became Warden in 1974. He played a major part in the wider ecumenical movement in Liverpool, and Shrewsbury House has played a significant role in defeating denominational tensions. In subsequent years the Warden's principal focus has been on the church and the local community at large in Everton. The fortunes of the Youth Club have depended primarily on the calibre, charisma and devotion of a succession of Youth Leaders (John Hutchison, now Chairman of the Board of Management, Peter Brennan and David Brereton being prominent among them), and upon their capacity to attract volunteer helpers.

In common with many similar institutions, controls on staffing, together with health and safety regulations, have had a major impact upon Shrewsbury House. Its financial basis is still precarious. The grant which the Liverpool City Council makes towards the salary of the Youth Workers and the maintenance of the fabric has recently been cut. Money is raised by the Club itself, by renting accommodation, the club premises and the minibus. It is also financed by gifts from Old Salopians and by fund-raising initiatives at the School. Regular Sponsored Walks in aid of Shrewsbury House have featured prominently among other initiatives launched in its support.

The social environment in which Shrewsbury House is situated has changed drastically during the last thirty years. The high-rise flats have been demolished. There has been a consequent reduction in the population and open spaces have been created. The catchment area of the Community Centre has also been extended. But the Christian ethos which informed the Club at its foundation still permeates all its activities. Wide-ranging discussions, usually on Tuesday evenings, still provide an opportunity for the discussion of ethical issues and choices. The community which has been built during the century in which Shrewsbury School has been associated with Everton remains as strong as, and wider than, it has ever been. Shrewsbury House is at the centre of it, but it is a very different kind of community from that which existed fifty years ago. In Everton, as in the nation as a whole, 1963 was a year which presaged dramatic change.

Throughout the 1970s and 1980s the hostel accommodation was filled with a stream of young Christian men and women, attracted to the inner city and the learning experience they could gain through helping out in the club, church and community. And the club in particular benefited enormously from the input and efforts of those people, maybe some 150 in total. As Gap Year opportunities have broadened and become more exotic, this factor has become less prominent, but the centre is still able to offer a unique experience for those keen to take up service in areas such as Everton.

And then there were the celebrations, which did much to strengthen the community which had formed round Shrewsbury House. John Hutchison, the Youth Leader, planned the 75th Anniversary celebrations in 1978 in the knowledge that the Club's tradition had suffered a severe break in the prolonged move from Portland Place. Accordingly he invited as preachers former Missioners, including James Hill and Roger Sainsbury, whose presence would emphasise links with the past. He made a great effort to attract to the celebrations recent members who had observed and would represent the traditions of the old location. (Sadly, a third designated preacher and former Missioner, Eric Treacy, who had become known as 'The Railway Bishop', had collapsed and died shortly before on Appleby station, while waiting to photograph one of his beloved steam locomotives.) A joint relay of Salopian masters and boys, with members of the Club, brought the best wishes of the School for the success of the celebration. The famous city-car, 'The Shrew', constructed by Ted Barber and the boys, was raffled to contribute to the purchase of a long-wheel-base Ford Transit minibus for the Club. A group of Salopians listened enthralled to the description, delivered in the broadest 'Scouse' by a Club lad, then a reformed character, of 'life inside'. In less dramatic vein, a large gathering of Salopian masters and other friends of Shrewsbury House, together with members of the management committee and Club lads past and present, assembled for a cheese-and-wine evening.

In July 1999 the twenty-fifth anniversary of the new building was celebrated with a Children and Young People's Day, at which Rt Revd Roger Sainsbury and his wife Jenny, Adrian Struvé and his wife Brenda, and Terence Harvey, great supporters of the Club over many years, were among those present. In 2003, 'the Shewsy' celebrated its centenary with a year-long programme of reunions, events and visiting preachers in St Peter's, culminating in a service with the Bishop of Liverpool, James Jones, in the Anglican Cathedral. At every reunion, former club members spoke of the impact the Club had had upon their lives, giving them values that held them in good stead, opening up opportunities they might otherwise not have thought of, making friendships that lasted, and building a good foundation for life. In 2013 a lovely week of events was held to mark the 110th anniversary.

The Club continues to serve the Everton community and beyond, and especially its children and young people. Henry Corbett succeeded Julian Charley as Warden in 1987. Henry's wife Jane has been a local councillor for the Everton Ward since 2002. Her work and influence in this capacity have, in many respects, reinforced and complemented that of the Club; and the Club has former members, such as John Dumbell, as key members of the staff. The Social Studies courses continue to serve the School's Sixth Form. Five groups of twelve pupils visit the Club each year, and there are increasing exchange visits for plays and special events, with an annual Club weekend visit to the School in the spring, including a service in Chapel. On the School's Speech Day, the Club's archive group put on a display, with pictures ranging from the early years to the present. The Club, with St. Peter's, also continues to produce the community newspaper *The Everton Telegraph*, and the Shewsy works carefully, in partnership with other organisations in the area, to support and strengthen the Everton community and its families, for example with the West Everton Community Council, the Friends of Everton Park, the Whitechapel Centre and local schools.

In the 1980s and 1990s the Club contributed, with local residents and other agencies, to the transformation of the area's housing. It saved the Langrove houses, immediately adjacent to the Club, from demolition and then went on significantly to improve the housing conditions across the area. The local Primary School in West Everton is now Faith Primary School, a joint Church of England and Roman Catholic initiative. Such an interdenominational association would not have been possible when the Club was a Protestant boys' club. But from the 1960s onwards the Club has not only welcomed girls as members, but has also been an important agent in further easing the long-standing tensions between Protestants and Catholics, helping the churches and communities to work effectively together. The Club has been innovative, too. One notable example is the inauguration of an Encouragement Academy, formed under the leadership of Kathy Riley, a local club helper and qualified teacher, to help Primary School children with behavioural issues. So successful was the project that the City Council adopted the programme and implemented it across the city.

The Everton area has changed dramatically since 1903. Housing has developed from terraced houses with an outside toilet, first to tower blocks and then to a much improved housing plan, which has also recovered and exposed the great view from the top of Everton hill. Encountering, in turn, the sectarian problems of the past, the unemployment problems of the 1970s, the drugs problems of the 1980s, and, in 2014, the second highest child poverty figures in Liverpool, the Shewsy has consistently shown a way ahead with compassion and courage.

What is the secret of the Shewsy's success? The Warden, writing in 2013, suggests that it is not buildings, though they help; it is not money, though it is needed. It is the quality of the people involved. He pays tribute to an outstanding team led by Youth Leader, Dave Brereton, with ex-Club member John Dumbell as assistant, ex-Youth Leader John Hutchison as Chair, and Frances Croft, ex-Club member as Vice-Chair, Treasurer and one of a team of motivated volunteers. But there is one person whom he does not mention, namely himself. Henry was associated with the Club for more than a decade before his appointment as Warden, but in that crucial capacity he has served with total devotion for nearly thirty years, more than twice as long as any of his predecessors. Dan Nicholas, a Salopian who had visited the Club in the 1970s as a boy returned thirty years on in 2009, as a housemaster, with a Social Studies group. He noted that although the environment had changed out of all recognition and the problems which the community faced were different,

Henry and his team are the real glue which makes this community one large family and, as public political figures come and go, some bringing promises only, while a few manage to deliver something, the Shewsy's work is what makes the real difference ... it was the fact that the future success of many former members of the Club was attributed to the formative years in the Shewsy which really struck me.

Henry Corbett and his team are the current guardians of a long tradition. This includes not only his faithful and distinguished predecessors, but also laymen like Barr Adams and David Bevan, Terence Harvey, and, most notably, Adrian Struvé, whose long service on the Management Committee and as Acting Missioner and Warden, made him the rock of the Club in his time. In March 2015 a meeting was convened under the chairmanship of Professor Donald Ritchie to inaugurate and discuss the future activities of *The Friends of Shrewsbury House*, an institution and an initiative which hold great promise for the future.

The plaque installed on one of the Club walls says it all: 'Welcome to the Shewsy, where people matter more than things'. Long may the Club continue to live up to that motto, to the great benefit both of the Everton community and of Shrewsbury School.

CHAPTER THIRTY-THREE

SHREWSBURY AND THE WIDER WORLD

Ut per ultimos Britannos nomen celebretur

Institutional and personal links

Shrewsbury has had strong links with the wider world throughout our period. Sandy Irvine's participation in the attempt on Everest, as far back as 1924, was an early and notable example of the Salopian taste for adventure, and both mountaineering and skiing trips have consistently been a feature of the Salopian holiday programme. The 1960s saw the English Speaking Union's Exchange scheme in full operation. This enabled Sixth Formers and their American contemporaries to spend a year on the other side of the Atlantic. Members of the Common Room in that decade were regularly given sabbaticals and returned enriched by the experience. Michael Hart led pioneering visits to Soviet Russia at a time when relationships between the Kremlin and the West were at a particularly low ebb. Salopian football players and oarsmen toured abroad: there was a notable football tour to Uganda in 1972. Since then, easier air travel and the inauguration of *Eurostar* have transformed the situation. During the course of the last thirty, and more particularly of the last twenty years, the theme has been one of dramatic expansion, so that now every holiday, and indeed every Exeat, seems to offer Salopians the opportunity to set off for foreign climes. The account which follows can scarcely hope to be comprehensive and does not claim to be so. It aims to demonstrate the variety and vibrancy of the picture, embracing institutional contacts, personal contacts, educational and cultural visits, foreign expeditions and sports trips abroad.

Shrewsbury's association with its International School in Bangkok is, of course, the most significant of the institutional links. There was an earlier, though, as it turned out abortive, attempt to forge such a link. In 1978 the then Headmaster, Eric Anderson, with a group of colleagues, consisting of Michael Charlesworth, Peter Hughes and Tom Wheare visited Iran, with a brief to report to the Pahlavi Foundation on how to establish a boarding school there. Consultations with Iranian education officials, the British Council and the British Embassy followed. There was a two-day visit to the proposed site of the school, by the Caspian Sea. A school of 450 boys was envisaged. Instruction would for the most part be in English. The staff of 45 would all be English too, except for the few colleagues needed to teach Farsi, Iranian culture and Islamic studies. Entrance to the school would be selective. 'O' and 'A' level examinations would be taken, and pupils would be prepared for entrance to British and American Universities. In the event, the plans came to nothing because, shortly afterwards, the Shah, who had strongly supported the proposal, fell from power.

The association with Shrewsbury International School in Bangkok, conceived on similar lines has, by contrast, proved to be firmly rooted and an outstanding success. The School continues to prosper mightily. Planned originally to accommodate 300 pupils, 670 were on the roll at the official opening on November 13th 2003. A first-class British education is on offer. The School follows British syllabuses, enters candidates for British examinations and prepares candidates for entrance to British and other universities. It is a co-educational day school, but the architect's key aim has been to create spaces to foster a greater degree of communication, both between staff and pupils, and between the pupils themselves, than the construction and facilities of most day schools would be able to provide. The A level courses followed are similar to those available in England, with variations such as Thai Studies, Chinese Studies and the Mandarin language, appropriate to the School's location and environment. As its first headmaster noted, the urge to learn demonstrated by all the pupils and the total lack of disciplinary problems make the teaching environment rather different from that of England.

The links between Shrewsbury and Bangkok were further tightened when Stephen Holroyd left Shrewsbury to become Headmaster of the International School in 2005. A member of the Shrewsbury Common Room acts as liaison officer between the two schools, and Shrewsbury provides two members of the International School's Governing Body. Members of each Governing Body have visited the other School. The Bangkok Governing Body has held a formal meeting at Shrewsbury. Some of its members were guests of honour at Speech Day in 2014. Members of the Shrewsbury staff regularly visit the Bangkok school. A Summer School was recently held in Shrewsbury for International School pupils and strong cultural links have been developed between the schools. Salopian musical ensembles have regularly performed in Bangkok. John Moore, the Director of Music, has visited Bangkok on several occasions to conduct the 'Last Night of the Proms' Concert: and in 2008 the combined orchestras of both Schools gave concerts both in Shrewsbury and in St John's, Smith Square in London. In 2013 Peter Fanning visited Bangkok to produce *The Bubble*, one of the finest of the home-grown Salopian musicals. There is now a steady stream of pupils who start their education at Shrewsbury International and graduate to Shrewsbury School UK.

Sabbaticals

Personal contacts between Shrewsbury and the wider world have been abundant. In the 1960s, sabbatical leave taken by members of the Common Room constituted one of the principal means of making them. Michael Tupper served as European Chaplain in Kisumu, Kenya; Lawrence Edbrooke taught in the University of Ibadan, Nigeria; Alan Laurie in the Kingston Collegiate and Vocational Institute in Ontario, Canada; Michael Charlesworth in Geelong Grammar School, Australia; Robin Moulsdale and Robin Trimby in St Mark's School, Massachusetts and Richard Raven at Berkeley in the University of California. Rodney Hoare went to pioneer the presentation of science on television in Sierra Leone and David Gee conducted research into the teaching of history in six European countries and the United States. Subsequently David taught at Rollins College, Florida and Simon Baxter at Scotch College, Melbourne, Australia. Several members of the Common Room have taken up headmasterships abroad, among them Stacy Colman at Melbourne Grammar School, Australia, Michael Charlesworth at Lawrence College, Pakistan, Michael Hart at the International School in Brussels, Robin Brooke-Smith at Edwardes College, Pakistan and Stephen Holroyd at Shrewsbury International School in Bangkok. David Smith, having served abroad in Colombia, Uruguay and Argentina, has been Headmaster of

St Julian's School, Carcavellos, Portugal, and is currently Headmaster of the International School in Leipzig. Michael Cross and Andrew Auster have also taken up headships abroad. Michael in Monteridio, Darjeeling, Ruwais, Cali, Dubai, Abu Dhabi and San Salvador and Andrew in Malaysia and Kazakhstan.

International Fellowships and Scholarships

International Scholarships were another means by which such contacts were established. The English Speaking Union Scholarships have already been mentioned. The Indian Scholarship, which was announced in October 1997 and inaugurated in February 1998, supported by Ted Maidment and nurtured by Hugh Ramsbotham, was another. Two half-fee Scholarships were offered and a strong field of thirty-one candidates applied. The prestigious Motley Morehead Scholarship at the University of North Carolina has been awarded to a number of Salopians, including Tom Geddes (Head of School 1995-1996) and Alastair McKeever (Head of School 2002-2003). Other Salopians have won awards and scholarships for Higher Education in the United States, based not only upon their academic attainments, but also upon their proficiency in music and in sport, particularly in rowing and football.

The Miles Clark Scholarship, a domestic award, was set up in 1994 to honour the life and achievements of Miles Clark (Severn Hill 1974-78), traveller, explorer, photographer and writer. This provided another opportunity for Salopians, in their 'Gap Year', to experience the wider world. Projects which have attracted awards have included teaching, charitable and conservation work and adventurous expeditions. The first awards were given for enterprises such as working in a leper colony near Calcutta; for teaching experience in a variety of environments - to Tibetan refugee monks in a Buddhist monastery in India, in an orphanage in Paraguay, and variously in Namibia, Morocco, Kenya and Fiji; for cycling from East to West across the United States; sailing across the Atlantic in a tall ship; working with street children in Harare; working at an Aids clinic in Uganda; and working with the terminally ill in a Jerusalem hospital. Many of these expeditions were sponsored to provide funds for specified charities. The wide variety of these initial projects is typical of the dozens of similar enterprises supported by the fund during its twenty years of operation.

The Harvard Fellowship, inaugurated in 1978, has brought over a succession of Harvard graduates, thirty-six in all, to join the Shrewsbury Common Room for one academic year. Together they have brought great enrichment and awareness of wider horizons to the School. A full list of their names is recorded in an Appendix. Their refreshing influence was further reinforced in the two decades after 1990 by the presence of 'Gappers', school-leavers, mainly from Australia, New Zealand and South Africa, who chose to spend their year between school and university at Shrewsbury. Many of these provided valuable support as sports coaches and classroom assistants.

One of the earliest of these 'Gappers', and one of the most fondly remembered, was James Meikle from Rathkeale College, New Zealand. He spent the academic year of 1990-1991 at Shrewsbury, and, by immersing himself wholeheartedly in a wide range of school activities, served as an exemplar for his successors to follow. Afterwards he kept in regular touch with members of the Common Room, but died, tragically young, in February

2005, after a long and courageous battle with a brain tumour. His affection for Shrewsbury was demonstrated by his legacy to fund a scholarship to enable future 'Gappers', from Rathkeale College or from Christ's College, to follow in his footsteps, and also for a prize to be awarded to the student considered to have made the most progress during the two-year Physical Education course to 'A' level. James is mentioned here as the representative of many other 'Gappers' who made their own committed and distinctive contribution during their year at the School.

Educational and Cultural Exchanges

Educational and cultural visits have played an important part in introducing Salopians to the wider world. Easter is the most popular time for such excursions. Low cost air travel and the proliferation of short Exeats has made exhilarating and exhausting excursions such as 'Paris in a day' and 'Barcelona in a weekend' possible. At a more leisurely pace, the prime movers in these enterprises have been the linguists, the artists, the musicians, the historians and the classicists. French trips and exchanges have been commonplace. At one stage a Versailles-Shrewsbury exchange was established. Subsequently there have been regular visits to Bordeaux, and more recently a Lower School link with Montpellier has been set up. The German Faculty had a long-standing and well-established link with the Alexander von Humboldt Gymnasium in Hamburg but in recent years this has been replaced by cultural visits to Berlin and Bavaria. Members of the Spanish Faculty have arranged visits to a variety of Spanish provinces and cities, initially to Valladolid and subsequently to Barcelona, Andalusia, Jerez and La Coruna. Since 2009 a still wider horizon has been opened by an exchange link with a school in San Bartolomé, Argentina. Michael Hart, as noted above, led a trip to Moscow and Leningrad more than fifty years ago. Louis Dunn followed him with the European Conference prize-winners in 2002. Peter Holgate set up an exchange link with a school in Ukraine.

Members of the Art Department have regularly led trips at Easter, to galleries in Paris, Berlin, Munich and Vienna, Madrid and Barcelona, Florence and Venice, and in 1998 to New York. The musicians established close links with the Czech Republic in the early 1990s and both chamber groups and the full school orchestra have played there several times during the last twenty years. The symphony orchestra has also performed in Boston, Paris, in the Rhineland and in Austria. A brass group has given concerts in Italy and on several other occasions musicians have travelled to contribute to occasions at the Shrewsbury International School in Bangkok, including a small group who performed at its official opening in 2003. The Classicists took part in a visit to Greece in 1996 and to Rome and the Bay of Naples in 2013, and they combined with the historians in a trip to Italy in 2009. The historians visited Istanbul in 2013. In 2014 members of the Third Form took part in a Battlefield tour, and a group drawn from the whole of the Lower School visited Munich and Nuremberg.

Expeditions and Adventures

Adventurous expeditions to foreign countries have been equally numerous and varied. Some of them can be described as 'the Everest Connection', the mountain having had a particular fascination for Salopians since Sandy Irvine's ill-fated attempt on the summit in 1924. The Irvine Lovett Everest Expedition of 2004 was launched to honour the memory of Sandy Irvine and Guy Lovett. Both Sandy (CJB, WHM (S) 1916-1921) and Guy (Ch 1988-1993) were remarkable sportsmen taken from us in the prime of their lives-Sandy while attempting Everest with George Mallory in 1924 and Guy, who was in the throes of organising an expedition to honour Sandy, a fellow élite oarsman, when he was tragically taken ill and died, aged 27. Another ex-Shrewsbury First VIII oarsman, Dan Morris (PH 1987-1992) was enlisted to realise the project. Accordingly on 28th May 2004, eight members of an Old Salopian climbing team stood on the icy North Col of the mountain.

Alister Hagger OS (PH 1986-1991) records that :

Seven days earlier, at Base Camp (BC), the entire expedition, including Guy's mother Val and sister Clare, had taken part in a moving Buddhist ceremony to dedicate a plaque and memorial cholten to the pair. With thick cloud enveloping the mountain as far down as BC, the group huddled together dressed in thick duvet jackets for prayer, followed by a rousing rendition of the Carmen Salopiense led by Martin Slocock OS (Rt 1948-1953).

In the following year, on 30th May 2005 at 6.40 am, Julian Thompson (SH 1989-1994) became the first Salopian known to have reached the summit, and Adam Booth (PH 1995-2000), at precisely the same hour of the day, 6.40 am on 13th May, 2013, repeated the achievement. Mark Twells also names Jonjo Knott (PH 1989-94), Murray Campbell (O 1992-97) and Richard Taylor (O 1994-99) in the roll of honour of those who have attempted to reach the summit during the course of the last dozen years.

Michael Hall's tours and his annual skiing trips to Villars have lured scores of Salopians abroad. These have included several visits to Turkey, but also to Egypt and South India, to Syria and Jordan, Romania and the Baltic States, to Borneo and to the Guyanas and the Caribbean, to Morocco and Spain, to Malaysia and Thailand. The Rovers' many expeditions, which did so much to instil the love of adventuring in Salopians, were in the earlier years mainly concentrated in the British Isles and are described in the section on Outdoor Activities.In the last quarter of a century they have launched international expeditions, of which the Mount Kenya Expedition in 1989 and the Karakorum expedition in 1991 were the most notable.

Bicycling feats have figured prominently in the annals of Salopian adventure. Salopian cyclists have travelled across North America, both from east to west and from west to east, across Africa, and across South America. Pride of place must surely be given to Alastair Humphreys (Rt 1990-1995). His was an epic journey of 46,000 miles along the length of the Earth's three great landmasses (Africa, the Americas, Eurasia) which took more than four years to complete. Sir Ranulph Fiennes paid tribute to it in the following words:

It was probably the first great adventure of the new Millennium. Alastair's journey was an old-fashioned expedition: long, lonely, low-budget and spontaneous. It was a life on the road rather than a whirlwind break from home.

It seems that Salopian enthusiasm for this kind of challenge remains undimmed. Will Loxton (R 2001-2006) cycled from the north to the south of America and then from the west coast to the east, a total of over 4,600 miles. Will Hodson (Rt 1990-1995) is proposing to spend another three years riding his bicycle 100,000 kilometres 'right the way around the planet' dressed in a superhero costume, hoping to be the 'first person ever to cycle across all seven continents'. Al Humphreys and Will Hodson were not only in the same House, they were also in the same year. Several other Salopians have also tackled tough cycling challenges in recent decades.

During the second half of our period, and more particularly during the last twenty years, there has been a very considerable development in Salopian adventure at sea. Before that there had been a long, if intermittent tradition of dinghy-sailing on Whitemere, but the longer stretch of time required meant that this could not be accommodated in the Thursday afternoon programme. Much wider horizons were opened when, at the turn of the century, J.M. Barr, a School Governor and a generous benefactor, placed his 37-foot yacht, berthed in Corsica, at the disposal of members of the staff and School who might wish to take advantage of the offer, on condition that pupils were always involved. Ted Maidment asked Philip Lapage to respond and since then he and Trish Wells have led a series of expeditions, to Corfu in 2001 and 2002, then three or four more, in and after 2003, based at Athens, to sail round the Greek islands. Subsequently there were two trips across the English Channel, one to Honfleur in 2004 and the other to Brittany in 2005. Mid-term Exeats have been used for short trips round the Isle of Wight in 2013 and around Anglesey in 2014 (the latter presenting significant challenges of navigation). Apart from the first year in JMB's boat, the yachts have always been chartered.

The School is now registered by the Royal Yachting Association as an accredited shore-based teaching centre. Philip teaches Day Skipper and Yachtmaster courses as a Thursday afternoon activity. Recently he has also branched out into Astro Navigation. Sailing trips are then used to complement the theoretical instruction he has given with practical experience. During the voyages Salopians attain two levels of proficiency. The first level provides training in steering and managing the sails, in the well-known phrase showing trainees how 'to hand, reef and steer'. The second involves watch-keeping, navigation and night-work. Philip monitors his pupils' progress carefully, aiming at each stage to set a task only slightly more challenging than the level of competence a pupil has already demonstrated. The location of the voyage is equally carefully chosen, a trip round the Greek islands (which involves no night-work) being deemed easier than a long Channel crossing. Now that Philip is a cruising instructor he is able to assess candidates up to Day Skipper practical level over six days or three weekends.

The Old Salopian Yacht Club grew out of these earlier initiatives about ten years ago. Membership is open to all Old Salopians and the Club now puts out two crews annually for the Arrow trophy. Yachts are chartered from *Sunsail* and skills are tested in an annual race between former members of Independent Schools. The races take place in the Solent. About twenty crews take part and Old Salopians have already reached fourth place.

Members of the CCF have specialised in expeditions to Norway. There have been three such expeditions during the last twenty years. The 1997 expedition was the first which had been organised for cadets in the history of the CCF. The subsequent expeditions in 2007 and 2012 followed the same pattern in which cadets had to learn the technique of cross-country skiing, navigation in winter landscapes, the procedure to be followed to survive if one had fallen through broken ice while skiing, and how to be comfortable when sleeping in snow holes! Another Salopian, Chris Lloyd (Rt 2000-2005), gained Arctic experience too, when he joined a scientific expedition on Svalbard in 2004. Candidates for the Duke of Edinburgh's award have also moved further afield, training in Bavaria and Croatia in 2008. The last decade has witnessed a series of scientific expeditions, twice to Honduras (2004) and (2007), to Venezuela (2009), Indonesia (2011) and Madagascar (2013). Finally there has been a couple of expeditions with the specific objective of assisting the work of the Medic Malawi Charity (in 2012 and 2014).

Sports trips abroad

In addition to all these expeditions, the regular sports trips abroad should be mentioned. After their tours of Massachusetts (1996), Uganda (1972) and California (1981), the footballers have conducted pre-season training during the last twenty years in a wide variety of European countries, including France, Spain, Italy, the Netherlands, the Czech Republic and Sweden. The cricketers have toured Barbados (three times), South Africa and Sri Lanka. Salopian oarsmen have competed in Australia, South Africa and the USA, and have recently established a tradition of competing annually in the Head of the Charles River race in Boston. Members of the Hunt have trained in Lanzarote and in East Africa. Rugby players have toured Canada and Ireland and tennis players have trained in Portugal, Sri Lanka and Majorca. In many Christmas holidays Salopian parties have travelled on skiing trips to France, Italy, Switzerland or Austria.

In the annals of Salopian travel and adventure perhaps no name is better known than that of Michael Palin (R 1957-1961), who famously sang the *Carmen* on national television and it is surely appropriate to conclude this chapter by quoting a line from it.

Ut per ultimos Britannos nomen celebretur.

In the last sixty years Salopians have spectacularly surpassed the aspiration with which Dr. Alington challenged them.

LIST OF APPENDICES

Appendix 1

Headmasters of Shrewsbury School

Thomas Ashton	1561-1571
Thomas Lawrence	1571-1583
John Meighen	1583-1635
Thomas Chaloner	1637-1645
Richard Pigott	1646-1662
Thomas Chaloner	1663-1664
Andrew Taylor	1664-1687
Richard Lloyd	1687-1723
Hugh Owen	1723-1727
Robert Phillips	1727-1735
Leonard Hotchkis	1735-1754
Charles Newling	1754-1770
James Atcherley	1771-1798
Samuel Butler	1798-1836
Benjamin Hall Kennedy	1836-1866
Henry Whitehead Moss	1866-1908
Cyril Argentine Alington	1908-1916
Harold Athelstane Parry Sawyer	1917-1932
Henry Harrison Hardy	1932-1944
John Frederick Wolfenden	1944-1950
John Magnus Peterson	1950-1963
Arthur Donald Robert Wright	1963-1975
William Eric Kinloch Anderson	1975-1980
Simon John Bartholomew Langdale	1981-1988
Francis Edward Maidment	1988-2001
Jeremy Wynne Ruthven Goulding	2001-2010
Mark Turner	2010 on

Appendix 2

Chairmen, Chaplains and Bursars

Chairmen of the Governors

Captain Sir Offley Wakeman Bt	1935-1956
Duncan Norman, Esq (OS)	1957-1960
Sir Fred Pritchard (OS)	1960-1968
Dr Walter Hamilton	1969-1981
Sir Peter Swinnerton-Dyer	1982-1989
Sir David Harrison	1989-2004
Sir David Lees	2004-2007
Richard Burbidge, Esq (OS)	2008-2013
Matthew Collins, Esq	2014 on

Chaplains

Revd A.L.E. Hoskyns-Abrahall	1933-1936
Revd Prebendary E. Moore Darling	1936-1937
Revd H. Beevor	1937-1941
Revd C.G. Furnivall	1941-1966
Revd A.A. Conn	1966-1973
Revd P. de N. Lucas	1973-1977
Revd. D. Allcock	1977-1993
Revd. T.O. Mendel	1993-1995
Revd. G.J. Williams	1995-2002
Revd. G.W. Dobbie	2003 on

Bursars

B.L.H. Alder	1947-1958
B.M. Edwards	1958-1964
M.M. Jones	1965-1973
J.T. Dixon	1973-1975
Wing Commander R. Harrison	1975-1985
Air Commodore D.J. Crompton	1985-1996
I.P. Somervaille	1996-2002
S.J. Dowson	2003-2010
M.J. Ware	2010 on

Appendix 3

Deputy Headmasters and Directors of Studies

The title of the Deputy Headmaster has varied during the last sixty years, between *Senior Master* in the earlier period and *Second Master* in the latter. The former use arose from the tradition that the senior member of the Common Room by appointment informally fulfilled the role, when occasion required. The latter use was adopted when the Headmaster made a formal appointment. The title of the chief academic administrator has similarly varied during our period. The position of the colleague now known as *The Deputy Headmaster (Academic)* and before that as *the Director of Studies* was, still earlier, called the *Second Master*. Hence 'Second Master' has been used over the years to apply to two quite different roles.

Deputy Headmasters
J.M. Street	1949-1960
J.R. Hope Simpson	1960-1964
D.J.V. Bevan	1964-1971
M.L. Charlesworth	1971-1981
R.N.E. Raven	1981-1990
P.T.C. Cox	1990-1993
S.S. Caney	1993-1999
G.C. Woods	1999-2003
S.M. Holroyd	2003-2005*
P.A. Fanning	2003-2012*
M.J. Tonks	2005 on*

*Between 2003 and 2012 there was both a Second Master and a Senior Master.

Directors of Studies
A.J. Hagger	1964-1972
D.E.P. Hughes	1972-1979
F.L. Duffield	1980-1987
R. Auger	1987-2003
M.J. Cropper	2003 on

Appendix 4

Housemasters and Housemistresses

Boys' Houses

The School House

The Headmaster	1882-1932
H.G. Broadbent	1932-1933
J.R. Hope Simpson	1933-1948
A.E. Taylor	1948-1952
A. Chenevix-Trench	1952-1955
M.L. Charlesworth	1955-1961
M. Hart	1961-1967
G. Garrett	1967-1973
M.A. MacKinnon	1973-1976
A.C. Struvé	1974-1976
T.D. Wheare	1976-1983
H.M. Ramsbotham	1983-1995
G.C. Woods	1995-1999
G.St J.F. Bell	1999-2013
H.R.D. Besterman	2013 on

Day Boys' Hall

W.H. Witherby	1904-1906
Revd E.W. Huntingford	1906-1909
J.R. Pound	1909-1910
J.B. Oldham	1910-1911
Revd J.O. Whitfield	1911-1917
R.F. Bailey	1918-1921
R. Sale	1921-1929
J.M. West	1929-1940
W.J. Pendlebury	1940-1949
D.S. Colman	1949-1961
H.L.B. Saint	1961-1966
A.D. Ellis	1966-1971
Dr D.H. Gee	1972-1983

Appendix 4 continued

Port Hill

W.G. Harvey	1984-1992
J.M. Gladwin	1992-1999
M.J. Barratt	1999-2002
Mrs S.L.Hankin	2002-2007
S. Hellier	2007-2011
A.S. Barnard	2011 on

Radbrook

S.B. Roberts	1984-1987
J.C. Peat	1987-1995
D. Kirkby	1995-2010
D.M. Hann	2010-2014
Dr R.A.J. Case	2014 on

Rigg's Hall

Revd J. Rigg	1861-1872
Revd G.T. Hall	1872-1900
W.D. Haydon	1900-1932
J.M. Street	1932-1947
Revd R.H.J. Brooke	1947-1962
W.J.A. Mann	1962-1970
A.G. Phillips	1970-1976
R. Auger	1976-1987
S.B. Roberts	1987-1993
D.W.N. Aston	1993-2001
M.A.J. Mostyn	2001-2011
P.J. Middleton	2014 on

Churchill's Hall

Revd C.J.S. Churchill	1875-1910
T.E. Pickering	1910-1926
Revd J.O. Whitfield	1926-1943
A.E. Taylor	1943-1948
A.L. Binney	1948-1963
A.C. Struvé	1963-1967
R.M. Blomfield	1967-1977
P.J. Owen	1977-1983
P.D. Morris	1983-1994
P.H. Lapage	1994-2005
S. Hellier	2005-2007
R.T. Hudson	2007 on

Appendix 4 continued

Moser's Hall

E.B. Moser	1884-1911
F.T. Prior	1911-1933
H.G. Broadbent	1933-1938
A.H. Phillips	1939-1954
C.P.E. Hawkesworth	1954-1962
A.R.B. Moulsdale	1962-1976
P.T.C. Cox	1976-1991
D.R. Field	1991-2002
S.A.A. Fox	2002-2010
Dr P. Pattenden	2010 on

Chance's (No.40 The Schools)

A.F. Chance	1886-1925
C.W.Mitford	1925-1943

Moore's (No.6 The Schools)

F.E. Bennett	1889-1906
C.J. Baker	1906-1918
W.H. Moore	1918-1929
J.H. Tombling	1929-1946

Severn Hill

J.H. Tombling	1943-1946
P. Childs	1946-1960
A.W. Laurie	1960-1968
R.N.E. Raven	1968-1981
R.S. Funnell	1981-1988
J.M. Williams	1988-1990
Dr D.H. Gee	1990-1997
S.M. Holroyd	1997-2003
N.P. David	2003-2006
P.R. Vicars	2006-2012
D.A.G. Nicholas	2012 on

Appendix 4 continued

Ingram's Hall

Revd F. Sergeant	1900-1908
F.M. Ingram	1908-1929
R. Sale	1929-1945
J.M. West	1945-1957
M.G. Powell	1957-1965
D.M. Main	1965-1973
M.A. Eagar	1973-1979
N.V. Bevan	1979-1988
R.E.D. Case	1988-2001
M.J. Tonks	2001-2005
S.H. Cowper	2005-2010
M.P.J. Wright	2010 on

Ridgemount

Revd W.S. Ingrams	1903-1921
Revd H.E. Kendall	1921-1925
A.E. Kitchin	1925-1943
D.J.V. Bevan	1943-1954
R.M. Connell	1954-1965
P. Gladstone	1965-1971
A.D. Ellis	1972-1983
R.E.W.B. Field	1984-1998
M.A.C. Humphreys	1998-2009
W.A. Hughes	2009 on

Oldham's Hall

J.B. Oldham	1911-1932
S.S. Sopwith	1932-1947
W.E. Matthews	1947-1962
Revd M.H. Tupper	1962-1972
R.W. Trimby	1972-1983
J.W.R. Goulding	1983-1989
G.C. Woods	1989-1995
R.N.R. Jenkins	1995-2009
M.D.B. Johnson	2009 on

Appendix 4 continued

The Grove
P.A. Fanning   1988-2003
M.J. Lascelles   2003-2009
D.A.G. Nicholas   2009-2012
S.H. Cowper   2012-2014

Girls' Houses

Mary Sidney Hall
Mrs S.L. Hankin   2008-2012
Ms A. Peak   2012 on

Emma Darwin Hall
Mrs K Weston   2011 on

The Grove
Mrs C Wilson   2014 on

Appendix 5

Heads of Faculties

Heads of Faculties were first recorded in Brown Book in 1972.
Before that date the names are drawn from other records.

Art
A.E. Broadbent 1939-1969; J.H. Alford 1969-1989;
P.N. Woolley 1989-2014; Mrs R Shawe-Taylor 2014 on.

Biology
J.H. Woodroffe; I.H.W. Lacey 1972-2002; A.J. Allott 2002-2015

Business Studies
H.M. Ramsbotham 1975-1986; D.R. Field 1986-1991;
M.J. Barratt 1991-2007; C.W. Kealy 2007 on.

Chemistry
R. Auger; P.F. Cann 1979-2004; B.J. Evans 2004-2009;
A.D. Briggs 2009 on.

Classics
D.S. Colman; W.B. Cook; A.J. Bowen 1967-1984;
J. Godwin 1984-2014; P.G. Fitzgerald 2014 on.

I.C.T.
M. Twells 1993-2014; with J.S. Heir 2003-2005;
with P.A. Kaye 2005 on.

Careers
A. D. Ellis; H.M. Ramsbotham; S.S. Caney 1986-1993; C.W.
Conway 1993-2013; Dr Kate Daubney 2013-2015.

Computer Studies
R.G. Roscoe 1973-2003

Craft, Design and Technology
E.T. Barber 1969-1983; D.Nickolaus 1983-2012;
K.M. Lloyd 2012 on.

*Divinity (subsequently Religious Studies and then Philosophy
and Theology)*
A.A. Conn; J.D. Stuart 1973-1976; M.H. Tupper 1976-1978;
D. Allcock 1978-1979; J.W.R. Goulding 1979-1984; D.H. Gee
1984-1998; M.J. Tonks 1998-2001; S. Hellier 2001-2005;
A. Dalton 2005 on.

Appendix 5 continued

Economics
G.E.L. Spragg; M.A. Eagar; H.M. Ramsbotham;1978-1981
Economics not offered during the intervening period.
P.A. Merricks-Murgatroyd 2003 on.

English
W.J. Jones 1959-1976; R.S. Funnell 1976-1982; P.A. Fanning
1982-1988; M.A. Schützer-Weissmann 1988-2005;
J.W.D. Marshall 2005-2009; Mrs K. Leslie 2009 on.

French
P.W. Twelves 1975-1998; T.C. Whitehead 1998 on.

Geography
D.E. Brown; W.R. Marsh 1977-1978; G.A. Brook 1978-1984;
G.C. Woods 1985-1989; J.M. Gladwin 1989-1992; M.W.R.
Worster 1992-1998; T.R. Foulger 1998 on.

German
P.T. Holgate 1973-1989; C.J. Minns 1989 on.

History
M. Hart 1956-1961; D.H. Gee 1962-1968; A.L. Le Quesne
1969-1980; D.H. Gee 1980-1982; M.E. Ling 1982-1998;
M.M. Morrogh 1998-2011; Miss L.J. Whittle 2011-2015.

Learning Support
Mrs. K. Balcombe 2005 on.

Mathematics
H.L.B. Saint; F.M. Hall 1967-1995; D.R. Harrison 1995-1996;
F.M. Hall 1996-1997; M.J. Cropper 1997-2003; J.C. Armstrong
2003 on.

Modern Languages
F.L Duffield after whom the position was in abeyance until
T.C. Whitehead 2012 on.

Appendix 5 continued

Music
J.R. Stainer 1950-1958; S. Lester 1959-1976;
J.W. Yarnley 1976-1979; C.G. Edmundson 1979-1982;
A.H. Auster 1982-1989; J.F. Moore 1989 on.

Physical Education
B.C. Pitt 1964-1968; P.D. Morris 1968-1973;
D.J. Lang 1973-1977; A.S. Bartholomew 1977-1987;
M.D. Dickson 1987-1988; P.R. Scales 1988-2004;
W.A. Hughes 2004-2010;
P. Greetham 2010-2014; A.J. Murfin 2014 on.

Physics
J.J. Crowhurst; R.G. Roscoe 1973-1981;
J.H. Furniss 1981-1999;
S.F. Adams 1999-2010; M.A. Kirk 2010 on.

Science
D.E.P. Hughes; J.H. Furniss 1980-1999; S.F. Adams 1999 on.

Spanish
S.H. Cowper 1998-2005; M.P.J. Wright 2005-2010;
S.H. Cowper 2010 on.

Drama and Theatre Studies
R.E.D. Case; J.W.D. Marshall 2005-2007;
D.M. Hann 2007-2012; B.D. Parsons 2012-2014;
Miss H.R. Brown 2014 on.

PSHE
Mrs E.M.A.Lascelles 2003-2009; A. Dalton 2009-2014.
Ms A.R. Peak 2014 on.

Appendix 6

Pillars of the Common Room

The composition of the following list requires a careful explanation. The Brown Books of 1950-2014 contain the names of more than 650 members of the academic staff, both full-time and part-time, excluding the visiting members of the Music Faculty.

The Brown Books do not always make a clear distinction between the full-time and the part-time members at any given time (though they do so more often than not); and some colleagues have served, at different times, in both capacities. More than 400 of these 650 colleagues have been full-time members of the staff during their time at Shrewsbury.

To list the 650, or even the 400 names in the form in which they appear in Brown Book, would constitute an element much too preponderant for the balance of the present book, nor would it exactly serve its purposes. However, a full account of the contribution which all members of the Common Room have made to the School during the last sixty years seems to be a worthwhile objective for a future, separate project.

Yet the timing of the arrival and departure of members of the Common Room, both individually and in groups, the roles they occupied, the influence they exerted, and their length of service do have great significance and immediate relevance to the character of the community, which is the primary concern of this book. A brief appraisal of this appendix will reveal that there are specific years, or small clusters of years, in which the simultaneous, or near-simultaneous arrival of a number of teaching staff who later became prominent in the community, clearly endorses that assertion. The number and role of Old Salopians in the Common Room also constitutes a significant element.

The names are listed in order of appointment. In order to produce a manageable amount of material for the present specific purposes, I have restricted mention in the following list in the first instance to those who have served as members of the Common Room for ten years or more, though I have included all Housemasters, clergy, heads of major faculties, masters in charge of major sports and a few others who, by general consent, 'loomed large' upon the Salopian scene, irrespective of their length of service. The resulting list still contains more than 220 names. I realise that this selection involves an arbitrary element and that there may appear to be omissions and anomalies, for which I apologise: but it is intended to illustrate and support my stated conviction that 'it is the people who make the city'.

In each case I have provided the dates of arrival and departure of members of the full-time staff, together with a note of longer part-time service before or after, when that is known and when it has made a significant contribution. This is followed by the principal subject taught, a note of housemasterships where appropriate, of extra-curricular activities of which a colleague was in charge, and a further note of other school activities in which he made a prominent contribution. I have provided the first name of a member of the Common Room in the form which was commonly used among his staff colleagues.

As a further means to keep the material within a manageable compass, I have omitted the educational provenance, the degrees and other qualifications of teaching staff which have customarily been given in the Brown Books of their times: and also any details of their subsequent careers after leaving Shrewsbury, which the School Register would have provided.

I have used the abbreviations RSSH and RSSBC to denote the Hunt and the Boat Club respectively. The present Philosophy and Theology Faculty was previously known as the Religious Studies Faculty and before that as the Divinity Faculty.

JMS - Street, Jimmy, 1916-1960, Classics. Housemaster of Rigg's 1932-1947, Senior Master to 1960, i/cFourth Centenary Appeal.

HND - Dawson, Harry, 1919-1954, Classics. Editor of the Salopian Register Vol II.

JMW - West, Col. James, 1922-1957, Form Master. History and French. Housemaster of Day Boys 1929-39, and of Ingram's 1945-1957 *Editor of the Salopian Newsletter* OS (FMI 1910-1914): Mayor of Shrewsbury 1952

JRHS - Hope Simpson, Russell, 1924-1965, Form Master. History and Classics. Senior Master 1960-1964. Housemaster of School House 1933-1948. Senior Master. Rowing Coach. RSSBC.

AHP - Phillips, Alan, 1925-1964, Chemistry. Housemaster of Moser's 1939-1954. Master i/c football Fives.

GMS - Simmons, George, 1927 - 1965, Form Master. French and Spanish. Producer of School Plays.

DSC - Colman, Stacy, 1928 - 1966, (1928-32, 1935-36, 1938-66) Head of Classics. School Librarian and Archivist. Housemaster of Day Boys. 1949-61, RSSBC 1st VIII coach. OS (WHM 1920-1924)

AET - Taylor, Tom, 1928 - 1952, Physics. Housemaster of Churchill's 1943-1948 and of School House. 1948-1952, Master i/c football.

DJVB - Bevan, David, 1929 -1971, Form Master. Housemaster of Ridgemount 1943-1954, Senior Master 1964-1971.

PC - Childs, Patrick, 1929 -1966, Mathematics. Housemaster of Severn Hill 1946-1960. Master i/c Rovers.

WEM - Matthews, Bill, 1930 - 1970, Physics. Logic. Housemaster of Oldham's 1947-1962.

ALB - Binney, Alec, 1931 - 1969, English. Housemaster of Churchill's. 1948-1963.

JRMS - Senior, Murray, 1932 -1951, History.

RHJB - Brooke, Revd. Hugh, 1933 -1969, Form Master. Housemaster of Rigg's 1947-1962. Master i/c Cricket.

FSH - Hadland, Frank, 1934 -1967, Mathematics. RSSBC.

CPEH - Hawkesworth, Peter, 1935 - 1962, Form Master. Housemaster of Moser's 1954-1962.

FMcE - McEachran, Frank, 1935 -1960, Taught post-retirement until 1975. Modern Languages, Divinity, 'Spells'.

MGP - Powell, Mike, 1936- 1969, Form Master. Housemaster of Ingram's 1957-1965. RSSBC. 1st VIII coach.

AEB - Broadbent, Arthur, 1939 - 1969, Head of Art.

CGF - Furnivall, Revd Guy, 1941 - 1966, Form Master. Chaplain.

VKC - Chew, Ken, 1946 - 1957, Physics.

AJH - Hagger, Arnold, 1946 -1974, Mathematics. Second Master 1964-1972. Director of School Plays.

JHW - Woodroffe, John, 1946 -1972, Head of Biology. Master i/c School Time-Table.

RGH - Harwood, Reg, 1946 -1971, Music. Chapel Organist.

DEB - Brown, David , 1946 - 1979, Geography. Master i/c Talargerwyn.

RMC - Connell, Rex, 1946 - 1971, Form Master. Modern Languages. Housemaster of Ridgemount 1954-1965.

FRE - Ewing, Felix, 1946 - 1979, Head of Modern Languages.

JPK - Knight, Peter, 1946 - 1958, English.

HLBS - Saint, Basil, 1946 -1971, Head of Mathematics. Housemaster of Day Boys 1961-1966

MLC - Charlesworth, Michael, 1947 - 1981, History. Housemaster of School House 1955-1961. Second Master 1971-1981. Acting Headmaster 1972, 1975 and 1980. Editor of the Salopian Register Vol.III. Producer of Plays. Fives. Athletics. Editor of the Salopian Newsletter. OS. (O 1932-1937)

ACT - Chenevix-Trench. Tony, 1948 -1955, (1948-51 and 1952-55) Classics. Housemaster of School House 1952-1955 OS (SH 1932-1937.)

AWF - Fowler, Bertie, 1948 - 1979, Biology. OC Shrewsbury School CCF.

MHT - Tupper, Revd Michael, 1948 - 1979, Form Master. Head of Divinity. Assistant Chaplain. Housemaster of Oldham's 1962-1972.

LRE - Edbrooke, Lawrence, 1950 - 1984, Classics. Form Master. Master i/c Rovers. Rugby.

AWL - Laurie, Alan, 1950 - 1970, History. Housemaster of Severn Hill 1960-1968. RSSBC.

JRS - Stainer, John, 1950 - 1958, Director of Music.

FLD - Duffield, Lyn, 1950 - 1986, Head of Modern Languages. Director of Studies 1980-1987.

ACS - Struvé, Adrian, 1950 - 1986, Modern Languages. Housemaster of Churchill's 1963-1967 and of Headroom (School House) 1974-1976. Master i/c RSSH. Master i/c 1982 Appeal. Friend and Acting Warden of Shrewsbury House.

ALLeQ - Le Quesne, Laurence, 1951 - 1989, (1951 - 1956; 1961 - 1963; 1969 - 1989) Head of History 1969 - 1980.

ARBM - Moulsdale, Robin, 1951 - 1981, English. Housemaster of Moser's 1962-1976. Master i/c football. Fives. OS (I 1942-46)

RPH - Hoare, Rodney, 1951 - 1971, Physics. Master i/c Social Services. Director of Staff Revues.

PG - Gladstone, Peter, 1952 - 1971, Form Master. Biology. Housemaster of Ridgemount 1965-1971. Master i/c RSSBC. 1st VIII coach.

DMM - Main, Revd Canon David , 1952 - 1973, Physics. Housemaster of Ingrams 1965-1973. OC Shrewsbury School CCF.

ADE - Ellis, Arnold, 1952 - 1986, History. Master i/c Careers. Housemaster of Day Boys 1966-1971 and of Ridgemount 1972-1983. OC Shrewsbury School CCF.

WBC - Cook, Bill , 1955 - 1967, Head of Classics.

MH - Hart, Michael, 1956 - 1967, Head of History. Housemaster of School House 1961-1967.

DEPH - Hughes, Peter, 1956 - 1979, Head of Science. Second Master 1972-1979. CCF.

RMB - Blomfield, Roger, 1957 - 1986, History. Housemaster of Churchill's 1967-1977. Master i/c RSSBC. 1st VIII coach.

JHA - Alford, John, 1958 - 1989, Head of Art.

DHG - Gee, Dr David, 1958 - 1998, (also 1998-2004, 2007-2012) History. Housemaster of Day Boys 1972-1983 and of Severn Hill 1990-1997. Head of History and subsequently of Divinity. Acting Chaplain 2002. Editor of the *Salopian Newsletter*. RSSBC.

MJM - Maloney, Michael, 1958 - 1966, Chemistry. Master i/c Rugby.

MM - Mortimer, Mark, 1958 - 1994, Classics, Form Master. RSSH. Master i/c Time-Table.

RWT - Trimby, Robin, 1958 - 1983, History. Housemaster of Oldham's, 1972-1983. Master i/c Football. Cricket.

SL - Lester, Stan, 1959 - 1976, Director of Music. OC Shrewsbury School CCF.

ACG - Grant, Alan, 1959 - 1972 , Mathematics. OC Shrewsbury School CCF. Shooting

WJJ - Jones, Willie, 1959 - 1977, Head of English. Master i/c RSSH. Director of School Plays.

AGP - Phillips, Geoffrey, 1960 - 1976, Geography. Housemaster of Rigg's 1970-1976. Master i/c Cricket. Fives. OS (O 1944-1949).

RNER - Raven, Richard, 1960 - 1993, Classics. Housemaster of Severn Hill 1968-1981. Second Master 1981-1990. Football. Fives. Rovers. OS (M 1945-1950).

GELS - Spragg, Graham, 1962 - 1969, Economics.

BRC - Coulson, Brian, 1963 - 1970, History and Economics.

JJC - Crowhurst, John, 1964 - 1973, Head of Physics.

GG - Garrett, Graham, 1964 - 1973, Head of Mathematics. Housemaster of School House 1967-1973.

BCP - Pitt, Barry, 1964 - 1968, Head of Physical Education.

JBL - Lawson, James, 1965 - 1995, History. School Librarian and Archivist.

AAC - Conn, Revd. Alistair, 1966 - 1973, Divinity. School Chaplain.

MWC - Cross, Michael, 1966 - 1973, Chemistry. First Head of Basic Year. OS (Ch 1951-1957).

MAM - Mackinnon, Dr Alexander, 1966 - 1976, Chemistry. Housemaster of School House 1973-1974 and Doctor's (School House) 1974-1976.

SDB - Baxter, Simon, 1967 - 2005, Mathematics. OC Shrewsbury School CCF. Tudor Court. RSSBC. Fives.

AJB - Bowen, Anthony, 1967 - 1990, Head of Classics. Form Master. Director of School Plays.

DCC - Christie, David, 1967 - 1983, Economics. Form Master. Bee-keeping. Master i/c RSSBC. 1st VIII coach.

JRD - Drummond, Hamish, 1967 - 1999, Music. Violin. Head of Strings.

MAE - Eagar, Mike, 1967 - 1979, Classics. Economics. Form Master. Housemaster of Ingram's 1973-1979. Careers. Master i/c Cricket.

FMH - Hall, Michael, 1967 - 1995, also 1996 - 1997. Head of Mathematics. Head of Basic Year.

BS - Storey, Barry, 1967 - 1991, Music. Clarinet. Head of Wind. Basic Year.

CJE - Etherington, Chris, 1968 - 2000, Modern Languages. Warden of Tudor Court. Master i/c Rugby. Jazz Band.

PDM - Morris, Peter, 1968 - 1977, also 1983-1994. Physical Education and Mathematics. Housemaster of Churchill's 1983-1994.

WRM - Marsh, Wally, 1968 - 1978, Head of Geography. OC Shrewsbury School CCF. RSSBC.

RA - Auger, Richard, 1969 - 2003, Head of Chemistry. Housemaster of Rigg's 1976-1987. Director of Studies. 1987-2003. Basic Year.

ETB - Barber, Ted, 1969 - 1983, Head of Craft, Design and Technology.

PTCC - Cox, Peter, 1969 - 2003, Mathematics. Housemaster of Moser's 1976-1991. Second Master. 1990-1993. RSSBC. Basic Year.

FRP - Pattison, Frank, 1969 - 1973, German.

MEL - Ling, Michael, 1970 - 2007, Head of History. Head of General Studies. Cricket.

NGD - Darrah, Noel, 1970 - 1984 , Mathematics. Master i/c Cricket. Fives.

NBB - Britton, Revd Neil, 1971 - 1973, Divinity. Form Master, Assistant Chaplain.

RPK - Kennedy, Richard, 1971 - 1977, Mathematics. Head of General Studies. Athletics.

MWK - Knox, Martin, 1971 - 2003, Part-time 2003-2012. Languages (Latin, French, German and English). Form Master. Chairman of the Sports Committee. Football and Cricket.

PJO - Owen, Peter, 1971 - 1983, Biology. Housemaster of Churchill's 1977-1983. RSSBC 1st VIII Coach.

NVB - Bevan, Nick, 1972 - 1988, Geography. Housemaster of Ingram's 1979-1988. Master i/c RSSBC. 1st VIII coach. OS (O 1955-1960)

IHWL - Lacey, Ian, 1972 - 2002, Head of Biology.

REWBF - Field, Richard, 1973 - 2005 English. Housemaster of Ridgemount 1984-1998. Registrar 1998-2005. Basic Year.

PTH - Holgate, Peter, 1973 - 1996, Head of German. Examinations Officer.

P de NL - Lucas, Revd. Paul, 1973 - 1977, Divinity. Form Master. School Chaplain.

SWM- Martin, Selby, 1973 - 1993 , Modern Languages. Form Master. Basic Year. Bee-keeping.

RGR - Roscoe, Gilbert, 1973 - 2003, Head of Physics. Head of Computer Studies. Information Technology. Basic Year.

PWT - Twelves, Peter, 1974 - 2001, Head of French. RSSBC.

AWH - Hayes, Alan, 1974 - 2009, Mathematics. Master i/c Time Table. Football. Basic Year. Refereeing.

RP - Parker, Bob, 1975 - 1997, Physics. Master i/c RSSH. Climbing.

PFC - Cann, Dr Peter, 1975 - 2005, Head of Chemistry. Basic Year.

HMR - Ramsbotham, Hugh, 1975 - 1999, Head of Economics and Business Studies. Careers. Housemaster of School House 1983-1995. Children Act Liaison Officer. Editor of the *Salopian Newsletter*. Hon. Asst. Secretary and later President of the Salopian Club.

RSF - Funnell, Simon, 1976 - 1988, Head of English. Housemaster of Severn Hill 1981-1988.

TDW - Wheare, Tom, 1976 - 1983, History. Housemaster of School House 1976-1983. Director of School Plays.

JWY - Yarnley, John, 1976 - 1979 , Director of Music.

ASB - Bartholomew, Alister, 1977 - 1987, Physical Education. Master i/c Rugby. Fives.

CMBW - Williams, Mark, 1977 - 1986, Mathematics. Master i/c Cricket and of Fives.

DA - Allcock, Revd David, 1977 - 1993, Head of Divinity. School Chaplain.

GAB - Brook, Geoffrey, 1978 - 1984, Head of Geography.

MDD - Dickson, Mark, 1978 - 2006, History. Master i/c Football.

JWRG - Goulding, Jeremy, 1978 - 1989, Head of Divinity. Classics. Form Master. Housemaster of Oldham's 1983-1989. Headmaster 2001-2010. RSSBC.

SBR - Roberts, Stewart, 1978 - 1993, Physics. Housemaster of Radbrook 1984-1987 and of Rigg's 1987-1993.

CDTS - Smith, David, 1978 - 1987, English. Form Master. Head of General Studies.

CWC - Conway, Chris, 1979 - 2013, Chemistry. Head of General Studies. Careers. Director of Staff Training. Friend of Shrewsbury House. Fives.

CGE - Edmundson, Colin, 1979 - 1982, Director of Music.

AFUP - Powell, Andrew, 1979 - 1990, Biology. RSSBC Diving. Bee-keeping.

MT - Twells, Mark, 1979 - 1985 also 1993-2014. Mathematics. Head of Information Technology. Head of Basic Year.

(* A single asterisk with initials denotes a female member of staff. **** Four asterisks after an initial date indicates that the person is still on the staff)

GCW - Woods, Gordon, 1979 - 2003, Head of Geography. Housemaster of Oldham's 1989-1995 and of School House 1995-1999. Second Master 1999-2003. RSSBC. 1st VIII coach.

LJC* - Tanner, Lucy, 1979 - 1982, Physics. First full-time female member of the staff.

SDG - Guise, Stuart, 1980 - 1987, Business Studies.

IJW - Walton, Julian , 1980 - 2004, Chemistry. Football.

ICB - Browne, Revd Ian, 1980 - 1982, Assistant Chaplain. Divinity.

REDC - Case, Robin, 1980 - 2002, English. Master i/c Drama. Housemaster of Ingram's 1988-2001. Registrar 2005 – 2011.

JHF - Furniss, John, 1980 - 1999, Head of Science. Basic Year.

WGH - Harvey, Gawen, 1980 - 1992, Chemistry. Housemaster of Port Hill 1984-1992. Basic Year.

JCP - Peat, Jonathan, 1980 - 2008, Physics. Housemaster of Radbrook 1987-1995.

PNW - Woolley, Philip, 1980 - 2014, Head of Art.

PAF - Fanning, Peter, 1981- 2012, Head of English. Housemaster of The Grove 1998-2003. Senior Master 2003-2012. Author and Director of School Plays and Musicals.

AHA - Auster, Andrew, 1982 - 1987, Director of Music. Rugby.

PHL - Lapage, Philip, 1982 **** Chemistry. Housemaster of Churchill's 1994-2005. RSSBC 1st VIII. Sailing.

DN - Nickolaus, David, 1982 - 2012, Head of Craft, Design and Technology.

PB - Broad, Peter 1983 - 1987, Director of School Plays. OS. (S 1967 - 1971)

SSC - Caney, Lt.Col. Stephen, 1983 - 1999, Religious Studies. OC Shrewsbury School CCF. Careers. Second Master., 1993-1999.

JMW - Williams, Joe, 1983 - 2008 Biology. Housemaster of Severn Hill 1988-1990. Master i/c Cricket.

JMG - Gladwin, Jeremy, 1984 - 1999, Head of Geography. Housemaster of Port Hill 1992-1999.

JG - Godwin, Dr John, 1984 - 2014, Head of Classics. Chapel Organist.

CJM - Minns, Dr. Chris, 1984 **** Head of German. French. Form Master. Head of General Studies. Child Protection Officer. Football.

RJK - Kendall, Bob, 1984 - 2011, Mathematics Examination Officer. Football. Warden of Tudor Court.

DAH - Hart, Revd. David, 1985 - 1987, Divinity. Assistant Chaplain.

DRF - Field, Robin, 1986 - 2007, Head of Business Studies. Housemaster of Moser's 1991-2002. Fives. Salopian Ventures.

JB - Balcombe, John, 1986 **** Physics. International Young Physicists Tournament.

RB-S - Brooke-Smith, Dr Robin, 1986 - 1994, History. Master, i/c Rovers. School Archivist 2014 on. OS. (S 1961-1966)

DK - Kirkby, Duncan, 1986**** Biology. Housemaster of Radbrook 1995-2010. Master i/c Rugby.

DWNA - Aston, David, 1987 - 2001 Geography. Housemaster of Rigg's 1993-2001. RSSBC.

SMH - Holroyd, Stephen, 1987 - 2005, English. Housemaster of Severn Hill 1997-2003. Second Master 2003-2005. Master i/c Cricket.

PRS - Scales, Peter, 1987 - 2004, Head of Physical Education. Diving.

ASMW - Went, Alex, 1987 - 2009 , English. Author and Director of Plays.

MJB - Barratt, Michael, 1988 - 2002, Head of Business Studies. Housemaster of Port Hill 1999-2002. Master i/c RSSH.

MHH - Hansen, Martin, 1988 **** Mathematics. Rovers. Basic Year.

TK - Kidson, Trevor, 1988 - 2004, Craft, Design and Technology. OC Shrewsbury School CCF.

MASW - Schützer-Weissmann, Michael, 1988 **** Head of English.

MSS* - Sourbès, Mylène, 1988 - 1998, French.

DJS - Stanton, Revd David, 1988 - 1990, Divinity. Assistant Chaplain.

GStJFB Bell, Giles, 1989 **** Religious Studies. Housemaster of School House 1999-2013. Football. Cricket. Sleuth of Blue Chairs. Admissions Tutor.

JRB - Burke, Rhodri, 1989 **** Physics. Diving.

JFM - Moore, John, 1989 **** Director of Music. Composer and Musical Direction of School musicals.

MMM - Morrogh, Dr Mike, 1989 - 2014, Head of History. School Librarian and Archivist.

MSVP - Partridge, Mike, 1989 - 1997, English, RSSBC. 1st VIII coach.

CMP* - Pringle, Caroline, 1989 - 2002, Art.

AJA - Allott, Andrew, 1990 **** Head of Biology. Bee-keeping.

DBN* - Nightingale, Dympna (Cadden), 1990 **** Music. Chamber Choir. Higher Education Adviser. Shrewsbury House.

APP - Pridgeon, Paul, 1990 **** Physical Education. Cricket Professional. Football.

JHU* - Upton, Jay, 1990 -1995, Modern Languages. European Liaison.

MWRW - Worster, Martin, 1991 - 1998, Head of Geography. RSSBC. 1st VIII coach.

HRWP - Peach, Huw, 1991 **** Modern Languages. European Liaison. RSSBC. Model United Nations.

FDE* - Douineau-Evans, Françoise, 1991- 2010, French.

RNRJ - Jenkins, Lt Col. Nick, 1992 - 2014, Classics. Children Act Liaison Officer. Housemaster of Oldham's 1995-2009. Director of the Salopian Club.

GJW - Williams, Revd Gavin, 1992 - 2002, Religious Studies. School Chaplain.

MJL - Lascelles, Mark, 1992 - 2009, Geography. Housemaster of The Grove 2003-2009. Master i/c successively of cricket, fives and football. OS (SH 1982-1987).

SLH* - Hankin, Sara, (Saxton) 1992 **** Modern Languages. Housemaster of Port Hill 2002-2007 and Housemistress of Mary Sidney Hall 2008-2012. Deputy Head (Staffing).

MDHC - Clark, Matthew, 1993 **** Classics. Sixth Form Admisssions Tutor. Oxbridge co-ordinator. Football. Tennis.

TOM - Mendel, Revd Tom, 1993 - 1995. Religious Studies School Chaplain.

TCW - Whitehead, Tim, 1993 **** Head of Modern Languages. Head of French. RSSBC.

MJC - Clarkson, Michael, 1994 - 2006, Classics. Administrator of School Plays. Rugby. Tennis.

SAAF - Fox, Steve, 1994 **** Geography. Housemaster of Moser's 2002-2010. RSSBC. 1st VIII coach.

MACH - Humphreys, Martin, 1995 - 2010, History. Housemaster of Ridgemount 1998-2009. Director of Communications. RSSBC.

M(J)C - Cropper, Martin, 1997 **** Head of Mathematics. Deputy Head (Academic). Director of Studies 2003 - 2013.

GMB - Barnes, Graham, 1997 - 2005, Physics. Master i/c Rovers. Rugby.

ADB - Briggs, Dr Andy, 1997 **** Head of Chemistry.

JCA - Armstrong, Jerome, 1998 **** Head of Mathematics.

SHC - Cowper, Stuart, 1998 **** Head of Spanish. Housemaster of Ingram's (2005-2010) and of The Grove (2012-2014). Director of Teaching and Learning.

TRF - Foulger, Dr Tim, 1998 ****Head of Geography. Master i/c RSSH.

MAJM - Mostyn, Matthew, 1998 - 2012, Modern Languages. Housemaster of Rigg's 2001-2011. RSSBC.

WJDS - Sayer, Bill, 1998 - 2002, Biology. RSSBC. 1st VIII Coach.

MJT - Tonks, Mike, 1998 **** Head of Religious Studies. Housemaster of Ingram's 2001-2005. Second Master 2005 on.

TDJW - Warburg, Thane, 1998 ****Modern Languages. Chairman of School First Committee. Cricket. Rugby.

SFA - Adams, Steve 1998 **** Head of Science. Physics. Master i/c GPR

KHB* - Balcombe, Kath 1999 **** Learning Support. Head of Department 2005 on.

NPD - David, Lt Col Nick, 1999   **** Business Studies and Economics. Housemaster of Severn Hill 2003-2006. Director of Activities. OC Shrewsbury School CCF.

EMAL* - Lascelles, Amber (Finch), 1999 - 2009, Geography. PSHE.

SH - Hellier, Struan, 1999 - 2015 Head of Religious Studies. Housemaster of Churchill's 2005 - 2007 and of Port Hill 2007 - 2011. Head of Sixth Form.

DMJ - Joyce, David, 1999 **** Music. Violin. Head of Strings.

MAO - Orviss, Martin, 2000 - 2007, Mathematics. RSSBC 1st VIII Coach.

CMS* - Samworth, Dr Christine, 2000 **** Chemistry.

ALMD - Dunn, Louis, 2001- 2009, Modern Languages. Russian. School Charites.

JWDM - Marshall, James, 2001 - 2008, Head of English.

TSM - Morgan, Dr. Torin, 2001 **** Biology. Head of Third Form.

FOLR - Reid, Fergus, 2001 **** Art. OS (M 1981-1986).

PRV - Vicars, Paul, 2001 **** Geography. Housemaster of Severn Hill 2006-2012. Deputy Head (Pastoral).

JG - Gabbitas, Jarrod, 2002 **** Art.

DP - Portier, Dimitri, 2002 **** French. Quiz Society.

GWD - Dobbie, Revd Gary, 2003   **** Philosophy and Theology. School Chaplain.

JAS - Sheppe, Jim, 2003**** Classics. English. Polo. Beagling.

ASB - Barnard, Andy, 2003 **** Geography. Housemaster of Port Hill 2011 on. Master i/c Cricket. Fives.

JMMB* - Burge, Jenny, 2003 **** Mathematics.

RTH - Hudson, Richard, 2003 **** English. Housemaster of Churchill's 2007 on. Editor of *The Salopian*. Climbing. OS (M 1967-1972)

CWK - Kealy, Colm, 2003 **** Head of Business Studies. Rugby.

PAMM - Merricks - Murgatroyd, Paul, 2003 **** Head of Economics.

MPJW - Wright, Mike, 2003 **** Head of Spanish. Housemaster of Ingram's 2010 on.

BJE - Evans, Ben 2004 - 2009 Head of Chemistry. Football. Cricket.

WAH - Hughes, Will, 2004 **** Physical Education. Director of Sport. Football. Cricket. Housemaster of Ridgemount 2009 on. OS (G 1988-1990).

TTJ - Jesdale, Todd, 2004 - 2007, Also 2010-2012. RSSBC. 1st VIII Coach.

KMW* - Weston, Kait, 2004 **** Biology. Housemistress of Emma Darwin Hall 2011 on.

PP - Pattenden, Dr Paul, 2005 **** Physics. Housemaster of Moser's 2010 on. RSSBC.

AD - Dalton, Andrew, 2005 **** Head of Philosophy and Theology.

MDBJ - Johnson, Marcus, 2005 **** Mathematics. Housemaster of Oldham's 2009 on. Rugby.

PAK - Kaye, Paul, 2005 **** Head of ICT. Master i/c Time-Table. Mountain-Biking.

RHM - Morris, Rob, 2005 **** Geography. Cricket. Football.

LJW* - Whittle, Laura, 2005 - 2015. Head of History.

DMH - Hann, Des, 2006 - 2014, English. Housemaster of Radbrook 2010-2014. Director of School plays.

NDJH - Henderson, Nick, 2006 - 2009, 29th Harvard Fellow. RSSBC. 1st VIII Coach.

CWO Oakley, Dr Charlie 2006**** Second in Mathematics, Assistant to the Deputy Head (Academic) RSSBC. Quiz Society.

MJH - Harding, Myles 2007 **** Business Studies: Economics. Tennis. Squash.

DAGN - Nicholas, Lt. Col. Dan, 2007 **** History. Housemaster of The Grove 2009-2012 and of Severn Hill 2012 on. Diving. OS (O 1975-1980).

TPP - Percival, Toby, 2007 **** Classics. Head of Middle School.

RWA* - Adams, Roxanne, 2008 **** Also 2003-2008. Economics.

PJM - Middleton, Peter, 2008 **** English. Housemaster of Rigg's, 2011 on Master i/c RSSH.

CHLW* - Wilson, Clare, 2008 **** Philosophy and Theology. Housemistress of The Grove 2014 on. RSSBC.

RAJC - Case, Dr Richard, 2008 **** Biology. Housemaster of Radbrook 2014 on. OS (PH 1991-1996).

KL* - Leslie, Kristina, 2008 **** Head of English.

SJB - Biggins, Steve, 2009 - 2015, Master i/c Football. Cricket.

PG - Greetham, Paul, 2009 - 2014, Director of Sport.

NJB* - Bradburne, Nicola, 2010 **** Head of Girls' Games.

MAK - Kirk, Martin, 2010 **** Head of Physics.

SKPC - Cooley, Seb, 2011**** Mathematics. Physics. Master i/c Fives. Football. Cricket.

ATH - Hundermark, Athol, 2012 **** Geography. Master i/c RSSBC. 1st VIII Coach.

ARP* - Peak, Anna, 2012 **** Geography. Housemistress of Mary Sidney Hall 2012 on. Mistress i/c PSHE.

HRDB - Besterman, Hugo, 2013 **** Biology. Housemaster of School House 2013 on.

Appendix 7

Members of the New House 1913-1978

Two masters spent a second period in the New House.
This is indicated by printing their names in italics on the second occasion.

1913-1915	E.H.L.Southwell	1943-1946	J. Key
1913-1915	M.G.White	1946-1947	D.W. Scott
1913-1918	H.E.E. Howson	1946-1948	H.T.G. Forster
1913-1921	R.F. Bailey	1946-1957	V.K. Chew
1913-1913	W.C. Fletcher	1947-1951	F. McEachran
1915-1916	R.A. Knox	1947-1947	L. Guppy
1915-1918	S.A.Wadsworth	1948-1952	W.J.A. Mann
1917-1917	T.A. Moxon	1948-1965	J.R. Hope Simpson
1917-1918	J.O. Whitfield	1948-1949	G.R. Grice
1918-1918	R. Sale	1951-1954	D.E. Brown
1918-1919	J.M. Veitch	1952-1964	P. Gladstone
1919-1927	H.J.E. Bailey	1955-1957	F.L. Duffield
1919-1921	H.E. Kendall	1955-1956	J.N. Coldstream
1919-1919	J.M. West	1956-1958	W.B. Cook
1919-1924	H.N. Dawson	1957-1965	D.M. Main
1921-1923	M.H. Gilkes	1958-1960	R.G.L. Holmes
1921-1936	K.B. Banks	1959-1959	R.W. Trimby
1921-1922	J.M. Harrison	1959-1967	D.H. Gee
1922-1929	*J.M. West*	1961-1978	A.W. Fowler
1923-1925	E.H.C. Hickox	1964-1970	B.R. Coulson
1924-1926	K.S. Snell	1965-1969	*R.W. Trimby*
1926-1930	R.A.R. Tricker	1965-1969	A.C. Grant
1926-1927	E.O. Connell	1967-1968	A.J. Bowen
1927-1933	G.M. Simmons	1968-1969	R.P. Murray
1927-1928	D.S. Crawford	1969-1976	S.D. Baxter
1928-1929	R.P. Wilson	1969-1972	F.R. Pattison
1929-1931	D.S. Colman	1969-1970	R.D. Taylor
1929-1938	D.J.V. Bevan	1970-1977	M.E. Ling
1930-1936	W.E. Matthews	1970-1970	P.J. Macdonald
1931-1934	R.St J. Pitts-Tucker	1971-1972	D.J. Lang
1933-1939	R.H.J. Brooke	1971-1972	M.W. Knox
1935-1937	C.P.E. Hawkesworth	1972-1973	R.J.B. Parkes
1936-1940	M.G. Powell	1973-1973	P.J. Knowles
1937-1939	A.D.C. Peterson	1973-1978	R.B. Parkes
1937-1942	F.S. Hadland	1973-1974	H.C. Purslow
1938-1941	H. Beevor	1973-1974	A.J. Seymour
1940-1941	A.L. Binney	1974-1974	R.A. Brown
1940-1940	E.R.L. Gough	1976-1978	A.S. Gray
1940-1946	G.S. Tothill	1977-1978	A.S. Bartholomew
1941-1946	F.R. Medlow	1977-1978	R. Higson
1941-1946	C.B. O'M. Owen	1977-1978	C.M. B. Williams
1941-1946	C.R. Oldham	1977-1978	P. B. StJ. Duguid

Appendix 8

Missioners and Wardens of Shrewsbury House

Revd Digby Kittermaster	1903-1910
Revd E.M. Cooke	1910-1914
Revd H.E. Kendall	1914-1916
Revd F. H. Davies	1916-1919
Revd J. W. Isherwood	1920-1921
Revd Ralph Clayton	1921
Revd F.H. Keatch	1921-1926
Mr R.F. Millard	1926-1927
Mr D.C. Temple	1927-1928
Revd Eric Treacy	1930-1936
Mr S Bayliss-Smith	1937-1939
Mr F.H.C. Tatham	1939-1942
Revd J.C. Hill	1942-1952
Mr John Turner	1953-1955
Revd David Street	1955-1962
Revd Roger Sainsbury	1963-1974
Revd Julian Charley	1974-1987
Revd Henry Corbett	1987 on

Appendix 9

Harvard Fellows 1978-2015

1978-1979	The Hon. T.A. McC Potter
1979-1980	J.P. Relman
1980-1981	M.B. Downing
1981-1982	D.M. Otto
1982-1983	P.E. Sax
1983-1984	A.D. Soutter
1984-1985	T.G. Peyser
1985-1986	A.C. Hodges Jr.
1986-1987	R.J. Lyman
1987-1988	A.M. Roe Jr.
1988-1989	F.R. Davis
1989-1990	J.M. Frates
1990-1991	J.C. Tedeschi
1991-1992	J.C. Bates
1992-1993	B.W. Hewitt
1993-1994	M.T. Kirsch
1994-1995	J.F. Hammond
1995-1996	C.S. Torres
1996-1997	A. Cummings
1997-1998	H.A. Sanchez
1998-1999	J. Linnoila
1999-2000	G. R. Oxnard
2000-2001	J.C. Dewis
2001-2002	J.Y. Stern
2002-2003	D.A. Rosenthal
2003-2004	B. A. Flanagan
2004-2005	C.B. Moffo
2005-2006	R.M. Pennoyer
2006-2007	N.D.J. Henderson
2007-2008	P.G. Hamm
2008-2009	M.D. Chalfin
2009-2010	Miss A.K. Kendrick
2010-2011	K.J. Hirt
2011-2012	N.E. Sceery
2012-2013	-
2013-2014	R.W. Lothman
2014-2015	Miss N. Paine

Appendix 10

Heads of School

50-51	M.E. Kitchin (SH)	72-73	P.M. Blackburn (M)
	J.R. Holt (R)		R.S. Edbrooke (DB)
	J.R. Tusting (Rt)	73-74	D.S. Fitzsimmons (R)
51-52	J.A. Fooks (S)		D.F. Kerr (M)
52-53	C.D. St. Johnston (Ch)	74-75	H.F. Schroeder (R)
53-54	M.O. Slocock (Rt)		D.C. Chance (O)
	M.A. Hill (O)	75-76	D.C. Chance (O)
54-55	T.J. Lewis (R)		J.E. Parry (R)
55-56	W.R. Williams (SH)	76-77	C.J. Talbot (O)
	C. Hewetson (R)		A.J.G. Wright (O)
56-57	R.O. Quibell (SH)	77-78	R.A. Charnock (SH)
	M.N. Mitchell (Rt)		L.W.J. Baart (DB)
57-58	A.T. Macaulay (SH)	78-79	N.J.Wyse (O)
58-59	P.J.M. Robertson (Ch)	79-80	P.M. Scott (DB)
	D.L. Wright (S)		J.E.M. Cross (O)
59-60	G.M. Fallows (R)	80-81	J.E.M. Cross (O)
60-61	R.P.F. Barber (SH)	81-82	A.J. Berry (Ch)
	D.L. Egerton-Smith (M)		J.H.C. Lord (M)
	N.M.S. Dutton (I)	82-83	J.H.C. Lord (M)
61-62	R.A. Stone (SH)		C.B. Hayward (SH)
	N.W. Wilson (R)	83-84	C.B. Hayward (SH)
	P.B. Adie (SH)		M.R.Wormald (SH)
62-63	S.B.W. Brunskill (I)	84-85	M.R.Wormald (SH)
63-64	H.J. Dixon (SH)		A.J. Jebb (I)
	P.J. Renshaw (Ch)	85-86	J.A. Skelton (O)
64-65	E.R.C. Chovil (Rt)		J.R.T. Griffiths (R)
	E.B. L. Armitstead (SH)	86-87	R.J. Blakesley (Rt)
65-66	P.G. Saltmarsh (R)	87-88	A.J. Mowat (S)
	F.A. Wright (S)	88-89	M. MacDougall (PH)
66-67	R.A.E. Grazebrook (M)	89-90	M.A. Eckersley (Ch)
	G.C. Sprot (O)	90-91	A.R.C.Cox (PH)
67-68	R.H. Gilkes (M)	91-92	E.J. Lewis (R)
	C.C. Wright (S)	92-93	C.H. Wilson (SH)
68-69	A.V. Hill (O)	93-94	R.A. Booth (O)
	C.J.B. Kemp (Ch)	94-95	C.M.T. Wright (S)
69-70	A.C.G. Eddy (O)	95-96	T.A. Geddes (SH)
	R.P.B. Duncan (SH)	96-97	I.J.W. McCarter (S)
70-71	P.St J.Worth (M)	97-98	M.J. Howse (R)
	T.M. Lamb (SH)	98-99	R.G. Hillman (M)
71-72	A.V. Le Grice (Ch)	99-00	M.J. Nichols (O)
	A.E.McFarlane (M)	00-01	E. Munir (SH)

Appendix 10 continued

01-02	O.A. Maitland (I)	09-10	B. Williams (Rt)
02-03	A.M. McKeever (S)	10-11	A.R.G. Collins (S)
03-04	I.R. Massey (Rt)	11-12	W.R. Hunter (Rt)
04-05	P.G.A Duncan (SH)	12-13	M.J. Kimpton-Smith (O)
05-06	J.P. Cummins (I)	13-14	R.I.C. Fraser (Ch)
06-07	L.H.B. Taylor (Ch)	14-15	E.K.B O'Keeffe (MSH)
07-08	W.C.W. Brennand (O)		J.R.C. Plaut (S)
08-09	R.F. Griffiths (I)		

Notes

Ninety-one boys (and one girl) have been Head of School since 1950. E.K.B. O' Keeffe is the first girl to have occupied this position.
House total are as follows:

School House 18
Oldham's Hall 14
Rigg's Hall 12
Severn Hill 10
Moser's Hall 9
Churchill's Hall 9
Ridgemount 8
Ingram's Hall 6
Day Boys 5 (3 from the combined House and 2 from Port Hill)

Mary Sidney Hall 1

There were no Heads of School from The Grove. An interesting feature is that Heads of School not infrequently seem to be produced in 'clusters' from one generation in an individual house.

Appendix 11

Old Salopian Members of the Common Room

Their names are listed in order of their appointment to the common room.

Common Room		School	
1922-1957	J.M. West	FMI (I)	1910-1914
1928-1966	D.S. Colman	WHM (S)	1920-1924
1947-1981	M.L. Charlesworth	O	1932-1937
1948-1955	A. Chenevix-Trench	SH	1932-1937
1951-1980	A.R.B. Moulsdale	I	1942-1946
1960-1976	A.G. Phillips	O	1944-1949
1960-1993	R.N.E. Raven	M	1945-1950
1966-1973	M.W. Cross	Ch	1951-1957
1972-1988	N.V. Bevan	O	1955-1960
1983-1987	P. Broad	S	1967-1971
1986-1994	Dr R. Brooke-Smith	S	1961-1966
1989	J.W. Anderson	M	1978-1983
1990	D.M. Towers	O	1990-1991
1991-1994	J.S. Taylor	O	1991-1994
1992-2009	M.J. Lascelles	SH	1982-1987
2001 on	F.O.L. Reid	M	1981-1986
2003 on	R.T. Hudson	M	1967-1972
2004 on	W.A. Hughes	G	1988-1990
2007 on	D.A.G. Nicholas	O	1975-1980
2008 on	Dr R.A.J. Case	PH	1991-1996
2012 on	T.A.C. Corbett	R	1996-2001

Appendix 12

The Sidney Gold Medal

This is the School's highest academic award, originally intended to recognise an outstanding Classical Scholar. First instituted in 1838, the practice of conferring it was interrupted between 1854 and 1899. Since 1980 the award has been opened to candidates from any academic disciplines who have produced work of great distinction. The winners since 1950 are listed below. Further information about the Medal is to be found in the chapter on Academic Changes.

Year	Winner	Year	Winner
1950	R.N.E. Raven	1992	D.S. Morris
1951	M.W.B. Townsend	1993	D.C. Pratley
1952	D.E. Peckett	1994	M.J.R. Bordewich
1953	J.M.B. Edwards	1995	N.R. Wilson
1957	W.I.J. Thorne	1996	D.A. Simon
	M.N. Mitchell	1997	R.P. Stokes
1958	M.J.C. Lowry	1998	C.R.E. Wilson
1959	N.C.F. Barber	1999	M.R. Miller
1966	H.D. Dicum	2000	E.A.R. Clive
1972	P.J. Davenport	2001	No award
1976	C.J.R. Manby	2002	Stephen Burgess
1978	S.A. Marston	2003	No award
1981	J.W.R. Watson	2004	John Frew
1982	J.St C. Wade	2005	Christopher Lloyd
	E. Welbourne	2006	Robert Hughes
1983	R.C.G. Brindley	2007	Jeremy Lloyd
1984	R.H.T. Dixon	2008	Hugh Williams
1985	M.R. Wormald	2009	Philipp Legner
	A.C.A. Woode	2010	David Kell
1987	S. Christmas		Max Emmerich
1988	S. Agnihotri	2011	Tom Elliott
1989	R.E. Reeve	2012	Jack Flowers
1990	D.F. Talbot-Ponsonby	2013	Edward Elcock
1991	P.G.B. Rickett		

Appendix 13

School Numbers

No consistent records of the total numbers of boys in the School at any given time were kept until about 1830, but there are occasional indications of the numbers on specific occasions prior to that which Basil Oldham lists in his History of Shrewsbury School.

Sixteenth-century records show that there were 266 boys in the School in 1562 and 360 in 1581. In 1586 Camden states that the number of boys at Shrewsbury was the greatest in all England.

In the seventeenth century, a source in Charles II's reign claims that the number sometimes reached 600.

The eighteenth century was, in general, a period of decline. 26 boys are recorded in 1719 and 16 in 1723. A recovery occurred in the middle of the century, bringing the numbers to 85 in 1735. It was reported that there were 'more than sixty in the Headmaster's House alone' in 1754, but this was followed by further reductions until there were fewer than 20 (some accounts claim fewer than 12) in 1798.

Under Butler (1798-1836) the numbers rapidly and dramatically recovered, to about 70 in 1814, 120 in 1818, 160 in 1821 and 285 in 1827.

After that, Oldham is able to provide an average number of boys for each succeeding decade, as follows:

1831–40	238	1891–1900	299
1841–50	123	1901–10	275
1851–60	101	1911–20	406
1861–70	164	1921–30	498
1871–80	177	1931–40	509
1881–90	233	1941–50	466

The average number of pupils for the decades after 1950 (continuing Oldham's method of calculation) were:

1951–60	535
1961–70	560
1971–80	642
1981–90	666
1991–2000	697
2001–2010	703

Appendix 13 continued

Oldham noted that the lowest number in the nineteenth century (88) was recorded in 1851 and that the highest number (309) was reached in 1890 and 1894. In the first half of the twentieth century the lowest number (240) was in 1909 and the highest (545) was reached in the Summer Term of 1952.

During the last sixty years the numbers in the School have grown dramatically by two hundred, from about 550 to over 760.

The 550 mark was passed in 1964; 600 was reached in 1970 and 650 in 1976. 700 was attained in 1992, and this total was reached again between 1997 and 1999 and in 2001. In and after 2007 the total number in the School consistently exceeded seven hundred. The first intake of girls helped to bring the numbers up to 721 in 2010, and after the opening of the second girls' boarding house the total (in 2012) was 748.

In the Lent Term of 2015 the total number of pupils in the School was 764, of whom 617 were boys and 147 were girls. The numbers in the Sixth Form and the Lower School are now almost equal, with 379 Sixth formers and 385 members of the Lower School. The Lower Sixth constitutes the largest age-group in the School and there are girls in every form except the Fifth.

The detailed breakdown is as follows:

Form	Boys	Girls	Total
Third	117	36	153
Fourth	100	10	110
Fifth	122	0	122
Lower Sixth	153	56	209
Upper Sixth	125	45	170
Total	617	147	764

It is thought that currently the Shrewsbury Sixth Form is numerically the largest among the co-educational boarding schools in the country.

Appendix 14

Carmen Salopiense

The Latin original is by Dr C.A. Alington (Headmaster 1908-1916) and the English translation by Mark Mortimer (Master 1958-1994)

Rex Edwarde, te canamus	To King Edward from the loyal
Pium Fundatorem,	sons of his foundation
Nec sodales sileamus	hymns are due, and to his royal
Regiam sororem	Sister salutation.
Mente prosequamur grata	Let us, friends, acknowledge proudly
Regem et reginam,	king and queen as founders,
Fautricemque amoena prata	and with 'Hail Sabrina' loudly
Resonent Sabrinam.	fill the fields around us.
Non tacemdumst hic priorum	Next be praise to those accorded
Nobilem cohortem	who were here before us,
Plenam vitam huic honorum	one who crowned a life much lauded
Pleniorem mortem:	with a death more glorious,
Illius nec nomen turpis	and another (ever splendid
Obruat robigo,	his renown) who teaches
Qui humanae docet stirpis	humankind from whence descended
Unde sit origo .	theirs and every species.
Ceteri dum magistrorum	Others mourn headmasters plundered
Lugent breve fatum	almost ere they've seen them:
Fas iactare Informatorum	we boast three who spanned a hundred
Hic triumviratum:	years and more between them.
Nostra tum iubente nympha	in their day Salopian learning
(Rudis forte si sis)	(all must know the story)
Exardebat Cami lympha	set both Cam and Isis burning
Exardebat Isis	with Sabrina's glory.
Nimiis stipata turbis	Scholars long by cramps vexatious
Annis plus trecenis	cabin'd and frustrated
Sedem schola liquit urbis	from their town to fields more spacious
Imparem Camenis ;	finally migrated
Nescit stadium mutari	Sites may change, but not ambition:
Quique alumnos pridem	ours has never faltered
Nominis amor praeclari	and our forebears' high tradition
Nos exercat idem.	we maintain unaltered.
Editique caro colle	On our hill, to serve our Mother
Matri quam amamus	fame through art we'll give her,
Arte, libro, remo, folle	fame in learning, as we love her,
Gloriam petamus;	fame on field and river.
Sic futuros hic per annos	Praise on praise be hers, and never
Laus accumuletur	may we fail to seek it,
Sic per ultimos Britannos	praise that shall be heard wherever
Nomen celebretur.	British tongues can speak it.

WHO'S WHO

The primary purpose of the following list is to identify persons who have been mentioned in the text. Although the names of many of the teaching staff appear in this list, the reader is referred to the appendix entitled 'Pillars of the Common Room' for a more substantial record of their contribution to the School.

Text in bold at the end of an entry indicates a contribution to the named section of the book, which I thereby gratefully acknowledge.

Adams, Steve: Master 1998 on. Head of Science: **International Young Physicists: Astronomy**

Alder, B.L.H: Bursar: 1947-1958.

Alford, John: Master 1958-1989. Head of Art. **Visual Arts.**

Allcock, Revd David: Master 1977-1993. Divinity. School Chaplain.

Allen, Revd Richard: Leader of the team ministry in Everton in the 1960s and founder of the *Everton Telegraph*.

Alington, Cyril Argentine: Headmaster 1908-1916.

Allott, Andrew: Master 1990 on. Head of Biology. **Biology Olympiad: Bee-keeping**.

Anderson, Sir Eric: Headmaster 1975-1980. President of the Salopian Club. **Interview. Foreword**

Anne, HRH Princess: Opened the new Shrewsbury House in 1974.

Argent, Christopher: Master 1994-2003. Organist and Choirmaster.

Argyll, Princess Louise, Duchess of: Royal visitor, January 19th 1898.

Armstrong, Jerome: Master 1998 on. Head of Mathematics. **Mathematics Olympiad**

Ashton, Thomas: Headmaster 1561-1571.

Atcherley, James: Headmaster 1771-1798.

Attenborough, Sir David: Visitor. Unveiled the Darwin Statue, September 9th 2000.

Auger, Richard: Master 1969-2003. Chemistry. Housemaster of Rigg's 1976-1987. Director of Studies. Basic Year. Rugby. Master-minded the preparations for the 1994 OFSTED inspection. **Academic Changes.**

Auster, Andrew: Director of Music 1982-1987. Rugby coach.

Baart, Leonard: Local architect who planned the conversion of the (Old) Darwin Buildings into the new Art School.

Baccanello, Maximillion: OS (Rt 2001-2006). Sculptor, some of whose work may be seen in Chapel.

Balcombe, John: Master 1986 on. Physics. **International Young Physicists Tournament.**

Barber, Nicholas: OS (SH 1954-1958). School Governor. Presided over the staff conference to mark the millennium.

Barber, Ted: Head of Craft, Design and Technology 1969-1983.

Barham Johnson: Director of Music to 1950. Keen advocate of congregational singing.
Barnard, Andy: Master 2003 on. Geography. Housemaster of Port Hill 2011 on. Master i/c Cricket and of Girls' Fives. **Cricket. Fives.**
Barnes, Graham: Master 1997-2005. Physics. Master i/c Rovers. Rugby.
Barnsley, J.R.K: Architect who converted the gymnasium into the Ashton Theatre.
Barr, J.M: OS (SH 1940-1945). Patron of Salopian sailing.
Barr Adams: Devoted supporter of Shrewsbury House.
Barratt, Michael: Master 1988-2002. Housemaster of Port Hill 1999-2002. Head of Business Studies. Master i/c RSSH.
Bartholomew, Alister: Master 1977-1987. Physical Education. Master i/c Rugby.
Baxter, Simon: Master 1967-2005. Mathematics. RSSBC. OC Shrewsbury School CCF. Fives. Steward of Tudor Court. **RSSBC.**
Beard, Professor Mary: Classical Scholar. Fellow of Newnham College, Cambridge. While at Shrewsbury High School she was a pupil of Frank McEachran ('Kek').
Bell, Giles: Master 1989 on. Religious Studies. Housemaster of School House (1999-2013). Master i/c Social Services. Admissions Tutor. **Blue Chairs.**
Bevan, David: Master 1929-1971. Senior Master. Form Master. Housemaster of Ridgemount 1943-1954. **Author of Recollections.**
Bevan, Nick: OS (O 1955-1960). Master 1972-1988. Housemaster of Ingram's 1979-1988. 1st VIII rowing coach.
Biggins, Steve: Master 2009 on. Master i/c Football. **Football.**
Birch, Peter: OS (DB 1966-1971). RSSH. Huntsman. OS Hunt. **RSSH.**
Blomfield, Roger: Master 1957-1986. History. Housemaster of Churchill's 1967-1977. Master i/c RSSBC. **Author of The History of Rowing at Shrewsbury.** 1st VIII rowing coach.
Booker, Christopher: OS (Rt 1951-1956). Author and Journalist. Private Eye.
Booth, Adam: OS (PH 1995-2000). Huntsman. Reached the summit of Mt Everest on 13th May 2013.
Bowen, Anthony: Master. Head of Classics. Director of School Plays, including A Beggar's Opera and Macbeth. Subsequently Fellow of Jesus College, Cambridge and University Orator.
Bowring, Peter: OS (JOW (Ch) 1936-1941). School Governor and benefactor.
Brain, Richard: OS (Rt 1942-1947). Literary editor.
Branckner, Thomas: Winner of the Ireland Scholarship at Oxford University while still at Shrewsbury (1831).
Brewster, Malcolm: Steward of Kingsland Hall.
Brooke, Revd Hugh: Master 1933-1969. Modern Languages. Form Master. Housemaster of Rigg's 1947-1962. Master i/c Cricket.
Broadbent, Arthur: Master 1939-1969. Head of Art.
Bridgeman, Major-General the Viscount: School Governor.
Briggs, Dr Andy: Master 1997 on. Head of Chemistry. **Chemistry Olympiad**
Britton, Revd Neil: Master 1971-1973. Assistant Chaplain.

Brooke-Smith, Dr Robin: OS (S 1961-1966). Master 1986-1994. History. Rovers. **School Archivist 2014 on.**

Brown, David: Master 1946 -1969. Geography. Master i/c Talargerwyn. New House. Host of 'The Brown Jug'.

Brown, Helen: Director of Drama 2014 on.

Brown, Keith: School Boatman.

Browne, Revd Ian: Master 1980-1982. Assistant Chaplain.

Burbidge, Richard: OS (Ch 1955-60). Chairman of the Governing Body 2008-2013.

Burke, Rhodri: Master 1989 on. Physics. Diving. **Diving.**

Burningham, Kathryn: Academic staff 2008-2011. Choirmistress.

Butchard, Grant: Master 1974-1979. Physics. BP Build-a-Car competition.

Butler, Samuel: Headmaster 1798-1836.

Campbell, Murray: OS (O 1992-1997). Climber on Everest 2002.

Cardus, Sir Neville (1888-1975): English writer. Music and cricket correspondent. Cricket coach and secretary to the Headmaster at Shrewsbury 1912-1916.

Case, Robin: Master 1980-2002. Drama and English. Housemaster of Ingram's 1988-2001. Registrar 2005-2011. **Author of Shrewsbury School 1552-2002. Drama.**

Cassidy, Adrian: OS (R 1984-1989). International oarsman.

Chaloner, Thomas: Headmaster 1637-1645 and 1663-1664.

Chance, A.F: Master 1880-1930. Senior Master. Housemaster of Chance's 1886-1925.

Charlesworth, Michael: OS (O 1932-1937). Master 1947-1981. Housemaster of School House 1955-1961. Second Master. Acting Headmaster and Bursar. President of the OS Club. Author of **Behind the Headlines (1994)**.

Charley, Revd Julian: Warden of Shrewsbury House (1974-1987). Influential in the ecumenical movement in Liverpool.

Childs, Patrick: Master 1929- 1966. Mathematics. Housemaster of Severn Hill 1946-1960. Master i/c Rovers.

Christie, David: Master 1967 -1983. Economics. Form Master. Master i/c RSSBC. 1st VIII rowing coach. Bee-keeping.

Clark, Andy: Current (2015) School Boatman.

Clark, Dr Matthew: Master 2012 on. History, **Debating.**

Clark, Miles: OS (S 1974-78). Traveller, explorer, photographer and writer, in whose memory a 'Gap' Year scholarship has been founded.

Clarke, Alex: OS (Rt 1982-1987). Composed his Rock Requiem while at school.

Coade, Thorold: Donald Wright's headmaster at Bryanston. Coade's collected papers are published as 'The Burning Bow'.

Coleraine, Richard Kidston Law, 1st Baron: OS (SH 1915-1919). School Governor. Chairman of the Committee which set up The Friends of Shrewsbury.

Collins, Matthew: Current (2015) Chairman of the Governing Body.

Colman, Stacy: OS. Master 1928-1932, 1935-1936, 1938-1966. Head of Classics. Housemaster of Day Boys, 1949-1961. 1st VIII rowing coach.

Conn, Revd Alistair: School Chaplain 1966-1973.

Conway, Chris: Master (1979-2012). Chemistry. Careers. Head of General Studies, Director of Staff Training. Fives and Rugby coach. Medic Malawi. Shrewsbury House.

Cooley, Seb: Master 2011 on. Mathematics and Physics. Master i/c Fives. *Fives*.

Corbett, Revd Henry: School Governor. Warden, Shrewsbury House, Everton (1987 on). **Shrewsbury House**.

Cowburn, Dr Philip: OS (SH 1931-1936). **Author of A Salopian Anthology**.

Cowper, Stuart: Master 1998 on. Head of Spanish. Housemaster of Ingram's 2005-2010 and of The Grove (2012-2014). Director of Teaching and Learning. Rovers.

Cox, Chris: OS (M 2004-2009). Joint composer of the Darwin Cantata while at school.

Craig, Alex: Master 2001-2005. History. Strong supporter of Debating.

Craig, Patrick: OS (Ch 1982-1987). Now singing with The Tallis Scholars.

Craigen, Stephen: OS (I 2004-2009). Joint composer of the Darwin Cantata while at school.

Crompton, Air Commodore Derek: Bursar 1985-1996.

Cropper, Martin: Master 1997 on Head of Mathematics. Deputy Headmaster (Academic). **Academic changes**.

Dacey, Richard: Master 1987-1994. Organist and Choirmaster.

Dark-Woolley, Victoria: Art. Ceramics: Designer of the wall plaques in Chapel.

Darrah, Noel: Master 1970-1984. Mathematics. Master i/c Cricket. Fives.

Darwin, Charles: OS. Entered Shrewsbury 1818. Author of On the Origin of Species by Means of Natural Selection (1859).

David, Nick: Master 1999 on. Business Studies and Economics Housemaster of Severn Hill 2003-2006. Director of Activities. **Outdoor Activities.**

Dearsley, Simon: Master 2003-2008. Organist and Choirmaster.

Dehn, Paul: OS (CWM (S) 1926-1931). Author of Call-Over, **A Masque for Shrewsbury School's Fourth Centenary 1952.**

Dickens: School Boatman.

Dickson, Mark: Master 1978-2006. History. Master i/c Football 1981-2005. **Football.**

Dillon, Jane: Fabric designer whose work can be seen in Chapel.

Dixon J.T: Bursar 1973-1975.

Dobbie, Revd Gary: Master 2003 on. Religious Studies. Chaplain. **Chapel.**

Dowson, S.J: Bursar 2003-2010.

Drew, Mrs Lesley: Academic Staff 2011 on. English. Chair of the Charities Committee. **Charities.**

Duffield, Lyndon: Master 1950-1986. Head of Modern Languages. Director of Studies. Supervised the changes required by the substitution of GCSEs for the previous O level examinations.

Duncan, Miles OS: (SH 1960-1965). RSSBC Benefactor.

Eagar, Mike: Master 1967-1979. Economics. Housemaster of Ingram's 1973-1979.
 Careers. Master i/c Cricket. Fund raiser. **Cricket**.

Edbrooke, Lawrence: Master 1950-1984. Classics. Form Master. Rugby.
 Master i/c Rovers.

Edinburgh, H.R.H. Philip, Duke of: Royal visitor October 24th 1952.

Edmundson, Colin: Director of Music 1979-1982.

Edward VI: King of England 1547-53. Founder 1552.

Edward, Prince of Wales, Royal visitor 1932.

Edwards, B.M: Bursar 1958-1964.

Edwards, Ian: First Director of the Shrewsbury School Foundation, 1991 on.

Elizabeth I: Queen of England 1558-1603. Second Founder.

Elizabeth II: Queen of the United Kingdom, 1952 on. Royal visitor, October 24th 1952.

Elizabeth, the Queen Mother: Royal visitor, November 5th 1969.

Elliot, Dr Mark: Master 2008 on. Physics. **Astronomy**.

Ellis, Arnold: Master 1952-1986. History. Housemaster of Day Boys 1966-1971 and
 of Ridgemount 1972-1983. OC Shrewsbury School CCF.

Eteson, Richard: OS (G 1989-1993). Now singing with the Swingle Singers.

Etherington, Chris: Master 1968-2000. Modern Languages. Master i/c Tudor Court.
 Master i/c Rugby. Jazz Band. **Rugby**.

Evans, Sir Charles: OS (DB 1932-1937). Strong supporter of the Rovers.

Fanning, Peter: Master 1981-2012. Head of English. Housemaster of The Grove
 1988-2003. Senior Master. Director of School Plays and Musicals. **Drama**.

Fisher, H.A.L (1865-1940): OM, FRS, PC. Distinguished historian and educator.
 Liberal politician and President of the Board of Education in Lloyd George's
 coalition government 1916-1922.

Field, Richard: Master 1973-1988. English. Housemaster of Ridgemount 1984-1998.
 Registrar 1998-2005. Basic Year.

Field, Robin: Master 1986-2007. Head of Business Studies. Housemaster of Moser's
 1991-2002. Salopian Ventures. School Fives coach.

FitzHugh, Richard: OS (I 1989-1994). Composer of a Requiem while at school.

Foot, Paul: OS (SH 1951-1956). Writer and journalist.

Foulger, Dr Tim: Master 1998 on. Head of Geography. Master i/c **RSSH**.

Fowler, Bertie: Master 1948-1979. Biology. OC Shrewsbury School CCF. New House.

Fox, Steve: Master 1994 on. Geography. Housemaster of Moser's 2002-2010. RSSBC.
 1st VIII rowing coach. **RSSBC**.

Fraser, Ian: OS (Ch 1944-1949). Founder Member of the Old Salopian Hunt.

Funnell, Simon: Master 1976-1988. Head of English. Housemaster of Severn Hill
 1981-1988.

Furnivall, Revd Guy: School Chaplain 1941-1966.

Gee, Dr David: Master 1958-1998. Head of History and of Divinity. Housemaster of
 Day Boys 1972-1983 and Severn Hill 1990-1997. Acting chaplain 2002.
 Editor of the Salopian Newsletter 1986-1999.

Gibbs, Mrs Jane: Headmaster's secretary and Personal Assistant 1987 on.

Gilkes, A.H: Master 1873-1885. Greatly influenced the establishment and promotion
of school football on Kingsland.

Gladstone, Peter: Master 1952-1971. Form Master. Biology. Housemaster of
Ridgemount 1965-1971. Master i/c RSSBC. 1st VIII coach.

Godwin, Dr John: Master 1984-2014. Head of Classics and Chapel Organist.
Latin translations.

Goliah, Miss: Member of the music staff and of the school orchestra in the first
decade   of our period.

Goulding, Jeremy: Master 1978-1989. Head of Divinity. Classics. Housemaster of
Oldham's 1983-1989. RSSBC. Headmaster 2001-2010. **Interview.**
Chapel preaching.

Grainger, Sam: OS (SH 2004-2009). Joint composer of the Darwin Cantata while at school.

Greetham, Paul: Master 2009-2014. Director of Sport. Sport: Introduction.

Hagger, Arnold: Master 1946- 1974. Mathematics. Second Master. Director of
School Plays, including Call-Over, the Masque of 1952. Presided, in the
1960s, over the substitution of the 'Block system' of A level subjects for the
'Sides' on which Sixth Form subjects had previously been based.

Halifax, George Savile, Marquess of Halifax (1632-95): OS. 'The Great Trimmer' who
gave his name to the eponymous staff dining society.

Hall, Michael: Master 1967-1995, 1996-1997. Head of Mathematics. Master i/c Basic
Year. Rovers.

Hamilton, Dr Walter: Chairman of the Governing Body 1969-1981.
Master of Magdalene College, Cambridge and Fellow of Eton College.

Hankin, Peter: Part-time teacher of English and joint author of school musicals.

Hankin, Sara, wife of Peter: Member of the Common Room since 1992, who has
the unique distinction of having been both the Housemaster of a boys' house
(Port Hill) and the Housemistress of the first girls' house, Mary Sidney Hall.
Deputy Head (staffing)

Hansen, Martin: Master 1988 on. Mathematics. Rovers. Basic Year.

Harrison, Sir David: Chairman of the Governing Body 1989-2004.

Harrison, Wing Commander Ron: Bursar 1975-1985.

Hart, Aidan: Painter who, during the last decade has contributed frescoes, a tryptych
and an icon to the decoration of Chapel.

Hart, Revd David: Master 1985-1987. Assistant Chaplain.

Hart, George: PE instructor and football coach in the 1950s.

Hart, Michael: Master 1956-1967. Head of History. Housemaster of School House
1961-1967.

Hartshorne, Ernest: School Porter 1932-65.

Harvey, Terence: OS (AEK (Rt) 1940-1945). Devoted supporter of Shrewsbury
House in Everton.

Henderson, Nick: Master 2006- 2009. Harvard Fellow 2006-2007. RSSBC. 1st VIII
rowing coach.

Hewetson, Venerable Christopher: OS (R 1951-1956). Author of the verse composed in the metre of the Carmen in tribute to Hugh Brooke.

Higson, Richard: Master 1977-1980. Mathematics. Member of the New House.

Hill, Revd James: OS (O 1928-1933). School Missioner, Shrewsbury House, Everton 1942-1953.

Hoare, Adrian OS (S 1976-1980), son of Rodney Hoare, Architect of Hodgson Hall. See James.

Hoare, Rodney: Master 1951-1971. Physics. Pioneer of the School's Social Service activities. Director of a series of staff revues.

Hodson, Will (Rt 1990-1995) OS cyclist.

Holloway, John: Master 2009-2014. CDT. He supervised the design and successful racing of electric cars.

Holroyd, Stephen: Master 1987-2005. Second Master. English. Housemaster of Severn Hill 1997-2003. Master i/c Cricket. School cricket and football coach. Principal of Shrewsbury International School, Bangkok since 2005. **Cricket**

Hoskyns-Abrahall, Revd A.L.E: School Chaplain 1933-1936.

Howarth, Ian: Master 2010 on. History. RSSH. Master i/c Athletics.

Hudson, Richard: OS (M 1967-72). Master 2003 on. English. Housemaster of Churchill's 2007 on. **Editor of The Salopian magazine. Editor and publisher of this book. Debating, Satire. Social Changes.**

Hughes, Mike: OS (SH 1975-1980). **Cricket and Fives.**

Hughes, Peter: Master 1956-1979. Chemistry. Head of Science. Second Master. **Academic changes.**

Hughes, Will: OS (G 1988-90). Master 2004 on. Physical Education. Housemaster of Ridgemount 2009 on. Director of Sport.

Humphreys, Alastair: OS (Rt 1990-1995). Adventurer and long-distance cyclist.

Hundermark, Athol: Master 2012 on. Geography. RSSBC Shrewsbury House 1st VIII rowing coach.

Hutchison, John: Chairman of the Board of Management of Shrewsbury House.

Ingrams, Richard: OS (Ch 1950-1955). Journalist and Author. Private Eye.

Irvine, Andrew: OS (CJB: WHM (S) (1916-21). RSSBC. Everest expedition 1924.

James, Adrian OS (S 1976-1980) Architect of Hodgson Hall. See Hoare.

James, Walter: Eminent educationist whose remarks, quoted in the chapter on Ethos, were originally made in an Address to the newly-formed Friends of Shrewsbury in the 1960s.

Jamieson, Angus: Medical officer. Rovers.

Jamieson, Chris: OS (G 2004-2009). **Contemporary school slang.**

Jarvis, David: School Boatman

Jeffreys, George, 1st Baron Jeffreys of Wem (1645-1689): OS (1652-1659). Lord Chancellor who presided over the Bloody Assizes after the Duke of Monmouth's rebellion in 1685.

Jesdale, Todd: Master 2004-2007, 2010-2012. RSSBC 1st VIII rowing coach, whose crew won the Princess Elizabeth Cup in 2007.

Jones, Anthony: OS (O 1934-1937). **School Slang.**

Jones, 'Micky'. Bursar 1965-1973.

Jones, Willie: Master 1959-1977. Head of English. Master i/c RSSH. Director of School Plays, including Othello, An Elizabethan Evening and A Victorian Evening. Subsequently Professor in the University of Hokkaido, Japan. **RSSH.**

Kaye, Paul: Master 2005 on. Head of Educational ICT. Master i/c Academic Timetable. Master i/c Mountain Biking. **Mountain Biking.**

Kealy, Colm: Master 2003 on. Head of Business Studies. Challenge of Management. **Challenge of Management.**

Kendall, Bob: Master 1984-2011. Mathematics. Examination Officer. School Governor. School football coach.

Kennedy, Benjamin Hall: Headmaster 1836-1866.

Kennedy, Henry: Researcher and historian of Shrewsbury House. **Shrewsbury House.**

Kent, H.R.H Duchess of: Royal visitor 1832.

Kidson, Trevor: Master 1988-2004. CDT. CCF. Rovers.

Kirk, Martin Master 2010 on. Head of Physics. **Physics Olympiad.**

Kirkby, Duncan: Master 1986 on. Biology. Housemaster of Radbrook 1995-2010. Master i/c Rugby. **Rugby.**

Kitchin, A.E: Master 1909-1943. Housemaster of Ridgemount 1925-1943. RSSBC 1st VIII rowing 1910-1940.

Kittermaster Revd Digby: OS. School Missioner in Everton 1903-1910.

Knott, Jonjo: OS (PH 1989-1994). Climber on Everest 2006.

Knowles, Dr P.J: Master 1972-1974. Chemistry. Fives. Joint author of **A History of Eton Fives.**

Knox, Martin: Master 1971-2003. Languages. School Football and Cricket Chairman of the Sports Committee. **Cricket. Support staff. Proof reading.**

Knox, R.A. (Ronald): 1888-1957. Priest, theologian, author and broadcaster. Member of the New House 1915-1916.

Kraenzli, Herr: Temporary Assistant Master who arranged the 1st football XI's tour of Nazi Germany in 1937.

Kwiatkowski, Marek: Director of the Foundation.

Lang, David: Master 1970-1975. Rugby.

Langdale, Simon: Headmaster 1981-1988. **Interview.**

Lapage, Philip: Master 1982 on. Housemaster of Churchill's 1994-2005. RSSBC. 1st VIII rowing coach. **Sailing. RSSBC.**

Larguier, Mlle: Part-time member of the academic staff in the 1950s.

Lascelles, Mark: OS (SH 1982-87). Master 1992-2009. Geography. Master i/c successively of cricket, football and fives. **Cricket. Football and Fives.**

Laurie, Alan: Master 1950-1970. History. Housemaster of Severn Hill 1960-1968. RSSBC.

Leach, Professor Colin: OS (O 1945-1951). **Author of A School at Shrewsbury: The Four Foundations (1990).**
Lees, Sir David: Chairman of the Governing Body 2004-2007.
Legner, Philipp: Joint composer of the Darwin Cantata while at school.
Le Quesne, Laurence: Master 1951-1956, 1961-1963, 1968-1989. Head of History. Long-serving cricket umpire. **Frank McEachran. The Summer of 1969. Donald Wright. The School Site. Salopian Satire.**
Lester, Standish: Master 1959-1976. Director of Music.
Ling, Michael: Master 1970-2007. Head of History. Head of General Studies. School Cricket. Member of the New House.
Lloyd, Chris: OS (Rt 2000-2005). Member of the Svalbard Expedition 2004.
Lloyd, Kevin: Master 2012 on. Head of Craft, Design and Technology. **CDT.**
Lloyd, Revd Paul: Master 1961-1962. Assistant Chaplain.
Lovett, Guy: OS (Ch 1988-1993).
Loxton, Will: OS (R 1990-1995). Cyclist.
Lucas, Revd P. de N: Master 1973-1977. School Chaplain.
Lycett, 'Mr': of Adnitt and Naunton, supplier of stationery to the School.
Lyster, Denny: Master 1979-1986. Organist and Choirmaster.
Lywood family: Benefactors to the RSSBC.

Macleod, Fergus: OS (Rt 2001-2006). Violinist and conductor.
Maidment, Ted: Headmaster 1988-2001. **Interview.**
Main, Revd Canon David: Master 1952-1973. Physics. Housemaster of Ingram's 1965-1973. OC Shrewsbury School CCF.
Maloney, Michael: Master 1958-1966. Chemistry. Master i/c Rugby.
Manser, Paul: OS (DB 1974-1979). **RSSBC.**
Margaret, HRH Princess: Royal visitor to the School May 13th 1984.
Marsden, Guy: Rugby coach.
Martin, Selby: Master 1973-1993. Modern Languages. Form Master. Basic Year. Bee-keeping. **Bee-keeping.**
Mason, Alex: Master 2011 on. Director of Chapel Music.
McEachran, Frank: Master 1935-1960. Modern Languages and Divinity. Proponent of *Spells*.
Meighen, John: Headmaster 1583-1635. 'Old' School Buildings constructed in his time.
Mendel, Revd T.O: Master 1993-1995. School Chaplain.
Middleton, Peter: Master 2008 on. English. Housemaster of Rigg's 2011 on. Master i/c RSSH. **RSSH.**
Miller, Nigel: OS (S 1947-1952). Founding Member of the Old Salopian Hunt.
Minns, Dr Chris: Master 1984 on. Head of German. Form Master Head of General Studies. Child Protection Officer. Football. **Proof Reading.**
Moore, John: Master 1989 on. Director of Music. Composer of school musicals. Music and Musicals.

Moore Darling, Revd Prebendary E: School Chaplain 1936-1937.

Morgan, Arthur: Master 1974-1980. Art.

Morland, David: Master: 1973-1980. Football and Rugby.

Morris, Dan: OS (PH 1987-1992). Organiser of the Irvine Lovett Everest
        Expedition 2004.

Morris, Peter: Master 1968-1977 and 1983-1994. Physical Education and
Mathematics. Football. Housemaster of Churchill's 1983-1994.

Morrogh, Dr Michael: Master 1989-2014. Head of History. **School Librarian
        and Archivist.**

Mortimer, Mark: Master 1958-1994. Classics. Form Master. RSSH.
        Master i/c Time-table. Satirical poet. Keen participant in the RSSH.

Moss, Henry Whitehead: Headmaster 1866-1908. Moved the School
        to Kingsland 1882.

Moulsdale, Robin: OS (I 1942-1946). Master 1951-1981. English. Housemaster of
Moser's 1962-1976. Master i/c 1st football XI. Fives. President of the Salopian Club.

Newhouse, Hugh: Master 1973-1979. Physics. Rugby.

Nicholas, Dan: OS (O 1975-1980). Master 2007 on. History. Housemaster of
        The Grove 2009-2012 and of Severn Hill 2012 on. **Diving.**

Nichols, Paul: OS (S 1966-1971). Captain of Cricket, Fives and Football. **Cricket.**

Nickolaus, David: Master 1982-2012. Head of Craft, Design and Technology.

Nightingale (Cadden), Dympna: Staff member 1990 on. Music. Conductor of the
        Chamber Choir. Careers department. Higher Education Adviser.

Norman, Duncan: OS. Chairman of the Governing Body 1957-1960.

Nugent, Robin: OS (DB and PH 1983-1988). Co-ordinator of the
        Old Salopian Rovers.

Oakley, Dr Charlie: Master 2006 on. Mathematics. RSSBC. Quiz Society. **Quizzing.**

Oldham, Basil: OS. EBM (M 1896-1901)Housemaster of Oldham's Hall (1911-
1932).   **Author of A History of Shrewsbury School 1552-1952.** (1952).

Orviss, Martin: Master 2000-2007. Mathematics. RSSBC. 1st VIII rowing coach.

Owen, Peter: Master 1971-1983. Biology. Housemaster of Churchill's 1977-1983.
        RSSBC. 1st VIII rowing coach.

Palgrave Brown, Alan and Alastair: OS (SH 1936-1941). Generous benefactors to
        several major new sports facilities.

Palin, Michael: OS (R 1957-1961). Writer, traveller, actor and television presenter.

Parker, Bob: Master 1975-1997. Physics. Master i/c RSSH. Rovers. **RSSH.**

Partridge, Mike: Master 1989-1997. English. RSSBC. 1st VIII rowing coach.

Peach, Huw: Master 1991 on. Modern Languages. RSSBC. European Conferences.
        Model United Nations. European Liaison Officer. **Model United Nations.**

Pearson, Jemma: Sculptress of the Darwin statue

Peat, Jonathan: Master 1980-2008. Physics. Housemaster of Radbrook 1987-1995. Rugby.

Pemberton, Christopher: Master 1955-1958.

Peterson, John Magnus ('Jack'): OS (SH 1915-1921) Headmaster 1950-1963.
Phillips, Alan: Master 1925-1964. Chemistry. Housemaster of Moser's 1939-1954. Master i/c Football. 1st X1 coach.
Phillips, Geoffrey: OS (O 1944-1949). Master 1960-1976; Housemaster of Rigg's 1970-1976. Master i/c Cricket. Fives.
Philomathes: Effigy on the wall of the Moser Building, depicting the novice Salopian as a lover of learning.
Pitt, Barry: Master 1964-1968. Master i/c P.E. Football.
Pitts-Tucker, Jim: Master 1931-1944. Founder member of the Rovers.
Polymathes: Effigy on the wall of the Moser Building, depicting the Salopian leaving school, as an educated man.
Portier, Dimitri: Master 2002 on. French. Quiz Society.
Powell, Andrew: Master 1979-1990. Biology. RSSBC. Diving. Bee-keeping.
Powell, Mike: Master 1936-1969. Modern Languages. Housemaster of Ingram's 1957-1965. Commander of the Guard of Honour for Her Majesty the Queen in 1952. 1st VIII rowing coach.
Pridgeon, Paul: Master 1990 on. Cricket professional. Cricket and Football Coach. **Cricket**.
Pringle, John, OS (Ch 1964-1969) Architect of the Maidment Building.
Pringle, Caroline: Member of Staff 1989-2002. Art.
Prior, F.T: Master 1891-1933. Housemaster of Moser's 1911-1933. Helped to establish Fives at Shrewsbury.
Pritchard, Sir Fred: OS (FTP (M) 1913-1917). Chairman of the Governing Body 1960-1968.
Pugh, John Edwin: OS. Died of wounds November 12th 1918. Commmemorated in the School Boathouse.

Ramsbotham, Hugh: Master 1975-1999. Business Studies. Careers. Housemaster of School House 1983-1995. Hon Asst Secretary and later President of the Salopian Club. Challenge of Management. Children Act Liaison Officer.
Randall, Nick: OS (O 1972-1976). RSSBC 1st VIII. Captain of Sabrina Club. **RSSBC**.
Raven, Richard: OS (M 1945-50). Classics. Housemaster of Severn Hill 1968-1981. Second Master. President of the Salopian Club. Football. Fives.
Ritchie, Professor Donald: Devoted supporter of Shrewsbury House.
Roach, Julian: Sometime scriptwriter for *Coronation Street* and joint author of School musical *Bubble*.
Rolfe, John: Current Director of Shrewsbury School Foundation. **The Foundation**.
Roscoe, Gilbert: Master 1973-2003. Head of Physics and Computer Studies. The inspiration behind the technical developments in the Ashton theatre.
Rowland, Dan: OS (Rt 1958-1960). RSSBC. Member of the victorious crew in the Princess Elizabeth Cup competition. Professor of History in the University of Kentucky.
Rushton, Willie: OS (Ch 1951-1956). Actor, author, cartoonist, broadcaster. Co-founder of *Private Eye*.

Russell, Bruce: OS (SH 1971-1975). Member of the King's Singers.

Sainsbury, Rt Revd Roger: School Missioner in Everton, Liverpool. 1963-1974.
Saint, Basil: Master 1946-1971. Head of Mathematics. Housemaster of Day Boys 1961-1966.
Sale, Dick: Master 1912-1949. Housemaster of Day Boys 1921-1929 and of Ingram's
    1929-1948. Master i/c Football. Coach of 1st XI.
Sawyer, Harold Athelstane Parry: Headmaster 1917-1932.
Sayer, Bill: Master 1998-2002. Biology. RSSBC 1st VIII coach.
Scales, Peter: Master 1987-2004. Physical Education. Diving.
Sheppe, Jim. Master 2003 on. English and Classics. Master i/c polo and beagling. **Polo.**
Sidney, Sir Philip (1554-1586): OS 1564-1568.
Silk, Dennis: Headmaster of Radley College, after whom the inter-school cricket
    trophy, competed for *inter alios* by Shrewsbury, Eton and Uppingham,
    is named.
Simmons, George: Master 1927-1965. Modern Languages. New House. Director of
    School Plays.
Slocock, Martin: OS (Rt 1948-1953). RSSBC. President of Sabrina Club.
Smith, David: Master 1978-1987. English. Form Master. Head of General Studies.
    Football.
Somervaille, Iain: Bursar 1996-2002.
Sopwith S.S: Master 1915-1948. Housemaster of Oldham's 1932-47.
Southwell, Evelyn: Master 1910-1915. Member of the New House. Killed in France 1916.
    One of the *Two Men* to whose memory the eponymous book was dedicated
    in 1919.
Spiby, Ken: Head Groundsman. 1957-1994.
Stainer, John: Master 1950-1958. Director of Music. Composer of music for
    Call-Over, A Masque for Shrewsbury School's Fourth Centenary.
Stanton, Revd David: Master 1988-1990. Assistant Chaplain.
Starkie, Professor W.F: OS (EBM and FTP (M) 1909-12). Author, scholar, violinist.
    British Council. Author of *Scholars and Gypsies.* Pupil of the *Two Men,*
    Evelyn Southwell and Malcolm White.
Stephen, Ross: Visiting Australian cricket coach, who spent several seasons at
    Shrewsbury c 2000.
Stone, Mike: Catering Manager. 1969-2002.
Street, Revd David: School Missioner in Everton, Liverpool. Pioneer of Social Studies
    Courses at Shrewsbury House 1955-1962.
Street, Jimmy: Master 1916-1960. Senior Master. Housemaster of Rigg's 1932-1947.
    Author of *Changes and Chances.* Conducted the Fourth Centenary Appeal.
    Changes and Chances.
Struvé, Adrian: Master 1950-1986. Modern Languages. Housemaster of Churchill's
    1963-1967 and of Headroom (School House) 1974-1976. Master i/c RSSH.
    Founding Member of the Old Salopian Hunt. Master i/c 1982 Appeal. Friend
    and Acting Warden of Shrewsbury House. **Shrewsbury House.**
Sturges, Gerry: School Boatman 1954-1988.

Swinnerton-Dyer, Sir Peter: Chairman of the Governing Body 1982-1989.

Taylor, Jimmy OS (R 2003-2008) England cricketer.
Taylor, Tom: Master 1928-1952. Housemaster of Churchill's 1943-1948 and of School
        House 1948-1952. Master i/c Football. Coach of 1st XI.
Taylor, Mary: Tom's wife and long-serving Assistant Bursar.
Taylor, Richard: OS (O 1994-1999). Climber on Everest 2004.

Tedder, Lord (1890-1967): Marshal of the Royal Air Force. Guest of Honour at the
        Fourth Centenary Celebrations.
Thomas, Alex: Master 2005-2008. History. Promoter of School Debating.
Thompson, Julian: OS (SH 1989-1994). Reached the summit of Mount Everest on
        May 30th 2005, the first Salopian known to have done so.
Thring, Edward: Headmaster of Uppingham, through whose influence Shrewsbury
        adopted the game of Eton Fives.
Tonks, Mike: Master 1998 on. Head of Religious Studies. Housemaster of Ingram's
        2001-2005. Second Master. **Administrative changes**.
Travers, Jack: OS (I 2000-2005). Long-distance cyclist.
Treacy, Rt Revd Eric: School Missioner 1930-1936.
Trimby, Robin: Master 1958-1983. History. Housemaster of Oldham's 1972-1983.
        Master i/c Football 1962-1981. School Cricket. **Football**.
Tupper, Revd Michael: Master 1948-1979. Housemaster of Oldham's 1962-1972.
        Assistant Chaplain 1948-1979. Founder of the football referees' society.
Turner, Ian: Former School Boatman
Turner, Mark: Headmaster 2010 on.
Twells, Mark: Master 1979-1985 and 1993-2014. Mathematics. Head of Information
        Technology. Master i/c Basic Year and Outdoor Pursuits. Rovers.

Victoria, Princess, later Queen of the United Kingdom (1837-1901): Royal visitor 1832.
Virgo, Paul: Former Director of Marketing.

Wainwright, Nicholas and Michael: OS. Sponsors of the Boodles ISFA Cup
        competition.
Wakeman, Captain Sir Offley: Chairman of the Governing Body 1935-1956.
Wales, HRH. Charles, Prince of: Royal visitor, 21st February 2001.
Wales, HRH. Edward, Prince of: Royal visitor 1932.
Walton, Julian: Master 1980-2004. Chemistry. Football.
Ware, Maylin: Bursar 2010 on.
Wareing, Steve: Current senior caretaker.
Watkins-Pitchford, R.N: Fund raiser.
Wells, Patricia: Part-time member of the academic staff. Biology. Sailing.
Went, Alex: Master 1987-2009. English. Writer and Director of plays.

West, Col James: OS. (FMI (I) 1910-1914) Master 1922-1957. Housemaster of Day Boys (1929-39) and of Ingram's (1945-1957). Commander of the Guard of Honour for the Prince of Wales, 1932. Mayor of Shrewsbury, 1952.

Wheare, Tom: Master 1976-1983. History. Housemaster of School House, 1976-1983. Director of School Plays.

Whelan family: Benefactors to the Cardus Cricket Centre.

White, Malcolm: Master 1910-1915. Member of the New House. Killed in France 1916. One of the *Two Men*, to whose memory the eponymous book was dedicated in 1919.

Whittle, Laura: Academic staff 2005 on. Head of History. **Debating**.

Williams, Revd Gavin: Master 1992-2002. Divinity. Chaplain.

Williams, Joe: Master 1983-2008. Biology. Housemaster of Severn Hill 1988-1990. Master i/c Cricket and Rugby.

Williams, Mark: Master 1977 -1986. Master i/c Cricket and Fives.

Williams, Revd Tom: Master 1959-1960. Assistant Chaplain.

Willis-Bund, The Revd Frank McCarthy: Master 1933-1945. Chaplain of Balliol College, Oxford. School Governor.

Wilson, Rt Revd Roger: Master 1928-1934. Founder Member of the Rovers. Bishop successively of Wakefield and Chichester.

Wolfenden, Lord: Headmaster 1944-1950.

Wood, Stephen: OS (M 1998-2003). Music. Organist and conductor.

Woods, Gordon: Master 1979-2003. Head of Geography. Housemaster of Oldham's 1989-1995 and of School House 1995-1999. Second Master 1999-2003. RSSBC. 1st VIII coach.

Woolley, Philip: Master 1980-2014. Head of Art. **Visual Arts**.

Worth, Peter: OS (M 1965-1970). Chairman of the Shrewsbury School Foundation. Benefactor to Fives. President of the Salopian Club.

Wright, Donald: Headmaster 1963-1975.

Yale, Mark: OS (S 1976-1981). Benefactor to RSSBC.

Yarnley, John: Director of Music 1976-1979.

Young, K. L. ('Pat'): OS (JHT (S) 1929-1932). School Governor and financial controller.

Zvengintzov, Brigadier D.D: Fund raiser.